Escape from Germany

# Escape from Germany

## TRUE STORIES OF POW ESCAPES IN WWII

Introduction by Air Commodore Graham Pitchfork

The National Archives

First published in 2009 by
The National Archives
Kew, Richmond
Surrey TW9 4DU
United Kingdom

www.nationalarchives.gov.uk

The National Archives brings together the Public Record Office,
Historical Manuscripts Commission, Office of Public Sector Information
and Her Majesty's Stationery Office.

A catalogue card for this book is available from the British Library.

ISBN 978 1 905615 49 0

JACKET, TYPOGRAPHIC DESIGN AND TYPESETTING BY
Ken Wilson | point918

INDEXED BY
Alan Rutter

PRINTED IN MALTA BY
Gutenberg Press

COVER ILLUSTRATIONS
*Above*: A view of Colditz Castle, a 16th-century fortress which
became an officers' camp and gained a reputation as the 'escapers' gaol' (Topfoto).
*Below*: POWs at Stalag IIB at Fallingbostel greet their liberators, 16 April 1945;
photograph by Sgt Smith, of No 5 Army Film and Photographic Unit.

# CONTENTS

During the late afternoon of 4 September 1939, the RAF mounted its first bombing raid of the Second World War. Of the fifteen Blenheim Mark IV bombers that took part, four from No. 107 Squadron, based at RAF Wattisham, were shot down in the target area near Wilhelmshaven, and ten of the aircrew lost their lives. The observer and the air gunner of one of the Blenheims survived, although badly injured, and were taken into captivity. Hence Sergeant G. F. Booth and AC 1 L. J. Slattery became the first Allied airmen to become prisoners of war (POWs). When Germany surrendered five years and eight months later in May 1945, they were repatriated together with 13,020 other British and Dominion Air Force former prisoners.

This large body of young, able-bodied men had led an alien life and gained unique experiences. Although no longer able to fight the enemy, they, together with the tens of thousands of other Allied POWs, had tied up a significant element of Germany's resources and manpower. During their captivity, the British and international support for them grew from an almost non-existent and ill-prepared organization to a large, specialized and sophisticated one geared for their particular needs.

As soon as the war was over, the Air Ministry recognized the unique nature of life as a POW and the difficulties that confronted potential escapers. They decided to commission a full account of the organization, methods and experiences of those who attempted to escape. In addition to providing a detailed reference, they also recognized the value of such an account as a guide to those who might find themselves facing the same situation in the coming years.

The invitation to compile the account was made to Squadron Leader Aidan Crawley—a former journalist who had served in the RAF as a fighter pilot, been shot down, and who had made a number of escape attempts during his four years spent in captivity. Over the next two years he gathered information from former prisoners and produced a narrative for the RAF's Air Historical Branch. By the time the narrative was ready for publishing commercially in 1951, British forces were engaged in the war in Korea and against communist guerrillas in the jungles of Malaya. Under these circumstances, it was decided that it would be unwise to release the narrative to the general public and, therefore, it appeared only as an Air Ministry confidential document. In 1956 an edited version was released commercially, but it was not until 1985 that a full unexpurgated version became available. It is the original official narrative that is reproduced here.

The book has become acknowledged as a definitive account of the methods of escape used by RAF and Dominion airmen during the Second World War, and it has formed the backdrop to many other books that have related individual escapes or life as a prisoner of war. However, although books such as *The Great Escape, The Wooden Horse, Colditz Story* and other personal accounts have become classics in their own right, they have necessarily been restricted to their own particular events and experiences. It is this book, *Escape from Germany*, which provides the wider perspective and embraces all the facets of escape; it thus retains its value and importance and fully deserves its excellent reputation.

As its title indicates, this book deals with escape, so at the outset it is important to draw a distinction between 'escapers' and 'evaders'. The former are those who have been taken into captivity, incarcerated in a prisoner of war camp and subsequently escaped. Evaders have avoided capture, remained 'on the run' and finally made their way to freedom.

During training it was impressed on all aircrew that it was their duty to escape, but the longer they delayed their attempt, the more the odds of success would reduce dramatically. Hence they were advised that an escape attempt should be made as soon as possible after capture since, in the early stages, they would almost certainly be in the hands of front-line troops or local police forces who had no specialist knowledge of guarding or imprisonment. As the prisoner was moved to Germany, he would come under the control of more competent guards until arriving in a prison camp, an establishment that was specifically designed and organized to keep him in captivity. The difficulties of achieving a delayed escape are graphically illustrated by the statistics. Over 5,000 airmen 'evaded' capture or escaped in transit—just 29 managed a successful escape from a German prisoner of war camp. Once a man had escaped from the camp, he became an evader. He then faced the almost insurmountable problem of being deep inside enemy territory with no hope of any outside assistance, unlike those who came down in the occupied countries and avoided capture.

Aidan Crawley uses the first part of his narrative to set the scene by describing the organization for escape. He gives a valuable insight into a prisoner's psychology and, in order to fully grasp the mindset and attitude men have in captivity and their attitude towards escape, it is important for the reader to appreciate this unusual and alien environment. Camps became sophisticated and unusual social places where men of vastly different backgrounds were thrown together. Their collective knowledge, initiatives, experiences, cultural backgrounds and attitudes created a unique society that most of us will never experience and thus, understandably, have some difficulty comprehending.

After describing the problems of escaping, Crawley then outlines the organization of escape. In the early days there was little co-ordination, and many escape attempts were organized and attempted on an individual basis. Success under these circumstances was almost negligible. It was almost two years into the war before Flight Lieutenant Harry Burton (later Air Marshal Sir Harry Burton) made the first successful escape, and by the end of 1941 just two men had made a 'home run'. The many individual efforts often jeopardized the safety of fellow prisoners and other escape attempts and it became apparent that a formal organization had to be established if there was to be any success. This led to the formation of Escape Committees, which started to appear by the end of 1941.

As Crawley makes clear in his earlier chapters, escape was an extension of a military operation and, under the control of the Escape Committee, it was conducted in such a way. Gathering, collating and interpreting intelligence was essential, as was detailed briefing. The organization had to be capable of producing tools to aid an escape and the appropriate escape materials, be they maps, clothing, forged documents or other requirements. It was in these departments that the huge variety of talents amongst the prisoners (or *kriegies* as they were known) played such an important and valuable role. Many worked under the guise of making theatre stage sets or costumes, printing camp newspapers, gardening, education classes and many other and varied activities. In this way, they could disguise many of their clandestine tasks, some on an almost industrial scale, in support of escape. These activities had an important indirect value since those involved, whilst not part of an escape, experienced a sense of community spirit and a great boost to their morale.

As experience was gained, the organization for escape became increasingly sophisticated, and one's admiration of what was achieved under immensely difficult circumstances is boundless. The escape of 76 men from a 336-foot tunnel at Stalag Luft III at Sagan on the night of 24 March 1944 encapsulates an amazing array of talent, skill, ingenuity and sheer bloody-mindedness, not to mention courage. We can only marvel at their achievements, sadly at such a great loss. Without doubt it was one of the most remarkable episodes of the Second World War and graphically illustrated that, even in captivity, it was still possible to carry the fight to the enemy and create havoc behind enemy lines.

It only needed a small party to escape for a national alarm to be initiated and many thousands of Germans were diverted to scouring the country—men who would otherwise have been available for other essential duties in the defence of their homeland. This nagging and continuous requirement whenever prisoners were at large was a form of sabotage and it remained a constant weapon which allowed the prisoners, as a force, to continue to contribute to the war effort.

In the main body of *Escape from Germany*, Crawley devotes much of his effort to writing about the Air Force camps, the *Lufts*. This is understandable since the great majority of escapes were made from these large camps. However, an understanding of the German approach to accommodating prisoners of war is an essential backdrop to the main activities in the Air Force camps.

At the beginning of the war all prisoner of war affairs were the preserve of the German High Command, the *Oberkommand der Wehrmacht* (*OKW*), and the camps were run entirely by army personnel. However, *Feldmarschall* Hermann Goering, Commander-in-Chief of the Luftwaffe, was determined that the detention of air force prisoners should come under his control and, in due course, separate camps were established for them. Despite his very many faults, Goering still held a certain sense of chivalry dating from his experiences in the First World War. He was also concerned that his captured aircrew would be well treated, two considerations that shaped his attitude towards the imprisonment of air force personnel.

By July 1940, two Air Force camps had been established. *Durchgangsler der Luftwaffe* (*Dulag Luft*) at Oberursel near Frankfurt became the initial reception and interrogation centre for all captured airmen. The first permanent camp, *Stalag Luft I*, was at Barth-Vogelsang on the Baltic coast, but this camp soon filled up. In October 1941 Goering ordered a new camp to be constructed, but it was not until March 1942 that the very large camp at Sagan, *Stalag Luft III*, was completed. This became the main camp for all air force prisoners, although separate compounds were established for officers and NCOs. Until the Sagan camp was completed many air force prisoners were sent to various army camps where a great deal of escape activity took place, but from which there were very few successful escapes. This period up to the middle of 1942 receives little attention by Crawley, but it is an important backdrop to what developed in the later years. The historian Charles Rollings covers this period in great detail in his two books *Wire and Walls* (2003) and *Wire and Worse* (2004), and these books are strongly recommended for those with a deeper interest in the history of RAF prisoners of war.

When Aidan Crawley wrote this narrative he was briefed to restrict his account to describing the support organization for, and the escapes from, prisoner of war camps. Furthermore, at the time of his research for the narrative, a great deal of material relating to the policy, organization and training for escape had not yet been released. There is, therefore, a good deal of important and highly relevant background material that has not been covered in *Escape from Germany*, and it is worth describing the important elements of this wider organization in some detail.

Throughout the First World War there still existed a somewhat old-fashioned notion that to be captured by the enemy was some kind of disgrace. There was, therefore, little encouragement to escape, although this did not stop some determined men from trying, and some were successful. It was not until 1917 that there was the realization amongst the military intelligence staff that there was a potentially large untapped source of intelligence material available from returning escapers. To exploit this opportunity the War Office established a small intelligence directorate, known as MI 1a.

With the end of the 'war to end all wars', little attention was paid to the possibility of other major wars in the foreseeable future, least of all to the need to maintain a support organization for escapers and evaders. However, by late 1938 war was again looking very likely, and two staff officers began to give some attention to the need for an organization similar to the old MI 1a. Captain A. R. Rawlinson, who had been a young officer on the staff of MI 1a at the end of the First World War, was mobilized in the summer of 1939. He was tasked to review arrangements for the interrogation of enemy prisoners, and the support for escape and evasion. The other officer was Major J.C.F. Holland, who had been appointed to a research branch to study irregular warfare. Amongst the subjects he reviewed was the need to provide prisoners of war with support for escape attempts, and in October he submitted a detailed paper outlining the organization that would be needed. Others had also started to give attention to the needs of prisoners of war and escapers, including those who had experience of such activities in the First World War, and a series of conferences was arranged to discuss the way forward.

From the outset of these discussions, it was apparent that a joint service approach was necessary, and the Director of Naval Intelligence (DNI) and the Director of Intelligence (D of I) at the Air Ministry were consulted. The outcome of these various initiatives was the establishment on 23 December 1939 of a new section within the Directorate of Military Intelligence (DMI), MI 9, to combine the work of all the departments. The brief minute to establish MI 9 was given a very limited circulation to MI 5, MI 6, the naval and air intelligence branches and DMI's two deputies. This significant document, Conduct of Work No. 48, was brief and to the point. It read:

1. A new section of the Intelligence Directorate at the War Office has been formed. It will be called MI9. It will work in close connection with and act as agent for the Admiralty and Air Ministry.
2. The Section is responsible for:
   a. The preparation and execution of plans for facilitating the escape of British Prisoners of War of all three services in Germany or elsewhere.
   b. Arranging instructions in connection with above.
   c. Making other advance provision as considered necessary.
   d. Collection and dissemination of information obtained from British Prisoners of War.
   e. Advising on counter-escape measures for German Prisoners of War in Great Britain, if requested to do so.
3. MI9 will be accommodated in Room 424, Metropole Hotel. [off Whitehall in London]

Placed in charge of MI 9 was Major Norman Crockatt DSO, MC. He had served with distinction in the First World War, and was to provide the section with focused and dynamic leadership for the remainder of the war. It was divided into two halves: one to deal with enemy prisoners and the other with British and Commonwealth prisoners, escapers and evaders. Rawlinson was put in charge of the section dealing with the enemy prisoners, called initially MI 9(a). MI 9(b) was responsible for all aspects relating to Allied prisoners and evaders. Following the German bombing of London in September 1940, Crockatt moved his organization to a country house at Wilton Park in the Chilterns where it became known as Camp 20, Beaconsfield.

The work of MI 9 expanded to such an extent that it resulted in the establishment in December 1941 of a Deputy Directorate of Military Intelligence (Prisoners of War) — DDMI (PW). Crockatt was promoted to Colonel, and subsequently Brigadier, to become the Deputy Director of this new organization. On 1 January 1942 the new MI 9 was re-organized into two sub-sections. MI 9(b) dealt with co-ordination, distribution of information and liaison with other services, government departments and overseas commands. MI 9(d) was responsible for arranging preventive training to combatants of the three services, the issue of escape and evasion equipment, and the promulgation of information to units at home and MI 9 organizations overseas.

Crockatt emphasized the value of getting back service personnel and containing additional enemy manpower on guard duties. He also outlined the methods to be adopted to achieve his objectives, and he split these into three categories. Two of these became fundamental pillars of the escape and evasion scene — the third was to devise methods of maintaining the morale of prisoners of war. The first series of measures were geared to preparing combatants before they went on operations. These included 'preventive training' (instruction in escape and evasion), and the issue and regular updating of a new publication, the MI 9 Bulletin, which passed on information on all aspects of escape and evasion including sanitized reports of successful evasions. Other measures were the technical research and production of escape aids, including special maps, the issue of these aids and 'blood chits', and the preparation of plans for escape and evasion. The second series of measures were geared to obtaining and distributing post-evasion information, which included the interrogation of escapers and evaders. The information obtained was embodied in reports and sent to all three services, and much of it was then used for briefing purposes, and the development of new escape aids.

To meet Crockatt's remit to prepare combatants before they went on operations MI 9(d) set up a school in Highgate in north London in January 1942. It was given the non-committal title of Intelligence School 9 (IS 9) — this title also provided a convenient cover for the secret work of MI 9's field activities. The school's main task was to train intelligence officers from all three services who were capable of briefing the men in their units on the intricacies of escape and evasion. All intelligence officers at the RAF's Operational Training Units and operational stations attended the course before returning to their units to brief all aircrew.

With the huge expansion of RAF operations in 1942 and 1943, particularly those of Bomber Command, it soon became apparent that the scope of the school had to widen in order to provide aircrew with knowledge on escape and evasion techniques. Travelling MI 9 lecturers toured military units and by the end of August 1944, they had given almost 1,500 lectures to RAF personnel, with 290,000 attending. First World War escapers joined the teams, as did those who had recently successfully evaded capture and returned to their units. Needless to say, these tended to concentrate on evasion techniques rather than methods of escape. Aircrew were also briefed on their rights under International Law, the conditions in Occupied Europe, how prison camps were organized and the conditions prisoners could expect to find once they arrived in captivity.

An important aspect of MI 9's work was to devise and develop escape aids for aircrew. This was the domain of a former First World War pilot, Christopher Clayton Hutton, variously described by the hierarchy as 'the most wayward and original of them all' and as 'eccentric, he cannot be expected to comply with ordinary service discipline'. He had always had an interest in magicians and escapologists, and he collected from second-hand bookshops all the escape books that he could find and had them summarized. By talking to First World War escapers and evaders, Hutton learnt that the most valuable aids were a map, a compass and food in concentrated form.

He first set about producing maps, and by the end of the war his department had produced well over a million silk maps to cover every theatre of war. After perfecting his map-making techniques, he turned his attention to the manufacture of magnetic compasses that could be hidden in various pieces of clothing or in routine objects such as pencils, pipe stems and buttons. Many of his aids, including mini-cameras, saws and knives, were designed for smuggling into prisoner of war camps; while some could be carried in by prisoners, most were sent concealed in 'loaded' parcels disguised as private parcels or donations from charitable organizations. Perhaps the most valuable aid to emanate from Hutton's fertile mind was the escape aid box, designed to carry concentrated food. It was made from a pair of acetate plastic boxes, one fitting closely inside the other, and filled with concentrated foods, such as Horlick's tablets and chocolate, together with water purifying tablets, a small rubber water bottle and a fishing line. The box fitted into a pocket and was waterproof.

Before flying on operations, aircrew went through a routine of dressing in their flying clothing, collecting survival equipment and, for those flying long-range sorties, in-flight rations. A crucial part of this pre-flight routine was the collection of escape and evasion equipment. Many aircrew had maps and compasses already hidden in their flying clothing and uniforms, and they were issued with the standard aid box. For aircrew operating over Germany, where no help could be expected from the population, a supplementary aid box was carried that contained sufficient nourishment for seven days. Aircrew were also issued with a coloured purse containing the equivalent of £12 in notes of the currency of the countries in which they may have to travel to evade capture, the appropriate silk map, a compass and a hacksaw. Finally, they carried one or two photographs of themselves in civilian clothing that could be used on forged identity documents.

One aspect that could not be covered by MI 9 lectures or individual briefings for security reasons was the organization of the escape lines, one of the most important aspects of MI 9's work. When Crawley wrote his narrative, much still had to be discovered about the running of these lines established in northwest Europe, and there was still great sensitivity about those involved and their gallant and clandestine activities. Therefore in his narrative his descriptions of the successful escapes say little about the experiences of the escapers once they got into the hands of the escape lines.

Of the 29 escapees from German prisoner of war camps, nine travelled through France and into Spain. Of course, many 'evaders' also travelled down these lines. There were four principal organizations, two of which carried the majority of evaders. The 'Pat' Line had its origins from the time of the British and French withdrawal from northern France in the spring of 1940. Centred on Marseille, a line had been established by Captain Ian Garrow who had avoided capture at Dunkirk. He made contact with MI 6 and co-ordinated the establishment of a route from Paris, through Marseille to the Perpignan region where evaders left to cross the Pyrenees or were picked up by boat from a nearby beach. By the middle of 1941, Garrow had laid the foundations of the escape line when 'Lieutenant Commander Patrick O'Leary' appeared on the scene. He was Albert-Marie Guerisse, a Medecin-Capitaine in the Belgian Army who had escaped from Dunkirk to England where he joined the Special Operations Executive (SOE), who gave him his alias as a French-Canadian and a commission in the Royal Navy. He was persuaded to take over the running of the line, which he did until a former British Army sergeant turned traitor betrayed him, allowing the Gestapo to infiltrate the line in early 1943. O'Leary survived his time in a concentration camp and was later awarded the George Cross. The line never fully recovered, but was able to continue on a reduced scale. Over 600 Allied airmen owe their freedom to the gallant members of the Pat Line.

The 'Comet' Line had its beginnings in Brussels, and came into being during the summer of 1941. It was co-ordinated by a 24-year-old trained nurse, Andrée de Jongh (known as Dédée). She personally made 18 crossings of the Pyrenees, and the Comet Line passed over 800 Allied evaders into the Basque region of Spain. In early 1943 the Gestapo infiltrated the line and Dédée was captured as she made her 19th crossing. Most of the heroic Belgian and French members of the line were captured, but one key member, Elvire de Greef (Tante Go), remained free, and she kept the line open, the last airman crossing into Spain on 4 June 1944. Dédée, unlike many others, survived her ordeal in Ravensbruck Concentration Camp. She recovered to become a missionary. The George Medal was among her many awards, and the King of Belgium made her a countess.

A third line was the 'Marie-Claire' Line run by the remarkable Mary Lindell, Comtesse de Milleville. The 'Marie-Claire' line operated by collecting evaders from many parts of France before moving them to safe houses in the Ruffec area. Once six or seven had been gathered, 'Marie-Claire' took them to the Pyrenees where she handed them over to Spanish mountain guides. This line was also infiltrated and Marie-Claire went to Ravensbruck, an ordeal she survived.

The fourth line, established in January 1944, had a relatively short life. Co-ordinated by a French-Canadian soldier, the 'Shelburne Line' exploited the short sea crossing between Brittany and Devon using the Royal Navy's fast motor torpedo boats based at Dartmouth. By the time of the liberation of France six months later, 365 Allied airmen had been rescued. There were further lines, some starting in Holland, and they linked into the other lines, all of which passed through Paris.

Most returning escapers and evaders were interrogated in London. MI 9 was very conscious of the welfare aspects of those returning, many of whom had been 'on the run' for many months, and others who had suffered particular hardships and gruelling experiences. The main report contained information on an escape or evasion up to the point where the individual passed into the hands of 'an organization'. No names of persons were mentioned, nor any descriptions given that might have identified helpers. These reports had a considerable influence on future policy and the re-design of escape aids. As the number of airmen returning after being shot down and making a successful evasion increased, the reports were of particular value to those responsible for the expanding training organization.

The work of the 'helpers', many of whom paid with their lives for their courage and service, has always created the closest possible bond with those who were helped. Many 'helpers' remained anonymous, but the establishment of the RAF Escaping Society in 1945 ensured that thousands of them, and their dependents, were given support. Although the Society has now disbanded, other organizations devoted to the memory of the helpers continue to give support where it is needed.

Those readers with a particular interest in the work of the escape lines are recommended to read Airey Neave's book *Saturday at MI 9*. Numerous other works describe in detail the work of individual lines and those who organized them.

The final words of this brief introduction should be left as a tribute to Aidan Crawley, the author of this book. Many will wonder who he was and how he came to write this specialized and detailed narrative.

Crawley was ideally placed to be the author of *Escape from Germany*. His modesty prevented him from recording that his Hurricane fighter had been shot down over North Africa and he became a guest of Adolf Hitler, soon finding himself in a German prisoner of war camp.

An Oxford graduate and a journalist, Crawley joined No. 601 (County of London) Squadron of the Auxiliary Air Force and trained as a pilot. He was mobilized at the outset of the Second World War and by the middle of 1941 was flying Hurricanes with No. 73 Squadron during the North African desert campaign. Whilst strafing enemy troops on 7 July 1941, he was shot down by ground fire and captured. A few weeks later he was at Dulag Luft, and by mid-1942 he was one of the first inmates of Stalag Luft III at Sagan. His first stay was short, and after being transferred to Oflag XXIB at Schubin in Poland, he was involved in an audacious escape (see pages 232–235). He joined a team digging a tunnel from a cesspit and on 5 March 1943 was one of the 33 men who broke free. He was well prepared with a passable suit, money, forged papers and a supply of food.

Once outside the camp, Crawley made contact with a Polish family who sheltered him, before he made his way by bus and train to Berlin. Very proficient in German, he was able to negotiate various checkpoints, but Allied air raids had disrupted the train service to Munich and he was forced to stay in a hotel for a few days. In due course he arrived in Munich before travelling to Innsbruck. However, as he travelled on a local train towards the Swiss frontier, an inspector became suspicious of his papers and he was arrested. He was the last of the Schubin tunnellers to be caught, and his magnificent effort had come close to success. Crawley always thought that his attempt was worthwhile since thousands of German troops had been used to look for him and his fellows.

Crawley remained at Stalag Luft III for the rest of the War. He was a member of the Escape Committee and worked in the information section. He made another escape attempt, but was soon apprehended. He also acted as camp interpreter, which included the occasion when the Senior British Officer, Group Captain Willis, announced that 50 officers had been shot following their capture after the Great Escape. As the evacuation of Sagan seemed imminent in early 1945, Crawley was appointed to gather information and documents to be used after the war. Despite the rigours and privations of the 'Long March', he was able to retain his valuable archives. His services as an interpreter proved invaluable during this ordeal, and he was able to barter for better conditions and food on behalf of his colleagues. A few days after the capitulation of Germany, he and his fellow prisoners were flown home by the RAF.

It is fitting to conclude this introduction with the words of the distinguished former Head of the Air Historical Branch, the late Air Commodore Henry Probert, who wrote; 'The volume Aidan Crawley wrote is in one sense a tribute to his personal courage and achievements as a prisoner of war. At the same time—and he would be the first to admit—its essential purpose is to honour those many thousands who for much of the war could only contribute to the Allied effort by causing the Germans as much trouble as possible'. Of that, and of its lasting fascination, there is no doubt.

GRAHAM PITCHFORK
May 2009

C.D. 1073

Copy No. 204

THE SECOND WORLD WAR
1939 — 1945
ROYAL AIR FORCE

# ESCAPE FROM GERMANY

Promulgated for information and guidance of all concerned.

By Command of the Air Council.

*J. H. Barnes*

ISSUED BY THE AIR MINISTRY (A.H.B.)

1951

*This volume records the methods of escape used by members of the Royal Air Force during the 1939–45 war. It is a history only, and should not therefore be confused with the publications describing current evasion and escape policies issued by the Joint Services through Air Ministry (A.I.9).*

## PREFACE

Since no written records about escape were kept in prisoner of war camps much of the material contained in this book has been obtained verbally or from accounts written some time after the events which they describe; for certain sections the author, Mr. Aidan Crawley, has drawn largely on his memory. As many prisoners learned to memorise with great accuracy the result is dependable in the main, but occasionally even the best sources have disagreed and it has not always been possible to be sure of a date or a figure.

To acknowledge all the help received would be impossible. Of the many manuscripts sent in, two, running into tens of thousands of words, form the basis of the description of the great tunnel at Stalag Luft III and were written by Commander P. E. Fanshawe, R.N., and Squadron Leader R. G. Kerr-Ramsay, R.A.F, two of the officers chiefly responsible for its success. Some of the descriptions of unsuccessful attempts were written by those who made them on odd scraps of paper before they left Germany during the last few days of the war.

But without the help of one man the book could not have been written at all. Squadron Leader C. B. Flockhart, R.A.F., who as Warrant Officer Flockhart was one of that small band of men who escaped from a prison camp in Germany and reached England, devoted himself to the interest of prisoners of war on his return. When the war was over, as the result of hundreds of interviews, he compiled a record of events in every camp in Germany in which Air Force prisoners had been held. For Part II of this book his work, which runs into many volumes of typescript, has been an essential and sometimes the only source of information. In addition, Squadron Leader Flockhart wrote the first draft of the chapters dealing with N.C.O.s' camps and with the Escapers' Camp at Colditz, and went through the whole text with great care to make sure that the experience of the N.C.O.s was adequately covered.

# INTRODUCTION

In the war against Hitler the meaning of the word Escape became so enlarged that a distinction must be made. In previous wars, fighting was mainly between fleets and armies and prisoners were military; even when portions of a country were overrun, civilians usually accepted occupation with stoicism but without organised resistance. But in the last war, with most of Europe occupied by the Germans and whole races subjected to extermination or slavery, thousands of men and women devoted themselves to underground hostilities. For them the problem was not so much how to escape as how to evade capture; and although the business of escape and evasion often overlapped, the word Evasion came to have a special significance.

Evasion can be said to have begun in 1934, when the Jews in Germany had to flee from the Nazis. As the stream of refugees grew, stories of hardship and adventure, and later of torture and concentration camps, became familiar in England and other countries which gave asylum to the Jews. But so long as these events were confined to Germany, no widespread consciousness of what was happening existed in the rest of the world.

With the attack on Poland the stream became a flood. From September, 1939, up to the time of the German occupation of the Balkans in the spring of 1941, tens of thousands of Poles crossed the frontiers of Hungary and Rumania to find their way back to France or England and to continue the fight. Some of these Evasions were mass movements, whole regiments and divisions crossing into neutral territory to be interned until one or another of the Allies could arrange for their reception. But many thousands escaped alone or in small groups, often crossing the mountains in mid-winter, and always suffering agonies of suspense. The endurance of these people and the patriotism which led them to leave their homes and fight anywhere and in any way against those who had invaded their country makes one of the most moving stories of the whole war.

From the end of 1941 onwards the need for Evasion spread into almost every quarter of the globe. Wherever the Allies had to give ground, in Greece, Africa, Burma, Malaya, and above all in Russia and Western Europe, men and women found themselves in enemy territory faced with the prospect either of surrender or of evading capture and carrying on the battle by underground methods, or of escaping and reaching Allied lines. The greatest difficulties were undoubtedly experienced in the Far East, and those who remained at large and fought with guerillas in Malaya or China, or who reached Australia or India, were few in number and endured hardships even more severe than those encountered in the European or African zones. In Greece and Crete some British troops evaded capture and managed to live in the mountains throughout the war; others reached the coast and with the help of courageous Greek sailors ran the gauntlet of German naval patrols to land in Turkey or on the shores of Egypt. In the African desert, owing to the speed of advance and retreat and the frequent operations of the Air Force and airborne troops, men of all arms constantly found themselves hundreds of miles behind the enemy front line. Some, performing extraordinary feats of endurance, got home by themselves; many more were helped by Arab tribes who continued their nomadic existence on the fringe of the fighting and who sometimes rendered the same service to both sides. In Russia the scope of those who evaded capture in the vast areas covered by the German advance has been convincingly demonstrated by captured German documents, which show the number of German divisions occupied in suppressing sabotage or in waging guerilla warfare hundreds of miles behind the German front line.

It was in Western Europe, however, that Evasion was most highly organised. An underground network, under regional commands but closely linked between the various countries, spread over the whole of the German occupied territories from the Baltic to the Pyrenees. All kinds of military activity from mountain warfare and large-scale sabotage to whispering campaigns, the distribution of pamphlets, or individual assassination were constantly undertaken by thousands of men and women who lived in hiding for four years. One of their chief tasks was the rescue of Allied airmen shot down over Western Europe, several thousand of whom were passed along the famous "lines" of the underground organisation to be taken to safety by submarine, aircraft, or couriers crossing the Alps or Pyrenees.

From its nature the history of Evasion has few records, but many books have already been written of a fictional or semi-biographical kind, and much first-hand evidence has been collected. Many of the chief characters have already been rewarded. It is to be hoped that one day a comprehensive history will be written of what must have been the most relentless of all the operations of war.

The story told in this book begins where Evasion broke down. For every airman passed along the underground "lines" to freedom, at least ten fell into enemy hands. Some were captured immediately their aircraft crashed or soon after they landed by parachute, others spent many days and months in hiding. Nothing was more heart-breaking for those whose duty it was to interrogate prisoners newly arrived in camps in Germany than to hear how, after being passed along some "line" and escorted, perhaps from Holland to Perpignan, a man was suddenly and inexplicably identified by the S.S. He might have lived securely in a farmhouse or in the centre of Brussels or Paris and have been fed and housed by agent after agent; he might have been travelling on a train with some of those gallant and outwardly insignificant middle-aged ladies who often acted as escort; he might have arrived at some destination in a remote part of the country where he was to meet another of these ladies or perhaps a farm-hand; and instead, quite suddenly, he would be met by two members of the S.S., and both he and his escort would be taken to jail.

For the agents the sequel was invariably death. For the airman, if he could establish his identity, it meant the end of Evasion and the beginning of captivity, and perhaps—of Escape.

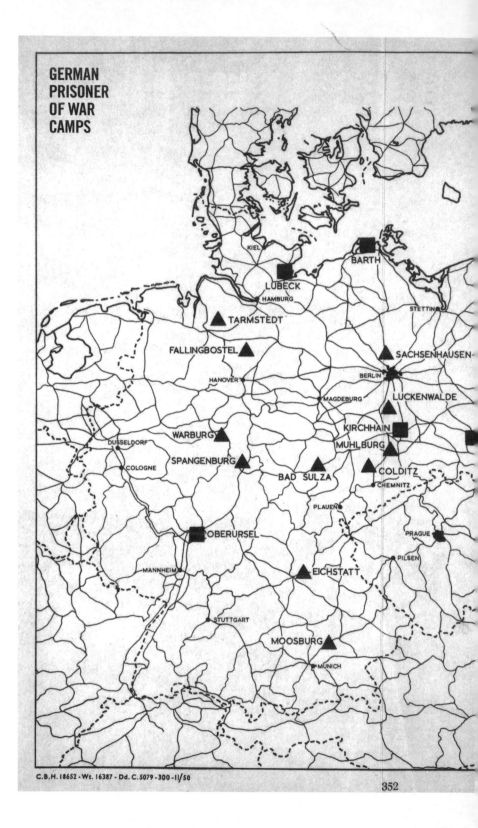

**GERMAN PRISONER OF WAR CAMPS**

BARTH

KIEL

LUBECK

BARTH

HAMBURG

STETTIN

TARMSTEDT

FALLINGBOSTEL

SACHSENHAUSEN

HANOVER

BERLIN

MAGDEBURG

LUCKENWALDE

KIRCHHAIN

WARBURG

MUHLBURG

DUSSELDORF

SPANGENBURG

BAD SULZA

COLDITZ

COLOGNE

CHEMNITZ

PLAUEN

OBERURSEL

PRAGUE

MANNHEIM

PILSEN

EICHSTATT

STUTTGART

MOOSBURG

MUNICH

C.B.H. 18652 · Wt. 16387 · Dd. C. 5079 · 300 · 11/50

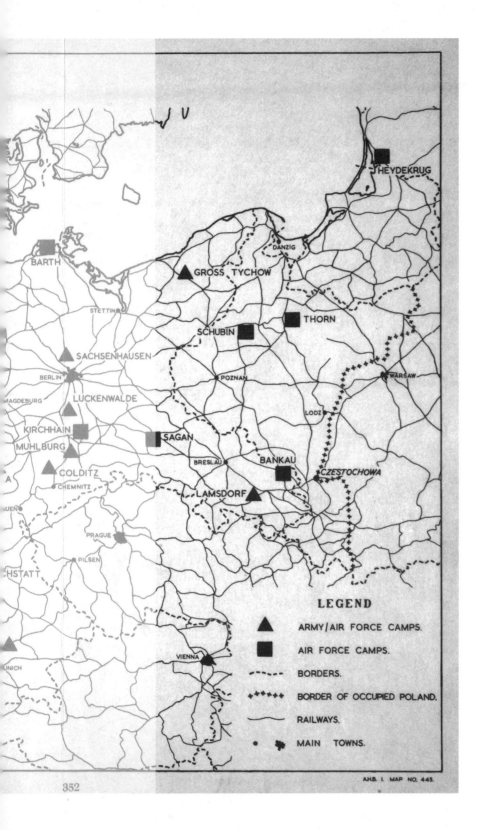

HEYDEKRUG

DANZIG

BARTH

GROSS TYCHOW

STETTIN

THORN

SCHUBIN

SACHSENHAUSEN

BERLIN

POZNAN

WARSAW

LUCKENWALDE

MAGDEBURG

LODZ

KIRCHHAIN

SAGAN

MUHLBURG

BRESLAU

BANKAU

COLDITZ

CHEMNITZ

CZESTOCHOWA

LAMSDORF

PRAGUE

PILSEN

HSTATT

VIENNA

UNICH

## LEGEND

▲ ARMY/AIR FORCE CAMPS.

■ AIR FORCE CAMPS.

---- BORDERS.

+++++ BORDER OF OCCUPIED POLAND.

—— RAILWAYS.

• MAIN TOWNS.

A.H.B. I. MAP NO. 445.

# Part One

# The Organisation

## CHAPTER 1 · PRISONER'S PSYCHOLOGY

It is not easy for those who have never been prisoners to understand the problem of escape. People are apt to imagine that when captured a man automatically longs to get away and that it is only the physical difficulties which prevent him. This is not true. Only a small percentage of prisoners of war ever make persistent attempts to escape; sooner or later the majority accept captivity and try to endure it with as much cheerfulness as possible.

Fundamentally the reason for this is that in captivity the instinct for survival re-asserts itself with great force. In battle that instinct often has to be suppressed, but when a man finds himself alone, without arms and in the hands of an enemy to whom his life is worth less than that of a beast of burden, it becomes his duty to survive. A live prisoner is a hindrance to the enemy, a dead one saves him trouble; from the first moment of capture there is in the back of every prisoner's mind a firm determination to come through with a whole skin.

But most attempts at escape do not involve serious risks and the reason that so few are made has less to do with fear than with inertia. A few rare people, who live for action, are never in any doubt what they should do. For them capture is always unbearable and escape their only interest from the start; but for the great majority the immediate difficulties often seem insuperable and the arguments for postponing the attempt overwhelming. This is particularly true during the first few hours or days of capture, when, if prisoners did but know it, their chances of escape are best, yet it is just then that their initiative is apt to be at its lowest.

For airmen during the Second World War these difficulties were increased by the manner in which they fell into enemy hands. On the sea, capture was sometimes the result of violent action, with perhaps many hours spent in the water, sometimes (in the case of merchantmen) of formal surrender; on land, although many hundreds of Commandos were captured singly while undertaking some particularly hazardous operation, the great majority of soldiers were taken prisoner in large numbers as the result of strategical defeat; surrender was formal and the men went into captivity with their units and among their friends. But, except for a few who were captured at sea or on the ground in France and the Mediterranean theatre of war, all airmen who arrived in prison camps had been shot down. In the space of a few hours they had been transferred from the comfort of an Air Force station to the middle of enemy territory. Instead of being supported by the *espirit de corps* of an operational unit they found themselves alone, either being hunted by the enemy or in his hands. Whatever the action in which they had been engaged, they had narrowly escaped death from anti-aircraft or machine-gun fire and had been compelled to crash or jump by parachute, probably for the first time in their lives. Sometimes they had undergone even more tense experiences, as the brief but graphic official records show. A fighter pilot reported:—

"The aircraft was hit and caught fire and I baled out landing on the telephone wires by the side of a railway line. My parachute was caught in the wires; I freed myself quickly and was about to approach some French civilians on the road when two Focke-Wulfs dived towards me at about sixty feet. They did not hit me, and I took off my Mae West immediately and left it by the side of the hedge, going off in my battledress."

Those who escaped from bombers operating at night often had even greater difficulties. An account taken at random reads:—

"I was second pilot of a Whitley which took off from Leeming at 2100 hours on the 28 June, 1941, to bomb Bremen. We reached the target and bombed it but on the return journey were shot down by flak at 0030 hours on 29 June over the coast. We baled out and came down in the sea. We were picked up by a German mine-sweeper."

This pilot was lucky to survive a parachute landing in the sea and to be picked up so soon; it was more common for bomber crews who landed in the sea to have to take to a dinghy. The longest period men are believed to have survived in a dinghy was fourteen days; but many spent more than a week on the water in mid-winter, and although some died while afloat or soon after reaching land, others found their way through German hospitals to prison camps.

Sometimes the escapes seemed providential. It was quite a common experience for fighter pilots to be knocked unconscious and blown out of their aircraft at 25,000 feet or more, to come to their senses when within a few hundred feet of the earth and then to pull the cord of their parachutes and land safely. On at least three occasions men jumped without para-chutes at all, and yet survived. One, after falling for nearly two miles through the night to what he imagined was certain death, hit another man whose parachute had just opened and whose body had swung out hori-zontally, clear of the envelope. The body must have been at the beginning of its downward swing, or the impact would have severely injured both men. The man who was falling free clung instinctively to the object which he hit, and finding it to be a pair of legs, held on. His saviour turned out to be another member of his crew. Both came down on the same parachute, receiving only minor injuries on landing.

Another man, a sergeant air-gunner, fell 18,000 feet without a para-chute and landed on the side of a steep hill in a deep snowdrift. Thereafter his chief difficulty was to convince the Germans, and later his fellow pris-oners, that his story was true. After much argument he managed to per-suade his captors to take him back to the scene of his fall, and as they could find no sign of his parachute and were able to confirm many other details, they signed affidavits on his behalf. Once they had heard his story none of the prisoners in the camp to which he was taken doubted his word.

Collisions in the air were frequent, particularly between bombers. One officer, aged twenty, flying a Lancaster, hit a Halifax over his target, and while interlocked and on fire hit another Halifax on the way down. All three machines were burnt out and he was the only survivor.

Most of those who reached the ground uninjured tried to get away, and many succeeded. For those who failed on the other hand capture was often a great relief. A man might have been alone and on the run for many days, or have spent a long time in the hands of some underground organisation; in either case he had suffered prolonged nervous strain. Once in enemy hands the temptation to relax was almost irresistible. He was no longer hunted. Instead of having to take lightning decisions, any one of which might cost him his freedom, the power of decision had passed from him. Events had taken charge and the sensible course seemed to be to recuperate and wait until a chance of escape presented itself. It required almost super-human qualities to *wish* to be hunted again immediately and to begin to contrive a means of escape rather than to wait for one to be presented.

Inside a prison camp the force of inertia was equally great. Once again the prisoner's first sensation on reaching the seclusion of the barbed wire was one of relief. At last he ceased to be "on show". Having been stared at, pointed at, segregated from those around him by special guards, perhaps interrogated for long hours, he was among his own people. The sound of his own language raised his spirit and he could laugh once more without a guilty feeling that he was fraternising with an enemy; within the limits of the camp he could move how and where he pleased.

When these early sensations had worn off, others took their place. The mere fact of being a prisoner offered endless possibilities. A man might dream of reading Shakespeare, of learning languages, of playing the piano, of doing some of the things he had often longed to do but for which he had never found time. He felt with urgency that this was a far better way of spending his days than thinking of escape which, at best, had such a slender chance of success.

From the first moment of captivity, therefore, there began in every prisoner's mind a conflict which lasted often until the day of liberation. Should he, or should he not, try to escape? Ought he to spend his time in what would almost certainly be fruitless endeavour, or should he use it to equip himself to be a better citizen later on?

There were many who from the start decided on the course of self-improvement. They argued, with great force, that however heroic escape might appear the odds against success have always proved so enormous that the realistic and truly patriotic thing to do was to put the idea out of their minds. In any war the number of those who reach home from prison camps is small; in this last war, out of the ten thousand British Air Force prisoners who were in permanent camps in Germany less than thirty ever reached Britain or neutral territory; and that despite the most energetic and highly organised attempts. The proportion of successful attempts among the other services was no higher. To every thinking man, therefore, the wisdom of spending years in such hopeless effort must at some time have seemed questionable and no one could blame those who decided escape was not worthwhile. Provided they stuck to their guns and held their point of view with tolerance they were often most valuable members of the community.

Nevertheless, for a number of people the arguments in favour of trying to escape were overwhelming. In the first place, it was laid down that should a prisoner see a reasonable chance of escape, it was his duty to take it. Suppose a prisoner had suddenly been deserted by his guard and instead of trying to rejoin his own forces deliberately sought captivity again, he would have been the equivalent of a deserter. Obviously the question turned upon what a man considered a reasonable chance, and it was left to each individual to decide. However, he was not left without guidance. In previous wars it was open to any man who wanted a quiet life to give his parole to the enemy; in this war parole could only be given for periods of twenty-four hours for the purpose of recreation or medical treatment and even this was discouraged by most senior officers. Plainly the authorities hoped that men would look for reasonable chances, and not take a passive attitude.

The official view was not a matter of form. Escape was a duty because the return of a prisoner had considerable military value. In total war manpower is the greatest of all problems and every able-bodied man is a vital asset. A prisoner who had been out of action for some time might no longer be fit for front line service or capable of piloting the latest aircraft, but there were thousands of other less spectacular things he could do. Assuming that in this last war one German was equal to one Englishman the mathematics of the position concerning Air Force camps were that for every four men immobilised as prisoners only one German was immobilised as a guard; in some camps the ratio was much higher. To remain a prisoner, therefore, was to play the least economic of all parts.

Secondly, escaped prisoners often supplied valuable information. Should they escape early their reports might affect a battle; but even when a man had spent months or years in prison camps he was still able to confirm much information that had come from less trustworthy sources. On journeys between camps or during his escape itself he might have passed through towns or seen factories which had been bombed, and he might have been able to describe much that was not ascertainable from photographs. His impressions of the general morale of the enemy, both from his contact in prison camps and from what he saw while escaping, were probably less biased than the reports of even the best secret agent. In peacetime, when regular information is received from diplomatic missions, Foreign Office officials are glad to talk to ordinary travellers and to gain first-hand opinions; how much more glad must a military intelligence officer have been to meet a man who had travelled through the heart of enemy territory.

Even if attempts at escape failed, as they generally did, still they were of military value. It was very evident in this last war that at certain Allied prison camps, where little or no attempt at escape was made, very few German troops were needed as guards; in Air Force prison camps, on the other hand, there was not only one guard to three or four prisoners but a large staff of highly qualified German officers and technicians. When any major escape took place tens of thousands of extra troops were turned out all over the country to hunt for the fugitives and to patrol roads and bridges. As the War went on the high bargaining value placed on prisoners by the German Foreign Office and the fear that British prisoners might join underground organisations made escape a matter of first importance. If more than five prisoners got away the matter was at once reported to the High Command and often received the personal attention of Hitler himself.

The effect of escapes on the morale of German civilians was also valuable. Those who remember reading accounts of the escape of German or Italian prisoners from English prison camps will remember the slight sense of surprise and irritation caused by the knowledge that a prisoner should still think it worthwhile to try and get home. The Germans were far more sensitive. Many hoped seriously that prisoners would come to admire Germany and even want to stay there and there is no doubt that the increasing number who escaped as the war went on depressed the people.

Most important of all, the effort to escape preserved the morale of the prisoners themselves. One of the great difficulties of prison life was that almost all effort, apart from the business of feeding and existing, was directed to goals which could be achieved only in the indefinite future. The mere fact that in preparing for a mass escape hundreds of people were co-operating in an enterprise which held the prospect of an immediate result was the best tonic a prison camp could have. In building a tunnel, making clothes, forging papers or preparing maps men took part in a common effort and once again got the feeling of serving a community. Instead of being thrown in upon themselves they began to rely upon and to judge each other by qualities more positive than unobtrusiveness.

No doubt at any given moment in any prisoner of war camp there were always a majority who were neither preparing nor contemplating escape; but in Air Force camps most people at some time made an attempt, and at all times were ready to help even if it meant considerable effort and inconvenience. As a result, the organisation of almost every Air Force camp was geared to escape. Every other activity and every other consideration, except the care of the sick, was subordinated to it. Even those who regarded the whole business as a waste of time accepted the inevitable with good grace.

## CHAPTER 2 · THE PROBLEM OF ESCAPE

If a prisoner was really determined to escape, what were his chances? The answer is that they were best in the first few hours or days after capture and the longer he remained in captivity the more slender they became.

Imagine a man who landed in Germany by parachute. By ill luck, perhaps, he had been seen coming down and fell into the hands of the local police. He was taken to the village gaol. In remote parts of the country this was often the policeman's house and as likely as not the prisoner was shown into the kitchen. The news of his arrival would spread quickly in the village and he would become an object of interest. One or two of the more prominent members of the community would come in to see him and very probably he would be offered food and drink; in a short time all would be talking together on quite a friendly basis and even the policeman might soon be off his guard. No doubt he would telephone the nearest military headquarters to have the prisoner taken away, but meanwhile there would be an hour or two to wait and it was quite possible that the prisoner would have to spend the night under the local policeman's care.

Obviously in such circumstances there were opportunities to get away. In the cells of village gaols the bars were apt to be rusty and insecure and endless excuses for leaving the cell for a few moments could be contrived;

if no other opportunity presented itself the policeman might be overpowered.

Opportunities grew progressively fewer. From the village gaol the prisoner would probably be taken to a town or to a military garrison and from there to a Gestapo Headquarters or to a military transit camp. At each stage security improved. Yet, even so, a prisoner still had a far better chance of getting away than he would ever have once he reached a permanent camp for the simple reason that he was on the move. In a train, in a lorry, in a crowded railway station, in the streets or villages and towns there might be opportunities of distracting the attention of the guards and slipping away. Furthermore, instead of being trained specially to watch prisoners the guards themselves were ordinary soldiers who could not help regarding the job of escort as something of an outing. No doubt they had been warned that they would be court martialled should the prisoner escape but they rarely managed to resist friendly advances and were usually on excellent terms with their captive after a few hours.

Even the Gestapo were inefficient when dealing with prisoners of war. They were so used to dealing with political prisoners who had been subjected to terror that they did not understand a prisoner who was unafraid. For them the chief danger to be guarded against was suicide and as soon as any man entered one of their prisons they took away his braces or belt, his razor and anything else that might conceivably be used as a lethal weapon. Although this was inconvenient, to a prisoner of war it was not fatal; if a chance of escape presented itself he could always find some means of keeping his trousers up. When he left their care the Gestapo always restored to him not only his braces and razor but any civilian clothes or money he had possessed when he arrived. Liaison between the Gestapo and the administration of prisoner of war camps apparently did not exist.

The proof that the earliest chances are best is found in the official records. In the year 1943 alone more members of the Air Force reached home by escaping on the way to a permanent prison camp than escaped from such camps during the whole war. Two members of the crew of an aircraft who succeeded in reaching England reported:—

"A German Corporal called out an escort of two men, youths of about 17 or 18 years of age. We had to follow these; they were very casual and kept their rifles slung; we walked for about ten minutes. There was a ditch on one side. My companion asked them for a light. As the guard gave it to him, he hit out at him, and I knocked the other one over. There was very little scuffling. We pushed them into a ditch, which was very swampy, and ran for the woods. We do not know whether we had merely knocked them unconscious or whether they were more seriously injured."

Another successful escaper stated:—

"We were then put on a train, from which I escaped after it had passed Rouen (about 23 August). There were German guards and prisoners in alternate compartments so that I had no difficulty in getting out at the carriage window."

In another case, while riding in a motor-cycle combination a prisoner waited for the moment when the German driver was looking at the side of the road and then, seizing the handlebars, jerked the combination into the ditch and escaped before his captors recovered.

The truth was that in all escapes luck played a great part, and a man could chance his luck easily while he was still outside the barbed wire. If more people had realised this, and realised from the outset that with an enemy who took prisoners at all there was nothing to lose in attempting to escape, more prisoners would have got home.

Once inside a permanent Air Force camp the prospects of escape altered drastically for the worse. Whether the prison was a medieval castle, a nineteenth century fortress, or a modern hutted and wired compound, it was designed deliberately to prevent its inmates from getting out and was equipped with all scientific aids for that purpose. The prisoner was at a tremendous disadvantage.

Surprisingly enough, even during Hitler's war, the most old-fashioned prisons were also the most formidable. Spangenberg, an old hunting lodge belonging to the family of Hesse, was a typical example. It was a gaunt castle standing on the top of a conical hill and surrounded by a broad dry moat flagged solidly with stone. Inscriptions carved in its panelling bore witness that it had been used for housing prisoners of war from the seventeenth century onwards. The reason was plain. The ground under the castle was solid rock so that from the interior it was impossible to tunnel. The moat was lit by searchlights and the wall on the far side was sheer, and twenty-five feet high. The parapet was guarded by German patrols.

Escape from such a place needed great ingenuity. Attempts to scale the moat failed ignominiously. Plans for launching a glider from the steep roof of the castle or for making a trolley-car to run across the moat on the telephone wires were discussed but never materialised. The only successful escapes from this camp, which housed prisoners from 1939 until 1945, were made by walking through the gates in disguise.

Luckily for the majority of Air Force prisoners it was only during the first eighteen months of the war that they were housed in such buildings. From the spring of 1942, when Goering's much-vaunted camp at Sagan was opened, they began to be segregated from the Army and to be kept in a few hutted camps of their own. For them, therefore, the problem was less often how to cross a moat or get out of a window than how to get outside the barbed wire.

The camp at Sagan was a model of what a prisoner of war camp should be – from the captor's point of view. A rectangular clearing measuring about a mile by two miles had been cut out of the pine forest which stretches southward from the town of Sagan to the Czechoslovakian border, and three compounds, two for prisoners and one for the German guards, had been built. Later the camp was enlarged and four more compounds were added, one of these in more open country three miles away. All except the German compound, which was in the middle of the north side of the clearing, were surrounded by two barbed wire fences ten feet high and between six and seven feet apart.

Each prisoner's compound was roughly of the same pattern. In the centre were wooden huts in which the prisoners lived. They were arranged in rows and each was designed to hold a hundred men, although they often contained double that number; four or five huts, usually standing a little apart, were set aside as kitchen, latrines and washhouses. Round the outside of the huts was an open space never less than forty yards wide, and beyond it the wire.

As the camp had been erected in a hurry the stumps of the trees which had been cut down were still in the ground when it was opened and it was left to the prisoners to remove them. When this had been done, the ground inside each compound was either dust or mud according to the weather. Except at the northern end of the camp, where the roofs of the town of Sagan were visible, the outlook was bounded by fir trees beyond which it was impossible to see at all. A drearier site could not be imagined.

The defences of the camp were thorough. Between the double wire of the perimeter fence loose coils of barbed wire lay thick on the ground so that it was impossible to walk across the intervening space. Exactly above the fence, at intervals of about a hundred yards, stood watch towers on each of which was a machine gun covering the interior of the camp. To the prisoners they were known as "Goon boxes". Immediately inside the wire was an area of dead ground six to fifteen yards wide, bounded by a low rail; if any prisoner crossed it, he could be shot without warning. At night boundary lights lit the perimeter of the whole camp and from each guard tower searchlights swept the compounds. To detect tunnelling microphones were let into the ground at intervals of twenty yards outside the wire and connected to a listening post in the German compound.

At Sagan these defences were manned by units of the German Air Force, the quality of which varied according to whether they were reservists or front line troops sent back for a rest. Quite frequently the guard company was composed of troops who had been withdrawn from the Russian front. The number of troops increased as the war went on but at no time was there less than one guard to four prisoners.

The duties of the guards were to man the towers, to patrol the wire, to guard the gates and to escort all vehicles and people going in and out of the prison compounds. There were seventy guard towers in all, each manned by one man who in addition to the fixed machine gun had a rifle and a "tommy" gun for use in case a prisoner got into an area which the machine gun could not cover. The patrols on the ground normally carried rifles, but if an escape had recently taken place some would carry automatic weapons. All guards in the towers and on the wire were relieved every two hours. At night additional guards patrolled inside the compounds with Alsatian dogs.

In addition to the ordinary guards, German Camp Headquarters consisted of an administrative staff and a special security unit whose duty was the prevention of escape. This unit was divided into sections of one officer and six or more N.C.O.s for each prison compound. The N.C.O.s were hand-picked and many of them had been with the Air Force prisoners since the beginning of the war. Dressed in dark blue overalls and armed with torches and screwdrivers of abnormal length, they patrolled the compounds in pairs from dawn till dusk probing anywhere and everywhere for any signs of preparation for escape. They could enter rooms unannounced, listen at windows, hide under floors or inside roofs and search or arrest anyone they pleased. To the prisoners they were known as "ferrets".

The chances of escape from a camp such as this were limited. They were better than from a medieval fortress because wire can be cut whereas the only way to reach the other side of a moat or wall is to climb or tunnel; and it was easier to tunnel from a large camp than from a flagged courtyard. Nevertheless, opportunity had to be carefully contrived. From the first day that barbed wire compounds were occupied men racked their brains for new ways out. After the first year or two few were found; "over, under or through" summed up the possibilities and newcomers had little option but to try old methods with greater thoroughness.

Most men began by tunnelling. This was one of the safest methods of getting outside the wire because while the tunnel was being built no one was in danger of being shot, and when finally completed there was a good chance of crawling away unobserved. Tunnelling also demanded less from an individual than most methods of escape. With the exception of the experts who designed the entrance and did the skilled work, those who built tunnels worked in teams and did as they were told. Most of the operations became a drill which needed perseverance and stamina but little more, and by working in teams men built up an *esprit de corps* which was otherwise so difficult to achieve in prison life.

Although tunnelling was exhilarating at first, it was apt to pall. The discomfort of the work, the time spent keeping watch in cold and draughty corners and the irregular hours soon wore down enthusiasm. The proportion of successful tunnels in Air Force camps in Germany was one in

thirty-five and even from those which were successful only a small proportion of the men who had built them got away. After working in a few
unsuccessful tunnels people often became discouraged and many decided
that the chances of escape were so small that it was their duty to spend
their time in other ways. For the intrepid, however, there was still the alternative chance of going "over" or "through" the wire.

To climb over the wire was the more difficult. If a prisoner had been
taken to an empty prison camp to carry out a test when there were no
guards, he would probably have managed to get across any double wire
fence within a quarter of an hour. When a camp was guarded, this could
be done only in very exceptional circumstances. Twice in 1942, in blinding
snowstorms, men went boldly up to the wire, climbed over it and walked
away without being seen. Thereafter in every camp there were plans to
take advantage of snow or fog, but few materialised.

Even thick fog or snow implied risks which few men were prepared to
take. At any moment a change in the wind or a gap in the fog might have
disclosed a man laboriously climbing the wire within a few yards of a
machine gun. Most men preferred less danger. The obvious time to try and
climb the wire was at night. If the boundary lights and searchlights could
be put out even for a few minutes, anyone might have a good chance of
succeeding. The electric system at all camps therefore was carefully studied and once a major scaling operation was performed successfully. Sometimes a change occurred unexpectedly. Every now and then German airmen
came to repair the wire, or to check the electric cables running above it, thus
providing an opportunity for impersonation. It was taken successfully on
more than one occasion.

However it was easier to go through the wire than to climb it for the
simple reason that in every compound there was a gate. The mere fact that
a gate opened and shut many times a day and that all manner of traffic
passed through it offered opportunities. Of course the gate was guarded
by a special sentry and to go through a man must either have acquired the
necessary pass or have hidden in some sort of vehicle. Even if he was
caught there was no risk, for he was simply arrested and taken off to the
camp gaol. If he succeeded he gained his freedom with less effort and usually with better equipment than was possible in any other way.

The only other method of going through the wire was to cut it. At all
times this involved considerable risk because by day or night there was the
danger of being seen and any man found close to the wire was liable to be
shot without warning. At night searchlights cast long shadows and by the
clever use of tree-stumps or folds in the ground it was possible to creep to
the guard-rail unobserved; but the dead ground between the rail and the
wire was usually bare sand and even if the guards in the towers noticed
nothing, beyond the wire was a sentry who must pass any given spot once

38

ESCAPE
FROM
GERMANY

*The*
*Organisation*
*of Escape*

every few minutes. In addition each compound was patrolled by police dogs every two hours. In daylight the danger of trying to cut the wire was so obvious that most men never contemplated it; yet on one occasion it was accomplished successfully in the middle of the afternoon and several times attempted in snowstorms. By night the wire was cut many times and almost always the prisoners got away from the camp.

Although, therefore, it was easier to escape before entering a permanent prisoner of war camp than after, no prison camp has yet been invented from which escape has proved impossible. No soldier has ever had so strong an incentive to keep prisoners in as prisoners have to get out. If he devoted all his time and energy to making his plans a prisoner of war was likely to find a way out in the end. That did not mean that he reached home, but to some prisoners of war a few days freedom were worth the effort of years.

## CHAPTER 3 · THE ORGANISATION OF ESCAPE

In the 1914–18 war, if one may judge by the books written, it was a common maxim that if a prisoner wanted to escape he should have nothing to do with Escape Clubs or Committees. So many plans were given away by loose talk that security alone appears to have dictated that as few people as possible should know when an attempt was being made.

During the 1939–45 war the fact that the prisoners of any one nation were usually segregated made the maintenance of secrecy easier; but the meaning of security was in any case more generally understood. The wide use of radio communications and the ease with which it could be tapped, as well as the greater speed and range of offensive weapons, created a more imminent sense of danger among combatants and non-combatants alike. In prison camps awareness became almost a sixth sense.

Carelessness in the early years caused so much effort to be wasted that prisoners learnt how dependent they were upon each other's help and discretion. At a comparatively early stage, therefore, an organisation was established in Air Force Camps in Germany on which prisoners who wished to escape came to rely entirely. Only an occasional eccentric attempted to plan an escape without its help. Although in some instances almost every individual in any compound or camp knew when escaping operations were in progress, only a few people knew the full details of any plan and the rest learned not to ask questions.

The control of the majority of activities in each compound of Air Force camps in Germany came under two headings. On one hand was the ordinary compound administration headed by the Senior British Officer and his adjutant and consisting of prisoners-in-charge of education, the distribution of Red Cross food, clothing, books, sports, theatres and all other camp activities, even down to the arranging of showers. All these departmental heads were appointed and each selected his own staff. Parallel, and at some points overlapping, was the Escape Organisation. This again was headed by the Senior British Officer but instead of the adjutant being the Chief Executive a Compound Escape Committee was appointed; this Committee in turn, appointed the heads of the various departments responsible for different kinds of manufacture or service, such as map-making and the collection of information. In some camps representatives were elected by the occupants of each of the barracks and these assisted the Escape Committee as advisers and executives. In N.C.O.s' compounds the Compound Leader was not necessarily the senior N.C.O. but was elected. The Germans permitted the Compound Senior Officers and Compound Leaders in each camp to hold conferences at frequent intervals to discuss administrative matters.

39

ESCAPE
FROM
GERMANY

*The
Organisation
of Escape*

## Officers' Compounds

In the general running of Officers' Compounds escape had priority over everything else, except care of the sick. For example, the supply of fuel was essential to general welfare but if the officer-in-charge of the distribution of coal saw a chance of promoting an escape from the coal dump, no fear of having supplies cut off as a reprisal was allowed to prevent the attempt. The same may be said of every other department.

Organisation did not come at once, however. In the early days of the war escape was looked on as a personal matter and permission to make an attempt was supposed to be obtained from the Senior Officer or Compound Leader. This was not always done and often control broke down. On one occasion, after the Senior Officer of the camp had carefully organised working parties for officers in order to create further opportunities for escape, one officer, quite unequipped and without even announcing his intention, walked off alone and so ruined the whole scheme. He was caught within 48 hours. In the same camp a prisoner who had been given special treatment in hospital, a concession which had been obtained with difficulty, saw a nurse's cap and coat hanging in the waiting room and decided suddenly to put them on and walk out. Unfortunately he had also forgotten that he was wearing a moustache and flying boots. He was recaptured almost at once with the result that hospital treatment was restricted, to the detriment of the wounded.

A more serious offence was committed by the prisoner who made an attempt to escape from an organised walk on parole. He was caught very soon afterwards and was spared a court martial only because the German Camp Commandant took a lenient view and thought the man partly insane. This breach, however, had repercussions in the German High

ESCAPE
FROM
GERMANY

*The
Organisation
of Escape*

Command and the number of parole walks which were allowed was restricted for the rest of the war.

Sometimes it was the Senior Officer himself who was at fault. By keeping the control of escape too much in his own hands he laid himself open to charges of favouritism and through lack of co-ordination would allow separate schemes to get in each other's way. Two teams engaged in digging tunnels might find themselves dispersing earth in the same place and each would accuse the other of jeopardising their schemes; men making clothes might find that others doing the same thing did not post sentries and ran grave risk of being caught. Strong though a sense of equality is among prisoners, when all are reduced to the same material level, rank without responsibility carries little weight and experiences such as these forced even the most independent prisoner to realise the need for organisation. Early in the existence of the first permanent Air Force camp at Barth, on the Baltic coast, the Senior Officer instituted an enquiry into escape, and as a result a policy was laid down upon which all subsequent organisation was based. For when new camps were opened old prisoners were always sent to form the nucleus of the administrative staff and naturally they passed on their experiences.

In officers' compounds the Senior Officer himself remained responsible for all final decisions on matters of escape but detailed organisation was put in the hands of an executive officer. At first the organisation was elastic. Whenever an escape involved several people and separate operations the Chief Executive chose one officer to be responsible for each particular job. If a tunnel was being built one officer would be in charge of digging, another of the dispersal of earth, another of carpentry, another of equipment for those intending to escape, and so on. In the case of individual attempts, the Chief Executive would examine each scheme with great care and ensure that no one attempt interfered with another. Within a few months results improved greatly. In order to make the organisation more democratic an advising committee was formed of one representative from each barrack and this system lasted until the end of the war.

In April, 1942, when Air Force officers were concentrated in the East Compound at Stalag Luft III Sagan, this organisation was developed further. Contingents of officers had come to Sagan from several Army camps in different parts of Germany and brought with them a varied experience, and as the war plainly had several years to run a tremendous effort was made to pool their skill and get people home. The Executive Officer who had been in control at Barth was put in charge, and the same type of committee was formed. In addition to the elected representatives a Compound Intelligence Officer was appointed who found his own staff, and whose duty it was to obtain all possible information about the German defences of the camp and about conditions in Germany and the occupied countries.

41

ESCAPE
FROM
GERMANY

*The
Organisation
of Escape*

When any officer had an idea for escape he first discussed it with his barrack representative and if it was approved they would bring it before the Escape Committee together. If the Committee approved the scheme the barrack representative became responsible for its operation and for seeing that any help that was needed was forthcoming.

By the middle of the summer of 1942 even this organisation proved inadequate. The number of schemes put forward had increased steadily and in that summer alone more than forty tunnels, varying in length from 10 feet to 400 feet according to when they were discovered, were dug. Every form of vehicle which entered the compound was boarded and every possible disguise from that of a German soldier to a top-hatted and soot-besmeared sweep was used in attempts to get through the gate. The wire was cut successfully on several occasions; and for every attempt made, at least a dozen schemes were planned. The work was more than one man from each barrack could manage.

The whole organisation was therefore revised. Barrack representatives were retained and continued to sift schemes and present them to the Committee, but a new and smaller committee was formed to decide priorities and questions of policy. It consisted of eight members, of whom five were deputed to supervise different types of escape. These, by then, had been classified under five broad headings:—tunnels, attempts to cut the wire, attempts to walk out of the camp in some sort of disguise, attempts to board transports, and "miscellaneous". Carelessness was still the chief cause of failure and an officer was put in charge of the security of all escape operations and told to organise his own staff. Both the Security Officer and the Intelligence Officer were *ex-officio* members of the new committee.

This committee worked well. Although its personnel changed, its pattern never altered. It met daily, functioning simultaneously as a Cabinet and Court of Appeal. At the height of the escaping season, in spring and summer, it had a full programme. At about 9 o'clock each morning its members would wander out to some point near the football clearing and lie down apparently to doodle in the sand. The Germans suspected that the meetings had something to do with escape and thought it was an escaping club, but as it met every day they took no particular notice.

The morning would begin with discussion about the progress of tunnels or the state of preparation of any individual attempts. With tunnels the difficulty was always the disposal of the earth which had been dug up. The places where this could be put were few and when several tunnels were being dug at the same time disputes were inevitable. One tunnel organizer might complain that men dispersing earth from another tunnel were moving in too steady a stream and were likely to arouse suspicion. Another might complain that new earth which had been dumped in the

42

ESCAPE
FROM
GERMANY

*The
Organisation
of Escape*

open had not been covered properly; another might suggest that as his tunnel was nearing completion work on all others might cease in order to reduce the risk of discovery.

This last would be a question of major policy to be decided according to the Committee's information about German suspicions. If it was known that the Germans believed that a tunnel was nearing completion, but did not know from which hut it was proceeding, it might be wise to let all tunnels continue in the hope that when the Germans discovered one they would be satisfied. If the Germans thought that no tunnel was nearing the wire it might be possible to work day and night on one tunnel and complete it before their suspicions were aroused. Sometimes attempts to walk through the gate in disguise or to cut the wire were staged deliberately in order to make the Germans think that for the moment tunnelling had been abandoned.

At intervals throughout the morning, while discussion on policy was going on, prisoners in ones and twos would stroll up and join the Committee to put forward new ideas. These were infinitely varied, but it was a rule that nothing too fantastic was to be ruled out. The wire was the obstacle, and anything which would land a man on the other side of it was worth considering. Perhaps the most ambitious were the schemes which aimed at leaving by air. A chemist noticed that the stench from the latrines was exceptionally powerful one summer and carried out experiments in the hope of filling a balloon with marsh gas, but he could find no material light enough to make an envelope. Several people designed gliders to be made from sheets, and in one camp parts of an aircraft were finished; but apart from the difficulty of launching a glider, it was almost impossible to hide the parts which had been made. Telephone and other wires which ran overhead across the barbed wire were another obvious opportunity, and in an American Compound a trolley was constructed to run along them. When it was launched, however, the wires sagged more than had been expected and the trolley crashed into the barbed wire fence. The man aboard was fortunate that he was not shot. One plan which was approved aimed at fusing all the lights round one of the compounds by catapulting a piece of iron over the electric cables which ran round the boundary fence. A wire was to be attached to this weight, which would short-circuit the current, and when the lights went out teams of men carrying ladders were to run to the wire and climb over in the darkness. The distance from the nearest hut to the fence was about 60 yards, and the plan was to construct a catapult in one of the rooms of the hut and project the weight and wire cable through the window. Experiments were carried out on a small scale in order to determine the type of catapult which would do the work required. Progress was satisfactory, and eventually a full scale catapult was constructed. To get the necessary leverage it was decided to use the walls of

43

ESCAPE
FROM
GERMANY

*The
Organisation
of Escape*

one of the small rooms at the end of the hut as uprights and when this had been done a further trial without the weight was made. A watch was set and with the aid of several men the catapult was stretched and secured to the trigger catch which went through the wall into the passage. The door of the room was shut and locked and the window opened. There was no doubt whatever that the catapult had worked. There was a terrific noise and the end of the hut shook visibly, but when the banging and clattering had subsided and the door had been opened, it was found that the wall of the room had collapsed and that the end of the hut itself was in danger of doing the same. Expert opinion was confident that had the weight and cable been in position it would easily have cleared the fence, but for want of more substantial uprights this scheme had to be abandoned.

The best schemes were usually less elaborate. On two separate occasions prisoners were packed in laundry bags and dumped successfully with the washing at the outer gate, but each time German soldiers saw the bags moving, and thought the phenomenon sufficiently unusual to warrant investigation. In both cases the prisoner was nearly suffocated. A similar fate nearly overtook a prisoner who lay at the bottom of a dung cart. He reached the gate, but he was almost overcome by fumes and had to climb out of his own accord. Another prisoner saw an opportunity in a horse and cart which daily left the camp with empty tins. He acquired a sack and carefully sewed hundreds of tins on until the sack was invisible. Having arranged to have the driver's attention distracted, he was then sewn into his sack and placed on the cart. The driver noticed nothing and continued on his round piling several hundred more tins on the cart before going down to the gate. However, on this occasion Compound Escape Intelligence had broken down; unknown to the prisoners an order had shortly before been issued that all carts leaving the camp were to have their loads prodded with a spear. Unfortunately the tins proved insufficient protection.

The Committee debated every idea thoroughly, taking particular care to ensure that no new scheme interfered with others already in operation, and before a new idea was approved hut representatives would be called in to give their opinion. But the number of plans in preparation steadily increased, and even the revised organisation became overstrained. Artists who had spent hours laboriously forging passes began to suffer from eyestrain, and indicated that they wished to draw something more inspiring than letter headings or police stamps. The few experienced tailors, leather workers and hat makers were also tired and perhaps discouraged by frequent failures. Regular departments therefore were formed for the making of clothes, maps, tools and other equipment and for the preparation of food and forging of documents. At the head of each was an officer who, though not on the Escape Committee, had access to it whenever he wished.

44

ESCAPE
FROM
GERMANY

*The*
*Organisation*
*of Escape*

The nucleus of his team consisted of a few of the original enthusiasts who stayed on long enough to train others and the rest were made up of volunteers. From then onwards it was seldom that an escape was postponed because of the failure to provide the necessary equipment.

All this imposed a great strain on security. Just as in flying the great majority of accidents are due to the human factor, so in escape failure was due in almost every case to carelessness. After the Chief Executive, therefore, the most important man in the whole escape organisation was the Security Officer, and his department was by far the largest. He alone, under the Senior Officer, had the right to call on prisoners on other than a voluntary basis. Had the purpose been solely escape the duties he imposed might not always have been performed willingly, but as the security system was also responsible for the protection of the secret radio on which all prisoners depended for news, there was seldom any difficulty. A successful escape, when it came, owed more to the security department than to any other.

### N.C.O.s' Compounds

In N.C.O.s' compounds the organisation of escape developed on parallel lines, but suffered from two handicaps. In the Officers' Compound discipline was maintained by the Senior Officer, who held his position and exercised his authority by virtue of his rank. In the N.C.O.s' compound seniority in rank was not recognised among the prisoners, and the Compound Leader was elected by majority vote. He maintained his position by virtue of his popularity and could not give orders. The N.C.O.s' Escape Committee therefore had no official standing and no means except persuasion of enforcing its wishes. The second difference was that only a small proportion of the N.C.O.s were deeply interested in escape; the majority did not feel it their duty to make an attempt. An Escape Organisation was first formed about September, 1941, by the Air Force N.C.O.s at Stalag IIIE Kirchhain, half-way between Berlin and Dresden. This Organisation formed the nucleus from which grew virtually all subsequent N.C.O. escape organisations in Germany.

Each barrack elected an Escape Representative, and these formed an Escape Committee under the chairmanship of the Camp Leader, who was also elected by majority vote. This Committee organised two mass escapes; one by breaching a wall and the second by means of a tunnel. Because of the nature of the operation, little organisation was needed in connection with the first escape beyond a diversion of the attention of the Germans at a critical time. On the other hand, the construction of the tunnel required much ingenuity, careful planning and security. As work on the tunnel progressed virtually every man in the camp was required to perform some function in connection with the scheme.

During the months of April and May, 1942, the Air Force N.C.O.s from

45

ESCAPE
FROM
GERMANY

*The
Organisation
of Escape*

Kirchhain, Stalag Luft I Barth, Stalag IXC Bad Sulza, and most of those at Stalag VII IB Lamsdorf were transferred to one compound at Stalag Luft III Sagan. This was known as the Centre Compound and was next to the Officers' Compound which has already been described. Batches of new prisoners arrived at intervals until October, 1942, when the strength was 1,800 N.C.O.s, and the compound was much overcrowded. At first there was no organisation of escape, and although a number of attempts were made by small groups of enthusiasts who attempted to build tunnels, all were discovered during the early stages. As a result, with the approval of the Compound Leader, the N.C.O. who had been chairman of the escape committee at Kirchhain formed Committee of three. The activities of this Committee were confined to considering schemes proposed by individuals and acquiring escape aids of various kinds, but in late October, 1942, at the instigation of the Senior Officer, it was arranged that a member of the N.C.O.s' Committee should visit the Officers' Compound secretly in order to learn how the Officers' Escape Organisation functioned. The transfer was successfully accomplished and the N.C.O. remained for two weeks without the knowledge of the Germans. As a result some alterations in the N.C.O.s' organisation were made, but owing to lack of discipline results continued to be disappointing.

In the autumn of 1942 the camp at Sagan broke up temporarily. The numbers of Air Force prisoners had increased so rapidly that the two compounds built originally were unable to house them. The construction of a new compound was begun at once, and, to avoid congestion through the winter, two hundred officers from the East Compound were sent to a camp at Schubin, in Poland, and one hundred and fifty N.C.O.s were sent from the Centre Compound to the camp at Barth, which was reopened. Among the N.C.O.s who volunteered to transfer to Barth in October, 1942, were a number who did so with the object of attempting to escape. Four enthusiasts formed themselves into a committee and attempted to build up an escape organisation. But as at Sagan, lack of discipline ruined their plans, and in January, 1943, the Camp Leader asked the German Commandant to make arrangements for two British Air Force officers to be sent from Sagan. The Germans agreed, and about three weeks later two Senior Officers, appointed by the Senior Officer at Sagan and approved by the Germans, were transferred to Barth.

Almost immediately escape was reorganised along similar lines to the Officers' Escape Organisation at Sagan. There was a marked improvement in security and in the acquisition of escape aids, such as forged passes, maps and clothing. But the number of successful attempts continued to be disappointing. In July the senior of the two officers quarrelled with the Commandant, and both were sent back to Sagan. But before leaving the Senior Officer appointed a camp leader and an N.C.O. to take charge of escape,

ESCAPE
FROM
GERMANY

*The
Organisation
of Escape*

and under their authority the organisation worked smoothly until the camp was evacuated in November. Meanwhile, an entirely new camp for N.C.O.s was prepared at Heydekrug, between Tilsit and Memel in East Prussia.

This camp was completed by June, 1943, and the N.C.O.s from the Centre Compound at Sagan were transferred there in batches of two hundred at a time. Thereafter the Centre Compound was used for American officers. In November, 1943, the N.C.O.s at Barth, who had increased to one thousand two hundred, were also transferred to Heydekrug, where the British were accommodated in one new compound and the Americans in another.

When the N.C.O.s were transferred to Heydekrug the Committee which had been in existence at Sagan assumed control of escape. But once again the old difficulties began to reassert themselves, and although the Compound Leader gave moral support to the committee, because of the "democratic" attitude of the prisoners, most of whom were of equal rank, he was unable to issue orders.

To counter this a propaganda campaign was started in which members of the Escape Organisation made speeches in all barrack rooms, outlining the ideals of the Escape Organisation and suggesting how every individual could help. In particular, prisoners were asked not to trade with Germans because this was to be done on an organised basis by selected individuals. At the same time the names of the selected traders, most of whom were able to speak German, were announced.

A great improvement followed, but as some private trading continued a propaganda display of various items of escape equipment, such as German uniform, maps, cameras and photographic materials was arranged and all Barrack Room Leaders and others who held positions of trust were invited by the Compound Leader to see what had been obtained by organised trading. At the meeting the Compound Leader announced that he had decided to forbid unauthorised trading with Germans and asked all those present to give him their support. They agreed and in due course told the occupants of the rooms under their control. The new order proved to be effective and from then onwards unauthorised trading was rare.

When the N.C.O.s from Barth arrived at Heydekrug in November, 1943, a second compound was opened, and those members of the Escape Organisation from the original compound were transferred. With their help escape was organised jointly; intelligence was pooled, documents were forged in one compound only, and no escapes were allowed without the consent of the parent committee. Even when the Americans arrived and a further compound was opened the same procedure was adopted, so that escape in this camp was more thoroughly organised than in any which had previously been inhabited by N.C.O.s. Prisoners bore the discomforts inflicted by the Germans as reprisals with good humour and active opposition was confined to a few individuals. In July, 1944, this camp was evacuated owing to the Russian advance, and the majority of British N.C.O.s were transferred to Stalag 357 at Thorn. But by then the end of the war was in sight and escape was a secondary consideration.

## CHAPTER 4 · INTELLIGENCE

The basis of escape, like any other military operation, is intelligence. In order to escape from a well-defended camp of the type used for Air Force prisoners a detailed knowledge of German routine and counter-escape measures was necessary. Suppose a prisoner wished to cut the wire, first he had to study the disposition of the defences of the camp, know exactly where he would be covered by the least number of machine-guns and be visible to the least number of guards; next he had to know what Germans were likely to be inside the camp at any time and what they would be doing; then he would want to know when the guards in the towers over-looking the wire and those who patrolled the wire on the ground outside were changed, and whether further patrols in the woods beyond had been instituted or not. Finally, he would want to know what immediate meas-ures might be taken by the camp authorities should his escape be discov-ered quickly, in particular whether dogs would be used.

Once outside the camp the more information a man had the better were his chances of travelling successfully through Germany. Generally there were two schools of thought about methods of travel, the first favour-ing the railway and relying on the fact that there were always between nine and ten million foreign workers in the country; the second believing that the best chance of getting away lay in being seen by as few people as poss-ible and travelling hidden either in goods trains, barges or some other form of transport or walking during the hours of darkness.

When travelling by train as a fare-paying passenger a man needed con-fidence and a capacity for bluff, and the more he knew about the routine of German travel the better. Certain knowledge was essential; for example, passengers were allowed to sit—even to sleep—in station waiting rooms provided they had their railway tickets; but without a ticket they were arrested. At barriers on certain main line stations identity cards had always to be shown. A prisoner who was doubtful about the quality of his forged card might try to squeeze past in the rush without showing it, but if he did, he was almost certain to be caught, whereas merely by holding out the card he was certain to survive such a perfunctory check. It was possible to stay in an hotel, but if a person stayed more than three days the police made enquiries.

Those who travelled on foot or by hiding in goods trains also needed information. In the early days of the war many of those who got outside the wire were caught through the most elementary ignorance. One party, walking boldly down the side of an autobahn disguised as workmen were surprised to find themselves arrested. They had not known that pedestrians were not allowed on these roads. Another prisoner strolled through a village smoking a cigarette. He was arrested and asked why he was smoking when everyone knew that it was forbidden in that village because of the proximity of ammunition dumps. Another party was seen to be drinking water from a stream out of tins, and as this was something no-one who had legitimate business in Germany would need to do, they were followed and caught.

When nearing a frontier, knowledge became still more important. At one part of the Swiss frontier there was a line of listening posts equipped with sound-detectors at intervals of about five hundred yards. Other frontier areas were guarded by electrified wire. Elsewhere, the frontier zigzagged so that it was possible to cross and re-cross it within a few hundred yards. A man who knew nothing of all this would have very little chance of getting through. For all this information the main sources were:—

NEW PRISONERS. After being shot down, men often spent a long time in German occupied territory or made long journeys across Germany. When such individuals arrived in a camp they were able to give a considerable amount of information concerning conditions of living and travel in the greater part of Europe.

GERMAN MILITARY. The majority of German officers were proof against bribery but in every camp there were one or two who, either out of hatred for the Nazis or from other motives, were prepared to part with information.

The rank and file of German soldiers were frequently corrupt. The fact that prisoners had such delicacies as chocolate, coffee, cigarettes and tobacco was a great temptation and, whatever type of unit was guarding a camp, there was always a fairly lively exchange of food for information or goods. Poles who had been forced into the German Army and Austrians or Germans who had had Communist sympathies before the war usually were ready to talk, and in every unit there were weak men who liked to be on good terms with the prisoners and who could be counted upon to give away details.

GERMAN CIVILIANS. The number of German civilians who came into any prison camp was small, and usually they were old men who were under-fed or former Communists who were forced to do the dirty work of the country. Occasionally both Poles and Frenchmen were sent in to do plumbing or constructional work of some kind, and in camps such as Schubin, which was in Poland,

Poles came in every day. Although some attempt was made to guard them and to make them spy upon one another nearly all such civilians proved useful. Some were very ingenious. One old German who did cement repairing used to take all kinds of articles into a camp in a box which he hid under the wet cement in his bucket. His mate was a Nazi and used to spy on him, but he was never caught. Others hid small things in their midday rations, or went into partnership with the German soldier who was guarding them and who was much less likely to be searched at the gate.

GERMAN NEWSPAPERS. German national newspapers were available at almost all times, local papers usually through corrupt Germans. The national papers were useful as an indication of the German mood at any moment, and also contained a great deal of accurate fact. A standstill order for ships in the Baltic or new regulations for railway travel would be announced in the national papers; the details for any particular locality in the local papers. All changes in ration cards, identification papers, leave papers and all the many dozens of other permits which existed in Germany in wartime were also published nationally and locally, so that it was possible to keep abreast of most of the restrictions.

ESCAPED PRISONER LIVING OUTSIDE CAMP. A prisoner escaped from one camp with the sole object of organising an escape route for those who should follow him. He adopted the guise of a foreign worker in Germany and moved about over a wide area for more than three months acquiring information and endeavouring to arrange a chain of helpers, mainly Poles, from his camp to a Baltic port. Throughout this period he was in constant touch with his colleagues in the camp through the agency of a German on the camp staff who was strongly opposed to the Nazi regime. Information obtained by this means was invaluable.

PRISONERS ON SICK LEAVE AND ESCAPED PRISONERS RETURNING TO CAMP. Prisoners left camp frequently to go to hospitals for treatment and occasionally for courts martial. Before departure from the camp such men were always carefully briefed to look out for information which was required, and quite often they obtained it. Experienced escapers who were recaptured and returned to camp were an invaluable source of information on almost every subject.

The organisation through which these sources were tapped was known as the Escape Intelligence Section. It consisted of a departmental head and a number of specially selected prisoners known as "contacts," most of whom were able to speak German. These "contacts" tried to win the confidence of those Germans or foreign workers whom they met in the camp, and as far as possible the same individuals were always dealt with by the same prisoner. This rule could not always be kept because those who were being bribed liked to get as much as possible out of the prisoners and sometimes showed resentment if an attempt was made always to refer them to one man.

Besides collecting information, "contacts" were responsible for carrying through deals for wireless parts, cameras, compasses, maps, railway guides, or anything else which might be required. All this involved a great deal of patient work. Sometimes it meant hours of boring conversation over cups of tea, listening to grievances or the family history of some soldier, or even more wearisome hours waiting for a particular German to arrive at the camp gate or some other rendezvous. It might be weeks before sufficient confidence was established for a definite understanding to be reached. A prisoner in one camp, who dealt with a junior "ferret" named Rudi, has stated:—

> "My main task during the early days was to distract Rudi's attention from various activities such as tunnel digging and the dispersal of sand. Soon I discovered that my quarry was not over fond of work and much preferred to smoke English cigarettes beneath the trees. It was from these early conversations that I discovered that his father had been a cavalry officer, though now dead, and that his uncle was a well-to-do Essen business man. He informed me also that he was married and had one son, and that his mother lived with his family at Essen. Gradually I gained his confidence, mainly by asking for nothing and giving cigarettes and chocolate in return. I discovered that he hated the Nazi party, having had most of his belongings stolen from him by Brownshirts when he returned from a holiday in Italy before the war. Owing to the danger of other members of the German Security Squad—and especially its head, Corporal Griese, who was nicknamed "Rubber-neck"—we devised a system of signals and agreed never to recognise each other in public.
>
> "Having received instructions to obtain various articles which were forbidden to us, eventually I began by asking for small things such as mapping nibs or ordinary ink. These were readily forthcoming and later Rudi was supplying the camp with more useful commodities such as rubber-stamp ink and pads, printing inks, stencil blocks and eventually a radio.
>
> "By this time I had managed to form an estimate of Rudi's character. He was reasonably well educated, cunning enough to keep away from the front-line, astute enough to deceive his compatriots, and sly enough to deceive me if someone else should offer him a better bargain. I sensed also that the way to his heart was to show a keen interest in his family."

Not all Germans responded as well to treatment as Rudi; one or two were impervious to blandishments of any kind. In the same camp the best known were Glimnitz, a Luftwaffe sergeant who had lived in America and spoke excellent English, and Karl Pilz, a Hanoverian who was always known as "Charlie."

"Charlie" was the most interesting. Tall, dark-haired, with a sallow complexion and lugubrious expression, he had once reputedly been a Social Democrat and suffered nine months' solitary confinement in the early days of the Nazi regime. Thereafter he had sold his soul and become not merely a Nazi but a determined enemy of Britain. "Charlie" had been with Air Force prisoners from the time that the special Air Force camp was opened at Barth in 1940 and stayed with them until the Russians relieved the camp at Luckenwalde, near Berlin. Owing to the fact that he had not served at the front he did not rise above the rank of corporal and this was a constant grievance; but whether from fear or conviction, his allegiance to the Fuehrer remained unshaken.

"Charlie" was a curious mixture of humanity and unscrupulousness. He had a genuine understanding of what a prisoner's life was like and frequently overlooked small irregularities which it was his duty to report. Often he would collect cigarette-lighters which had been confiscated and give them back to prisoners, or procure extra supplies of timber when they wanted furniture or some domestic gadget. He had some sense of sportsmanship and appreciated that escape was a game with rules. Tunnels in particular he regarded with the eye of an expert; if they were the effort of new recruits he would pour scorn on them and ask why they were wasting their time; on the other hand a good tunnel aroused his admiration and he would take endless photographs for his escape museum.

Nevertheless, "Charlie" was a most dangerous opponent. He spent so much of his time in the camp that he seemed to know by instinct when anything was afoot. He had an uncanny knack of finding entrances to tunnels when all his subordinates had looked for them in vain, and he was untiring in his efforts. Frequently when off duty he would take the Alsatian puppies which were being trained as police dogs for walks round the camp in order to get a fresh view of it from the outside. At his suggestion special camouflaged hiding places were constructed in the woods from which he and others used to watch the camp from a distance through field-glasses, and more than once he spotted unusual activities in this way. Sometimes in order to avoid the check kept by prisoners on those who entered the gate, he would climb the wire in some far corner in the hope of arriving in the camp before anyone became aware of his presence.

His morale was remarkable. Before the invasion of Europe he was always contemptuously confident that the Allied troops would never succeed in breaking through the Atlantic Wall. Afterwards, although far too clever not to realise that the success of the invasion meant the end of Germany, he would never give way or admit the possibility of defeat.

The seamy side of Charlie's character appeared in his dealings with his fellow Germans. At all times during his career with prisoners Charlie had accepted food and cigarettes from them as gifts, but whenever he thought it would pay he never hesitated to lay traps for his own subordinates and report them for exactly the same practices. The other "ferrets" were fully aware of this and after they had received cigarettes or coffee used to bury them in the prisoners' compound and retrieve them when on night duty. After one escape, when the Gestapo were putting pressure on the German security staff, Charlie deliberately spied on certain German guards and denounced them. One was sentenced to three years' imprisonment as a result and another is alleged to have been shot. Many Germans swore to get their revenge for this and all were delighted when Charlie's frequent demands for promotion were turned down.

What happened to Charlie after the war is not known. It has been reported that he was seen in a long column of German prisoners in Russian hands who were being marched away from Luckenwalde, but the report has never been substantiated.

Glimnitz was a very different character. A German who had lived for some time in America, he spoke fluent English and had a friendly and bluff manner. Prisoners liked him because, as far as was known, he was one of the few incorruptible Germans and yet had a sense of humour. Glimnitz was never depressed and enjoyed what he thought were wisecracks. "Well, why are you not digging to-day? It's bad weather to be above ground," or "I hear that the Allies have selected Sagan as the place at which to open their Second Front," were typical sallies. Glimnitz was talkative and observant, going frequently into prisoners' rooms and haranguing them on politics or any other subject; yet all the time he was on the look-out for signs of escape activity.

But Glimnitz was also humane and did what he could to help the prisoners in their endeavours to improve their surroundings, provided that it did not facilitate the digging of tunnels. After repeated requests through normal channels had failed, it was he who persuaded his superiors to allow Red Cross crates into the compound in order that the prisoners could make armchairs and sofas. He kept a check on the number of crates and the amount of furniture made and satisfied himself that none of the timber was being used for tunnels. He also persuaded the Security Officer to allow the prisoners in one compound to make a golf-course, on condition that the bunkers were not too close to the wire.

Until the end of the war Glimnitz kept up his spirits and refused to admit the possibility of defeat. On the march from Sagan he did much to help the prisoners to obtain billets. It is said that he was seen subsequently

as a prisoner in England doing road repairs in Southampton and, when
hailed by one of his former charges, shouted out gaily that it was his turn
now and that he was a very good prisoner.

Glimnitz and Charlie were characters; some of the other Germans with
whom prisoners dealt were more interesting or sinister. One of the most
useful was a small fair-haired Corporal known as "Harry", whose real
name was Hesse. He was a member of the headquarters staff at Sagan and
had worked in many different departments of the camp administration
including the censorship. Harry was a genuine democrat and was prepared to take considerable risks to do anything which he considered might
bring an end to the Nazi regime. Once his confidence had been gained he
supplied a great deal of information and also made suggestions about
British propaganda to which he listened on the radio. He pointed out that
the lack of an Allied policy towards post-war Germany was having a bad
effect amongst an increasing number of Germans who, from the time of
Stalingrad onwards, realised that the war was lost. Statements by Allied
Ministers that there were twenty million Germans too many or that the
only good Germans were dead ones completely nullified the arguments of
the British Political Warfare Department which was trying to win Germany for democracy.

Within the camp itself there was little that Harry was not prepared to
try to find out, and as he often had access to the German Adjutant's office
or walked out with one of the girls who acted as typists, he kept the prisoners well informed about orders which came from Berlin and about camp
administration generally. Changes in the regulations governing entrance
to and exit from the compounds, alterations in passes and changes of German personnel were all reported accurately.

When a typewriter was needed for the production of spurious documents he arranged for one to be brought into the compound from his own
office. Later he did some typing for the forgery department and at other
times kept watch whilst the typewriter belonging to his sergeant was used
by one of the prisoners. If the sergeant entered the office he would distract
his attention. Perhaps the bravest thing he did was to agree to a plan by
which two prisoners were carried out of a compound in crates which were
supposed to be full of books and dumped in his office. They had to pass
through a gate where the cart carrying the crates in which they were concealed was examined by a sentry, and afterwards spent the whole of one
day and the following night hidden in the loft above Harry's book store. At
dawn the following morning they walked out of the main gate of the camp
dressed as Russian prisoners. For this escape Harry had stolen from the
main guardroom some of the special passes which were issued to the
Russians and had lent them to the forgery department for copies to be
made. He also bought two original Dutch identity cards from some Dutch

workers in his home town of Freiburg. These were not used on this occasion, but a Dutch airman who escaped through a tunnel carried one and reached England.

Harry also made it possible for food to be given to the Russians who were working in the camp and who were segregated from the other nationalities. The rations which they received from the Germans were inadequate and, as they had no parcels from home, Red Cross food parcels were sent into the book store disguised as books, from where, with Harry's connivance, they were taken by the Russians at night.

Harry had one or two narrow escapes. Once some typewritten forged documents were traced to a typewriter which was in his office and he was questioned closely. Later a prisoner who was due to be packed in a crate of books which was being sent out of the camp was found in the loft of the hut in which Harry worked. Fortunately the Germans discovered that the prisoner had been fed by the Russians and once again Harry was cleared of suspicion.

Eventually Harry was posted. He took away with him testimonials signed by British Officers sealed with a rubber stamp bearing the arms of the Royal Air Force which had been made from the rubber heel of a boot. He survived the war.

Quite a different type of man was a small sergeant of the Luftwaffe from Saxony who was in charge of the kitchens of two British compounds. His name was Deutsch. He was a cheerful little rogue who had more than once been up against the authorities and would do anything for gain. Being in charge of the kitchens, not only had he access to more than one compound, which was exceptional, but he travelled to various nearby towns for the purpose of buying supplies. Deutsch, therefore, was able to shop on behalf of prisoners on quite a large scale. In return for generous supplies of Red Cross food he bought wireless parts and even small radio sets, and brought them into the camp on his food cart. When mass escapes were in prospect and the demand for letters and passes was too great for the forgery department to deal with, he arranged to have letters typed by one of his friends in Dresden and Leipzig—towns far enough afield to be safe.

In Dresden he had a photographer friend who undertook to print the photographs which had been taken in the camp and were needed for forged identity papers. Owing to a shortage of paper the prints were never made, but the photographer supplied some materials which enabled printing to be done in the camp itself. Towards the end of the war the "Kitchen Feldwebel," as Deutsch was called, was caught, a complete Red Cross food parcel having been found in his home by the Gestapo. He was arrested and later sentenced to three years' imprisonment; but as he remarked to a British officer who occupied a neighbouring cell in the camp jail, this was the best thing that could have happened to him because he had far more chance of coming out of the war alive than if he had been sent to the Front.

Another German who was thoroughly corrupt was a man named Rickmers, who joined the administrative staff of the camp at Sagan in 1943. He was known to be a dangerous man and was dealt with by the Head of one of the Escape Committees and by no one else. Rickmers' prices for information or material were always high and he seldom kept the whole of a bargain, but certain information and materials were obtained from him which could not have come from any other source.

Towards other Germans Rickmers was a blackmailer. All were afraid of him and suspected him of being an agent of the Gestapo. He used deliberately to try to discover illegal connections between German soldiers and the prisoners and then, instead of denouncing them he maintained control over them. After he had been in the camp for some months the whole of the German censorship staff, including the officer in command, were in his power. When mass escapes caused the Gestapo to conduct an investigation in the camp, Rickmers is known to have denounced both this officer and several other Germans in order to save his own skin.

A number of very useful German "contacts" were made by the N.C.O.s at Heydekrug, the most important being Eddie Munkert, an interpreter, and Sommers, who was the official photographer. Munkert, who had lived in America for many years before the war, claimed that he had been a member of the former Centre Party in Germany for several years before the Nazis seized power. He was an idealist and, once his confidence had been gained, did everything in his power to help the prisoners. A small man with a quiet voice, who wore thick-lensed spectacles, he made the most of his insignificant appearance. As a member of the camp administrative staff he was able to visit the prisoners frequently without arousing suspicion.

He did everything that he was asked to do. He supplied good quality second-hand suits, overcoats, hats and German uniforms, all of which he or his wife had obtained on the "black market" and which he brought back to the camp upon his return from leave. He took them into the compound by wearing or hiding them under his uniform. All his passes and other official documents were available whenever required for copying, and on several occasions he typed spurious documents and gave advice on their compilation. Every scrap of information which he could obtain was passed on, and this often included warnings of searches or changes in the German camp defences. He was one of the Germans responsible for counting the prisoners and for many weeks he helped cover the absence of a number who had escaped. Several times he visited Baltic ports in search of information which was required. For some months he acted as the link between the Escape Organisation and a prisoner who had escaped from the camp and was trying to organise a regular escape route to a Baltic port.

Eventually his activities were suspected and he was placed under arrest by the Gestapo. Although he knew the identity of all the principal organisers of escape in the camp, it is clear that he gave nothing away because no action was taken against these prisoners by the Germans. However, damning evidence of his connection with the prisoners was found amongst his personal possessions and it is believed that he was shot about April or May, 1944.

Sommers was quite a different type. He was born in Lodz of Polish parents and at the outbreak of war was a Polish Army Cadet. He had been taken prisoner by the Russians when they advanced into Poland in September, 1939, and was subsequently handed over to the Germans. Eventually, in order to obtain more food for himself and his widowed mother, he became a naturalised German and was conscripted into the German Air Force.

Sommers was about 25 years old, but looked much younger, having a chubby face and innocent expression. He too was a member of the German administrative staff and was chiefly engaged in taking photographs of prisoners for the official identity cards held by the German Anti-Escape Organisation. When not doing photographic work, he was used as a "ferret."

Soon after his arrival in the camp Sommers responded to the friendly advances of a "contact" and before long he supplied large quantities of photographic material which was extremely difficult to get. He divulged that he was a member of the Polish Underground Movement, and it is believed that much of the material was supplied by that organisation. After a time he worked in close collaboration with Munkert and another Polish naturalised German on the camp staff who also was a member of the Polish Underground. Sommers took a tremendous risk each time he carried contraband into the compound but he displayed no sign of nervousness.

Just before Munkert was arrested Sommers was suspected by the Germans of being connected with the prisoners' Escape Organisation. It is believed that he was able to clear himself, but a few days later he was re-arrested because a colleague of his in the Polish Underground had been killed in a shooting affray with the German police and a message had been found on the body connecting Sommers, in his real name, with the Movement. Sommers had been in the hands of the Gestapo on a previous occasion, and he hanged himself in his cell rather than risk divulging what he knew.

On the whole the Intelligence Service in Air Force camps was equal to the demands made on it. After a camp had been occupied for a few months there was little the prisoners did not know about the German organisation, and information about searches became so accurate that very little equipment was lost. Occasionally some change in the routine of the guards foiled an attempt to escape, but normally failure was due to causes beyond the control of the escape intelligence section. Once outside the wire, prisoners had enough general information to enable them to travel by whichever method they had chosen with a fair chance of success. Their papers were usually good enough to enable a man to pass through normal checks, but even genuine papers were not in themselves sufficient to ensure that special checks, especially those in frontier zones, could safely be negotiated. Sometimes information went much further and enabled a prisoner to obtain help or to board a ship unaided.

The barter which "contacts" carried on was also of great value. Without the valves which were secured, not even Air Force wireless technicians could have made and maintained their secret radios. Without ink and pens, forgery would have been impossible. Without cameras and printing materials, many passes would not have been made. Without tools, cement and many other things, the most successful tunnels could never have been constructed. Except where plans involved things as ambitious as balloons and gliders, few attempts were abandoned for lack of materials.

## CHAPTER 5 · INTELLIGENCE BRIEFING

As zero hour for an escape drew near the Head of the Escape Intelligence Section prepared all his information in the form of a series of briefs. If a long tunnel was being dug and a large number were hoping to go out, the first brief would be given five or six weeks before the tunnel was expected to be completed. Imagine the scene; after special sentries had been posted, thirty or forty men, dressed perhaps in shorts and singlets, many of them wearing beards and most of them showing signs of fatigue and strain, would crowd into one of the small lecture rooms of a wooden hut. In front of them was a blackboard and on the wall a map of Central Europe. On one side of the blackboard was a plan of the camp and its surroundings and on the other some sketches of clouds or a genealogical tree, so that if a German came into the hut the "brief" could turn at once into a lecture on navigation or ancient history.

Until the briefing began perhaps most of the tunnellers had thought of the Germany beyond the wire only as a daydream. They all had picked up a good deal of information in the course of conversation, but did not know how much of it was accurate or what changes had taken place in the last few months. Probably they had pictured themselves travelling in trains or walking through the woods at night but had never come down to earth and imagined just what they themselves would do in all the circumstances they might meet. As they sat there and listened it occurred to them, perhaps for the first time, that they did not know what the entrance hall of a German railway station looked like; what to say when they wanted to buy a ticket; how to find out what time the trains left; what the German word for a platform was and what the normal notices in a German station were and meant. If they were to travel on foot perhaps they began to wonder how to cross rivers; whether all bridges were guarded; whether it was safe to walk through a village at night; what time farmers started work in the morning; whether it aroused suspicion to walk across fields by day; whether German troops patrolled the roads and if so at what time.

Illustrating his remarks by the plan on the blackboard, the Intelligence Chief would first go through the details of the locality, pointing out what was known about the defences and the movement of Germans. Prisoners were reminded of the beats of sentries and the times at which they changed guard; of the fact that the attention of all guards was concentrated inwards on to the camp; that the bright lights which surrounded the camp made it difficult for them to see anything at all in the blackness behind them, but that the searchlights on the corner towers could light up a segment of country beyond the wire.

Warning was given of the dangers a prisoner might run into in his first few moments of freedom. Perhaps a farmer at one corner of the camp had an Alsatian dog which ran loose at night; or a power station over the railway had a permanent German picket; or perhaps the German guards used certain paths on their way back from the local pubs in the evening. Every camp had a team of Alsatian police dogs which might be dangerous if the tunnel were discovered soon after the prisoners had left. They were told to carry pots of pepper to sprinkle at the tunnel opening and occasionally on their tracks. At the end of half an hour the prisoners knew that unless they were very unlucky they were almost sure to get clear of the camp if the tunnel could be completed successfully.

The second part of the brief would deal with the conditions in Germany and Europe. Many people found it difficult to make up their minds which way to go; they would be taken on an imaginary tour of Germany and Europe and given all the latest information about the frontiers and methods of travel.

At the beginning of the war the idea of stealing aircraft and flying to England was very popular. Everyone knew that Dutch and Norwegian airmen had succeeded in doing this after the Germans had occupied their countries and the simplicity of the plan made it attractive. Once off the ground it was assumed that a man would be very unlucky not to reach at least neutral territory, whereas by any other method there were a thousand hazards. The lay-out and terminology of the cockpits of several German aircraft were known.

In practice, however, the chances against such an escape proved overwhelming. It was seldom difficult to penetrate an aerodrome, for German security measures were as primitive as our own, and given a reasonable imitation of a German uniform, it was not very difficult to move about the aerodrome unmolested. On several occasions prisoners entered hangars, examined aircraft and pretended to be doing repairs without being discovered. But to find an aircraft of a type known to prisoners which was also serviceable, filled with petrol, and in a position from which they could get it out so as to take off, was asking more than Fate ever gave. More than one prisoner got into the cockpit of an aircraft, but it always turned out to be unserviceable or for some other reason would not start.

The nearest approach to success was achieved by two officers who escaped from Stalag Luft III, Sagan. They found an aerodrome and were hanging round a hangar dressed in overalls and field-service caps, waiting for an aircraft which would suit their purpose. A two-seater Junkers came in to land and the two prisoners, pretending to be on duty, walked out to meet it. The pilot and observer got out, and left the machine in their charge without saying anything which could not be answered with a salute and "Jawohl." The prisoners climbed in, took a quick look round, and had just begun to crank the engine when they saw the Germans coming back to the machine.

Realising that they would not get the engine started in time and unwilling to be caught, they changed their role and became once more the duty crew. They helped the Germans into their seats, started the engine and stood at the salute at the wing tips as the aircraft taxied away. They then moved off to wait for another opportunity.

For most pedestrians in the early days of the war Switzerland was the usual goal. It was the nearest neutral country and mountain climbers and skiing enthusiasts had detailed knowledge of some parts of the frontier. In addition, many thousands of Frenchmen, Poles and a few members of the British Army had crossed this frontier in 1940 and 1941 and certain stretches of it, such as the Schaffhausen Salient or the eastern end of Lake Constance, had been carefully mapped.

If prisoners were going by train they were told to what distance it was safe to travel on the main lines, and were given routes on secondary lines south of Munich or Ulm which had been used successfully. The frontier zone began south of those cities, and in that zone German patrols both on railways and roads were frequent and dangerous. Within five miles of the Swiss frontier was a line of listening posts between which guards patrolled with dogs. Prisoners were warned that in the villages near the frontier they might at any moment be stopped and asked for their passes and that on the frontier itself guards were stationed at intervals of two hundred yards with orders to challenge all by day and shoot without warning at night.

In 1941 the late Squadron Leader Bushell, one of the greatest figures in Air Force escape, reached the village of Stuhlingen on the Schaffhausen Salient before being recaptured, and in 1942 a Dutch airman, who spoke perfect German and had been given a ride on the motorcycle of a member of the S.S. for part of the way, reached the same village and was recaptured also. Both these prisoners drew detailed plans of this part of the country showing from which vantage points the frontier could be seen and which landmarks should be noticed. Armed with this knowledge, and later with large-scale maps which had been obtained, many prisoners felt that in spite of the density of the German guards the Schaffhausen gap offered the best chance. Provided they treated the last few miles as a deerstalker treats the last few hundred yards of his approach to a stag, there was a good chance.

As the war went on and the underground organisation of foreign workers in Germany improved, Switzerland became less popular. The western frontiers of Germany were long and in many stretches without patrols except on the main roads. It was known that hundreds of airmen who had been shot down had evaded capture and walked from Germany into France, Belgium and Holland without difficulty. Once there they had a good chance of falling in with the great Evasion Organisation and of being passed back to England.

From camps like Spangenberg and Warburg, which were west of the Elbe the advantages of this route were obvious; but Sagan, Lamsdorf, Barth and Heydekrug were in eastern and northern Germany and to reach the western frontiers the whole of Germany had to be crossed. This journey was usually undertaken therefore only by those who felt confident enough to travel by train as fare-paying passengers. They were advised to use expresses while in the centre of Germany and as they neared the frontier to take shorter hops and use either third-class trains, which were so crowded that identity checks were difficult, or workmen's trains on which identity checks were perfunctory or non-existent. Large centres like Leipzig, Dresden or Berlin were the safest at which to change. The crowds in the stations or in the streets, and the enormous numbers of foreign workers always in these places made discovery unlikely.

By 1943 the underground organisation, particularly among the French workers, had improved so much that even those who did not feel competent to bluff their own passage across the railways of Germany could be put into sealed wagons destined for Paris or Brussels by Frenchmen working on the railways. An American from Sagan who had been put into a truck at Guben, a town within forty miles of the camp, reached England via Paris. Many other similar successes were reported from Southern Germany, particularly Munich. In the first brief the addresses of the French workers and the passwords would be withheld, but the fact of their existence would be given and a rough estimate made of the chances.

The Baltic coast was the most popular route of all. Air Force prison camps, whether at Barth, Sagan, Schubin or Heydekrug usually were closer to the Baltic than any other of Germany's frontiers, and during most of the war regular ferries ran to Denmark and Sweden, and Swedish and Norwegian ships trading timber or other goods maintained a fairly regular service to the ports of Stettin and Danzig. The sailing times of the ferries from Helsinger, Copenhagen, Frederikshaven, Sassnitz and Warnemunde were checked constantly and news of the suspension of these ferries for longer or shorter periods was received fairly regularly, mostly through German sources. Not until 1944, when there was a general standstill of all Swedish ships trading with Germany, were movements so limited that escape by this route became impossible.

From the early days a fairly detailed knowledge of some of these ports, Sassnitz, Stralsund, Rostock and Stettin in particular, was available through prisoners who had attempted to escape by them and been recaptured. Later large scale maps of the docks of most of the North German ports were acquired and much was known about Danzig. In the brief, prisoners were told that these details were available and would be given to anyone who chose to go that way. More Air Force escapers reached home via Sweden than by any other route.

Lastly, there were Germany's eastern and south-eastern boundaries. Before the Balkans were occupied by German troops there had been opportunities for escape through Poland. From 1939 onwards the Polish Underground had been highly organised and several British army prisoners were helped into Hungary and Yugoslavia, to find their way back to England.

Once the Balkans were occupied, this escape route was virtually closed. A courier service of devoted Poles, some of whom were women, continued to run the gauntlet across the mountains into Hungary and organised a precarious service to smuggle news, and occasionally very important people, through Turkey or Greece to Egypt. The number who got out in this way were few and prisoners of war were not given high priority. From the summer of 1941 onwards, therefore, Poland was more or less ruled out as an escaping route; even Poles in the R.A.F. who were unlucky enough to be taken prisoner seldom tried to get back to their own country because of the danger to their families. From Schubin, which was in Poland, and from Sagan which was only sixty miles from its borders, less than a dozen ever attempted to cross the frontier.

For the N.C.O.s at Heydekrug which was only five miles from the Lithuanian frontier, the eastern route was naturally attractive. It was known that the East Prussian Lithuanian frontier was not heavily guarded; that Lithuania was not occupied by strong German forces; that the people were hospitable and would provide food and shelter. Some prisoners considered that although it was doubtful whether one could reach England before the end of the war by this route, nevertheless, it was worthwhile investigating the possibilities of reaching Sweden from one of the ports in Lithuania, Esthonia or Latvia; making contact with the Russian forces by penetrating the lines; or as a last resort remaining under cover until overrun by the Russians. A number of escapers from Heydekrug did attempt this route but all were recaptured.

To the south-east the Czech Underground Movement was at all times willing to hide and to help escaped prisoners of war; the small group of Czech pilots who found themselves in Air Force prison camps gave instructions and addresses when they dared. In 1941, while in transit from Lubeck to Barth, Squadron Leader Bushell and a Czech officer named Zaphok escaped from the tram and made their way to Prague. There they spent some months while the Czech tried to arrange a passage to Yugoslavia or Turkey; but in the round-up after the death of the German Gauleiter Heydrich they were caught and sent to Berlin where they spent some months in the hands of the Gestapo. This experience, the news of which soon spread, discouraged others from thinking of Czechoslovakia as a base of operations for some time.

In 1943 when the tide of the war was set against Germany and Air Force officers were concentrated at Sagan, only sixty miles from Czechoslovakia, prisoners began again to look in that direction. The country south of Sagan was heavily wooded and there were no patrols on the former German–Czech frontier, except on the railways and main roads. More than one prisoner succeeded in reaching Czechoslovakia and receiving help. Not only food, clothing and shelter, but passports and papers were provided and prisoners were escorted as far as possible towards the Swiss frontier. In 1943 a prisoner from Sagan after being in the hands of the Czech organisation for five weeks, was caught within fifty yards of the Swiss frontier at Bregenz, having made his way across Southern Germany with the help the Czechs had given him.

After the first brief, those who hoped to go out would go away and make up their minds about which route they wished to take and by what method they would travel. Then, within two or three weeks of the date the tunnel was due to be completed, they would go to the Intelligence Chief singly, or in pairs, and get the final details.

Take as an example an occasion when two prisoners decided to try to reach Sweden via Danzig from Sagan. One spoke a little Swedish, and the other a smattering of French. One was to travel as a salesman for a Swedish manufacturing firm and the other as a French electrician. First they discussed with the Intelligence Officer what papers they were to carry. The routine documents for such a journey consisted of an identity card, a travel permit stating that their place of work had been transferred from Goerlitz, or some other town south of Sagan, to Danzig, a police permit allowing them to travel and endorsing the transfer, and a formal letter from their employers confirming their bona fides and ordering them to work in Danzig.

At Danzig they had the address of a French prisoners' camp where it was known they could get help by the use of a pass-word, and that was their goal. It was quite possible, however, that they would be stopped in the street before they got there and questioned; they might even be asked to take the police with them to their new place of employment. Should they, therefore, have a change of clothes and a second set of papers describing them as Swedish sailors, for use in Danzig? After thorough discussion the prisoners decided that their only chance in Danzig lay in avoiding the police altogether; either they would get help or they would board a ship by night. Their chance of surviving any interrogation was so slight that it seemed wrong to ask for a second set of papers, especially when the forgery department was so busy.

Next they went through the railway time-table to decide on their exact route and to learn the possible connections; owing to the rigorous controls which had been imposed they were told that the junction of Posen was to be avoided at all costs.

As the journey involved a night they discussed also whether to spend it in the waiting-room of a station or to use an hotel. In the first two or three years of the war little was known about the possibility of using hotels except that passes were examined by the police and nobody was allowed to stay longer than three or four days without a special permit. In 1943, however, it was learned that it was possible to stay in hotels in Stettin and Danzig, and that inspection of passes was as perfunctory as at the barriers of a railway station, provided one did not stay too long. This decision, therefore, was left open.

Lastly, every detail of the train journey was carefully considered. When a prisoner began to envisage how to get from one place to another without arousing suspicion, it was extraordinary how many questions needed an answer. If all the seats on a train were taken, was one allowed to stand in the corridor? Was one allowed to put luggage in the corridor? Did one help ladies with their luggage, or did one attract attention if one failed to do so? Did people generally read books in trains or only papers? Were tickets collected on the trains or at the barriers? What words did the ticket collector use? Was it necessary to reserve a seat if travelling second class? How did one know whether a seat was reserved or not? Where were the waiting-rooms in German railway stations and how long could one stay in them? Could one get beer and coffee without ration tickets?

The most important thing to know was that nobody could stay in a waiting-room unless they had purchased their ticket and that frequent inspections of tickets were held. This rule had been made because both Germans and foreigners were apt to treat waiting-rooms as convenient free shelter. At almost every station it was possible to get beer and ersatz coffee, and a good meal of vegetables and perhaps fish, without ration cards. If it was necessary to spend three or four hours in a town during the daytime, cinemas, public parks, picture galleries and restaurants provided a sufficient variety of waiting places to pass the time safely and without monotony. When as many questions as possible had been answered, prisoners were assured that with so many millions of foreigners in Germany and such congestion on the railways, travel by train in the interior was much easier than they imagined. Provided a man knew how to ask for a ticket and had the necessary permits, almost every other difficulty could be overcome by adopting the attitude of the innocent and well-meaning foreigner. Generally the Germans were quite anxious to help.

In this case the real dangers began at the entrance to the Danzig docks. The information about docks varied. By 1943 large-scale plans of the harbours of Lubeck, Rostock, Stettin and Danzig had been acquired on which the quays normally used by Swedish ships were marked. Many important details had also been learned from those who had escaped and been recaptured. A plan of the ferry which left Sassnitz, on the island of Rügen, with all the best hiding places in the ship marked, had been made by a man who had spent 48 hours on board; by bad luck the ship went not to Sweden, as he hoped, but back to Stettin. The barman at the Sassnitz ferry was an agent of the Gestapo. Reports also had been received that Swedish and Norwegian ships willing to take prisoners from these ports would fly a red garment between two blue ones on their washing line, but no confirmation of this was obtained.

In Danzig and Stettin the addresses of French and Polish underground workers were known and also the cafes among the ruins where it was possible to make contact with Swedish and Norwegian sailors. For security's sake these addresses were withheld until the last moment then given verbally.

If prisoners intended to travel on foot the information they would need was different but no less detailed. As they intended to avoid meeting Germans, papers were unnecessary though most men liked to have an identity card in case of emergency. Maps varied according to the route. For Switzerland and the west there was a standard set of maps rising in scale as the frontier was approached. For the other directions there were small-scale maps and perhaps road maps for part of the journey, which had been acquired from the Germans. Free-hand sketches of towns, ferries, railway stations and docks were sometimes available from men who had previously escaped.

The first problem to settle was whether to travel by day or night. The advantages of moving by night were that men could avoid being seen at all and that they kept warm; but it was almost impossible to go across country in the dark and on roads there was a danger of running into patrols. Paradoxically, because no pedestrians or cyclists were allowed on them, autobahns were the safest and quickest roads to use, so long as they ran in the right direction. The light of any approaching vehicles could be seen a long way off and prisoners had plenty of time in which to hide.

However, if prisoners travelled by night they had to hide by day and this was not always easy. Barns were dangerous because of dogs or farm hands. The best cover was provided by young fir plantations, which were proof against anything except police dogs, but in many parts of Germany no such thing existed. In open country a ditch sometimes was the only place available. Often those who began with the determination to travel by night found progress so slow that they changed their minds and walked by day as well.

By day men could go across country without attracting attention, and unless a country-wide hunt was on they were unlikely to be challenged in villages or towns. Main bridges were guarded, but provided a prisoner joined a group of civilians going across he usually had no difficulty. It was important not to light fires in woods or the attention of foresters might be attracted, and care had to be taken not to be seen drinking from streams.

The greatest disadvantage to travelling by day was the cold at night. Even in summer it required considerable endurance to spend many nights in the open, and in winter they were frequently unbearable. Yet prisoners who had been driven to take shelter in barns had been caught all too often. Fortunately it was not necessary always to go only on foot. To jump a goods train was easier than most people imagined. Marshalling yards in Germany were large and at night almost deserted; there were seldom more than one or two railwaymen about. Surprisingly few prisoners who boarded goods trains were caught in the act; on the other hand they could never be sure that a goods train would continue in the direction they wanted, or would continue very far at all. Several times men found that they had been shunted into a siding and had to leave hurriedly before the trucks were unloaded. Often they were caught in this way or when leaving the train after it had turned in the wrong direction.

In this connection, a story which circulated in Air Force camps and is believed to be true, describes an encounter which sometimes used to be quoted as a sublime example of English insularity. A prisoner who had hidden in a goods train found it was going in the wrong direction and decided to leave it at the next station. It was night and when the train stopped he crept out, crawled under two neighbouring trains and then moved cautiously along the track. Suddenly a figure loomed up in front of him. He turned to run when a voice in perfect English said "Is that you Meredith?" Overcome with surprise he did not answer immediately and the figure disappeared. The prisoner was recaptured. To this day he does not know who, in the middle of Germany, at night, in a large marshalling yard, assumed that he might be Meredith.

The best way of all for those who did not wish to travel as normal passengers on trains was on a bicycle. For some reason people hesitate to stop a man on a bicycle and more than one prisoner covered large distances in broad daylight without being challenged. There was a risk because foreign workers, who often had bicycles were not allowed more than fifteen miles from their place of residence without a permit, and at any bridge or town permits might be demanded, but the chief difficulty was to steal a bicycle. They were nearly always padlocked, and even when they could be stolen they were apt to have weak tyres. One escaper who cycled from Bromberg, in Poland to Danzig, had a puncture just outside Grandenz, about half-way. He continued to the railway station, where he saw a German leave a new bicycle outside. He took this, leaving the old one in its place. With this he reached Danzig docks and within a few weeks was in England; but such good fortune was rare.

The aim of the briefing given by the Head of the Escape Intelligence Section was to give prisoners such a full background that when they found themselves outside the wire they felt at home, even in wartime Germany. Once all available information had been given, the initiative passed to the escaper. A keen man turned what he had learned over in his mind and went back for more and more detail. Also he made mental notes of the things he did not know but needed to notice as quickly as possible. He suggested himself into a cheerful and confident frame of mind. Once outside he usually found that a surprising amount of information came back to him when it was needed and helped him against everything except bad luck.

## CHAPTER 6 · FORGERY

There was a hard and an easy way to escape. The hard way was to tunnel or cut through the wire and then travel across Germany on foot or by hiding in goods trains. The easy way was to travel in disguise. But disguise by itself was not enough. During the war everyone in Germany needed a pass. They needed an identity card to get their rations or stay in an hotel, they needed more than one kind of pass to travel by train, and if they travelled by car they had to be able to show papers which justified their movements. Even the guards of a prison camp had to show a pass every time they went in or out of the gate. If, therefore, a prisoner wanted to escape in disguise he had to possess the right kind of papers.

It was not easy to obtain genuine documents. For a German the loss of a pass was a serious offence and for a foreigner in Germany at least an inconvenience. The theft of a pass from a prison guard was bound to be reported and there followed not only a rigorous search and perhaps reprisals, but the immediate alteration of all camp passes so that the one stolen became useless at once. Theft of passes for use outside the camp was rarely possible. Occasionally a guard would acquire the pass of some rela-tion or civilian who had been killed or called up for the forces, and would offer it for sale; but usually the most that prisoners could hope for was to steal, buy or borrow passes for long enough either to take a tracing or to copy the wording and memorise the general pattern.

Forgery was not an art of which any member of the R.A.F. acknowl-edged previous experience, and its practice had to be developed by trial and error. In the early days, when the organisation of escape was haphaz-ard, it was a matter for individuals. Anyone who wanted a pass had first to procure an original and then either make a copy himself or find someone to do it for him. Civilian workers who came into camps usually carried their passes in their coat pockets, and as they often hung their coats up while working it was fairly simple to steal a pass and return it without being seen. Quite a large variety of passes was obtained in this way.

Theft from guards was not so easy. In winter they usually carried their passes in the turn-back of the sleeves of their overcoats, in summer inside their coats. In hot weather they often took their coats off, but the loss of a pass was so serious to them that they kept a close watch. Thefts were suc-cessfully made both in winter and summer, but with guards bribery was more effective. So long as he could be convinced that he would get it back within half an hour there was usually one man in any guard company who would lend a pass at a price.

It was rarely that a man who wanted to escape was sufficient of an artist to do his own forging. Luckily artists were almost always willing to help, and one or two worked so hard and for so long in the first years of the war that their eyes suffered permanent damage. But when R.A.F. prisoners were concentrated at Stalag Luft III the demand for passes became too great to be dealt with by casual arrangement. One or two artists broke down and refused to do any more, and it became obvious that a forgery department would have to be organised if the work was to continue. Accordingly, the acquisition of passes was handed over to Contacts, and anyone who had any aptitude for drawing was asked to volunteer. The result was an organ-isation known in Stalag Luft III as "Dean and Dawson" which, from the summer of 1942 onwards, provided passes for all those who wished to walk through the gates in disguise and for all those who needed them on their journeys outside. The methods of "The Firm" were copied in other camps and not even the London travel agency from which the name was taken could have provided better service.

The founder and moving spirit of "Dean and Dawson" was the late Flight Lieutenant Wahlenn. In 1940 Wahlenn had spent some time in an Army prison camp and had there learned the rudiments of his trade. A quiet, mild-mannered officer with a large black moustache, he was not only an expert forger himself but taught a staff which, as more and more

R.A.F. compounds were formed, provided the nucleus of a series of Forgery Departments. In the two years from the spring of 1942 to March 1944, Wahlenn worked day and night at his job, and although very anxious to escape himself he several times gave up opportunities in the interests of the prisoners as a whole.

His greatest delight was the invention of passes. As every man and woman in Germany had to have a different identity card according to their nationality or occupation, and as there were anything from six to ten million foreigners in Germany during most of the war, there was a great variety of passes. Not even trained members of the Gestapo could recognise all of them at sight, and any authoritatively worded pass, well laid out and carrying the necessary police and departmental stamps, was almost certain to survive examination unless suspicion had already been aroused through some other cause. Wahlenn read the newspapers carefully, studied the official notices, mastered German officialese, and produced a series of passes which survived numerous examinations and in many cases brought prisoners safely through to England. In March 1944 when the great tunnel broke from the north compound in Stalag Luft III, his fellow prisoners insisted that he take his chance and he went with the rest. He was recaptured and murdered by the Germans.

It would be impossible to describe all the passes made by Dean and Dawson and its branches in the three years of their existence. They varied from a Dutch passport—a four-page booklet backed with stiff buckram containing thousands of words in a very small black print which took months to forge—to a simple typewritten travel permit stating that so-and-so was permitted to travel to such-and-such for a particular purpose. In the main, however, they fell into four categories.

First, came the passes which were necessary to get through the gate of a compound. Even for soldiers these were of many kinds; members of the Security staff had an elaborate, stiff-backed folding identity card bearing two photographs, one of which had to be side-face. The administrative and the medical staff had cards, each of a distinctive colour, the details of which were changed periodically. Commonest of all were the blue or green sheets of paper carried by the ordinary soldier or N.C.O. who guarded civilians or escorted prisoners in and out of the camp. These were partly printed, name, number and other details being typewritten in the spaces provided. Civilians usually had typewritten forms but, as no civilian was allowed into any compound unaccompanied by a soldier, a civilian pass alone was of little use to escapists. At all times, therefore, military passes were in urgent demand and, owing to the frequent changes in their details, there was no period at which some member of a forgery department was not working on one. All these passes had to be exact reproductions.

In the second category came the identity cards which both the military and civilians had to carry at all times during the war. For the ordinary soldier an identity card consisted of his pay book, a little grey notebook, on the first page of which was his photograph, number and service details. Most men carried these in a folding case covered with talc so they could be easily shown on demand. The inner pages contained the details of pay, but for purposes of forgery it was seldom necessary to copy more than the front page since the books were hardly ever opened. Civilian identity cards varied according to sex, occupation, age and nationality. German identity cards were not easily available and as far as is known only one was ever acquired; but as has already been said, the multiplicity of foreign passes was the forger's opportunity, and once two or three of these had been copied it was comparatively easy to change the wording to suit any nationality required.

The third category consisted of three different types of pass; temporary identity papers for use when Germans or foreign workers lost their permanent ones or when they were in the hands of the police for registration purposes; permits to travel; and permits to allow civilians to change their place of residence. All these papers were typewritten and varied so much from district to district that, once again, any well-worded and properly stamped document would almost certainly pass.

Lastly, in the fourth category came the letters of recommendation which both Germans and foreigners carried, and in which their business was explained in more detail than was possible on a form. These letters originated either from business firms or private employers and were often handwritten, sometimes in Gothic script. They carried imposing letterheads, much bolder than those used by British firms, and often in raised type.

The production of these letterheads became one of the specialities of forgery departments. They usually consisted of a trade mark, the address of headquarters and a branch office, and perhaps small drawings of messenger boys or telephones where telegraphic addresses and telephone numbers were given. "Dean and Dawson" usually chose the name of a well known firm such as Krupps or Siemens, which might have a branch anywhere in Germany. The results were so convincing that on one occasion even the camp Intelligence Officer, who knew most of the tricks of the forgery department, was completely taken in and asked in surprise where the original office paper had been acquired. German police who examined these letters after prisoners had been recaptured, were much impressed, and a collection of letterheadings formed one of the show pieces in the Escape Museum which the German Air Force accumulated at Stalag Luft III.

The length of time it took to forge documents varied with the amount, size and kind of lettering they contained and with the conditions under which the work had to be done. Recruits to forgery departments sometimes expected to find a fully equipped engravers' workroom and a first-class drawing office. They were sadly disappointed. The equipment usually consisted of pencils, a few bottles of ink, some very poor nibs and worse penholders, a few jagged and warped rulers, some set-squares which were never quite what they set out to be, a box of paints, and a box of mathematical instruments.

Paper, the most important material of all, was fairly easy to get. Lyles toilet paper, sent out from home, was excellent for tracing, and high-grade typing paper could usually be found in the Adjutant's office where it was used for administrative work and was not on parole. A double thickness of smooth water-colour paper, sent from home for the use of artists, was used for passes which were semi-rigid.

Printed documents took longest to make. They were in Roman or Gothic lettering and were forged with paint or brush and Indian ink. German mapping nibs were of such poor quality that it was practically impossible to get the fine line necessary for Roman type; unfortunately English mapping nibs only began to arrive in any quantity in the latter half of 1944. Whenever they were available the quality of the work soared and the spirits of the forgers showed a corresponding improvement. One forger consistently used a water-colour brush with Indian ink, and was able to get exceptionally fine results. This method of forging is to be recommended, as it lays the ink on the paper without damaging the surface in any way and looks much more like genuine printing. A Frenchman in another Air Force camp had an even more ingenious system. He placed a sheet of thin glass over the document to be copied and made a tracing of it on the glass in white paint. The glass then was turned over and the tracing retraced on the back of the glass in slow-drying black ink or water colour which was used to print a copy of the document. Additional copies were made by cleaning off the black ink and repeating the second half of the process. This method produced most excellent results.

As the working time available each day was seldom more than three hours it often took several weeks to produce one paper. Roman lettering was more difficult than Gothic. It took anything up to sixty hours—the equivalent of at least four weeks—to produce a leave pass or a return travel-permit in Roman, whereas a Service travel-order in Gothic type, although it might contain twice as much lettering, could be done in eight hours.

Typewritten papers presented a special problem. There was seldom a typewriter in the compound which was not on parole, and papers frequently had to be done by hand. Rather surprisingly, typescript was one of the easiest things to forge and could be done quite quickly with a fine water-colour brush and lamp black or ivory black ink. When there was a mass escape hand-work was too slow and some form of mass production became essential. It was quite easy to make a stencil on a typewriter by typing on thin paper without using the ribbon so that the letters punctured the paper instead of printing on it. It was also quite easy to make an ink roller. Given a flat surface it was then usually possible to take fifty copies before the paper tore. The printing was seldom perfect but could be touched up. In N.C.O.s' camps the master copy was often made by hand instead of with a stencil and transferred to gelatine, from which copies were taken; the "type" was cleaner but only about twenty copies could be made from each transfer.

But even for stencils, the difficulty of a parole-free typewriter remained. Occasionally a prisoner would hear that a typewriter had been despatched by the Swiss or Swedish Y.M.C.A. and would be able to smuggle it into the compound before the Germans were aware of its arrival, and keep it for several days. This, of course, was ideal. Sufficient stencils for several months could then be prepared and the typewriter smuggled out again and presented to the Germans as if it had newly arrived. "Contacts" who worked in the parcels or book store where there were German machines could sometimes do stencils themselves, or bribe guards to do them. But this always entailed considerable risk, and if a copy of the pass subsequently fell into German hands there was always the danger of the typewriter being traced.

A safer method was to bribe a German to take the typescript away with him, make the stencils on a typewriter some distance from the camp, and bring them back when completed. "Harry's" help in this has already been mentioned. Another German at Stalag Luft III, who took risks not only for what he could get in exchange but through a real devotion to democratic principles, was Private Fischer. His wife lived in Hamburg, and he went there for his leaves, taking the pencil drafts of passes with him. He would then type the stencils on his wife's machine, and bring them back. When asked why he took such risks—for German soldiers were frequently put through rigorous searches when returning from leaves—he replied that it was better to be in the German Air Force than in a concentration camp, and by being there he could do more to help the Allies. He never let "Dean and Dawson" down.

Stiff-backed passes such as an identity card or a passport were especially difficult to make. In pattern they were like a British driving licence, but of many colours. They were printed on stiff cloth or buckram, for which the only substitute available was architects' dressing linen. Many experiments had to be made and a great deal of valuable linen wasted before a suitable method was found of giving the cards the necessary rigidity, and of dyeing the linen to the correct colour without washing out the "type" or stretching it unevenly. Pocket books and folding photograph frames provided the necessary backing. Eventually this type of pass was so well made that it was difficult even for prisoners to distinguish them from the originals.

All documents of whatever kind bore official "rubber" stamps. These were usually cut from linoleum or from rubber taken from the heels of

R.A.F. boots. The stamp was drawn on the rubber in white ink and then handed over to the cutter whose tools consisted of a specially shaped ink ruling-pen and slivers of razor blades set in a wooden handle. The stamps were mostly circular with the German eagle in the centre and the name of the local police department written round the perimeter. The commonest stamps were those of the police and the local labour office who had to sanction all movements of workers in Germany; the name was generally drawn from a town near the camp. In addition a number of rectangular stamps were invented to lend an official touch to less official papers such as letters from business firms. It was found that the Germans were impressed by these.

Photography was an ancillary department. Identity cards and passports had to carry photographs and though photographic work usually came under the control of the forgery department it was done by a separate staff and in a different part of the camp. To obtain photographs in a prisoner of war camp was not easy, but fortunately the likeness mattered very little. Not one inspector in a hundred had time to consider the likeness, and what mattered was that the photograph should be of the right size, in the right place, and should carry the necessary police stamp somewhere across it.

In the early days of the war almost any photograph was used. Men who were reasonably like their fathers or brothers often used family snapshots, but any photograph which was not strikingly dissimilar was better than none. In N.C.O.s' compounds even pencil sketches were used with success. There was no case of a prisoner being recaptured through having the wrong photograph.

But in escape no unnecessary risk is worth taking, and from the outset great efforts were made to get a camera. At one period a German officer who wished to curry favour with the prisoners used to bring a camera into the compounds and take small groups of men in their rooms; some of these were occasionally useful. A much greater success was achieved during an identity parade held by the Germans. A German N.C.O. brought in a Leica and set it up on its tripod to take fresh photographs of those whose likeness on the official identity card was not considered good enough. His attention was diverted for a moment and the camera stolen. The identity parade was postponed and the N.C.O. and the guards scoured the camp looking for the camera. Meanwhile a studio was rapidly improvised by the prisoners and thirty-six "passport" photographs of the correct size were taken. The film was then removed and the camera returned to the German.

But photographs had to be developed and printed. Occasionally a German could be bribed to get this done, but all photographic work was under strict control in Germany and anyone with a licence to print ran a severe risk if he gave a special priority, so that prisoners often had to wait several months. It became increasingly necessary, therefore, to develop photographic departments within each camp.

At Sagan this was finally accomplished by the carpentry department under the direction of two officers, one of whom had been a watchmaker in civil life and the other a Naval officer who had been trained in photography. The foundation of their work was the lens of an epidiascope which had been sent to the camp by the Y.M.C.A. First an enlarger was made, and used for bringing the faces of individuals taken in groups up to the size necessary for passport photographs. Next a camera was ordered. This caused a good deal of discussion in the carpentry department, but eventually a design was agreed upon which it was believed would not only be efficient but could be dismantled and disguised in a way which would defy detection. The basis of the camera was a roll-type calendar which had certain unusual specifications. The top and bottom were detachable, fitting very tightly; when they were removed the back and front of the calendar fell apart. Inside were the necessary recesses to take the rolls showing the dates, but these recesses could also take standard size film. There was a small hole in the back, plugged to look like a fault in the wood but which, when the plug was removed, became the red window through which the film numbers were seen. Round the front of the calendar was some ornamental beading which could also be removed, leaving a groove into which fitted a cardboard box—the "box" part of the camera. When detached this box was used for cigarettes, but it had a movable bottom, and a lens could be mounted in one end. Both the calendar and the box sat on the table of the officer in charge of tools who, having made himself a pendulum clock, several model yachts, and gadgets of all kinds including two which turned out his light and opened his door from his bed, was regarded as an eccentric by the Germans. Though his room was searched many times they were never touched. Just when the camera was complete a new Kodak was brought into the camp through the usual channels, and the wooden camera was held in reserve. Film was too precious to use in trials but the experts had no doubt that it would have worked. The experience gained enabled the carpenters to build a printing machine which worked excellently.

In the N.C.O.s' camp at Heydekrug many months were spent in attempts to reproduce printed documents by photographic means. As nearly all German identity cards and passes were printed on poor quality rough-surfaced coloured card, the first task was to make a suitable photo-sensitive emulsion for printing. Several different chemicals were obtained, often with great difficulty, and hundreds of experiments were carried out before an emulsion was discovered which would give the right result—jet black printing on a white background which would be easy to dye.

Meanwhile all the original documents which could be borrowed from Polish workers or corrupt Germans were photographed to scale on ordinary film. The colour of the original document was checked against a shade card and the type of paper was compared with a sample book which had been built up over a period. Unfortunately, when these photographs were printed on normal bromide paper the background was grey instead of white, owing to the fact that the original documents were printed on coloured paper. Various methods of removing this greyness without reducing the strength of the lettering were tried in vain. It was therefore decided to use a combination of photography and hand forgery.

The artists in the forgery section made enlarged copies of the printed matter of all the documents required. These were then reproduced in black water colour on matt white paper to a scale six times the size of the original. Wooden extensions were made for the back of the plate camera so that plates of a larger size than those for which the camera had been constructed could be used, and the enlarged forgeries were mounted on boards, illuminated by photo-flood lamps, and then photographed. The focus was adjusted so that the photographs were the exact size of the original documents. These plates were satisfactory.

Attempts to print on poor quality paper failed and eventually hard bromide paper was used. The printing was deliberately overdone (with the aid of photo-flood lamps), the greyness of the background being cleared by a reducer. The back of each print was then rubbed with sandpaper to reduce the thickness of the paper. The prints were then dyed the correct shade having been obtained by soaking different coloured crepe paper in warm water. When dry, the prints of the back and front of each document were stuck together with glue and trimmed to the correct size. Results were so good that the documents looked as though they had just been received from the printer. This would have been fatal, so each card was handled by members of the Escape Organisation in order to give it the appearance of having been in use. It should be added that many of the men who carried out these experiments worked fifteen and sixteen hours a day for long periods.

The primitive tools with which most of the work had been carried out have been described; it remains to say a word about the general working conditions. In most compounds the room used by the forgery department was the canteen store. This was always a small room, congested with packing cases, and usually with a concrete floor, but its walls were lined with shelves on which stood articles for sale, such as inkpots, pens, writing pads, erasers and drawing instruments, which provided just the camouflage which was necessary. The rest of the furniture consisted only of a rickety table and one or two benches. Another room was available for temporary use in an emergency.

Each of these rooms had special hiding places in which documents and tools could be stored. In one of them a false bottom was made to a packing case which was released by a concealed catch and pulled out like a drawer.

The packing case contained odious Yugoslav tobacco which nobody tried to smoke more than once. In another a beer barrel was used and a watertight bottom constructed, the joint of which was covered by the usual iron band. If the Germans became inquisitive beer could be drawn from the barrel and during one search, when German soldiers were going through all papers very carefully, the German officer in charge sat happily on the barrel supervising operations. Other hiding places were made by putting false backs to clothing cupboards or by constructing concealed panels in the wooden walls. Comparatively little material was lost through the German searches within compounds.

Before work could be started a special watch had to be set with a special team of sentries. The apparatus of forging took quite a few seconds to conceal and adequate warning was essential; only men with a very high sense of duty or great enthusiasm were used. It was a tiresome, boring job involving many hours of standing at a window unable to do anything except look out for approaching Germans.

In the early days there were certain periods such as the lunch interval or from 6 o'clock until 9 o'clock in the evening when compounds were clear of Germans. At those times work was easy and great progress was made. At Schubin, in Poland, and from September, 1943, onwards at Sagan, the "ferrets" kept continuous watch in the camp and made the work of the forgery department much more difficult. The table at which they worked was always covered with architectural or other drawings which would account for the ink, pens and paper should work be interrupted, but too many interruptions soon affected the forger's nerves, and good work became impossible. Sometimes, when many warnings had been given, forgers found themselves jumping in their seats if the door opened even though they knew already that it was only a friendly visitor. Not unnaturally hands began shaking, and it was impossible to draw neat lines.

At Heydekrug the N.C.O.s overcame their difficulties by constructing a secret room. Permission was obtained from the Germans to carry out some alterations to the barrack containing the administrative offices and the library. The work was done by prisoners who were skilled carpenters and also members of the escape organisation, and in the course of it an extra partition was erected between the office and the library, forming a room fifteen feet long by six feet wide. Both partitions were fitted with doors which looked exactly alike, were exactly opposite each other and were always kept locked. From either the office or the library the partition appeared to be an ordinary wall and, as no one ever used the doors, no suspicion was aroused. The inside walls of the room were lined with thick brown paper to prevent light filtering through.

It was considered that this room was reasonably secure from discovery by the Germans as the structural alterations had been made within a few hours at a time when no Germans were in the compound. However, in order to provide a reasonable excuse in case of an accident, two prisoners who repaired prisoners' watches were installed there during the hours of daylight as well as the forgers. If asked why the walls had been covered with paper the watch-repairers would have stated that it had been done to prevent the watches being fouled by dust.

The forgers were all artists and had partly-finished drawings attached to their boards so that they could be used to cover their real work. If the Germans had asked why the artists chose to work in artificial light they would have replied that it was the quietest place in the camp.

Once built, this room came to be used for many other purposes connected with escape. Germans and Germanised Poles who were trusted were brought there by their "contacts" to hand over the goods which they had brought into the compound and to receive payment. This arrangement was a strain on the nerves of the artists who found the presence of a German disconcerting, but it was ideal for the Germans since no suspicion was aroused by their entering the compound offices or library. In the evenings, until 9 o'clock when all prisoners were locked in their barracks and counted, the hidden room was used for photographic work.

After several months the secret room was discovered by the Germans, but so effective was the camouflage that they made no comments and apparently were quite unsuspicious about it. The quality of the documents produced in it may be judged by the fact that one N.C.O. who escaped and travelled in North-East Germany for more than three months had his papers checked on hundreds of occasions. On one journey alone they were examined twenty-seven times.

Apart from security the greatest difficulties in forgery were the strain on the eyes and boredom. It was quite impossible for men to work for more than two hours at a time even in the best light without their eyes starting to ache and refusing to focus properly; this may partly have been due to inadequate diet. In some cases a permanent deterioration in sight resulted, and for this reason a rule was made in some camps that no forgery should be done by artificial light. However, when mass escapes were being prepared it was impossible to get all the work done without it and, despite the use of 100-watt lamps, all forgers suffered from headaches and loss of sleep after a few intensive evenings. The weather was another difficulty because in summer hands became hot and liable to smudge the paper, and in winter it was often so cold that it was impossible to keep hands steady.

Just how many hundreds of passes and papers were produced by forgery departments is not known. Large stocks of temporary identity cards and travel forms were hidden in the compounds, and many elaborate sets of papers were made for individuals.

To give one example. From the tunnel which was used successfully at Schubin, in Poland, in March, 1943, two officers planned to go to Denmark. They were supplied with all the papers necessary to support the roles they intended to adopt. On the journey from the camp to the coast they were disguised as Polish workers with the usual Polish identity cards and travel passes. Once near the coast they discarded their Polish identity and became Danish seamen whose ship had been mined by enemy action in the Baltic. This gave them an excuse for having lost all their Danish papers and instead they were supplied with the temporary pass for foreign workers, endorsed by the Danish Consul in Danzig. The Consul described the loss of their other papers by enemy action, and stressed that the present papers were only issued to them to travel to Copenhagen to join another ship. They also had a letter from the German Commandant of the "Home for Merchant Seamen" in Danzig, which again set out the facts of the enemy action. Both the letter and the pass for foreign workers bore an invented Danish consular seal and the usual police stamps of the Danzig Police. Each prisoner carried a set of these papers, and both reached Denmark. Neither, however, reached England, and it is feared that both lost their lives as the result of German action.

Of the thirty-three officers who went out of that tunnel, eleven were fully equipped with papers to travel by train, and two Czech officers had complete Polish papers including a very detailed and complicated Polish passport, all of which had been forged by hand. These documents enabled one prisoner to reach Kufstein, near Innsbrück, and survive seven examinations on the journey; another to reach Hanover, surviving three examinations; two officers to reach Cologne surviving six examinations; and the two Czechs to reach Warsaw and remain there several months. Unfortunately no one reached England. For a month before this escape two forgers worked almost continuously from 9.30 a.m. to 10 p.m. with an hour off for lunch. It was a period when the forgery staff was at a rather low ebb and pressure was such that there was no time to train new people.

For the great tunnel from the North Compound, Stalag Luft III, in March, 1944, the volume of work was even greater. More than 450 separate papers were produced, of which nearly two hundred were facsimiles of printed documents made by hand. The rest were typewritten. The work was spread over nine months and two hundred prisoners were equipped.

The results of an escape were of great importance to forgery departments. Provided some men got out and used their passes something was learned, and all who were brought back to the camp were closely questioned by the forgers themselves. If a pass had failed it was usually due to a fault in one of the police stamps, perhaps only a single letter.

Complete success was often tantalising. When a man got home a message would almost certainly be received saying that some pass had worked perfectly, and every forger felt compensated. But what they really wanted to know was just which passes had been shown at which points and what the inspector had said. This they might never learn at all. A few hints might trickle through in letters and eventually a prisoner might arrive who had heard a lecture given in England by the man who had escaped. He was at once pounced upon; but the last thing that men think about when on active operations is what may happen to them if they are shot down. Invariably men who had heard these lectures confessed that although they had thought them very interesting, they had never paid particular attention; they could never give more than a vague or inaccurate outline of what had been said. It was not until the forgers finally reached England after the war was over that they learned many of the details they had so badly wanted to know.

## CHAPTER 7 · MAPPING

For all prisoners maps had a great fascination. On a map they could see their own country and sometimes even their own home. Maps told them all that they knew of the war, and the pinning and flagging of the various Fronts was more than a pastime and provided the basis of much of their conversation. However, to those who were thinking of escape, maps had a special significance. They were not only one of the essential tools of the trade but a constant source of inspiration, for it was by studying a map and weighing the various obstacles presented by any particular route that prisoners came closest to the realities of escape. There were occasions when a good map of sufficiently large scale made all the difference between success and failure.

At the beginning of the war the only maps of Germany possessed by Air Force prisoners were small-scale handkerchief editions of a map of Europe printed either on rice paper or on silk. These were easy to conceal and were issued to members of aircrews, so that a good many reached the inside of prison camps. Although these gave a general sense of direction and were useful to any prisoner attempting to escape by train, they were of very little use to those who intended to travel on foot. The acquisition of local and larger-scale maps from Germans, therefore, was an important part of the trade to be done by the "contacts." They were fairly successful for, though the printing of civilian road maps ceased in Germany soon after the war began, Germans are fond of maps, and many families had kept those which they had used for hiking or touring and were prepared to exchange them for cigarettes or other barter. Large-scale maps always commanded a high price.

Sometimes the German propaganda machine itself supplied just the maps that were needed. For instance, the new frontiers between Germany and the Polish General Government and Germany and the Czech Protectorate were important because at certain points patrols and identity checks were often held. The general direction of these frontiers had been announced in the newspapers, but the exact line was not known until the Propaganda Ministry issued beautifully printed booklets setting out all the benefits that German rule was bringing to the newly-occupied territories, and showing exactly what those territories were. As the war went on more and better maps were obtained until most of the German frontiers were covered. Finally, on the marches through Germany in 1945, the mapmakers' dream came true and the most detailed German Air Force maps came into possession of prisoners through the connivance of the German officers and guards.

Original maps were far too precious and rare to be used by those who were attempting to escape; except for the pocket-handkerchief editions, of which there were occasionally enough, all maps had to be copied.

This copying was a long and tedious business. In the early days the number of originals was limited and every intending escaper had to borrow one in his turn and make his own tracing. This led to many losses, for when several people were tracing maps in different rooms in a small compound, discovery by a German sooner or later was inevitable. A dwindling stock of original maps and a demand for more and more copies gradually produced an organisation; and the organisation developed mass-production.

The method of duplicating maps was learned originally in an Army officers' camp in 1941, and, as soon as the Air Force officers were concentrated in Stalag Luft III, a map unit was set up. The basis of reproduction was gelatine. If this was obtained in a form which contained chemical impurities, these were removed by a thorough washing in warm water. The gelatine was then heated and poured into trays of a suitable size and allowed to set. A master copy of the map was traced on to a thickish sheet of paper with indelible ink of various colours, and laid on the gelatine so that the inks were transferred to the jelloid surface. Copies were taken by placing a sheet of paper on the gelatine, rolling it and lifting it off carefully.

In hot weather it was very difficult to obtain a hard surface on the gelatine because it took four or five hours to set, and the coolest places were often difficult to conceal from the Germans. In the snow the task was easy. The number of copies which it was possible to obtain from one transfer varied with the scale of the map. Small-scale maps with fine lines were the most difficult because less ink could be put into the lines and therefore less ink was transferred to the gelatine. If twenty-five copies of these were obtained from one transfer the mappers had done well. Large-scale maps of an inch to a mile or more were much easier and as many as forty-five copies were obtained at a time.

Like every other escape activity, map-making was handicapped by the need for secrecy, and it was seldom possible to do more than three hours' work a day. Tracings of small-scale maps usually took from four to five days and large-scale maps from two to three.

Once mass-production had been achieved the problem of supplying maps was largely solved. Escapers normally chose one of three or four routes from any camp and a set of maps covering each of these routes was made and as many as possible kept in stock. For instance, for the route from Stalag Luft III to Switzerland the set consisted of a small-scale map of Central and Southern Germany, useful to anyone going by train; a larger scale map of the Frontier Zone which began about one hundred miles north of Swiss territory; a map of one inch to a mile or larger of the Swiss Frontier itself; and lastly detailed maps and plans, including panoramic views, of the three or four sections of the frontier where it was known to be possible to cross.

Plans were usually drawn free-hand. At the beginning of the war a few prisoners who had been expert skiers or mountaineers knew parts of the German-Swiss frontier so intimately that they were able to draw quite useful plans from memory. Later, other prisoners who had escaped and been recaptured on or near a frontier drew plans of the areas they remembered. When the addresses of Polish, French, Danish, Belgian and Dutch underground workers who were prepared to help escaped prisoners became known, plans of the town in which they lived, showing the route from the main station to their house, were also drawn. Because these would have cost many people their lives if discovered by the Germans, special precautions were taken to hide them and neither an original nor a copy was allowed to be carried out of the camp; the routes had to be memorised. Towards the end of the war an invaluable set of plans of all the North German ports showing the quays where Swedish ships docked was obtained.

Many of the tools for map-making were the same as those for forging, and the work had many of the same difficulties. Eye-strain was a constant danger and to avoid it, in some camps, drawing-boards were constructed with a glass frame in the centre and an electric light bulb underneath. Although all work suffered from constant interruptions, sufficient maps were always ready even for the largest mass escapes. When twenty-eight officers walked through the gate of the North Compound at Stalag Luft III in June, 1943, each was equipped with a set of four to five maps and more than one hundred and fifty maps had been made. For the mass escape in March, 1944, from the same compound, in which two hundred officers hoped to go out and eighty eventually did so, one thousand five hundred maps were made and most officers carried six or more. Each of the fifty men who took part in the attempted mass escape by tunnel at Heydekrug in August, 1943, was provided with three or four maps. When Stalag Luft

III and Stalag Luft VI were evacuated towards the end of the war only the original maps were taken, stocks of several hundreds of copies being left behind or destroyed.

## CHAPTER 8 · FOOD

In ordinary life the quantity of food a man eats is limited by his income or his appetite; in escape it depended on the amount he could carry. Those who travelled by train as normal passengers could always get meals of vegetables without a ration card in any station buffet, and usually it was only when they left the railway towards the end of their journey that they had any difficulty. On the other hand those who travelled on foot had to sustain themselves throughout. In August and September when fruit was on the trees they could eke out their rations fairly easily, and in certain other months they could appease extreme hunger by eating raw roots; but their constant problem was how to carry the largest amount of the most sustaining food in the most compact form.

Stalag Luft III was fortunate in possessing an officer who was an expert on nutrition. Having worked at the Rowett Institute near Aberdeen, he had been co-author with Sir John Boyd-Orr of a small book on how to feed the people in wartime, which later was the basis of much of the British Governments rationing scheme. In 1940, feeling that he must do something more active, he joined the Royal Navy. In late July, 1941, as a Sub-Lieutenant Observer in an Albacore aircraft operating from an aircraft-carrier, he was shot down whilst engaged on a raid on Kirkenes in Northern Norway. An attempt to walk to Russia through the Tundra failed and in due course he reached Germany.

In prison he applied himself to the problems of food. They were considerable because the rations provided by the Germans were not of the same quality and quantity as those issued to German depot troops, as laid down in the Geneva Convention, but the lowest civilian grade designed for those who were too old to work. An average-size man leading the sort of life that is possible for a prisoner of war confined within a camp needs three thousand calories a day for full health. Had prisoners been able to sleep for the greater part of each twenty-four hours, they could have lived healthily on one thousand six hundred calories. The German rations averaged about one thousand six hundred calories a day and occasionally sank as low as eleven hundred calories. The deficiency had to be made good from other sources.

These supplementary sources varied from time to time. During the first year of the war prisoners were able to buy limited quantities of fresh vegetables and fruit through camp canteens and a small number of food parcels were received by individuals from the Red Cross Society, paid for by prisoners' relatives or friends. From the end of 1940 onwards larger quantities of Red Cross parcels, which were paid for by voluntary subscriptions and addressed to the Senior Officer, arrived in the camps and were distributed equally amongst the prisoners; but more often than not the demand was greater than the supply, due to the influx of new prisoners and the fact that until late 1942 it had not been possible to build up reserve stocks of parcels in the camps. Private food parcels continued to arrive, some from people in countries like Holland and Denmark where people barely had enough to eat themselves, but made great sacrifices in order that prisoners might benefit. Others came from the Dominions and Colonies, the United States of America and several of the neutral countries. Although these parcels, which were forwarded through the Red Cross Society of the country of origin, were of the utmost value, especially during those periods when the supply of the normal Red Cross parcels were irregular, they created a feeling of inequality among the prisoners. Food was usually shared as between the members of any one "mess," but some messes received these private parcels once or twice each week while others received none at all, and bad feeling was inevitable.

At the end of 1942 all private food parcels to British prisoners were stopped and from then onwards only the normal Red Cross parcels were received. These arrived fairly regularly until the invasion of France, but the closer the Allied ring tightened around Germany the more dislocated transport became and the more irregular prisoners' supplementary food supplies. In the winter of 1944 parcels failed to arrive for several months. The prisoners also cultivated as much of their compounds as possible, buying seeds from the canteen and occasionally receiving help from the camp administration; but as most Air Force camps were on sand this was not easy. Animal manure was not available and the only alternative source was open to objections on other grounds. Some remarkable tomato and marrow crops were grown but the total production of camp gardens was never large.

The contents of Red Cross parcels varied with their country of origin. Food which came from the Argentine was packed in bulk, that which was supplied from Britain, Canada, America and New Zealand was packed in parcels which contained a balanced diet of food designed to give a basic ration to one man for a week. Their food value was approximately 1,280 calories per day. When prisoners were getting a whole parcel a week, therefore, in addition to their German rations, they were being fed adequately, but there was no single year of the war in which Red Cross parcels arrived so regularly that the full diet was available throughout. With anything less than a whole parcel a week a prisoner suffered from a greater or lesser degree of malnutrition.

From these supplies escapers had to save enough food for their journeys. In the early days of the war anyone intending to escape had to save what he could from his own rations. Owing to the fact that prison diet was deficient in fats and sugar they tended inevitably to save the foods which contained these ingredients. The result was that they added to their own weakness before the escape took place and the food they took with them often proved too rich to digest. Under the direction of the Nutrition Officer the preparation of food for escape became more scientific. Men continued to save some of their Red Cross food such as chocolate, but a pool was established from which a balanced escaping diet could be supplied.

The basis of this diet was a "fudge," which consisted mainly of sugar, oatmeal, chocolate or cocoa, butter or margarine, dried milk or flour, Ovaltine or Bemax, and if desired some raisins. After being boiled and allowed to dry solid it was cut into flat cakes of a size convenient to carry. It was good to eat and could be stored almost indefinitely. Provided it was not held in too large quantities it could be kept quite openly in food cupboards along with chocolate and other rations; for though the Germans knew that it was used for escape they were very sensitive about Red Cross food and seldom confiscated any. Some fudge, therefore, was always available immediately. Larger quantities were packed in boxes and buried; and though mildew formed on the surface, it remained quite good to eat even at the end of a year. In addition to the fudge and to give bulk, a second mixture of powdered milk and oatmeal was prescribed, to be carried dry in small sacks. Raisins, chocolate, Horlicks tablets, a tin of corned beef and cheese completed the ration, which was normally designed to last a man for fourteen days.

Because neither unopened food parcels nor unopened tins were allowed in any prison compound the preservation of some of this food was difficult. In most camps this was solved by an institution known as "The Mart" or "Foodacco." Everything that a prisoner of war possessed had a barter value; an old pair of braces could be cut into wicks for a lamp; a worn-out pair of shoes could be made into covers for golf balls; an old shirt could be cut into dishcloths or handkerchiefs. Inevitably, therefore, exchange flourished. Prices fluctuated. In the summer of 1941, for example, in the transit camp at Salonica, food was so scarce and clothing so unnecessary that an officers greatcoat in perfect condition was exchanged for a single biscuit; in 1944 when food was running short, one prisoner was known to have given a cheque for £25 on his home bank for a single bar of chocolate. Normally, however, prices were reasonably stable and exchange could be organised centrally; this was the function of "Foodacco."

The basis of exchange was a points system. Every commodity, from a wrist-watch to a meat cube, was allotted a certain number of points by the committee which ran the exchange. When parcels were arriving regularly,

100 Players cigarettes would be priced at 40 points, a 14-oz. tin of condensed milk at 90 points, a 4-oz. bar of chocolate at 40 points. At one time matches were so short and cigarettes so plentiful that one match cost four cigarettes. The prices varied both according to the type of Red Cross parcel which was being issued, the regularity with which they arrived, and with the weather.

Though their food value was similar, the contents of Canadian, New Zealand, American and British parcels differed considerably. All Canadian parcels were standard and each contained pure butter, corned beef, full cream dried milk, raisins, prunes and a particularly popular kind of biscuit in addition to other items. Some United Kingdom parcels contained porridge and useful accessories like mustard and pepper. American parcels contained excellent cheese and prunes. When British or American parcels were being issued butter was at a premium; with Canadian parcels there might be a shortage of margarine and tea. In winter porridge, and in summer prunes commanded a high price.

The average value of a British Red Cross parcel was approximately 700 points, made up as follows:—

|  |  |  |
|---|---|---|
| 8 oz. biscuits | 40 | |
| 3¼ oz. cheese | 20 | |
| 4 oz. chocolate | 40 | |
| 8 oz. fish | 20 | |
| 12 oz. creamed rice | 20 | average 30 |
| *or* 8 oz. dried fruit | 10 | |
| *or* 12 oz. pudding | 60 | |
| 12 oz. jam | 55 | average 47.5 |
| *or* 8 oz. syrup | 40 | |
| 8 oz. butter | 60 | average 40 |
| *or* 8 oz. margarine | 20 | |
| 16 oz. meat or vegetable | 70 | |
| 12 oz. beef loaf | 40 | average 45 |
| *or* 12 oz. chopped ham | 50 | |
| 8 oz. bacon | 70 | average 60 |
| *or* 8 oz. sausages | 50 | |
| 8 oz. condensed milk | 90 | |
| 4 oz. sugar | 40 | |

```
2 oz. tea . . . . . . . . . . . . . . . . . . . . . . . . 25
10 oz. vegetables . . . . . . . . . . . . . . . . . . 10
8 oz. oatmeal . . . . . . . . . . 40 ⎤
      or                          |
5 oz. rolled oats . . . . . . . . 30   average 43.3
      or                          |
6½ oz. pancake flour . . . . . . 60 ⎦
4 oz. cocoa . . . . . . . . . . . . . . . . . . . . . . 30
1½ oz. dried eggs . . . . . . . . . . . . . . . . . . 40
2½ oz. soap . . . . . . . . . . . . . . . . . . . . . . . 1
                                    _____
                                     691.8
                                    _____
```

As prices varied it was possible for those who anticipated shortages of particular types of food to "play" the market. For instance, some British parcels contained a tin of mustard, the normal value of which was 10 points; Canadian parcels contained corned beef but no mustard. Suppose a rumour went round that British parcels were running short and that Canadian would soon be issued, a prisoner might buy up as many tins of mustard as he could and then, if the rumour proved true, sell them while Canadian parcels were being issued for 20 or 25 points a tin, making a profit of 150 per cent.

Playing the market became even more profitable in 1943 at Sagan when American Air Force officers were segregated from the British and put in an adjacent compound. Red Cross parcels were shared communally between the British and Americans but the latter continued to receive private food and tobacco parcels throughout the war. Americans therefore had many things such as cigars and extra supplies of butter and chocolate, which the British lacked. Moreover, their tastes differed. The Americans liked coffee, the British tea; the Americans liked American cigarettes, the British preferred British. So long, therefore, as the Germans refused to allow an amalgamation between the British and American "marts" there was a brisk "black market."

Cigars in a British compound were usually worth 60 points each, and tea 200 points per pound. In the American compounds cigars were worth only 10 points each and tea 160 points per pound. On the other hand 1 lb. of coffee was worth 240 points to the Americans, whereas to the British it was worth only 160. A British officer visiting the American compounds, therefore, might take in his pocket a 1 lb. tin of coffee, sell it for 240 points, buy 24 cigars, bring them back to the British compound and sell them for 1,440 points. As the coffee had cost him only 160 points in the first place his profit was 1,280 points, or roughly 800 per cent. Profiteering was so great that the "black market" was declared illegal by the Senior Allied

Officers and eventually the Germans were persuaded to allow the two markets to be run as one.

The existence of these food markets solved the problem of storage for escapers. A large quantity of food was always on the shelves, and though it changed hands rapidly there was always some in reserve. All that was necessary was for the Committee to have a credit from which food could be withdrawn on demand. When an escape was about to take place, those concerned were allotted a certain number of points and drew what they needed against the Committee's credit. Much of the escape ration, therefore, could be left on the shelves of the market until the last minute.

The credit of the Escape Committee was also used for bribery. Besides food, Red Cross parcels contained soap, cigarettes and tobacco, all of which were invaluable for corrupting Germans. Occasionally, for particularly valuable information or for some vital piece of contraband such as a wireless valve, a complete Red Cross parcel would be issued in payment; but normally the stocks of the mart sufficed and "contacts" who were dealing with Germans on the Escape Committee's behalf, were permitted to draw what they needed against the Committee's account.

## CHAPTER 9 · CLOTHING

When a convict escapes from a gaol one of the first things he must do is to get rid of his prison clothes. The same is true of any prisoner of war. It is quite true that the differences between the uniform of the Royal Navy and the German Navy, and of the British Air Forces and the German Air Force, were so slight that British officers, even when prisoners and accompanied by German guards, were frequently saluted in the streets by Germans. It is true also that, both in England and Germany, prisoners occasionally walked about openly in the uniform of their respective armed forces and went into restaurants and cinemas without being challenged. Probably the reasons were different in the two countries; in Germany the number and variety of uniforms, both military and civilian, was so great that any uniform worn with an air might pass easily in a crowd; in Britain the general public was so unmilitary in outlook that they took any uniform for granted. Nevertheless while a prisoner was wearing uniform there was the risk of running into somebody who would recognise it and, as far as travel in Germany was concerned, a uniform created difficulties rather than solved them. At any moment while walking in the streets a man in uniform might be asked to show his papers, and he could travel by train only with special Service authority.

On the other hand, to disguise oneself as a civilian in Germany was not very difficult. Though never untidy, German dress deteriorated during the war and towards the end all clothes were very mixed. In the large towns men clung to the respectability of complete suits and felt hats as long as possible, but in the country, in winter, Germans of all classes tended more and more to wear trousers or breeches, a thick three-quarter length coat, and either a ski-cap or a peaked "chauffeur's" cap. When the weather was hot, shorts, shirt and rucksack would pass anywhere in town or country and most men went hatless.

The presence of many millions of foreign workers in Germany and of more than five million prisoners of war, many of whom had considerable freedom of movement, made disguise easier still. Both foreign workers and prisoners had to have special permits to move away from their place of employment but, with so many in the country, any town or railway station was sure to be crowded with them and the confusion, both of dress and language, was complete. Many of the foreign workers wore a mixture of khaki and civilian clothes and French prisoners in particular, who often worked without any guard at all, retained their full khaki uniform and wore berets. Whatever a prisoner wore, therefore, provided it was not full British uniform, was unlikely of itself to excite comment.

As with most other escape activities, the clothing department was first organised properly in the summer of 1942 at Stalag Luft III. Previously, individuals had been responsible for their own disguises, but when several tunnels were being dug and more than one mass escape was in prospect, the volume of clothing to be made became so great that, for security reasons alone, division of labour was imperative. In each compound a single prisoner was put in charge of all escape clothing and he, like other departmental heads, was able to find professionals on whom he could call to form the nucleus of his team. The cutting and skilled tailoring was done by men who in peace-time had been tailors, bag-makers, leather workers and hat makers; except on the rare occasions when it was possible to get the use of a sewing machine, the sewing was done by a team of sempsters who quickly became professional.

The head of the clothing department was almost always the prisoner who distributed the clothing supplied by the British Government and forwarded through the Red Cross. This consisted of underclothes, shirts, socks, razors, ties, uniforms, greatcoats and boots, and arrived in bulk from England. It was necessary partly because uniforms quickly wore out in prison camps, but also because many prisoners had no proper uniform when they arrived. Some had been captured in civilian clothes which they had been given by friends in occupied countries while they were trying to evade capture, and many others had had their uniforms burned or ruined by a crash or by immersion in the sea. Others were captured in tropical dress. When captured the Germans issued such men with some sort of Allied uniform, usually French, Polish or Italian, but on arrival at a permanent camp these were exchanged for British regulation dress.

Supplies were limited but, with the help of private clothing parcels sent out by prisoners' relatives, there was usually enough for every man to have one complete set of clothes and to leave a reasonable stock for replacements. Should an escaper wish to convert his greatcoat into a German uniform, he would warn the prisoner in charge of clothing in advance and, having cut up his coat, apply for a replacement. It was a comparatively simple matter for the clothing representative to find a pretext on which to issue a new one. If an escaper wanted a pair of boots without toecaps or a pair of trousers which were threadbare, he simply exchanged his own boots or trousers for another pair.

There were two other sources of clothes. One was the German booty store in each camp which contained a variety of civilian and military garments captured from Allied armies and internees. The Germans kept a tight hand on their booty but if, as often happened, new prisoners came in who were so large that none of the stock sizes of British uniform would fit them, booty clothes would be issued to keep them going until their private parcels arrived. As both the prisoner and clothing representative were present on these occasions, the latter was able not only to keep a check on what the booty store contained, but, with the help of corrupt Germans or direct theft, to bring away many useful civilian garments.

The other source was the private clothing parcel weighing 11 lb. which every prisoner was allowed to receive from his relatives every three months. These private parcels were issued by another prisoner but, as often they contained clothes which were undeniably civilian, they came under much closer German supervision. Nevertheless, through bribery, smuggling or German laxity, such things as football shorts, tweed or woollen dressing-gowns, tweed blankets leather belts, golfing jackets and occasionally even flannel trousers, all of which might prove useful for escape, were acquired by the prisoners at one time or another.

On the arrival of any such garment the prisoner in charge of private clothing would inform the Escape Committee, who would pass the information to someone who was planning to escape. Theoretically the Committee had the power to confiscate, but as this could have caused ill-feeling it was invariably left to an intending escaper to conduct his own negotiations. It was seldom that there was any difficulty.

The work of the clothing department fell into two parts, the making of civilian clothes and the making of German uniforms. The best and simplest civilian suits were made from Naval officers' uniforms. Throughout the war members of the Fleet Air Arm were imprisoned with the other Air Forces and, though sailors were often the keenest escapers, they were always prepared to lend a pair of trousers or a coat, or both, if they did not happen to want them immediately for escape themselves. By the end of the war the only Naval uniform left to many of them was a pair of shoulder straps or a cap. Once a Naval uniform had been acquired, all that was necessary was to cut off the insignia and substitute civilian buttons. The pattern of civilian coats on the Continent is so varied that the slits in the back of a Naval officers tunic never caused comment and as a double-breasted dark blue suit they passed muster anywhere.

The next best civilian disguise was made from airmen's greatcoats. Cut to the right length and with some alteration to the lapels, they looked exactly like the double-breasted three-quarter length coat which so many Germans wore in winter. So long as a different coloured pair of trousers or breeches was worn it was unnecessary even to dye them.

A rather smarter, but less convincing, type of civilian jacket could be made from regulation airmen's tunics. Such a jacket was much tighter than the three-quarter length coat and had rather too pronounced a waist; but pleated pockets and high necklines are not uncommon among civilians in Germany and when worn with dark trousers and a gay coloured tie such converted tunics were unlikely to attract attention.

Full length civilian overcoats were most easily made either from French or Polish greatcoats from the booty store, or from Air Force officers' greatcoats. Airmen's greatcoats were so shapeless that they were apt to look odd and needed dyeing. The alterations to an Air Force officer's greatcoat were very simple; brass buttons had to be replaced by bone buttons set so as to offset the military waist, and the buckle of the belt had to be covered with some of the material taken from inside the coat. One officer who travelled right across Germany in such an overcoat, wearing a felt hat and carrying a rather dilapidated suitcase, heard a young officer who was walking with his sweetheart in the street remark, "I say, what a lovely coat," to which the girl replied, "Yes, but what a rotten suitcase." In fairness it should be added that the suitcase had fallen into a pond during a night walk through a forest.

The lower half of almost any disguise could be made from airmen's trousers. Not only were they practically indistinguishable from the trousers of the German Air Force, but, when old and nearly threadbare, could be made to look like grey flannels; alternatively, by threading a bootlace through the hem at the bottom and fastening them below the knees, they could be made into plus-fours. Worn with a light pair of stockings and brown shoes, plus-fours looked so unmilitary that any danger of their colour being recognised disappeared; those who wished, however, could dye them black or brown.

Hats were important. In summer anyone could go bareheaded without creating suspicion, but in winter German hats were distinctive. In large towns men usually wore felt "trilbies" or "Homburgs" and these were hard to come by because none were made during the war and civilians were loath to part with them, even for a considerable bribe. Attempts to make them out of paper or cardboard were unsuccessful and the few genuine felt hats which were acquired were reserved for men who were thought to have an exceptional chance of getting home. Outside the towns styles were more varied. Black ski-caps, peaked "chauffeur" caps without badge or band, fur caps and cloth caps of the ordinary British pattern were common, and nearly all Frenchmen wore berets.

Cloth caps and berets were easy to make. As no hat was expected to last more than a few weeks, any blanket was good enough material and either type could be mass-produced according to the following formula. Cut two ovals of material about 9 in. by 12 in. and sew their edges together; then cut a circle about 4 in. in diameter in one of the ovals and turn them inside out; scallop the rim of this circle fairly deeply, cut a half-inch strip of cardboard to the size of the head and then sew the cardboard on to the scallops; make a peak separately, cover it with cloth and sew it on, and finally sew a band of cloth over the cardboard headband. If anyone cares to experiment with these instructions he will find that after one or two attempts he can make a cloth cap which will pass muster even in comparison with a tailored object. Berets were made on the same principle and even more easily, and a large stock of both was always kept by the clothing department, hidden in places which were easily accessible.

Ski-caps were more complicated. The foundation was a R.A.F. field-service cap, the top of which had to be cut off and a new flat top sewn in. A cardboard peak covered with material was sewn on and civilian buttons replaced R.A.F. buttons on the front of the folded ear-flaps. The caps were then dyed a dark blue or black. For "chauffeur" caps it was necessary only to take the badge and band off an airman's peaked cap and dye it.

Occasionally demands for clothes were more ambitious. More than one prisoner grew his hair long, ostensibly to play a female part on the stage, but in reality to escape dressed as a woman. The clothing department made skirts and blouses from blankets and shirts, but though one officer imagined a striking likeness between himself and a dentist's assistant who came into the hospital, and another achieved a most effective disguise as an old woman with a vegetable basket, neither attempt ever materialised and the department's creations were in time relegated to the theatre.

Perhaps the most difficult work of all was dyeing. In the first year of the war dyes were obtained quite openly from the canteen, but when this was stopped permanganate of potash, gentian violet, indelible lead from pencils, tea, coffee, dye from beetroots or the coloured bindings of books, were all tried with only moderate success. Chloride of lime supplied by the Germans for wash-houses was used for bleaching. In the later years dyes were obtained from corrupt Germans.

For security, and because of the limited supply, as far as possible

clothes were dyed in the mass. Those intending to escape would be warned
that on a certain day dyeing operations would take place, and it was up to
them to have their clothes ready. A wash-house would be set aside for the
purpose, special stoves would be reserved for warming water, and special
guards set. For camouflage, a particularly heavy batch of laundry would be
dealt with at the same time and special containers would be borrowed
from the kitchen. On one occasion twenty complete outfits, consisting of
trousers, coat and cap, were dyed and dried within twenty-four hours, several of them being used successfully on long journeys shortly afterwards.

Nevertheless, dyeing was never entirely satisfactory. However much
trouble was taken, dyed coats and trousers somehow always looked as
though they had been dyed, and when prisoners came to realise that it was
less the colour than the line and general appearance of clothes which mattered, they tended to use dyeing only for caps, berets and trousers. The
making of German uniforms was much more difficult. Few officer's uniforms were attempted, but it is worthy of record that, by arrangement
with his wife, one prisoner had a new uniform specially made in England
which, by a few simple alterations, could be transformed into that of an
officer of the German Air Force. The uniform duly arrived and, despite a
difference in colour, survived German scrutiny and was delivered to the
prisoner. Unfortunately no opportunity of using it ever arose.

The Germans of other ranks who came into the British compounds
wore five different varieties of uniform according to their unit, their job,
or the time of year. Of these the two which were simplest to copy were the
least often worn. The loose and invariably dirty white coat and trousers
which German troops wore in the summer on organised working parties
could be made easily from more than one kind of pyjama or from the towels issued by the Germans, but the occasions for such parties were rare and
the chance of attaching extra men to them in broad daylight was slender.
Several attempts were made but only one was successful.

The uniform of the "ferrets" was also comparatively easy to copy. Summer and winter they wore dark blue one-piece boiler suits, boots, a leather
belt without holster or pistol and a field-service cap. They carried very
long screwdrivers or iron probing rods and torches. At various times two
or three genuine boiler suits were smuggled into the compound, but when
these did not fit or were not available, a good suit could be made from
sheets and dyed. The fact that such suits were usually stained and dirty
made the quality of the dyeing less important. Several attempts at escape
were made in this disguise and from the point of view of the clothing
department it was satisfactory that the most successful of all, that of a
Dutchman who walked out of Stalag Luft III in August 1942, was in a
camp-made suit.

Other German uniforms were more complicated. The normal dress worn by the camp staff consisted of a short buttonless tunic with a high collar fastened at the neck, trousers, black boots, field-service cap, belt and pistol. German Air Force blue is a little greyer than the uniform of the R.A.F. but the colours are so close that a little powdered chalk rubbed into R.A.F. material made it indistinguishable; Air Force trousers, therefore, needed no alteration and any boots that were without toecaps would do. On the other hand the tunic needed complete tailoring.

British battledress tunics had the right kind of buttoning in front, but were too short; all other R.A.F. tunics had open necks with lapelled collars and buttons outside. The difficulty was overcome by using large-size airmen's greatcoats which had plenty of spare material and could be re-cut entirely in front so that they buttoned to an under-flap. When their collars were opened up there was enough material to make a high neck, and it was easy to cut the coat short. This work was done almost entirely by professionals, the best of whom were Poles and Czechs. More than one British officer owes his escape to their labour, and particularly to a Polish officer named Mondschein who was murdered by the Germans after the mass escape in 1944.

In summer German guards on duty in the watch-towers and outside the wire wore the regulation buttoned tunics, trousers, high boots and field-service cap, and carried ammunition pouches and rifles. The tunic could be made from a regulation R.A.F. tunic, but as it was much shorter, the pockets smaller and the neckline again high, a great deal of alteration was necessary. German buttons were the colour of polished lead, made of composite material and embossed. They were difficult to counterfeit but easy to acquire either through bribery or theft. The pre-war type of black leather flying boot needed only to have the slit in the front sewn up to become a high boot, although the British leather was so much better than the German that there was always danger that a German might comment. This uniform was never copied as satisfactorily as the others.

In winter all Germans wore greatcoats. Their pattern was longer and fuller than British greatcoats, with pleats under a belt at the back, and the same grey buttons as on tunics. The pleats were the main difficulty and to achieve them either very large-size British greatcoats had to be used on small men or material had to be let into the back; this was a difficult thing to do well. Occasionally it was possible to steal Polish greatcoats of approximately the right colour from the booty store and these, being made more in the shape of capes, were more easily adaptable. Greatcoats had the great advantage that they covered the tops of high boots and that it mattered little what was worn underneath. Belts and ammunition pouches were worn outside.

Headgear was comparatively simple because the great majority of Germans wore field-service caps on all occasions. The R.A.F. field-service cap was of a slightly different shape, having a kink in the ear-flaps; it was necessary, therefore, to cut off the ear-flaps and sew on another piece of material which had an unbroken curve. Instead of buttons in front the Germans wore a red, white and blue roundel and above it an embroidered eagle, both of which could easily be made if they could not be procured through bribery. A little powder changed the colour and the result was a cap which even the Germans themselves admitted was indistinguishable except under close inspection.

Whatever the uniform, the insignia were similar. All ranks wore rectangular patches on their collars, the colour of which denoted the branch of the service to which they belonged. Yellow patches, the type usually needed by prisoners, denoted the general duties branch; medical orderlies wore blue, anti-aircraft units red, and the quartermaster's staff green, and so on. On each coloured patch were pinned little metal wings which indicated the wearer's grade. There were four grades of privates and five grades of N.C.O.s. Corporals and above wore silver braid round the bottom of their collars and round the edges of their shoulder-straps. Several N.C.O.s had stars, according to their grade, within the braid on the shoulder-straps. On both types of regulation tunics there was an embroidered eagle on the left breast and under it were worn the various efficiency badges. There were no eagles on greatcoats or overalls.

None of these insignia was very hard to make. Yellow patches were cut from ordinary dusters. The other colours came from handkerchiefs, football shorts and any other suitable piece of material. The metal wings were made from tin or cast from silver paper. Eagles, roundels and braid could often be bought from the Germans, but even when originals were not available roundels were easily made, eagles could be embroidered by hand, and the elastic from the waist of summer underpants or bootlaces made excellent braid when painted with silver paint. Very great skill, on the other hand, was needed in the making of belts, ammunition pouches and rifles, and for the last the escape clothing representative had to call on another department.

German belts were of plain dark brown leather about one and a half inches broad with a buckle in front. Occasionally prisoners had belts sent from home which were sufficiently near the required width to be used, but as these were usually confiscated on arrival it was necessary to rely on substitutes. The best was the tarred paper which lined the hollow wooden walls of the barracks. Folded thickly to the required width and glued, this paper was not only strong but took quite a high polish and was difficult to detect even at close quarters in daylight.

German buckles were not of the pronged type, but solid and rectangular, a large edition of the type of buckle often found on bathing shorts. They were the colour of polished pewter and embossed in the centre with a laurel wreath round which were inscribed the words "Gott mit uns". To make a buckle it was necessary to secure an original for long enough to take an impression of the inscription, either in clay or by hammering it out of tin; as Germans frequently took off their belts when they were working this was not difficult. A buckle made of tin was usually adequate from the prisoners' point of view, as it could be slipped over the fastening of the belt to cover the hooks or safety pins. However, more than one solid buckle was cast and these were used when the belt was made of real leather. There was no case of a belt or buckle being detected.

Ammunition pouches and pistol holsters were made from paper and cardboard held together by glue. Glue sometimes was brought into the camp for legitimate purposes, and though supplies had to be husbanded carefully there was usually enough to cover escaping needs as well. Taught by professional bag-makers and helped by practice in making properties for the stage, prisoners were able to turn out pouches and holsters which, when polished to the right colour with boot polish, would have survived even a dress parade.

Pride of place in craftsmanship, however, must go to the carpenters who produced the rifles. There were two standards, one for use at night and the other by day. At night anything which looked the right shape and had the gleam of metal at certain points was sufficient, but by day a rifle might have to pass much closer inspection. Once again they were made so that, to a glance even at close quarters, they were indistinguishable from the real object. Although made entirely of wood, bolts could be opened and shut and bayonets fixed and unfixed; and the appearance of metal was given by the use of ordinary lead pencil rubbed in and polished.

The work of the Clothing Department never ended. Attempts to escape in disguise were frequent and losses were high; what had taken many weeks to prepare might disappear into the German escape museum five minutes after it had been used. Replacements took time. Under extreme pressure, German tunics were made in forty-eight hours, but normally the tailors liked to have at least a week, and often they took much longer. Working hours depended upon security. So much sewing of all kinds was always going on in the camps that a good deal could be done without special precautions, but the cutting and tailoring of a German tunic or civilian suit meant an outlay which could not quickly be concealed and had to be done under the strictest secrecy. For this work only a few hours of any day were available.

While such clothing was being made, and especially after it had been completed, it had to be hidden in a place where it was easily accessible in case it was needed at short notice. Special wall panels were constructed, but if one of these became suspect, mattresses were often used. It is remarkable how difficult it can be to find something in a mattress stuffed full of straw or wood shavings, even if one knows it is there; and the Germans in their searches seldom had time to turn the contents of mattresses out on the floor.

Losses from carelessness were few. Once an officer with a long experience of escape forgot all that he had learned and chose to put the final touches to a German uniform while sitting in front of his closed shutters after dark. The shutters opened from the outside and the guard, who noticed a light shining through the chinks where no light should have been, opened them without warning and took all that he found; but such lapses were rare.

It would be wrong to judge the success of the clothing department by the number of prisoners who escaped. So far as is known, no failure was due to faulty dress and many of the failures themselves were the best possible advertisement for the disguises which had been made.

One of the most amusing attempts took place in 1941 at Barth. Each evening a party of six Germans entered the compound to close and fasten the shutters on the outside of the barrack windows and to lock the barrack doors. Two prisoners decided to try and tack themselves on to the end of the party as it left the compound. This was comparatively simple because, once inside the compound, the guards split up, each man going to a separate barrack and re-forming in his own time when he had completed his duties. The operation was quite casual, the last two men rejoining their ranks just before the party reached the gate; there seemed a reasonable chance that two extra men, tacking themselves on at the last minute, would not be noticed.

Full uniforms were made, with ammunition pouches, shoulder-straps and wooden rifles, and the bayonets could be fixed and unfixed in case it should be necessary to stay with the guard through the dismounting ceremony. On the night chosen all went according to plan. The two prisoners emerged from different barracks and took their places successfully in the rear of the party. The sentry at the gate made no comment and they marched off into the German compound. Here, however, the discipline of the German guards broke down. They were not supposed to talk while on duty, but a guard next to one of the prisoners suddenly turned and began a conversation. Not understanding German, the prisoner replied lustily "Ja". The German looked surprised and tried again. This time he received an equally lusty "Nein". As the second reply was no more suitable than the first the German became suspicious and the prisoner was discovered; whereupon all the guards, including the second prisoner, stopped marching and stood round in a group roaring with laughter and slapping each other on the back. The second prisoner joined in the fun and fortunately found it unnecessary to say anything, as in his case also this would have been fatal.

Just as the party was about to resume its march, to take the first prisoner to the Guard House, a German officer appeared to whom the whole story had to be recounted. The officer enjoyed the joke with the rest and ordered them to march on; whereupon, solely because of the presence of the officer, a check of the numbers was made, and it was found there was still one too many. Chaos ensued and every German started feverishly accusing his neighbour until finally the second British prisoner was unmasked.

In Stalag Luft III in the summer of 1942 there was another comic failure. Three officers had succeeded in getting out of the camp by a type of tunnel known as a "mole." The entry was in a drain near the wire and, once in the drain, the prisoners had dug their way through, pushing the earth back and sealing the tunnel behind them as they went. They kept themselves alive by making small air holes. Naturally this sort of tunnel had to be dug very fast and close to the surface. After the officers had escaped the tunnel collapsed where it passed under the wire, leaving a sort of irregular ditch. It was known that the Germans were going to fill in this ditch, and it occurred to two prisoners that they might perform the task themselves and at the same time reach the other side of the wire in comparative safety. Uniforms were made and a plan laid.

One of the officers spoke reasonably good German and it was to be his duty to walk up to the Germans in the watch-towers on either side of the "ditch," and explain to them that they had been ordered to fill in the ditch, and that in doing so they would have to climb over the wire. His companion was to carry a sack, out of the top of which would appear stakes which were to be used for holding up the loose coils of wire in the middle of the fence, while underneath would be the civilian clothes and the food they were to use once they were outside. Spades were to be taken from one of the many gardeners who had permission to use them inside the camp; but for reasons of security the gardeners were not told anything of the scheme and it was left to the two prisoners to assert their authority as "Germans."

The luncheon hour was chosen for the attempt and after putting on their German uniforms the prisoners marched out from their barrack, the non-German speaker carrying the heavy sack in the rear. They walked across the main street of the camp to a garden where some prisoners were digging and the German speaker said curtly that they needed the spades. The prisoners looked startled but let them take the spades without comment.

Much encouraged by the success of their disguise, the two "Germans" continued on their way to the wire. Having reached the "ditch," they dumped the sack and leant the spades against the warning rail; and while the officer who had been carrying the sacks stood and mopped his brow the other walked off slowly to the guard towers to explain their mission. Neither guard showed the least concern, and both replied with a bored "Jawohl."

Delighted at what seemed to promise certain success, the officer walked back to his companion and said in an undertone that all was O.K. and that they should go ahead leisurely. They picked up their spades and were just turning to cross the warning wire to begin their task when, to their dismay, they saw a third German, also carrying a spade but bearing unmistakable signs of authenticity, coming towards them. He was fifty yards away when he shouted something and waved to them cheerfully. The German-speaker of the two prisoners knew only too well that although his accent might survive carefully prepared sentences he would betray his identity at once in a running conversation, and as the real German came on steadily with the apparent intention of joining them at their work, he decided to beat a hasty retreat.

Spades and sack were picked up, and without a word the two set off at a smart pace for the nearest wash-house where their accomplices had stationed themselves in case of such an emergency. The real German stopped in surprise and shouted again. The guards in the boxes looked mildly interested but did nothing. The prisoner carrying the two spades reached the wash-house first and had the pleasure of watching his companion labouring under the heavy sack and doing his utmost not to run. They entered the wash-house and once again startled some prisoners who seemed to be engaged on their lawful occupations. As they tore off their clothes, swearing roundly in English, they were told that they had interrupted another escape operation.

It transpired later that the prisoners from whom the spades had been taken in the first place, having been informed that the camp was cleared of all Germans, were just about to bury some sand which had come out of a tunnel. The sudden appearance of two "Germans" had taken them completely by surprise and they had thought they were being discovered. They were greatly relieved when the "Germans" simply took the spades and walked off.

## CHAPTER 10 · TOOLS

If bad workmen complain of their tools, it might be claimed that workmen who not only do the job but make all their own tools beforehand are superlatively good. In prison camps the only tools with which most men began were small files which had been part of the escaping kit provided in their aircraft or which had been sewn into their clothes before they left England. Occasionally in the early years, a canteen would have a few penknives for sale but otherwise everything larger than a needle or a nib had to be stolen, made, or acquired by bribery.

The demand for tools was endless. Those who were digging tunnels needed shovels or scrapers and lamps, those who were shoring tunnels needed saws, hammers, chisels and bradawls, and those who were preparing the entrances to tunnels needed all those and cold steel chisels as well. These were just the beginnings. Trolleys to carry sand needed axles and ball-bearings, hooks and pulleys, long tunnels needed air-pumps and pipes, men who were hoping to climb or cut the wire needed ladders or wire-cutters, and men who were going out in disguise often needed keys or rifles which had to be exact reproductions. There was no tool from an axe to an iron bracket that was not useful.

Throughout the war theft was probably the most prolific source of supply. There was almost always some constructional work going on in a compound and it was difficult for workmen to be unceasingly vigilant against a community in which theft was a virtue; if guards accompanied the workmen they were easily distracted. But when thefts were reported to the German authorities reprisals were sometimes threatened and it was not always possible to keep what had been gained. Nevertheless guards were often afraid to report a loss and many workmen were Poles or men otherwise sympathetic to the prisoners, and from the day that the first camp was opened some real tools were available.

But the supply of stolen goods was never adequate; and as every prisoner at some time needed a hammer—or something that would serve for a hammer—for purely domestic purposes, any piece of metal was at a premium. Broken bits of iron, the bars of an old grate, old motor-car springs lying in a dump, the rims of cartwheels or the bands off a barrel were seized upon at once and guarded almost as carefully as food. Those whose hobby was the making of more refined tools would accept any piece of metal that a man could carry. Once prisoners' eyes had become attuned to the need it was remarkable how much metal a prison compound contained. Almost all wooden barracks had iron angles to strengthen corners and long bolts through their beams. Stoves had many bars and handles which were unnecessary. Compound kitchens had a variety of fire-irons and sometimes meat axes, bacon cutters and more than one meat saw. The wooden shutters of barrack windows had long iron hinges. Aluminium washing basins, tins of all kinds, and even silver paper had their uses.

As with every other aid to escape, the acquisition and use of tools was haphazard to begin with but gradually became organised. At first men were their own blacksmiths and carpenters, but experience brought specialisation and losses brought security and discipline. Ultimately in most Air Force camps there were teams of carpenters and metal workers who together or separately formed departments of the escape organisation and who besides being craftsmen, often acted as technical advisers on constructional problems. Under the security chief, they were responsible for hiding the tools they made and used.

SAWS. After the file, the first tool was almost always a knife saw. In its most primitive form this consisted of an ordinary table knife, the sharp edge of which had been filed into a series of jagged teeth. This saw had its limitations and took a long time to do its work, but with it men sawed through the floors of cattle trucks and with patience it could cope with most of the timber that prisoners used.

A great improvement on the knife saw was a frame saw with a gramophone spring blade. The chief difficulty in making these was to find the owner of a gramophone who did not mind it being ruined. Once made they were very efficient. The frame was of wood, held taut by twisted string, and with a round section handle the blade could be turned in any direction like a jig-saw. The frames could be made to any size but the saws were always light and liable to bend.

BORING TOOLS. Boring holes in wood with a red-hot poker is messy and inaccurate; a number of useful tools were evolved. For small holes nails or pieces of stout wire were set in wooden handles, the ends being fined down to form a bradawl. A high speed drill for small holes in wood or metal was made by mounting old dental drills in a round piece of wood; this was then pressed down on to the surface which needed holing and rotated at speed by a simple bow made from a coat-hanger and a leather boot lace. Large holes were more difficult and the best method was to make several small holes and then knock through a large iron bolt or wooden wedge.

PINCERS. The standard method of extracting nails was to force an ordinary table fork under the head and lift vigorously. This was so effective, and forks so plentiful that pincers were only needed for special jobs. They were made in much the same way as wire-cutters.

CHISELS. The best chisels were stolen, but extraordinarily serviceable tools were made by the metal workers from broken fencing rails, skate blades, shutter hinges and other odd bits of iron. All such metal needed tempering and it was only by trial and error that the right degree of heat and the proper rate of cooling was discovered. If the metal was cooled too quickly it became brittle.

In some camps sugar, with its high carbon content, was used for hardening. The end of a length of iron pipe was blocked, the sugar poured in and then the piece of metal inserted. Owing to the poor quality coal it was difficult to bring the sugar to the right temperature, but furious blowing with home-made bellows or anthracite stolen from German supplies eventually provided the necessary heat. As there was always a shortage of sugar this method was only used on special occasions, usually for wire-cutters.

WIRE-CUTTERS. Wire-cutters were made from skate-blades or shutter hinges. Skate-blades were harder and sharper but holes had to be driven through them for the hinge; shutter hinges had the holes already drilled but needed careful hardening. The cutting edges were made with files and hack-saws. These home-made wire-cutters were extremely effective and would cut normal barbed wire silently and swiftly.

The tools listed above are only a few of those made; the full list would include almost everything seen in a carpenter's shop and a few extra gadgets besides. Two specialities were the manufacture of keys and of air-pumps for tunnels.

KEYS. To pick locks or make keys a knowledge of the mechanism of locks was essential, and in every prison compound one or two enthusiasts made it their business to dismantle and study as many of the locks in use as possible. With some measurements and a mental picture of what was required it was then possible to make a set of lock picks which would cover a large range of door locks and padlocks. Where there were several locks of a similar pattern a master key could also be made and for some especially difficult locks a replica of the genuine key was the only solution.

The majority of fixed door-locks in German prison camps were of the "rim" type where the important variations are on the front of the key rather than on its face. This made them very easy to pick. All that was needed was a strong piece of wire about an eighth of an inch thick, one end of which was bent at right-angles and the other formed into a loop to serve as a handle. The short right-angled end would then be beaten with a hammer until it had a flat face and would then be cut to fit the entrance slit to the lock. The end of the face was then filed square. To pick the lock the wire key was inserted in exactly the same way as the ordinary key, but as it had no steadying extension the shaft had to rest on the forefinger of the free hand. By manipulation and feel the end of the wedge-shaped face could be made to raise the wards and free the bolt. With a set of wire-keys of varying lengths and widths, and with lots of practice most fixed door-locks could be picked in well under a quarter of a minute.

Picking padlocks was more difficult because the locks were smaller; the principle, however, was the same. In cheap padlocks all the wards were held in position by a single spring and by turning the padlock upside down and depressing one ward, all the others could be made to fall as well; the bolt could then be turned.

For a master key it was necessary to examine the locks and determine the essential variations. An original key or a duplicate could then be filed so as to avoid the safety precautions of any particular lock and still raise the wards and slide the bolt.

Duplicate keys had to be cast. First an impression of the original was taken in wet chewing gum, plasticine or putty. Then a blank key was cast in a mould. The best moulds were made from the German equivalent of "bath brick" which could be bought in the canteen. Four of these tablets made the two halves of the mould the joins being made smooth by rubbing the blocks together. Half the shape of the key would then be gouged out of each block, and before the two halves were laid together two grooves would be cut at either end of the key shape, one to allow the metal to be poured in and the other to allow the air to escape. The metal used was zinc, taken from wash-bowls and jugs supplied by the Germans. It could be melted easily and after being poured into the mould and allowed to cool, a slightly oversized blank key would result. This could then be cut and filed as required. The rate of cooling was important, because if the metal cooled too fast the key was apt to be brittle. Zinc keys in any case were soft and apt to wear or break unless accurately made; but many were so good that they did duty for years. Clay could also be used for moulds but the edges were less well-defined. Badges and buckles, however, were successfully made from clay moulds.

Yale locks were quite simply overcome by forcing the blade of a table knife between the lock and the jamb of the door. The curved end of the bolt receded as the knife-blade was forced down on it until it was finally clear of the catch. The drawback to this method was that it usually left traces on the woodwork of the door.

An example of successful lock-picking occurred in 1941, when the Royal Air Force were moved from Spangenberg to another camp. One officer decided to hide in the castle and try to escape when it was empty and less well guarded. A room was found in the top of the castle the entrance to which had been bricked up. The double doors remained, however, the first fastened by a yale lock, an ordinary lock and a heavy padlock and the second by an ordinary lock. It was decided to open the doors, pull down the bricks, install the officer armed with suitable tools, and then seal the room again.

The yale lock was forced with a knife-blade and as the door fitted badly and there was quite a wide gap between it and the jamb this was done without trace. The padlock was not picked, but the end of the hinge-pin was sawn off so that the clasp could be removed at the wrong end. The ordinary locks were picked in the normal way. The wall presented no difficulties and after the officer had been installed the bricks were put back and the doors re-locked.

The Germans soon discovered that a prisoner was missing and searched everywhere, except the sealed room which they thought inaccessible. They finally concluded he had escaped. The castle was not evacuated for a fortnight and the officer was visited daily and given food; he made his attempt a few days after the prisoners had left but unfortunately the rope by which he descended from his window was seen before he had time to get away.

AIR PUMPS. In the course of the war a great many different types of pump were invented to pump air into tunnels. In one army camp it is believed there was an electrically-driven pump and several rotary pumps were tried. Eventually, however, the most universally efficient turned out to be a pump made from an ordinary kit-bag, and once established this type was developed and improved throughout the war.

The bottom of the kit-bag was fastened to a square board in which there were two holes, one covered by a leather flap-valve on the inside and the other on the outside. The mouth of the kit-bag was fitted with a round board with a handle on the outside. A number of wire rings, with their ends twisted into lugs on either side, were then sewn on to the kit-bag and the whole was fitted on to a wooden base, of which the board at the bottom of the kit-bag formed the end. The lugs ran along the side of the base and prevented the bag from collapsing when compressed. All that was then necessary was for a man to sit beside the base and push the bag backwards and forwards along it, the air being sucked in through one valve at the end and driven out through the other into a pipe. This was made of tins which fitted into each other, and could be extended indefinitely. A man could work such a pump for several hours at a stretch without undue fatigue and in the last year of the war improved mechanism made the work lighter still. The pumps themselves lasted many months with very little overhaul.

## CHAPTER 11 · SECURITY

A love of secrecy is not a natural characteristic of the British race. At the beginning of the war there must have been many who, on hearing the title "Security Officer", wondered vaguely what it meant and thought it must be something to do with seeing that the locks of doors worked and that papers were not left lying about. Even as late as 1943 there were many who felt that all the precautions for secrecy were rather exaggerated, but not absurd. Yet only a day or two before the landing at Dieppe a German guard told a British Intelligence Officer in one of the compounds of Stalag Luft III, in the heart of Germany, that a real attempt at invasion would be made at that place within a few days. The failure of the attempt itself showed how bad security had been. Fortunately, by 1944, all this had changed and no secret was so well kept as that of D-Day.

In a prisoner of war camp such a large proportion of the things which were done had to be done without the knowledge of the enemy that a sense of security was learned more quickly. Besides all the work connected with escape, comparatively harmless activities, such as the making of clothes from German blankets or of furniture from parts of German buildings, needed to be concealed. Individuals not only became cautious themselves, but learned to understand the need for organisation.

In Air Force camps the security department was the largest and most elaborate organisation of all. On its efficiency depended the existence not only of the various escape departments, but of the secret radio, the safety of all articles that were hidden, and many less spectacular but almost equally important activities such as conferences held by the Senior Officer or Camp Leader. To these responsibilities, at the end of the war, was added the secrecy of the plans made to take over prison camps and their immediate surroundings in the hour of German defeat.

In the early years of the war no single security department existed. Theoretically the Senior Officer, or in N.C.O.s' compounds the Camp Leader, was responsible, but though he was ready at all times with help and advice, in practice any man planning to escape had to take his own precautions. As prison camps became larger and clandestine activities more numerous, failure and discovery forced men to accept more and more centralisation and control. It was not, however, until the autumn of 1942 in Stalag Luft III, when all the other departments were in operation, that a security department with overriding powers was created.

From that time onwards in officer compounds the chief security officer was second only in importance to the Senior Officer. He alone of all departmental heads could call upon any prisoner for duty, and his instructions had the full force of orders. At any time he could stop any activity within a compound which he thought might jeopardise an attempt at escape, and though these powers sometimes were resented, prisoners learned by bitter experience how vital security was and in the end accepted his decisions willingly.

In N.C.O.s' compounds, where such authority was impossible, security depended more upon voluntary co-operation. But the organisation of the department followed the same pattern and in many compounds equally good results were obtained.

The organisation of security followed the general pattern of the escape organisation itself. At the head was the Security Chief who worked in the closest touch with the Senior Officer or Camp Leader and with the head of the Escape Committee. Under him came officers representing their respective barracks who were responsible for everything connected with security within their own precincts. Theirs was a job which never ended and which called for men of considerable personality. Within this general system, and under the supervision of these officers, there existed also special security systems for special operations. The forgery department and the secret radio department had each a special team of "stooges" who were excused other duty; and any tunnel which ran a sufficient distance to have a reasonable chance of success tended to establish its own system with specially selected men.

The system by which security was enforced can conveniently be described as one of "Watch and Ward". "Watch" consisted of a network of sentries who were on duty in varying strengths through all the daylight hours, and when necessary through the night as well; "Ward" comprised the safekeeping of all secret equipment and apparatus for escape, and entailed the construction of special hiding places all over the compounds.

The foundation of any effective "Watch" was an accurate knowledge of how many and which Germans were in a prison compound at any time. As most compounds had one gate only any prisoner sitting at any window which commanded it could know exactly who came in and went out. "Duty pilots" therefore were established whose task was to write down in a book the name or description of all non-prisoners who came into the compound during the day and the exact time of their entry and exit. As the greater part of the perimeter of any compound was brightly lit this could also be done at night if necessary.

Such a task sounds simple, yet it was surprising how often mistakes were made. "Duty pilots" worked in pairs, one to watch and one to act as a runner, and were relieved every hour; yet time and again, when according to the book a compound should have been clear of Germans and escaping operations were under way, a guard would suddenly appear and create general panic. Somehow, perhaps because a friend had distracted him for a moment or because he had been reading a newspaper, the "duty pilot" had failed to keep his eyes on the gate for just the few critical seconds it took a German to pass through and out of sight. Because of this, "duty pilots" were at first recruited from volunteers who hoped to take part in an escape and who could be trusted not to let their attention wander; but as time went on and the value of security was more generally realised it was possible in many compounds to make each man take his turn on a roster. When a mistake was discovered all clandestine activities were closed down at once and a thorough search of the whole compound was made to ensure that no other Germans were there.

The Germans soon found out that they were being watched, but realising that it was something they were powerless to prevent, usually ignored it. Sometimes "Charlie" or another of the more experienced Germans would walk straight to the "duty pilots'" window after entering the compound and book himself in, and occasionally if a German was in a bad temper he would confiscate the lists; but new lists were started elsewhere immediately. If the "ferrets" were getting nervous about a tunnel, one of them sometimes would try and defeat the system by climbing over the wire in some far corner of the compound; but there were always so many prisoners about that it was difficult for them to do this unobserved and, of course, warning was given immediately.

All Germans who came into a prison compound were not equally dangerous, and in order not to hold up work unnecessarily they were divided into two categories. When a harmless German, such as the N.C.O. who looked after the kitchen, entered the compound no special action was taken; but when "ferrets" or other dangerous men entered special signals were put out where all could see them. If more than three dangerous men were in a compound at the same time all operations were usually closed down.

The "duty pilots" ensured that anyone who was interested could learn how many Germans were in a compound at any time; but unless work was to be confined to the rare periods when a compound was free of all Germans whatsoever, additional sentries had to be posted round each separate operation to give warning when Germans came closer. These sentries were known as "stooges". Stooging was, perhaps, the worst of all jobs. Often it meant standing or sitting in some inconvenient place, perhaps in an uncomfortable position, for many hours at a time unable to do anything but watch or give an occasional signal. Yet failure on the part of a "stooge" could be as fatal as that of a "duty pilot" and ruin the work of months in a few seconds. It could also cause a lot of unnecessary trouble. To give an example, a stooge in one compound used to sit in a chair outside a hut, and his signal that a German was coming was to get up and walk into the hut. After about a week of sitting, without ever having to get up, he suddenly decided one evening to go and get himself a more comfortable chair. As soon as he moved there was frantic activity in two huts from which tunnels were being dug. All diggers were brought to the surface at once and traps were closed. When the stooge returned to his chair he was surprised to find several prisoners standing round waiting for him, wanting to know where the German had gone and who he was. As with "duty pilots", "stooges" in the beginning were always volunteers, often the friends of those who were planning to escape, but by 1943 they had become part of the general security system and in officers' compounds anyone could be called on to take his turn.

Tactics for "stooges" varied. If the Germans were unsuspicious and if only a few escape operations were taking place, "stooges" would be hidden, and great care would be taken to ensure that the Germans did not notice them; but if, as was more usual, the Germans were aware that many escapes were in preparation, exactly the reverse policy was adopted, and obvious "stooges" were placed all over the compound in order that attention should not be drawn to any particular spot.

When this policy was in force signals were abandoned and warning was passed round by word of mouth. The Universal name for any German was "goon" and as a German approached a barrack the "stooges" outside would enter the main passage and shout loudly "Goon in the block", and all work would be hidden at once. The Germans had always been inquisitive about the word "goon" and when enquiring what it meant were told it was only another nickname, like "Jerry" or "Tommy". One day, however, the German General in charge of all prison camps paid Schubin a visit, and in the course of his tour entered a barrack, followed by the usual suite of obsequious German officers. Owing to a shortage of Red Cross parcels prisoners were particularly disgruntled, and instead of standing to attention as the General came in they remained where they were. One man with a particularly deep and sonorous voice gave the cry "Goon in the block".

The General was furious, rated the Commandant then and there for the ill-discipline of his prisoners, and demanded at once to know what the word "goon" meant. Research took time, but a week or two later an order was issued that if any prisoner was heard using the word "goon" he would be arrested. The Germans had discovered that the original "goon" was a sub-human being in a *Daily Mirror* cartoon, and from then on even inoffensive members of the guard company would become annoyed if they heard the word used.

One of the most important events which "stooges" had to guard each day was the reading of the B.B.C. News Bulletin. German news was relayed into each compound by loudspeaker and much of it was of considerable interest; the first page of the Bulletin therefore was a summary of this news, which might or might not be read but could always be given up to a German in case of emergency. On the rare occasions when a German took a news-reading by surprise this device was adopted, and the explanation given was that as so few prisoners could speak German a précis of the German news was read every day.

But most Air Force compounds also had a secret radio receiver and because knowledge of what was happening in the world outside did more than anything else to preserve the morale of prisoners the greatest care was taken to prevent the Germans from discovering it. A small team listened to almost all Allied broadcasts during the twenty-four hours, including the Soviet news, and a summary was made. Four or five copies then were written by hand and distributed to special readers. Reading took place in several barracks simultaneously and was covered by "stooges," who were concealed; when it was over each copy of the news was returned to the prisoner in charge of the service and destroyed. Radios had been discovered by the Germans in many prisoner of war camps and one or two sets and a number of components were discovered in R.A.F. compounds, but except for occasional interruptions owing to technical breakdowns, the radio service was maintained throughout the war, even when the prisoners were on the march at the end.

The system of "Watch" protected all active operations; the system of "Ward" ensured that when the equipment was made it should not fall into the hands of the Germans. By far the safest place to hide anything was under the ground. Even when a man had buried something himself, within quite a small area, it was often extraordinarily difficult for him to find it unless the spot had been marked with great care. For the Germans the prospects were hopeless. Not unless they had used hundreds of men and dug the whole surface of a compound systematically to a depth of at least three feet could they have made certain of finding all that had been hidden; and, of course, they never had the men or the time. However, things buried, even under the floors of barracks, were not always accessible at short notice. All kinds of wall-panels, false tops and bottoms to tins and boxes, secret drawers in tables, chairs and cupboards were therefore constructed, and equipment was distributed between them so that the discovery of any one hiding place would not mean the total loss of any one type of article. Inventories, which themselves had to be hidden carefully, were kept by the security staff, and checked after any search by the Germans.

When the Germans found a hiding place during a search they did not always take what was in it, but would sometimes leave it hoping that its discovery would not be noticed and that they might return later and make a complete haul of all similar hiding places in the camp. Prisoners countered this by using threads of cotton or transparent sticky-paper which, if broken, showed that a cache had been tampered with; in which case the contents of all similar hiding places throughout the compound were removed at once and messages sent to warn other compounds.

One of the most ingenious of all secret places was made by moving the whole of one side of a room. The partition walls inside the huts were double, made in wooden sections and lined with asbestos stuffing and paper sheeting; it was not difficult to move one half of such a wall into a room, leaving space between the double walls which might vary from a few inches to the dimensions of a prison cell. All the rooms in the barracks being rectangular and of a pattern, not one man in ten thousand would notice such a change.

In the summer of 1942 at Stalag Luft III one side of a partition wall was moved a full yard in order to conceal the entrance to a tunnel. This secret chamber survived a search of the barrack by "ferrets" and excellent progress was being made until one morning "Charlie" hid himself under the hut in the early hours. He was not seen when the early morning shift of tunnellers commenced work. He did not interrupt but watched and waited until the prisoners went on parade at 9 o'clock, when he climbed up into the barrack to find himself in a confined space and complete darkness. Thoroughly bewildered, he began shouting and hammering on the sides of his prison demanding to be let out. As no one did anything, finally he broke his way out and in a state of great excitement went in search of his superiors. The tunnel was lost.

The safety of some hiding places lay in the psychology of the Germans. Although they knew that prisoners were adept at making keys, for some mysterious reason they retained a pathetic confidence in locked doors. In most compounds one of the smaller rooms was reserved as a waiting room for German guards and when they went away they locked the door. Ordinary skeleton keys were quite sufficient to open and shut it without wasting time, and though such rooms could not be guaranteed always to be accessible, their walls were invaluable for storing reserve sets of maps or anything else which would not be needed at very short notice. So far as is known no search was made in any of them.

Although by the end of the war the Germans had discovered many of the different types of hiding place they never found more than a small fraction of escape equipment. As always, their difficulty was shortage of man-power. To have tested every tin, every piece of furniture, and each plank in each wall of all the barracks every few weeks would have taken more men and time than were available. The Germans therefore used to concentrate on one or two types of hiding place at a time, testing the walls under the window-sills one day, and perhaps probing mattresses and inspecting the backs of pictures or books another. Occasionally they were lucky and would discover some wall panel which gave them a good haul and earned them good marks with their Security Officers; but as a rule searches yielded little except cigarette-lighters or coloured pencils, and as the work of the "contacts" improved, even these could be bought back again for a few cigarettes. In the last two years of the war the information service was so good that the prisoners knew not only at what time and in which barrack a search would take place, but also the particular type of hiding place or object which the Germans were looking for.

If nothing was found, the German Security Officers would get so angry with their men that they would order a continuous series of searches which became very inconvenient. Often it was worthwhile, therefore, to leave a hack-saw or an unwanted map where they would be found, in order to keep the "ferrets" in a good temper. By the autumn of 1944 German morale had declined so far that searches were little more than a formality.

A responsibility of the British Security Chief which was not exactly "Watch" or "Ward" was the filling of vacant places in the daily parades. If a prisoner escaped, the longer his absence could be concealed from the Germans the longer start he would have before they started looking for him; someone therefore had to take his place during parades. Or if a tunnel was being dug and the Germans held a snap roll-call, it might easily happen that one or two men at the far end could not get back in time, and their places, too, had to be filled.

Roll-calls were usually held twice a day at fixed hours, but after a mass escape extra parades were often added, and occasionally there were as many as six in twenty-four hours. It was the normal practice for a number of prisoners to report sick each morning and to be counted in bed. Usually it was possible for one or two of them to jump out of their beds after being counted and reach another bed in another room further along their barrack while the German was checking another room. When tunnels were being dug the number of prisoners who reported sick was kept at a certain level so that the German who counted the men in bed would take time to do his rounds, and give those who were to act as substitutes plenty of opportunity.

If for any reason it was impossible for a prisoner to change his bed, sometimes a dummy was made. As the dummy would be covered by blankets the only part of it which needed careful construction was the head. Casts of prisoners' faces were taken in plaster of paris and masks were made from them in a mixture of soap and plasticine. These were painted and real hair, which was preserved specially by the barber, was fixed on. In the shadow thrown by an upper bunk, and half covered by a pillow, they looked convincing enough. The Germans knew that dummies had been used and often would go right up to a bed and poke the figure in the blankets to make sure that it was a man. Sometimes, therefore, dummies were made to move. Strong cotton pulleys were attached to whatever was serving for arms and legs and were passed through a hole in the wall and worked by a prisoner in the next room. When pulled they created the effect of a leg stretching or bending, or an arm rising under the blankets. Sometimes a football bladder placed where the stomach should have been and worked by a hidden pump, was used to produce the effect of breathing or a lighted cigarette was placed in the dummy's mouth. Though they were used on several occasions none of these dummies was discovered.

Evening parades were more difficult to arrange. Those who had reported sick in the morning were usually taken to sick quarters immediately after breakfast and either detained or declared fit; in either case they were not available to act as substitutes in the afternoon. As it was not always possible to ensure that other prisoners should go sick during the middle of the day without arousing suspicion, other methods had to be employed.

Fortunately the Adjutant, who was responsible for the discipline of prisoners on parade, remained outside the ranks and could go more or less where he pleased provided he looked as though he was doing his duty. Usually it was left to him to choose one of several different ways of deceiving the Germans.

The Germans so frequently got the count wrong themselves that it was often worth gambling on the Adjutant's powers of persuasion when they came to check the figures. On the other hand, if substitution had already taken place inside a barrack and the Germans nevertheless counted a man too few, it was up to the Adjutant to do all he could to discover where the Germans had made their mistake, and prevent them counting again. Fortunately the German officers and N.C.O.s who took parades were frequently lazy and would often accept the Adjutant's word.

If fast talking failed there were a great many other tricks to fall back upon. Sometimes the Adjutant himself would fall in the centre rank of one of the first squadrons to be counted, and then when the Germans had passed, casually stroll out on to the parade ground to take his place at the centre. Alternatively it could be arranged that the men should be found to be missing in one of the last squadrons to be counted, by which time the rest of the parade would have broken ranks and men would be passing from one squadron to another; the Adjutant then would try to arrange that the re-count should be taken from half-way. In an Army camp a dummy was dressed in uniform and held up successfully in the ranks by the man on either side; but though satisfying to those concerned, this was a risky performance. Provided that no more than three men were missing it was almost always possible to cover their absence for at least one parade, and it was often done successfully for several days.

Occasionally the Security Officer was relieved of all these anxieties by the presence of "ghosts" in a compound. If an escape had been made which the Germans did not immediately discover it was always possible for two or three prisoners inside the camp to pretend that they had gone out and to give themselves a chance to get away later without raising an alarm.

The process of hiding was not as easy as it sounds, for a prison compound is a bare place and with Germans constantly in and out of barracks a "ghost" either had to spend most of his time underground or be constantly on the move if he was to avoid being recognised. His existence was strenuous and uncomfortable. But if another prisoner escaped whilst a "ghost" was still in being he automatically filled the vacant place at roll-calls. He was unlikely to be recognised because the Germans were always so intent on counting that they never looked closely at faces: a pair of dark spectacles in summer or a scarf wound round the chin in winter was all the disguise that was needed. So successfully were "ghosts" used that on several occasions prisoners were recaptured in distant parts of Germany before the German Camp Administration knew that they had escaped.

However thorough the organisation of escape, security in the long run depended upon the habits of mind of prisoners as a whole. Quite early in the war it was learned from the Germans themselves that the way in which they discovered most escaping operations was by listening at the barrack windows after dark. Chance remarks in wash-houses, latrines, sick quarters, or other places where Germans and prisoners might be together without knowing it were also known to have given away information. The only way to ensure that nothing was lost through carelessness was to suppress casual talk about escape altogether. This took time, but by dint of ceaseless propaganda, and by publicising every failure which was the result of some slip in security it was achieved in many compounds. By the end of 1943 any new prisoner arriving in Stalag Luft III who did talk unnecessarily about escape could sense at once, and without being told, that he was committing an offence. He soon found that not to mention escape became part of his nature.

· 111

ESCAPE
FROM
GERMANY

*German
Counter-
Measures*

## CHAPTER 12 · GERMAN COUNTER-MEASURES

The defences of German prison camps have already been described; their efficiency depended upon the German Staff. In the early days of the war German Security Officers seemed to work on the theory that once inside the wire prisoners were comparatively harmless and that precautions need only be taken prior to that stage. Before the prisoners entered a camp, or whenever they were to be transferred to other compounds rigorous searches were made. Prisoners were sometimes stripped naked and made to do physical exercises over a mat in the hope that hack-saws, compasses and other escaping equipment would fall from the cavities of their bodies; before a contingent left one camp for another searches would often be conducted at 4 or 5 o'clock in the morning so that each man could be taken separately from his bed.

Inside the camps, prisoners were left comparatively unmolested. When special Air Force camps were first set up the German Administrative Staffs prided themselves on their adherence to the Geneva Convention which regulated the treatment of prisoners of war, and often resented interference from their own Security Officers. Prisoners were not slow to take advantage of this and frequently made complaints about the unnecessary restrictions which the German Security Officer imposed.

Inter-compound sports were an example. Camp Commandants liked to have contented prisoners and on condition that no escape would be made or prepared, would encourage athletic events. However, on the slightest pretext these would be forbidden by the German Security Officer who realised that no parole could prevent general conversation and that much useful information not connected with any particular escape would be exchanged.

The German High Command order about tins was another bone of contention. The work involved in emptying the contents of every tin before the food was allowed into the compounds was so great that German Administrative Staffs usually ignored the order; but when prisoners who had escaped were recaptured with unpunctured tins in their possession it was extremely difficult for the Commandant to defend himself. Should the Security Officer resign because the Commandant was not prepared to take the necessary precautions, the latter would be placed in an impossible position; on the other hand the prisoners had no means of

112

ESCAPE
FROM
GERMANY

*German
Counter-
Measures*

storing food except in tins, and if Red Cross food was wasted bitter complaints were made to the Protecting Power who in turn complained to the German Foreign Office.

Every Commandant faced this dilemma and, as the war went on, tended to come down on the side of his Security Officer. At Stalag Luft III the Commandant's last victory was over the question of the trees in the North Compound. When this compound was opened in 1943 the Commandant, a German gentleman of the old-fashioned school, expressed the hope that the prisoners would find it so comfortable they would remain in it patiently until the war was over. Each barrack had water laid on and was surrounded by groups of pine trees which, in spite of the protests of the Security Department, the Commandant had refused to have cut down. Prisoners were duly grateful and for a few weeks made unprecedented progress with every kind of escaping plan. Eventually some of their efforts were discovered and the Commandant, humiliated and angry, ordered the trees to be removed. From then onwards the Security Officer had the last word.

During 1943 the Gestapo rose to a position of absolute power in Germany and interfered more and more in the affairs of the armed forces, including prisoner of war camps. The Chief Security Officer was forced to have at least one member of the S.S. attached to his staff and these men became the real masters, interfering not only with the activities of the prisoners, but of the Germans who guarded them.

From the outset the staff of the German Security Officer was separate both from the camp administration and from the companies of prison guards. At his headquarters were two or three officers of the rank of Captain or Lieutenant and three or four sergeants; under them teams of five or six special men, with a corporal or sergeant at the head, were assigned to each compound. These were the "ferrets" whose activities already have been described.

To begin with the "ferrets" were as amateur as the prisoners. They wandered about aimlessly, occasionally stopping a prisoner and carrying out a perfunctory search, but generally staying disconsolately in corners not knowing what to do or where to look. At Barth and Dulag Luft, where the "ferrets" were first employed, their methods were so haphazard that although the entrances to tunnels were open holes under the huts in which prisoners lived, some of them were not found for many days and more than one tunnel nearly succeeded. It was not for many months that regular searches were instituted. The Germans had the sense, however, to keep the same men on this particular job throughout the war, and though new "ferrets" were added as the number of prisoners increased, most of those who began their work at Barth became skilful detectives.

In the early years of the war "ferrets" usually patrolled the compounds from 9 a.m. to 1 p.m. and from 3 p.m. to 6 p.m.; but from the summer of

113

ESCAPE
FROM
GERMANY

*German
Counter-
Measures*

1943 onwards their routine was changed and throughout all the hours of daylight at least two were always on duty. During the night, besides the special guard who patrolled the compounds with a dog, a "ferret" would pay intermittent visits. The German security staff copied the British escape organisation and placed a key man in each of the administrative departments of the camp. An agent of the German Security Officer was present when food, books, or clothes were distributed, and it was his duty not only to supervise, but to make the members of the administrative staff "escape conscious." When the Gestapo took over security this supervision was extended to the German guards as well, and a regular system of setting one German to spy upon another was introduced.

The German security staff relied upon four methods for detecting preparations to escape; they watched, they listened, they searched and they censored.

Besides maintaining a constant watch inside the wire the "ferrets" built concealed observation posts in the woods or fields which surrounded camps, from which they could watch the prisoners through field glasses. In this way they sometimes saw things which the prisoners were able to hide from their colleagues inside the wire, and they also got a bird's eye view of the camp as a whole. Any continuous movement, such as a stream of prisoners carrying water cans to a wash-house, or a group of prisoners in an unusual place, either of which might pass unnoticed by the guards in the towers attracted their attention. Sometimes a Security Officer, or one of the more experienced "ferrets" would go up into the watch towers themselves, to look and to instruct the guards how to look. Once they had spotted any suspicious activity the area of their search was narrowed and they were much more likely to discover what was going on.

Listening was equally important. Quite as much information was picked up from overheard conversations as from watching or searching the compounds. Microphones were installed in most camps but they were usually discovered quickly by the prisoners, and in any case they were so sensitive that, except at night, they picked up a babel of sound which was unintelligible. In Dulag Luft in 1940 it was said that a microphone had recorded prisoners' conversations on to sound film and that some useful information had been acquired in this way; but it was significant that a tunnel which had been under construction during the whole of the period concerned and had been discussed freely by the prisoners (who were then infants in security) was completed and successfully used.

According to the Germans themselves the most successful listening was done outside the windows of barracks at night when the shutters were closed but the windows open. It was possible to hear very distinctly all that was said, and in spite of the difficulty of understanding bed-time conversations in a foreign language, there is no doubt that they picked up a great

ESCAPE
FROM
GERMANY

*German
Counter-
Measures*

deal of information in this way. Clever "ferrets" were adept at hanging round places where prisoners might talk unguardedly and in drawing them into conversation. "Charlie" or Glimnitz were quite capable of confirming suspicions by a badly told lie.

To counteract tunnels special microphones were buried in the ground at intervals round the wire to a depth of three feet. They were connected with a special listening post in the German compound where a needle registered on a dial the intensity of vibrations in the ground. By day these microphones were of little use because, once again, they were too sensitive and picked up much of the normal vibration caused by people running about or walking near the perimeter of the compound; but by night, when prisoners were confined to their barracks, they would register any sounds which were being made near the wire, and may have been responsible for the discovery of more than one tunnel. The lesson was soon learned, however, and digging at night was either forbidden or done gently with knives and without talking. Once the range of these microphones was known there was little difficulty in passing between or underneath them.

The Germans listened most carefully of all for a wireless transmitter. Special listening apparatus was installed and tested frequently but as no transmitting was done from any Air Force camp until the last weeks of the war, their efforts were wasted. Special listening vans were sometimes brought into a camp, or driven round it, in order to try and locate the whereabouts of the radio receivers, but though searches were frequently carried out in the huts where the radios were hidden, plenty of warning had usually been received and it was seldom that anything was found.

For the prisoners, searches were much the most troublesome of the "ferret's" activities. The earliest and least effective was the individual "snap" search when a German would stop any prisoner haphazardly and run through his clothes. These were soon abandoned and thereafter the most usual form of search consisted of a thorough examination not of the prisoners themselves, but of their belongings. Gradually the Germans adopted a definite routine. In order to effect surprise, search parties would be kept out of sight until all the prisoners were on parade. Special guards would then enter the compound, surround a barrack and prevent the prisoners from returning to their rooms. A team of men under the supervision of the "ferret" would then go through each room. This type of search usually lasted three or four hours and though the Germans were reasonably careful the rooms and cupboards were usually left in a mess. As the Germans discovered the ingenuity and variety of hiding places which prisoners constructed, the character of searches changed. Not having enough men to go through every article, or test every wall, even in a single barrack, they would concentrate on one or two objects at a time, perhaps searching one day for forged papers, and another day for radio parts, or civilian clothes.

115

ESCAPE
FROM
GERMANY

*German
Counter-
Measures*

This meant that sometimes they would touch only books or papers or look for secret drawers and at others would concentrate on the walls and floors. This type of search did not take quite so long and was normally over within two hours.

If for any reason the Germans were convinced that a tunnel was being dug in a particular barrack and failed to find it in the course of a routine search, their methods became more rigorous. They would turn the prisoners out of the barrack indefinitely, allowing them to take their belongings with them and to lodge with friends in other huts, where they might sleep on the floor or wherever they could make themselves comfortable. The Germans would then set a permanent guard on the empty barrack and literally tear everything out of it until they found what they were looking for.

On one occasion in Stalag Luft III this procedure lasted for several weeks. The Germans were rightly convinced that a tunnel had been in operation for some months and that it was nearing the wire. Although they did not know it, they had already discovered two entrances, but in each case a short dummy tunnel had led them astray and the main tunnel had survived to be re-entered from another point. At the time in question it was almost four hundred feet long with two entrances in two different barracks which were ninety feet apart. Having searched several barracks in vain the Germans finally picked on one of the correct ones and searched it several times. The prisoners took the warning and after the second search filled in the vertical shaft which formed the entrance to the tunnel, taking great care to cover the last foot or two with pine needle mould to match the surrounding soil. The ground below was sand.

A day or two later all the prisoners were turned out and the Germans went to work. The floor was ripped up and many of the partition walls taken down; the whole of the ground underneath the barrack was probed and then sprayed with fire hoses. Still no sign of the tunnel was found. The Germans then began to clear away the top soil by hand. Just what betrayed the entrance was never known for certain, but it is thought that in spite of their care in trying to match the pine needle mould the prisoners may have failed by a few inches to do so; the soil which they put back may have sunk and when the Germans reached the sand they may have found a square of black earth. In any case they found the shaft and dug through to the tunnel.

At Schubin in the winter of 1942–43 tunnels were so frequent and the German Security Staff so scared that they adopted the practice of making prisoners change their barracks about once a month. Some had to move their quarters with all their belongings nine times in the six months they were there. It was seldom that the Germans found anything as a result, but they argued that these methods interrupted whatever work was in progress, and up to a point they were right. It was very cold and the business

116

ESCAPE
FROM
GERMANY

*German
Counter-
Measures*

of moving so often not only took up a lot of time but added to the general discomfort and irritation. Yet more tunnels reached the other side of the wire at Schubin than in any other Air Force camp and an unusually large number of prisoners escaped.

At Heydekrug, following a successful tunnel, the Germans introduced a new method of trying to find tunnels which gave the prisoners hours of entertainment. At about six o'clock one morning they were woken by an unfamiliar noise which sounded like a gas engine. Looking out of the windows they saw a motor-driven roller, which weighed about five tons, being driven around the compound by a member of the German Security Squad, a Corporal Heinz. This man was a young, arrogant Nazi, who was heartily disliked by both Germans and prisoners. On this occasion he was obviously delighted with himself. It is believed that the roller was his own idea and his bearing conveyed his self-satisfaction.

After the roller had travelled some distance it became stuck in a patch of soft sand and the smile on Heinz's face faded. The more he tried to extricate the roller by accelerating the engine, the more deeply it became embedded. Naturally the prisoners began to jeer, and Heinz, who understood English perfectly, became angry. Finally, after each fresh effort had been greeted with roars of laughter from hundreds of throats, he stalked off in a towering rage and returned with a small army of Germans carrying planks. The roller was extricated, but although it was used again Heinz never drove it; no tunnel was discovered in this way.

Organised personal searches were rare, but on one occasion when a personal search of a whole compound was held without warning a great haul was made by the Germans. For once the number of guards was adequate; there were two men to search each prisoner as he passed and a guard for every few men who were waiting in the queue; other guards were posted all round the compound to ensure that those who had been searched could not approach those who were waiting. It became clear that the Germans were prepared to spend the whole day at the job and all attempts to hurry or divert them failed.

When the prisoners saw that most of their usual ruses had been forestalled they began to drop as many articles as they could into the sand on which they were standing, burying them with their feet and taking a careful note of their bearings in order to be able to recover them later. Unfortunately one of the guards noticed what was going on and a platoon was sent immediately to fetch rakes. The Germans waited patiently until the search was over and then carefully raked the ground on which the prisoners had stood. As a result they reaped an unprecedented harvest of papers, hack-saws, compasses, maps and all kinds of other equipment. Yet, no doubt because it took too many men and too much time, this type of search was not repeated.

117

ESCAPE
FROM
GERMANY

*German
Counter-
Measures*

Censorship, though a vital part of general security, was not the responsibility of the Security Officer but came directly under the camp Commandant. Censorship was necessary to prevent information about Germany or adverse comments on prison life being given in prisoners' letters, and to stop literature and opinion dangerous to the Nazi regime from coming into the compounds where they might find their way into German hands. All letters, books and pamphlets were scrutinised by a staff of German girls working under German officers and two or three N.C.O.s, and a selection of each was sent to the head Censorship Office in Berlin. Books and papers were quite often banned, but as a rule very little was crossed out in letters and the chief inconvenience to prisoners was delay. Sometimes letters became so congested that the censors would skip the mail of one or two months altogether and unload it straight into the compounds.

On the whole German Security was thorough and reasonably successful. The German mind is not very subtle and Security Officers tended to bolt the door after the horse had gone; but supported as they were by absolute power, it was inevitable that they should discover the majority of attempts at escape. The dice were heavily loaded and a single mistake on the part of the prisoners, or a piece of bad luck, was usually sufficient to lead to discovery.

For the detection of tunnels the "ferrets" developed a routine. Under every barrack they dug a system of trenches which enabled them to examine the intervening surface with great thoroughness and they carried out regular inspections. Sometimes they would leave twigs in positions which they had marked, so that it was easy to see whether the ground had been disturbed; at all times they were on the look out for new sand in the cracks of floors or in the seams of prisoners' clothes. The "ferrets" also kept a constant check on the whole surface of a compound in order to ascertain whether sand from underground was being deposited in the open and it became very difficult to dispose of the sand from a tunnel without their knowledge.

Nevertheless, most of the discoveries of the "ferrets" were due to the fact that they were familiar with the prisoners' habits of life rather than to any particular trick. A knot of men gathered where usually a few people lay sunbathing, new friendships between experienced escapers and other prisoners, a change of room or a change of barrack between prisoners themselves, overcoats worn when the weather scarcely was cold enough to justify them were the sort of indications which gave them their clues. If they remained vigilant they could scarcely fail.

The very thoroughness of German methods throws into relief the way in which the best of schemes can be undermined by weakness in morale. Even at the height of German successes in 1941 there were some Germans who were disgusted by the arrogance of the Nazis and who loathed the

ESCAPE
FROM
GERMANY

*German
Counter-
Measures*

whole system, and after Stalingrad the number of the discontented in-creased steadily. The key men of a Security Staff, such as "Charlie" and Glimnitz, remained keen and generally efficient; but their subordinates grew more and more weary of the long hours they had to work and became oppressed by the fact that the prisoners took a more hostile attitude towards them than towards ordinary guards. They began to look for com-panionship and in this mood they were an easy prey for "contacts."

In the latter years of the war both the guards and the junior "ferrets" made less and less attempt to do their work thoroughly. This was notice-able particularly in searches. To the end the Germans turned clothes out of cupboards, pulled books out of bookshelves and generally gave an air of being busy; but unless an officer was in the room they made no serious attempt to find anything at all. When their officers were out of the way they would sit down and curse the whole business.

With the arrival of the Gestapo in prison camps a new fear entered every German's heart and he began to think more and more of his own skin and less and less of his duty. Every man knew that some of his com-rades were spying on him, and on more than one occasion "ferrets" and guards were denounced and imprisoned. Each man tried to obey the letter of the law and to do nothing either good or bad that would bring him to the notice of his superiors. If he was efficient he might be promoted and be asked to spy himself; if he was too lazy he might be accused of sabotage. Towards the end of 1944 the order was given that every able-bodied man below the age of fifty was to take his turn at the front unless his presence elsewhere was vital to the war effort. From then onwards the dread of every prison guard was that he should find his name on the list for posting and his only aim was to make himself as inconspicuous as possible.

The battle of Security between the prisoners and their custodians in Germany was a reflection in miniature of the great battle being waged in the world outside. The German camp organisation was well conceived, its details thoroughly thought out, its personnel adequately trained. Had faith in the Nazi cause been sufficiently all-embracing the system would have worked and attempts at escape would have become well nigh impossible. But the only belief which all Germans at one time shared was the superi-ority of their race; as the war went on and each man came up against dis-honesty, arrogance, corruption and brutality among his associates he either became contaminated or disillusioned. Disillusionment won.

# Part Two

# Escapes from Prisoner of War Camps

## CHAPTER 13 · DULAG LUFT

The history of Air Force captivity in Germany began on 3 September, 1939, the day war was declared, when a New Zealand officer who had arrived in England only a few days before was shot down on a reconnaissance flight in an Anson over the North Sea [Ed: this event occurred on 5 September. The first airmen were actually captured on 4 September. See p.7.] His opponent, in a German seaplane, landed alongside the wreck and took him prisoner; the two members of the crew were killed. During the next three months a few more officers and N.C.O.s were shot down or captured and by the end of 1939 thirteen of each were housed in the Castle of Spangenburg, near Kassel. At the beginning of December, 1939, the Germans began to segregate Air Force prisoners, and a party of five British and eight French Air Force prisoners were transferred to Dulag Luft, a camp on the outskirts of Oberursel, a suburb four miles north-west of Frankfurt-on-Main.

In later years a myth grew up that in these early days relations between the Germans and their Air Force prisoners had been almost medieval in chivalry and that prison life had been more like life in a country house. The facts were otherwise. It is true that the first Squadron Leader to be shot down was taken to see Goering and the latter uttered a few well-sounding phrases about Air Force chivalry and expressed his determination to see that Air Force prisoners were well treated. In practice, however, the lot of Air Force prisoners differed little from that of the other Services. Far from being lenient German discipline in the first few months was strict. The officers lived in permanent brick buildings, which had previously been an agricultural school, and for many weeks were locked in cells and prevented from living any sort of communal life. Only in the spring of 1940, when the permanent buildings were abandoned and the first huts in a small barbed wire enclosure were built, did camp life begin. Even then the Germans seemed nervous of their prisoners and were reluctant to give them the privileges due to them under the Geneva Convention.

While the leaflet raids were going on and prisoners amounted to only a few hundred, escape was scarcely a serious proposition; there still seemed a faint hope that the war in the west would not develop. But with the attack on the Low Countries and the fall of France in the summer of 1940, captivity took on a different character. Up to June, 1940, French and British had been living together amicably and making unhurried plans for escape, but with the influx of thousands of French prisoners the two races were segregated and the only trace of their former allies which most members of the R.A.F. saw from that time onwards were the mural decorations of a lively feminine character which adorned the communal sitting-room at Dulag Luft.

From July, 1940, Dulag Luft became the interrogation centre to which all British, and later many American Air Force prisoners were sent immediately after being shot down. Like all interrogation centres it was the exception to most prison-camp rules. On arrival the prisoners were put into solitary confinement where they remained for periods varying from twenty-four hours to a month. If for any reason the Germans suspected that they had information which might be of value, they were subjected to mild forms of third degree. Sometimes they were starved for twenty-four hours, or forbidden to read or write. Occasionally they were forbidden to wash, a deprivation which most prisoners found easy to bear. The most severe form of pressure was overheating of the prison cell. This produced thirst and after twenty-four hours was distressing enough to make most men angry; it was rare that they became pliant. A few men talked more freely than they intended, but so far as is known no information of value was obtained by the Germans in this way. Those who were rude or obstinate were sometimes subjected to the same treatment.

When the interrogation was completed the prisoners were sent from the cells into the compound, where they remained for anything from a few days to two or three months according to the rate at which prisoners were being shot down. The compound was like any other prison compound with wooden barracks and barbed wire defences, but the life differed in many respects from life in the camps to which the prisoners were afterwards sent. From the beginning of the war supplies of Red Cross food parcels were more plentiful at Dulag Luft than elsewhere, and gala dinners of four or five courses were given at least once a fortnight during the early years in order to prevent too large stocks of parcels from accumulating. Instead of ten or twelve officers to a room or between one hundred and two hundred N.C.O.s to a barrack, which was the rule in permanent camps, the rooms were normally shared by two or four men. Parole walks, visits to church and other outings were common. During the first two winters some of the prisoners went ski-ing with German officers and in the summer there were occasional excursions to collect berries in the woods. Wines and spirits which had been captured during the German advance into France were issued frequently from the German booty stores and prisoners could sometimes get a special supply for a birthday party or a farewell dinner.

On both sides this fraternisation was part of a deliberate policy. The Germans hoped not only to make the prisoners talk but to create an atmosphere in their first camp which would sap their aggressive spirit; the prisoners hoped to create an atmosphere which would cause the Germans to become lax and help them to escape. It would be difficult to say which side got the better of the battle. The Germans had concealed microphones in the barracks and in the early years conversations among prisoners were recorded on film. Although the only time the sound track of such a film was heard by a prisoner it was unintelligible it is quite possible that useful information was gathered in this way. There is also no doubt that a few prisoners were softened by the comparative luxury they found and did not recover their offensive spirit for the remainder of the war. On the other hand, by the end of the summer of 1941 not only had nineteen British prisoners escaped from the camp but five others had escaped from hospitals to which they had made special trips and a number had escaped from the trains in which they were sent away from Dulag Luft, helped by the preparations they had made there.

### Wing Commander H. M. A. Day

The escapes from the camp were not the first of the war but as they were inspired and organised by three men who between them were the mainsprings of escape in all Air Force officers' camps—and indirectly of the N.C.O.s' camps as well—they are of interest. As a rule the names of prisoners who are still living are not mentioned in this book unless they escaped and reached England. So many gallant but unsuccessful attempts were made that it would be invidious to single out the efforts of a few simply because their story was amusing or unusual. But one exception must be made. Wing Commander, now Group Captain H. M. A. Day, D.S.O., O.B.E., A.M., R.A.F., was shot down on 13 October, 1939, while in command of No. 57 Squadron operating in France. At that time, and for almost three years afterwards, he was the senior Air Force officer among prisoners of war in Germany. Throughout his career as a prisoner of war not only did he make escape his own first interest but saw that it became the primary interest of those under his command. He made no less than six escapes from prison camps himself and when finally sent to Sachsenhausen Concentration Camp he escaped again. He succeeded in reaching the Allied lines in Northern Italy on 15 April, 1945. But inspiring though his own attempts were, Group Captain Day will be remembered by prisoners mainly for the part he played as Senior British Officer in successive camps, and for his organising skill. It was he who laid the foundations of the escape organisation. The pattern of which spread to every Air Force camp in Germany with results which at times seriously embarrassed the German High Command.

The other two men most intimately connected with the organisation of escape in Air Force camps were Lieutenant-Commander J. Buckley, D.S.C., R.N., and Squadron Leader R. J. Bushell, R.A.F.V.R., both of whom afterwards lost their lives.

### Lieutenant-Commander J. Buckley

Buckley was shot down on 29 May, 1940, while trying to silence German guns which were harassing the men on the beaches at Dunkirk. He was one of the few airmen to have made the march from Calais into Germany, escaped on the way, was recaptured and sent to Dulag Luft. A small man, with dark hair and eyes which seemed always to be laughing, he had a passion for history and one of the few recreations besides rugby football which he allowed himself was to deliver lectures to some of the many educational classes. He was a born comedian and occasionally would also write and act comic sketches in theatrical shows. From shortly after his arrival at Dulag Luft until his escape from Schubin in 1943 he was the head of the Escape Organisation and several of those who reached home owe much to him. His death was tragic. After escaping from Schubin he reached Denmark with a Danish member of the R.A.F. named Thompson, and lay in hiding. Eventually they set out in a canoe to cross three miles of water which separates Copenhagen from Sweden. The night was calm but foggy. A day or two later Thompson's body was found on the beach just north of Copenhagen and examination showed that he had been drowned. There was no trace of Buckley. It is thought they may have been run down by a ship.

### Squadron Leader R. Bushell

Roger Bushell was a more flamboyant character. Thick-set and of medium height, his naturally aggressive appearance was enhanced by the fact that he had a cast in one of his eyes which gave the impression of a slight squint. Bushell had been at Brazenose College, Oxford, in the early 1930s where he had played rugby football and read law. He then became a barrister and joined No. 601 Squadron of the A.A.F. As a pilot Bushell showed all the characteristics that he possessed in ordinary life. He was efficient but daring and a signpost which he had decapitated when landing for a drink at a pub in a small private aircraft was one of the ornaments of his squadron's mess. But though swashbuckling in manner, Bushell was a first class leader of men. Early in 1940 he was given command of a Spitfire squadron, and was shortly afterwards shot down.

To his life as a prisoner of war he brought two special qualifications. Besides flying, ski-ing had been his main hobby, and he had not only acquired an intimate knowledge of sections of the German-Swiss frontier, but had made himself a first class German speaker. From the moment he was captured Bushell did all he could to turn these qualities to account; as time went on he added to them an unrivalled knowledge of everything connected with escape and a remarkable power of organisation. In the early days of the escape organisation Bushell held the post of Intelligence Officer. Later at Stalag Luft III he became the Chief Executive in the East Compound, and then the officer in command of all the tunnelling operations in the North Compound, under Wing Commander Day as Chief Executive. Bushell was one of the first to leave the tunnel which broke in March, 1944, and was one of those who was shot.

The tunnel at Dulag Luft was organised by Wing Commander Day and Lieutenant-Commander Buckley. It was dug from one of the barracks close to the wire and was designed to pass under the road which ran along the side of the camp. The road was raised a few feet above the fields on either side and it was intended that the tunnel should come out in the bank on the far side. The distance was not very great, but owing to the fact that the camp was very small and that Germans were constantly passing in and out of it, progress was slow.

Bushell laid other plans, which he designed to synchronise with the breaking of the tunnel. In the sports field which was just outside the compound itself there lived a goat, the memory of which will be fresh in the minds of all early R.A.F. prisoners. The goat possessed character. Prisoners were constantly playing with it and at the least provocation and sometimes without, the goat would attack them and butt them in the stomach. Some hardy spirits used to consider this a better game than football, with the result that the goat was seldom without company.

But the most important thing about the goat was that it had a kennel. From the beginning those prisoners who took an interest in the goat were constantly in and out of the kennel cleaning it or giving the goat food. But the kennel, being a kennel, was also a place in which a man could sit unobserved by German guards, and to Bushell this suggested a means of escape.

While the tunnel was being built therefore Bushell and a colleague dug a hole in the kennel just large enough to conceal a man, and covered it with a firm trap so that the goat should not fall through. They carried the earth away gradually during their many visits. Bushell planned to hide himself in the kennel on the evening before the tunnel was due to break and to climb over the single strand of wire which surrounded the football field later that night. There was so little difficulty in falsifying the count at roll calls that he was sure he would get at least twenty-four hours' start.

Both plans went smoothly. When the tunnel was ready Bushell hid himself and got away. The next night the tunnel broke and eighteen prisoners crept out of it unobserved. It was not until roll call the following morning that the Germans discovered they had gone and Bushell by then had thirty-six hours' start. The Germans always assumed that he had gone with the others through the tunnel.

Of the eighteen who got out of the tunnel none got very far. The best German speaker reached Hanover and two others were arrested while walking down the middle of an autobahn in broad daylight. They had not realised that neither bicycles nor pedestrians were allowed on these roads.

Bushell on the other hand was caught within a few yards of the Swiss frontier. Knowing Switzerland well and having read and thought more about escape than most other prisoners, he had made a detailed plan and followed it exactly. Dressed in a good civilian suit which he had bought from one of the German guards, he travelled by express tram to Tuttlingen and from there along the secondary line to Bonndorf where he began to walk. He had maps and was also able to buy guide books en route.

The weather was perfect, and confident of being able to sustain a casual conversation without giving himself away, he walked by day across country. As it turned out he met no one, and reached a point about five miles from the frontier without any difficulty.

As he himself said later, his greatest danger at this time was over-confidence and he often described how he sat down on a hill for several hours to calm himself and to plan a more cautious approach for the last few miles. He knew of the existence of listening posts and patrols and that same evening he reached a point for which he had been aiming and from where he could see Switzerland ahead of him; still he had not met a soul.

Again he sat down to consider his position. He had to decide whether to wait some hours for nightfall, and then to cross without being able to see clearly where he went, or to make a bold bid for it in daylight. Against all his inner promptings he chose the latter, and walked down into the village of Suhlingen. Half-way down the village street a man came out of a door and accosted him. It was a member of the frontier police and Bushell was at once arrested.

The success of the tunnel at Dulag Luft came as a shock to the Germans. One of their officers afterwards remarked that he ought to have realised what was happening from the number of shower-baths that prisoners used to take at all times of the day. For it was in the shower-baths that the diggers cleaned off the dirt from the tunnel. Once roused, however, the Germans took drastic measures. After they had been recaptured and served their sentences all those who had escaped were sent to Stalag Luft I at Barth, and thereafter escape from Dulag became less easy. No prisoner considered likely to attempt escape was ever allowed to stay long in the camp, and for the permanent British staff the Germans chose men who were temperamentally inclined to accept imprisonment passively.

In the summer of 1941 four prisoners escaped from Hohemark, the hospital about a mile distant to which the severely injured were sent. However from May, 1941, onwards Dulag Luft came to be regarded less as a jumping off ground for escape than as a place where airmen suffering from shock could recover before being transferred to permanent camps. It was a policy for which much could be said but which was frequently challenged by new prisoners because also it suited the Germans.

125

ESCAPE
FROM
GERMANY
*Stalag Luft I,
Barth*

## CHAPTER 14 · STALAG LUFT I, BARTH

The first permanent camp for Air Force prisoners was opened at Barth, sixteen miles north-west of the port of Stralsund on the Baltic coast in July, 1940. This camp had a chequered career. After housing some 800 R.A.F. officers and N.C.O.s for nearly two years it was closed in April, 1942, when Goering's larger Air Force camp was opened at Sagan in Silesia, only to be re-opened in October of that same year when the number of Air Force prisoners had again exceeded the accommodation provided.

From October, 1942, to November, 1943, Barth housed Air Force N.C.O.s only, the numbers rising to 1,200. In November, 1943, the N.C.O.s were sent to Heydekrug near Memel in East Prussia, which had been established as the main N.C.O. camp that summer, and Barth was re-converted into an officers' camp and considerably enlarged. A third compound was added to the original two and early in 1944 a fourth compound was built on the north side as the German administrative area, and was extended as required until the end of the war.

When the camp was relieved by the Russians in May, 1945, it contained approximately 2,000 British and Dominions officers and 8,000 United States Air Force officers. With the British contingent were between two and three hundred Air Force N.C.O.s and other ranks from Army camps who acted as orderlies. Although the majority of the compounds contained Americans only no attempt was made to separate the Allies after the end of 1943.

In spite of its steady growth as a camp, attempts to escape from Barth were far more numerous and successful in the first period, when it housed some 230 British Air Force officers and about 550 N.C.O.s than at any other time. The reasons for this were that German counter-measures were less effective in the early years of the war and that prisoners who were shot down before the great Allied offensive in North Africa had far more incentive to escape than those who were captured later.

The camp stood on the western side of a small flat peninsula projecting northwards into a large bay. It was of the usual type consisting of one-storeyed wooden barracks standing in rectangular compounds surrounded by barbed wire. From the point of view of escape it had certain peculiarities. In the early years the compounds were very small, which meant that tunnels from barracks had a comparatively short distance to go before they were outside the wire. Then the warning wire was only six feet from the perimeter fence which meant that there was very little ground where prisoners could be shot without warning. A disadvantage was that the water level was only six feet below the surface, so that no tunnel could go very deep; once ground microphones had been laid round the outside of the camp in the summer of 1941 it became increasingly difficult to dig tunnels which had any chance of success.

Nevertheless, in the period between July, 1940, and April, 1942, no less than forty-three tunnels were dug by officers and ten by N.C.O.s, and of these, two were completed after the installation of ground microphones. Of the four prisoners who escaped from these tunnels one reached England. At the same time a steady succession of attempts to escape by other means resulted in a further twenty-five officers and twenty-four N.C.O.s getting away from the camp, of whom again one reached England.

The first attempts were extremely amateur. When twenty-one officers arrived from Dulag Luft in July, 1940, the German camp staff contained no security department, and detection of escape was left to the casual observation of two camp interpreters. Nor was there any system of passes for Germans entering and leaving the compounds. In addition, Air Force N.C.O.s were allowed to leave camp on working parties and were thus presented with opportunities which, after the beginning of 1942, were never to recur. Yet there was no mass escape and almost all individual attempts failed through lack of organisation or equipment. Twelve N.C.O.s got away from working parties in the summer of 1940 but all were recaptured almost at once. In August, two officers who had impersonated N.C.O.s also got away and were unlucky to run aground off Stralsund in a sailing boat they had stolen. That same month three more officers brought off the same trick but were seen going into a wood and were rounded up by the Home Guard. A few days later five N.C.O.s, who were members of a working party on a farm, escaped from a barn but all were recaptured near Stralsund a few days later. And so it went on, but one attempt which deserved to succeed was made by an officer on the way to a game of football. The football field was a few hundred yards away from the compound and the prisoners were marched to it every day guarded by two sentries who walked at the back of the column. There was a right-angle corner on the road round which it was impossible to see and this suggested to the officer a simple method of escape. He made himself a German uniform which he wore under his greatcoat, and marching at the head of the column took off his coat immediately he was round the corner and then walked back past the column as a German. The two guards took no notice of him and he got half way to Stralsund, where he intended to catch the ferry, but he was caught on a train without a ticket.

127

ESCAPE
FROM
GERMANY

*Stalag Luft I,*
*Barth*

In January, 1941, the senior British officer, a Squadron Leader who later reached England and who had been indefatigable in helping those who wished to escape, was sent away to a court martial; his successor, another Squadron Leader and a Lieutenant-Commander of the Fleet Air Arm, began to organise escape more thoroughly and the methods of the prisoners improved.

In April, an officer of the Fleet Air Arm escaped in a box to which he had made a false bottom. He wrote:—

"When food parcels were issued, a wooden box containing empty tins was lifted on to a light cart by our own orderlies and pushed out of the camp. One day when a friend and I were watching the cart being pushed through the gate, he remarked: 'A great pity that the box is not just a little longer, or you might be able to think of some way in which you could hide yourself in it. I myself am far too big a man.' It was an idea, though I was rather doubtful if I could fit in the box, although I was about the thinnest man in the camp.

"After examining the box we decided it could be enlarged a little and a false bottom made without attracting attention. When the enlargements were complete we decided to make a test to see if I could stay inside for the two hours which would be necessary. I squeezed myself under the false bottom and found that the only way was to lie on my side with my head and neck bent in one corner and with my knees drawn up to my chin. It was going to be most uncomfortable because once inside I had to remain as I was, and I would just have to hope that I would not be attacked by cramp.

"Everything was ready and in the last week of April I decided to do a further test to see if, under the required conditions, I could stay the course and also to see if things worked out satisfactorily when the box was unloaded. I was locked in the box and though the cramp at times was almost unbearable I amused myself by thinking of the German N.C.O. standing right alongside and not suspecting I was there.

"One thing I had not taken into account was that the oils and juices remaining in the tins would seep through the cracks on top of me. This made things most uncomfortable, and as I did not want to emerge covered in grease we arranged that on the day we would have plenty of absorbent paper lining the false bottom. Otherwise the test was satisfactory.

"May 2nd was the day chosen, and after being pushed through the gate the box was lifted off the cart, and while the attention of the guard was distracted by the British orderlies I opened the hinged trap we had constructed, and on receipt of a pre-arranged whistle, crawled into a small wooden hut and hid under some timber until dark, then slipped out, a free man, into the woods."

*Stalag Luft I, Barth*

This escape was not discovered by the Germans for five days. Owing to bad weather the Senior British Officer was able to arrange for roll-call to be taken inside the barracks instead of on the parade ground, and by cutting trap doors through ceilings in two rooms a prisoner managed to be counted twice on each occasion. Even when they knew a man had gone the Germans never had any idea how the escape was made and on being recaptured on the Danish frontier a week later the prisoner said that he had climbed the wire, and the Germans believed him.

### Flight Lieutenant H. Burton

In May, 1941, Flight Lieutenant H. Burton made the first successful Air Force escape. He was serving a sentence in the "cooler"* for a previous attempt and managed to get out of his cell. He spent five nights loosening the bars across his cell window with the aid of a table knife. On the fifth night at about 11.00 p.m. he unscrewed the bars completely, removed them and climbed through the window. He undid some of the screws fastening the grille covering the window of the cell occupied by another officer, then crawled to the double gate leading to the German compound. Once there, he began scraping a hollow under the gates with a piece of metal which he had picked up, but while doing so the guard was changed and he had to crawl back and lie under his cell window at the side of the building to keep clear of the Alsatian dog which was allowed to run along outside the perimeter fence. While he was lying there one of his gaolers came out for a smoke and a chat with the sentry.

After he had burrowed under the gates, he ran across to the German Headquarters buildings and from there crawled to a perimeter fence, which was patrolled but not lit. He climbed this about 2.30 a.m. while the sentry was at the far end of his beat.

"When I climbed over the fence I was dressed in my Service trousers, which I had dyed black, and a battle-dress tunic. I took a blanket with me in which I wrapped my two bars of chocolate, shaving tackle and towel and a pack of cards. I walked to the railway on the west side of the town of Barth, then followed the tracks through the town towards Stralsund, until I reached some woods close to the railway, about five kilometres east of Barth, where

* The military gaol of the camp to which prisoners were sent for minor offences.

I hid for the day. The following night I set off again, following a track towards Stralsund. During the night it thundered and rained and I got very wet. About 2 a.m. on 28 May, I reached a lake about three miles west of Stralsund, where I got some water and filled a beer bottle which I had found.

129

ESCAPE
FROM
GERMANY

*Stalag Luft I,
Barth*

"About 4 a.m. I followed the railway line right through the town of Stralsund, walking down the main platform of the station. I carried on down the railway to the bridge between Stralsund and the island of Rugon, which I reached about 4.30 a.m., when it was beginning to get light. I decided to carry on across the bridge, rather than turn back and hide close to the town. After I had walked about 20 yards on to the bridge I noticed a sentry on the left-hand side. He had seen me, and as there was no chance of turning back, I carried on and crossed the remaining quarter mile of bridge, passing five sentries on the way whom I greeted with: 'Good morning'. That day I hid in a small wood close to the railway line.

"That night I followed the railway line and passed through the town of Bergen, after which I hid in a wood. The next night I resumed walking and in one village an Alsatian dog ran out, followed by its master, who was in semi-uniform. I was walking with my shoes in my hand as I always did through cobble-stoned villages; the old man spoke to me but did not seem to require any answer. Eventually I discovered that he wanted to know where I was going so I said: 'Sassnitz', after which he walked away.

"I reached Sassnitz at 3 a.m. on 30 May, climbed over a fence and walked towards the sea, only to find myself surrounded by coastal defence guns and anti-aircraft guns. Realising what they were I went away quickly and stayed on a cliff above the harbour, but before daylight returned inland to a wood, where I spent part of the morning.

"After washing I discarded my jacket and walked down into the town wearing an open-necked shirt and my dyed Service trousers. During my walk through the town I passed many German soldiers. I studied the harbour very closely, went further along the beach, had a bathe and a sunbath for the remainder of the afternoon, and watched the ships which left the harbour in order to discover at what time the Swedish ferry sailed. That night I returned to the wood in which I had spent the previous night, having discovered that the Swedish ferry left at 4.30 p.m.

"Next day at 3 p.m. I went to the docks and walked past the sentry who took no notice of me. There were quite a few sentries walking about when I passed, and there were several Naval vessels in the docks. Going down to the Swedish ship I found that it was surrounded completely by barbed wire. The alternative methods of getting on board were either to go through the entrance reserved for passengers, or through the entrance where the railway trucks were taken on board, which was well guarded. The only possible way seemed to be by going on the trucks.

"Having studied the trucks for some time I discovered which were

130

ESCAPE
FROM
GERMANY

*Stalag Luft I,
Barth*

being loaded for the ferry. I went round to the other side and got beneath an express mail van and hung on to the axle. At about 4.15 p.m. the trucks were pulled on board the ferry and I sat on the deck under the truck. I remained there till the ship had been at sea for an hour, then climbed into the mail van, where I remained for several hours.

"When the ship reached Trelleborg, I hung on to the underside of the truck whilst it was pulled off on to the quay side; this was at about 8.30 p.m. on 31 May. I gave myself up to the Swedish police who took me to the police station, and in due course I was sent to the British Legation at Stockholm. Some time later I was repatriated to the United Kingdom."

In June two N.C.O.s escaped from a working party by climbing through a lavatory window. They were recaptured about twelve hours later near Stralsund. Two other N.C.O.s escaped from another working party a few days later while one of their fellow prisoners engaged the guard in conversation. They walked along the main road towards Stralsund but when about five miles from Barth, a German from the camp who was driving a tractor along the road recognised one of them and took both of them back to the camp.

The next escape from a working party was made by two N.C.O.s who were employed near a railway line between Barth and Zingst. While the attention of the guards was distracted they slipped away and climbed on to the buffers of the rear coach of a train as it began to move off. However they were seen by a guard who fired some shots without effect. After the train had travelled a short distance and before it had gathered speed they jumped off and parted company. Both were recaptured a few days later.

That same month a party of officers which included Wing Commander Day, and Lieutenant-Commander Buckley, and many others who had escaped from the tunnel at Dulag Luft a few weeks before, arrived at Barth and a new chapter in the history of escape began.

At no time had there been any lack of enthusiasm and each Senior Officer in turn had given tireless assistance to anyone who wanted to escape. But with the arrival of more and more prisoners who were not regular members of the Air Force and to whom rank in a prison camp meant comparatively little, an organisation on a much broader basis became essential.

Wing Commander Day therefore ordered an enquiry into the organisation of escape and a few weeks after his arrival instituted the system, which has already been described, on which the whole future organisation of escape in the R.A.F. camps was founded. As the two officers who had been building up an organisation were both sent away by the Germans Lieutenant-Commander Buckley was put in charge and was ordered not merely to make the organisation of escape his own full-time job, but to set up any committees he felt necessary.

There is no doubt that this re-organisation produced results. Through June and July there were no individual attempts, but a tunnel was completed and preparations were made for twelve officers to go out of it. On 19 August the tunnel broke surface, but as the second man out was seen by a guard and shot at only three prisoners got away. Two of them reached Lubeck and were particularly unlucky not to reach home. Their report of their experience reads: —

"We boarded a Swedish ship and spoke to the cook and first mate, and asked them if they would hide us. They went away and we hid in a coal bunker. After we had been there about ten minutes our presence was discovered by a stoker, who reported us to the chief engineer. When he arrived he told us to go ashore, or he would report us to the police. We left the ship and boarded several others without being able to obtain help. Eventually we found a Swedish seaman who agreed to help us to stow away on his ship, but we discovered that we were being watched through binoculars by a policeman on the docks, so left the dock area.

"Later we decided that we should separate and attempt to get on board different ships."

One of them continues.—

"We parted and I returned to the docks, where I boarded a ship and stowed away amongst some auxiliary steering gear in the stern.

"On 31 August the ship sailed and when we were about eighty miles at sea I was discovered by a deck hand and taken to the Captain, who stated that he would have to hand me over to the Germans. He turned his ship about immediately and anchored near a watch-ship. On 1 September a pilot came on board and I was taken off and put on board the watch-ship. Some time later I attempted to steal a motor-boat moored to the watch-ship, but was captured in the act. Soon after a supply boat came alongside and I was taken to Wamemunde and handed over to the German Air Force. On 3 September I was returned to the camp."

The other prisoner was caught while still in the docks.

In September, 1941, two officers started a tunnel from an incinerator close to the perimeter fence which was intended to come out in the sports field beyond.

At 10.30 a.m. every day there was a football match and some of the prisoners always stood on top of the incinerator to watch the game. This provided cover for the two who were digging the tunnel. They left the trap open a little for ventilation and worked until about 5 p.m., when arrangements were made for spectators at another football match to stand on top of the incinerator to cover their exit. A table knife was used for excavation and the sand was carried from the face to the incinerator on a board, dumped in the incinerator and mixed with rubbish. No shoring was used.

The construction of the tunnel took only four working days, but work was interrupted by a series of searches which lasted for about three weeks. When completed the tunnel was about twenty-five feet long and was just large enough to enable a man to crawl through.

### Flight Lieutenant J. T. L. Shore

Six men hoped to use the tunnel, and in order that they should get into the incinerator after roll-call without being seen it was decided to wait for an air raid, when the camp lights would be put out. Flight Lieutenant J. T. L. Shore, R.A.F., the only man to get out of the tunnel, continued the story as follows:—

"On 15 October all preparations had been completed and we started nightly watches in order to take advantage of the first air raid warning. At 10.30 p.m. on 19 October I heard aircraft and the camp lights went out. I went and warned one of the party of five which was to follow me, then started crawling through my trapdoor in the hut. Unfortunately, I was wearing my greatcoat, which got caught when I was half-way through the trapdoor, and a German guard came along and almost stepped on me. He did not notice me, but walked on for about twenty feet and then stood still, watching something in one of the barrack rooms. Then the guard at the gate flashed his torch and the guard who was standing near me walked over to him. I walked after this guard, making my footsteps coincide with his, until I reached the barrack in which the man who had dug the tunnel with me lived, and called him.

"He came out just behind me, and I went across to the incinerator, thinking he would follow me. I got into the incinerator and banged the door at regular intervals to attract my friend's attention, but he did not appear. Then I went through the tunnel, which was partly waterlogged, and pushed up the trapdoor at the other end. Looking back into the camp I saw a German guard talking to someone through the window of my hut.

I got out of the tunnel and went across the football field to a ditch which had been dug by the Germans and crawled under the bottom strand of wire. As I made my way across the field I remembered that I had told my friend that I would wait half an hour for him in the wood. While waiting and watching the camp I saw two lights, and, fearing recapture, went on. After squeezing lemon over my boots and clothing to destroy the scent, as I knew that the Germans employed dogs, I set off down the main Barth-Planitz road."

Shore reached Sassnitz the morning of the second day of his escape, having walked by night. Twice he boarded trains which he hoped were being taken on to the ferry, only to find them moving off in the wrong direction. He also tried, unsuccessfully, to board a Swedish ship.

133

ESCAPE
FROM
GERMANY

*Stalag Luft I,
Barth*

"On the way back towards the harbour I saw two Pullman coaches and got into one of them and had another drink and a wash in the lavatory. I was feeling rather despondent, and got into a second-class carriage and went to sleep, not much caring if I was discovered. I woke up about 3 a.m. and left the carriage, as it occurred to me that there might be a ferry at about 4.30 in the morning as well as in the afternoon. I scrambled into a tarpaulin-covered truck filled with piping and from there saw the funnels of the ferry. A line of trucks was being taken on to the ferry, and I jumped off my truck, ran across the intervening fifty yards, and managed to scramble on to a low truck which was passing me at right angles. This truck contained a German lorry.

"The ferry sailed at about 3.30 a.m., and during the voyage the trucks were not searched. I sat in the driving cab of the lorry. When we arrived at Trelleborg a man on a bicycle noticed me sitting in the lorry, but I managed to slip out and tried to get out of the goods yard. However, I walked off in the wrong direction and was seen going through a gate by a Swedish guard, who came after me. I was arrested and taken to a small office, where I said I was an escaped prisoner of war and must speak to the British Consul. On being told that this was impossible I said I must see the police.

"Two policemen arrived in a car and took me to the police station. No particulars were taken and I just said 'Harry Burton' and they recognised the name of the prisoner who had escaped before me. Later that day I was taken to the railway station and sent to Stockholm. A few days later I was returned to the United Kingdom."

The man who followed Flight Lieutenant Shore to the incinerator was caught by the guards, and as the air raid ended soon afterwards no one else was able to use the tunnel.

During the winter of 1940–41 more and more Air Force prisoners who had been hiding in France were rounded up, and the camp at Barth became overcrowded. Already in the autumn there were rumours that Goering's boasted luxury camp for the R.A.F. was to be opened soon, and all those with plans to escape pressed on with their attempts before a move should come. In later years hard winters were a deterrent, but this year, between December and the beginning of April, when the move was finally made, eleven attempts involving seventeen officers, and five attempts involving twelve N.C.O.s were made; in almost every case the prisoners succeeded in getting away from the camp.

Snow, although it made conditions outside the camp more difficult, was sometimes useful. For instance, when the football field was covered in snow it occurred to one officer that he might be buried under it in the hope of being left behind when the players returned to camp, and so get away. He lay buried for five hours until he heard a bugle call in the compound

134

ESCAPE
FROM
GERMANY

*Stalag Luft I,
Barth*

which gave him the signal that it was dark. He then got up, climbed the unguarded fence of the football field, but found that he was unable to walk properly as his leg was frost-bitten. He was caught soon afterwards. In February, with the snow still on the ground, four other officers crawled under the gate which led into the German compound, covered in sheets. But they were caught before they could get any further.

During actual snow storms even bolder attempts were made. In a blizzard visibility is often cut down to a few yards, and sometimes the weather used not only to drive the German guards into the back of their watch-towers, but to cover the side windows of the towers overlooking the wire with ice. This offered an opportunity to climb the wire, even in broad daylight. The first officer to succeed in doing this was a Lieutenant of the Fleet Air Arm, who got over the wire in January, 1942, but was caught immediately by patrols on the other side. In March two other officers did the same thing. One of them wrote:—

> "A blizzard from the east had reduced visibility to anything between twenty and a hundred yards. Snow had been drifting for several days and the entanglement between two wire fences was covered with snow packed hard. The morning of the 10 March an officer noticed that the sentry in one of the corner watch-towers had retired into his box to get out of the wind, and that the windows of his box were snowed up. He decided to try to escape, and after a very hurried preparation chose a moment when visibility was at its lowest, and climbed the wire about ten yards from the box. The snow was so thick that no German in any of the other watch-towers could see him. Fifty yards from the wire he was lost from sight and in a few minutes the snow had filled in his footsteps, leaving no trace.
>
> "Inspired by his example, I decided to do the same. The guard was changed and the new guard was more conscientious, standing out in front of his box in such a way that I could not get near the wire without being seen. I plodded round the circuit for an hour, then noticed that this guard also was succumbing to the weather and was standing in the inside corner of his box where the windows were almost entirely covered. By walking directly up to the box and keeping these blind windows between myself and the guard, I was able to get right underneath his tower, and so climb the wire beneath the box without being seen. Unfortunately, the weather cleared soon afterwards, and I was spotted about two hundred yards from the camp. The guard opened fire without effect, and I reached the cover of some exercise trenches which had been used by a local anti-aircraft school. Unfortunately a member of this school saw me as I emerged from the trenches and brought me in."

The weather was so bad that the first prisoner was forced to give himself up after twenty-four hours.

135

ESCAPE
FROM
GERMANY

*Stalag Luft I,
Barth*

That same day another and very ingenious escape was made. The Continental chimney sweep was a familiar sight to most prisoners of war. According to an old tradition, which was maintained even in prison camps, he wore a top hat, a black tail coat and black trousers, and carried his weighting ball, wire and brush with him. As his face was also smothered in soot his appearance in the camp suggested the idea of impersonation. The sweep, however, had a special blue pass, and it was not until August, 1941, when an officer managed to borrow the pass for long enough to have a tracing made of it, that permission was given to make the attempt.

The sweep's visits came at intervals of two or three months, so that the prisoner had plenty of time to make his preparations. One of his difficulties was the colour of the pass, which was a rather deep blue. Forgery was still in its infancy, but after many attempts one of the camp artists got a reasonable imitation with water colour, over which he printed the rest of the pass in Indian ink. One of the theatre staff made a top hat from cardboard and the prisoner himself made his coat and trousers and coloured them with soot. The equipment was hidden and it remained only to await the return of the sweep. Twice he was seen in the neighbouring N.C.O.s' compound, and each time the equipment was hurriedly collected, but the sweep disappeared. Then suddenly in the middle of the blizzard which has just been described, the sweep arrived. The prisoner who was to impersonate him only heard about it after the sweep had already been in the camp for half an hour, but as rumours of a move were growing there was no question of missing the opportunity whatever the weather. Dates were hurriedly filled in on the pass, and while Polish R.A.F. officers detained the sweep, who was himself a Pole, the prisoner made his attempt. Describing it he wrote:—

"Carrying my imitation wires, weighting ball and brush I battled my way to the gate against a very high wind. The top hat caused me much anxiety as it threatened to disintegrate, but it just held together, and though the guard at the first gate gave the blue pass a close scrutiny he let me through, merely remarking on the depth of the snow. The guard at the second gate took no interest whatever. In order to follow the sweep's routine I had to pass close to the German guard house on my way, and as luck would have it an interpreter who knew me well came out just as I went by. The soot on my face and hands saved me, and he neither recognised me nor made any comment.

"Once outside the camp I got into a copse and there discarded my top hat and cleaned my face and hands as best I could with snow. I had a cap in my pocket for the next stage."

Unfortunately the weather again proved too severe, and after a night spent looking for somewhere to rest in 20° of frost, the prisoner was caught. The next eight days he spent in a small brick cell without heat and with only brick eye-holes for ventilation. He was given no blankets and very little food and was constantly interrogated. Perhaps he was lucky to survive.

One of the most remarkable feats of endurance was achieved by another officer who in similar weather crawled for nine hours across two compounds during the night and then climbed the wire fence under one of the watch-towers. His description gives an idea of the difficulty of moving in a prison compound under the glare of searchlights.

"After the football match was over I hid in one of the N.C.O.s' barracks until after the evening roll call. At about 6 p.m. I left the barrack, which had been locked up for the night, by getting through a concealed trapdoor in the floor. Two N.C.O.s who lived in the barrack asked if they could accompany me, but I refused, advising them to follow my tracks the following night if my attempt should be successful.

"I crawled diagonally across the N.C.O.s' compound towards the sentry tower on the south-west corner next to the Officers' football field. After traversing about two-thirds of this distance, I turned and crawled away from the sentry tower and parallel to the fence dividing the N.C.O.s' compound and the football field.

"In due course I reached the double gate in this fence, which was only about five yards from the gate leading into the German Administrative Compound where a sentry was on duty. An arc light was suspended above this gate and the area was well lit. Slowly I burrowed under the double gate leading into the football field. This took a long time because the ground was frozen and I could not make any noise on account of the sentry on the gate close by.

"In order to get through the hole which I had made under the gate I had to remove my greatcoat which contained my food, maps and wire-cutters. When I had crawled through to the other side, at about midnight, I was caught in the beam of a searchlight and had to roll away to rougher ground which afforded some shadow. I decided not to take the risk of attempting to recover my greatcoat. In due course I learned that when my greatcoat had been discovered by the Germans on 3 January, they assumed that it belonged to one of the two N.C.O.s who had attempted to follow me.

"I then crawled parallel to the fence towards the sentry tower on the south-west corner and climbed over this boundary fence at about 3 a.m. on 2 January at a point about five yards from the sentry tower and at a moment when the patrolling sentry was at the other end of his beat. The sentry in the tower was sweeping the N.C.O.s' compound with his searchlight over my head at the time.

"The two compounds over which I had crawled were swept by four searchlights. As far as possible I crawled directly towards, or away from, the nearest searchlight during the nine hours which it took me to carry out

137

ESCAPE
FROM
GERMANY

*Stalag Luft I,
Barth*

the operation. By doing this I had to travel a much greater distance, but my object was to ensure that the shadow cast by my body when illuminated would be confused with the shadow cast by a small hillock. The two N.C.O.s who attempted to follow me the following night did not heed my advice in this respect, but crawled diagonally across the beams of the searchlights. In my opinion, this was the cause of their failure.

"When I had climbed over the fence I crawled to a point about twenty yards outside the fence, then ran across the field to the wall surrounding the nearby anti-aircraft school. When I reached this I fainted. When I regained consciousness I discovered that my clothing was saturated and at first thought that this was due to having crawled over the snow, but closer examination showed that it was due to perspiration."

This officer was caught on his way to the ferry at Sassnitz. As he remarks, two N.C.O.s attempted to follow his example the following night but after getting under the gate they were seen crawling across the football field and fired upon. One of them, Sergeant J. C. Shaw, was killed.

On the eve of the evacuation of the camp, two N.C.O.s escaped hidden in packing cases which were supposed to contain books and which were being sent ahead to Sagan. One of them successfully boarded the ferry at Sassnitz, but to his dismay found that the boat was going south instead of north. He had not known that besides plying between Trelleborg in Sweden and Sassnitz the ferry also went down the coast to Stettin. He was caught on board.

The camp at Barth was finally evacuated in two stages and both officers and sergeants went to Goering's new camp at Sagan in Silesia. From each party prisoners managed to escape on the journey, three climbing out of a window which had been ineffectively nailed up by the Germans, and a fourth being packed in a crate and put among the stores. He got out of his crate, which had a specially constructed catch for him to open from the inside, and got off the train. All were recaptured after a few days.

### October, 1942–November, 1943

In October, 1942, the camp at Barth was re-opened. Allied airmen were being captured in such numbers that Goering's camp at Sagan was already overflowing and 150 N.C.O.s were sent back to Barth to prepare it to receive new prisoners. By October, 1943, the two compounds were housing 2,200 N.C.O.s in very cramped conditions.

All the N.C.O.s who came from Sagan were volunteers and a few of them at once formed a committee to organise escape. As has been said, lack of discipline made their task difficult, but eighteen tunnels were dug, two of which had passed under the wire before they were discovered and many determined attempts were made by individuals.

One tunnel deserves description. Nine tunnels, all of which had been dug at the same time, had been detected by the German listening apparatus. It was then discovered that the only part of the perimeter of the camp which was not protected by the system was the area close to the gate leading into the Vorlager. It was decided to construct a tunnel from a nearby wash-house to a point under the sentry tower at the side of the gate, where it was proposed to make the exit. The distance was approximately seventy feet.

The entrance shaft was made under the wooden steps leading into the wash-house. Although these were in the open they could not be seen by any of the guards in the tower and a watch was kept to give warning of the approach of any German through the gate. When work was not in progress the shaft was covered with boards over which sand was spread. When the vertical shaft had been sunk to a depth of about two feet a number of bricks were removed from the foundation wall of the wash-house and a space excavated in the sand below the concrete floor. From this stage onwards when work was not in progress the bricks were replaced and the vertical shaft under the steps filled with sand to the level of the surrounding area.

The tunnel itself was cut through the sand beneath the wash-house floor and needed a considerable amount of shoring because it passed beneath one of the showers. The shower was not used and the drain was plugged. At this stage the sand which was excavated was dispersed under barracks or dug into gardens. At the end of approximately four weeks the tunnel had reached the end of the wash-house, a distance of about 40 feet. In order to facilitate the disposal of the sand from the second half of the tunnel, which was very much darker in colour, the existing tunnel was enlarged to about four feet in height and five feet in width.

About this time the Germans became suspicious about the wash-house and conducted a surprise search while six men were underground. However, the entrance had been closed and by means of a pre-arranged signal the men were instructed to keep quiet. The Germans spent three hours in the area tapping the floor of the wash-house and prodding the soil around the building with crowbars but found nothing. Work was suspended for a fortnight as it was known that the Germans were watching the area through field-glasses from an anti-tank training school about two hundred yards away; but eventually the Germans gave up the search and work on the tunnel was resumed.

At the end of two weeks the tunnel had reached the area under the sentry tower and was ready for use. It was intended that seventy men should escape and it was decided that the attempt would be made at the end of the moon period about five days later. In the interval a prisoner who had just arrived in the camp used the shower above the tunnel. He removed the plug from the drain and ran the shower at full strength for some time

139

ESCAPE
FROM
GERMANY

*Stalag Luft I,
Barth*

and when it was discovered water was seeping through the loose bricks under the steps and a large area of damp sand was visible. The tunnelling team at once covered this with dry sand but the guard in the nearby sentry tower noticed something unusual going on and is believed to have advised the German Security Officer by telephone. A few minutes later a number of Germans entered the compound and, after breaking through the wash-house floor, discovered the tunnel.

One of the most remarkable individual attempts was made by a Royal Air Force Warrant Officer who climbed the wire in November, 1942. He was working in the cook-house which was in an outer compound and was allowed to go from the compound to the cook-house without an escort. One morning it was extremely foggy and the Warrant Officer asked the guard on the compound gate to allow him to take an assistant with him. No objection was made and the assistant reported to the cook-house in the stead of the Warrant Officer. Under cover of the fog the Warrant Officer climbed over the fence and began walking towards Stralsund. About four hours later he was stopped by German civilians and asked where he was going. In rather poor German he attempted to bluff but was taken to a house while the police were informed. Eventually he was taken to Stralsund and interrogated, then returned to the camp.

A few weeks later a similar escape was made by another N.C.O. This man had observed that when the prisoners had finished using the cook-house each day the German in charge of it locked up and went away. At meal times a party of prisoners was escorted from the compound to the cook-house to collect the food which had been prepared, using a hand-wagon for transport. This N.C.O. decided to get into the outer compound by hiding in the hand-wagon.

On the selected day, dressed in a Polish Army greatcoat and wearing civilian trousers made from a blanket, he was hidden in the wagon and conveyed to the cook-house by the ration party. While the attention of the escorting guard was diverted he climbed out and hid in a coal bin. He remained there until the Germans had locked up for the night and left the compound and then climbed over the fence. He was caught after a few hours.

On 12 May two Warrant Officers cut through the compound fence. They selected this particular day because it was stormy and the rain was sometimes very heavy. About 6 p.m. they hid underneath the stage of the camp theatre, which was out of bounds during the hours of darkness as it was close to the perimeter fence. At 10 o'clock, after the Germans had completed their nightly search of the theatre, the two prisoners burrowed underneath the wooden wall of the theatre at a spot which was partially obscured from the searchlights in the sentry towers, one of which was about forty yards away and the other twenty. They emerged in a patch of ground which had been dug for a vegetable garden. Having blackened

140

ESCAPE
FROM
GERMANY

*Stalag Luft I,
Barth*

their faces and drawn sacks over their shoes they crawled over the rough ground to a slight depression about twenty-five yards from the further sentry tower, just short of the fence.

At this point the grass was about eighteen inches high. The fence was lit by arc lamps at intervals of about twenty yards and patrolled on the outside by a sentry who passed the selected spot every five minutes. While one of the prisoners was cutting through the first fence his colleague watched the two sentry towers and the patrolling guard from a position about five yards behind. When he saw the patrolling sentry approaching on his beat he whistled softly and the man who was cutting the fence joined him. After the sentry had passed the man with the wire-cutters returned to the gap he had made, raised the coiled wire in between the fences on pegs and cut through the second fence. Then he threw the wire-cutters to his companion who buried them so that they could be recovered by the prisoner who looked after the garden, according to a pre-arranged plan. During this time the first prisoner crawled through the fence and then kept watch while the second followed. Both men got clear of the camp but were caught hiding in a goods train two days later.

In August a most daring escape was made by an N.C.O. who had previously devoted all his energies to the construction of tunnels. He had noticed that on some occasions there was a period of four minutes when one particular stretch of the compound fence was unguarded during the change of sentries. He made his preparations and, on the day chosen, saw that the fence was unguarded at noon. As he climbed over he was seen by two girls who informed the camp authorities, but he was able to hide in some rushes at the side of a nearby creek. He remained there until about 11.30 p.m. but was caught by a cycle patrol as he walked across a road a few minutes after leaving his hiding place.

In November, 1943, the N.C.O.s were evacuated to Heydekrug so that the camp at Barth could be used for Air Force Officers. A few remained behind to help settle in the officers, who were new prisoners.

### November, 1943–May, 1945

A few days after the last batch of N.C.O.s has been evacuated to Heydekrug the first contingent of British and American Air Force officers arrived and their numbers increased steadily until April, 1945. Two new compounds were brought into use early in 1944 and by the end of the war the camp held approximately two thousand British and Dominion officers and eight thousand American Air Force officers. In addition there were about one hundred and fifty British and Dominion Air Force N.C.O.s, including fifty who had elected to remain when the main body was evacuated, and a few British soldiers transferred from other camps, all of whom acted as orderlies.

141

ESCAPE
FROM
GERMANY

Stalag Luft I,
Barth

In those compounds which contained both, British and Americans occupied separate barracks. With the exception of the North Compound which housed Americans only, prisoners could pass freely from one point to another except during parades and the hours of darkness when the gates of all compounds were locked. The privilege of visiting the North compound was restricted to Compound Senior Officers and their assistants who attended weekly conferences with the Senior American Officer, to the orderlies engaged in dealing with the distribution of Red Cross parcels and other camp duties, and to an N.C.O. who acted as liaison between the Senior British Officer and the Senior American Officer.

Amongst the N.C.O.s who remained in November, 1943, were two members of the former N.C.O.s Escape Committee including the Chairman and they dealt with all escape matters until the officers formed their own committee about a month after the arrival of the first party. The two N.C.O.s continued to act in an advisory capacity until they too were transferred to Heydekrug in February, 1944, following attempts to escape. At first the British and Americans formed separate committees but after a month these were amalgamated and the constitution of the new Escape Committee was predominantly British, controlling all escape activity in mixed compounds. The North Compound being separated from the others had its own wholly American Committee.

With the exception of a few officers who had been transferred to this camp from Italy, the prisoners were new and inexperienced in escape. It was natural that most of their efforts should be directed to the construction of tunnels and approximately sixty were started within a year in the three compounds. Two of them reached beyond the perimeter fence but in each case the first two escapers to emerge were caught by the guards. A number of individual attempts were made, however, the first of which was an attempt by a Canadian officer to cut through the perimeter fence under cover of darkness. He was caught by a patrolling guard.

A further attempt to cut through the fence was made on 16 January, 1944, by the same officer accompanied by the Chairman of the former N.C.O.s Escape Committee. The officer could fly a Ju52 and their intention was to steal an aircraft of this type from the aerodrome a few miles from the camp. They were wearing R.A.F. battle-dress, camp-made German Air Force field-service caps and were in possession of forged German Air Force pay-books.

Before dusk they hid under the stage of the camp theatre which was out of bounds after dark and stayed there until the prisoners had been locked in the barracks. At 4.30 p.m. they crawled from under the theatre to a position which was partly screened by a potato store from the only sentry tower having a view of the spot. The officer kept watch while the N.C.O. cut through the nearby double fence into an enclosure around the

142

ESCAPE
FROM
GERMANY

*Stalag Luft I,*
*Barth*

cook-house. At this time the lights on the perimeter fence had not been switched on. It was necessary for the prisoners to be clear of the camp before 6 p.m. as both were well known to the Germans and were certain to be missed during roll-call.

Owing to the intense cold the N.C.O. was forced to stop before he cut through this fence, in order to have his hands massaged by his companion. While this was being done the lights on the fence were switched on. The N.C.O. returned to the fence, resumed cutting and succeeded in getting through the first part. He then saw two guards accompanied by a dog approaching for the usual nightly search of the theatre and he returned to his colleague in the shadow of the potato store. The Germans inspected the door of the store then entered the theatre. The dog sniffed at the two prisoners but did not bark and the Germans had some difficulty in calling him away after they had completed the inspection of the theatre. The N.C.O. then resumed cutting through the second part of the fence.

The delay meant that he would have to work at very high speed if they were to get clear of the camp before 6 o'clock. When he had made a gap sufficiently large in the second part of the fence he clambered through and signalled for the officer to follow. In doing so the latter injured his eye. They then crawled to the second fence which separated the cook-house from the unoccupied south-west compound which was guarded by one patrolling sentry. When they reached this the N.C.O. noticed that the guards had entered the compound for roll-call and he decided to risk being seen in order to cut through the fence more quickly. To do this he worked in a kneeling position instead of lying flat. He had cut through the first part of the fence, propped up the entanglements and was at work on the second part when the patrolling guard saw him. The officer had failed to see him first owing to his injured eye.

Six days later a New Zealand officer and the second member of the former N.C.O.s Escape Committee made an attempt which was more successful. Both were wearing civilian clothes made in the camp. They hid in the roof of the camp theatre and when it was dark crawled through a ventilator on to the roof. They crawled along the roof and dropped to the ground near the gate leading into the south-west compound which was unoccupied. Avoiding two patrolling sentries they climbed over the gate under cover of heavy rain, and then crawled across the compound to the western perimeter fence and climbed over a temporary gate which was about half-way between two sentry towers fitted with searchlights. As soon as they were clear of the camp area they walked south across country and about 8 a.m. the following morning arrived at the outskirts of Velgast and hid in a small wood until mid-day. When they left the wood they walked to the railway marshalling yard where they were arrested by four policemen as they attempted to enter.

143

ESCAPE
FROM
GERMANY

*Army
Officers'
Camps*

A Group Captain of the Royal Air Force and a Norwegian Lieutenant serving in the Royal Air Force made a daring but futile attempt to escape by cutting through several fences in the early hours of 22 May, 1944. After cutting through a gate and a double fence under cover of darkness, and with only one double fence in front of them they were delayed by an air-raid warning which brought out extra guards. By the time they reached the last fence it was already getting light and they were forced to give themselves up.

The only attempt made during this period by a British prisoner to escape by walking through the gates was carried out in June, 1944, by a Wing Commander of the Royal Air Force. He was wearing German Air Force fatigue dress consisting of a white jacket, field-grey trousers and field-service cap. By arrangement he hid beneath a pile of clothing which was being taken from the West Compound to the North Compound on a hand-wagon. This was pushed by a party of orderlies but as they had to cross a German compound they were accompanied by a guard. On the way the orderlies engaged the guard in conversation and at a signal the Wing Commander rolled off the wagon. His disguise enabled him to walk through the Vorlager gate into the woods. This was about 11 a.m. He walked through the woods until he came to a wire fence over which he was climbing when a German appeared. He dropped back into some under-growth until the German had gone then decided to wait until nightfall before making another attempt to get clear of the camp area. As he had not seen anyone during the day he made a second attempt before it was dark but was seen by a member of the camp staff and recaptured.

Shortly afterwards news of the murder of those who had escaped from Sagan was received and escape was banned by the Senior Allied Officer. The Germans left the camp and withdrew from the area during the night of 30 April, 1945. In accordance with plans made previously the Senior Allied Officer assumed control immediately. From the early hours of 1 May until the arrival of the Russians on 2 May the whole of the Barth area, including the aerodrome, was controlled by Allied prisoners. On 1 May parties began to clear the aerodrome of mines and bombs in preparation for evacuation by air. The evacuation took place without incident on 12 and 13 May.

## CHAPTER 15 · ARMY OFFICERS' CAMPS

As the camp at Barth became filled almost as soon as it was opened, the desire of the Germans to segregate the Air Force had to be postponed. A considerable number of prisoners were taken in the Battle of Britain and the fighter sweeps which followed as well as in bomber operations, and many of these were dispersed for a time in Army camps. From the beginning

ESCAPE
FROM
GERMANY

*Army
Officers'
Camps*

of 1941 until the spring of 1942, therefore, groups of Air Force prisoners were scattered all over Germany, the officers mainly at Thorn, Spangenburg, Warburg and Lubeck, the N.C.O.s at Lamsdorf, Bad Sulza and Kirchhain. In all these camps Air Force prisoners made frequent attempts to escape, sometimes alone sometimes in conjunction with friends in the British Army.

## Oflag IX A.H. Spangenburg

Spangenburg castle, twenty miles south of Kassel, looks almost as romantic as the castles of the Rhine. Typically German with a steep sloping roof, small round turrets and high forbidding walls, it stands on the top of a steep conical hill overlooking the town. It was built mainly in the twelfth century and later was used as a hunting lodge by the Princes of Hesse. Inside the rooms are smaller than one would expect, the walls being extremely thick. Even in pre-war days the only heating was provided from medieval carved and tiled stoves which were quite inadequate. The castle is surrounded by a deep and wide moat the outer wall of which is sheer and lined with stone too smooth to offer any foothold. The moat is dry.

In 1939 the castle had been used as a hostel for agricultural students. With fruit trees growing along the terrace above the moat, bird-boxes in all the windows and a glorious view on all sides with excellent agricultural land at its gates, it must have been almost ideal. Unfortunately it was even better suited as a camp for prisoners of war. According to a pamphlet which had been printed for the benefit of tourists it had been used to house prisoners as early as the Thirty Years' War and inscriptions carved on some of the woodwork showed that prisoners had found time heavy on their hands in the early eighteenth century.

From 1939 until 1945 it was used mainly to house Army officers but during the first two years these were joined for short periods by members of the British and Dominions Air Forces and from July to October, 1941, Air Force officers were in the majority. The Army officers had been far from passive. One tunnel from a gymnasium beyond the moat nearly succeeded in 1940 and in October of that year three Army Lieutenants escaped by cutting through the wire, but were recaptured almost immediately. Though the castle stood on solid rock reports reached Air Force camps later in the war that a tunnel had been started from the centre of the castle itself and was being patiently chipped away. It was discovered after almost a year's work.

Between July and September, 1940, three Air Force officers succeeded in escaping from the castle. One, by making a dash from the gymnasium across the sports ground and through the wire whilst under fire from the sentries; he was recaptured the following day. Soon afterwards two other officers disguised themselves as painters and walked through the castle gates carrying a ladder, but they too were caught within a short time.

The camp was closed down in February, 1941, the Air Force prisoners being transferred to Thorn, but they returned in July and between then and the following October nine separate escape attempts were made, three of which were partly successful. Of the failures two were particularly unfortunate. A prisoner who had a talent for amateur dramatics and spoke some German, planned to disguise himself as one of the German civilian workers who entered the castle and to take another prisoner through the gate with him as an orderly going to fetch coal. The disguise was good and all might have gone well if the impersonated civilian had not arrived outside the gate just at the moment the two escapers were endeavouring to persuade the guard to let them through.

ESCAPE
FROM
GERMANY

*Army
Officers'
Camps*

The following month another prisoner changed his identity with that of a British doctor who was being sent by the Germans to another camp. The substitution worked perfectly but unfortunately the "doctor" had no opportunity to jump off the train as he had hoped and arrived safely at his destination. There he discovered that the camp was seriously short of doctors and he was expected to do medical work at once. He had to admit to the Germans that he was not what he pretended to be and asked to be returned to Spangenburg.

A more successful escape was made on 22 August. With the help of British Army orderlies two Air Force officers were able to get into the cart which entered the camp to collect rubbish. They were covered with rubbish and after passing through the gate managed to get out of the cart and away from the camp without being seen. Next day they were picked up whilst attempting to cross a bridge in daylight.

Four days later there was another partial success. The camp laundry was done weekly by housewives in the nearby town of Spangenburg. The washing was wheeled down the hill in a small hand-cart by a team of orderlies accompanied by a guard. Again, with the help of orderlies the cart was modified so that two men could lie in it under the dirty linen. The plan was that once the cart was through the gate and out of sight of the camp one of the orderlies was to allow a wheel to go over his foot. He was to feign such a bad injury that two other orderlies would be required to carry him back to the camp. The cart would then be too heavy for the remainder to push and it would be necessary to leave it where it was. Provided the German guard returned to the camp with the orderlies, the men hiding under the linen could climb out and escape. On the appointed day the two escapers were packed under the linen and after a perfunctory search at the gate the cart was duly pushed down the hill and the plan carried out to perfection. The two officers got away with 15 minutes start and despite being pursued by dogs covered approximately 50 miles before being caught whilst boarding a goods train. Perhaps it is worth recording

ESCAPE
FROM
GERMANY

*Army
Officers'
Camps*

that at this time the Germans were particularly aggressive and made little attempt to observe the terms of the Geneva Convention concerning the treatment of prisoners of war. On their way back to the camp these two officers were made to march through the centre of the town of Spangenburg in the middle of the road while the guards followed them with rifles at the ready, a totally unnecessary display for the benefit of the civilians. On arriving back in camp both officers received a sentence of 34 days solitary confinement.

A most brilliant attempt was made in September. A locked room had been discovered at the top of the castle and after it had been broken into with the aid of a crowbar a complete German officer's uniform and some civilian clothing had been found. Armed with this equipment three officers decided to disguise themselves as a Swiss Mission with a German Army officer as escort. As the plan depended upon being able to deceive the sentry at the gate it had to be timed to take place shortly after the guard had been changed so that it could be pretended that the "Mission" had been passed into the camp by the previous guard party.

The mid-day change was chosen and shortly after noon the three officers, who had little knowledge of German, emerged from the castle into the courtyard attended by two British officers one of whom spoke fluent German and who kept up a conversation which the trio answered in monosyllables. The party dawdled a little before the gate and when it became clear that the guard was convinced by their disguise, the "Mission" and their "escort" said a formal goodbye and went up to the sentry. He opened the gate immediately and they passed through without a word being exchanged. The party had to pass the guard-room and those guards who were off duty unsuspectingly stood up and saluted. The trio disappeared round the corner which led down the hill to the town.

It must have occurred to someone to check the time of the "Mission's" entry, for in less than a minute the trick was discovered and every man of the guard party who could be spared set off in pursuit. However, luck was on the side of the prisoners. There were two paths down the hill and no one had seen which they had taken. All the Germans chose the wrong one and the prisoners got clear away. In order that a false description of them should be circulated they wore a change of clothing under their disguise, and having gained the cover of some woods emerged as three members of the German Air Force. Having tried unsuccessfully two aerodromes near Kassel, hoping to steal an aircraft, and having walked through the streets of that town exchanging salutes with German officers, they decided to turn west towards Cologne. By living on apples and vegetables they travelled more than a hundred miles before their luck deserted them. A solitary sentry in a village, through ignorance of what the German Air Force uniform looked like, became suspicious of their dress. He alleged, wrongly, that the caps were made incorrectly, but explanation proved too much for the prisoners' knowledge of German and they were arrested. Each received a sentence of 52 days in solitary confinement as a result.

147

ESCAPE
FROM
GERMANY

*Army
Officers'
Camps*

In October, 1941, the castle was evacuated again, the prisoners going to Warburg. It was re-opened early in 1942 and a batch of new Air Force officer prisoners was sent there from Dulag Luft, but by then the Germans were thoroughly on their guard and no attempts succeeded. The Air Force prisoners were not sorry to exchange the castle for the barbed wire encampment at Sagan where they were transferred a few months later.

## Oflag XX A—Thorn

The fortress of Thorn, which stands on the right bank of the Vistula, has played an important part in the wars of Eastern Europe since the days of Charlemagne. For two centuries it was garrisoned by the Teutonic Knights as vassals of Poland and then fell successively to Gustavas Adolphus, Charles XII of Sweden and to Prussia in the Second Partition of Poland in 1795. During the 1914–18 war the various forts comprising the fortresses were modernised by the Germans. Standing in a wide plain, these were built mostly underground. The walls, which are several yards wide, rise only a little above the surface and the interiors look more like pits than courtyards. They are surrounded by moats with sheer sides. Air Force prisoners were first sent to one of these forts in February 1941 and attempts immediately were made to scale both the walls and the moat; they were unsuccessful. One prisoner was caught on the roof of the fort and two others were seen when trying to scale the moat at night. They avoided being shot by dashing back into a storage cellar in which they had hidden before the attempt.

In May, 1941, four Air Force officers and an Army officer managed to leave the camp. One of the Air Force officers, who spoke German, was dressed in a camp-made German uniform. He talked to the sentry on the gate and told him that he wanted to take the other officers to the back of the camp to get some tools. This ruse succeeded. Two of the five made for an aerodrome intending to steal an aircraft and fly out of Germany. Unfortunately they were arrested on the aerodrome after making an unsuccessful attempt to start an aircraft. The three others walked in a southerly direction until dawn next day then hid in a straw barn. Setting off again at nightfall they walked until dawn the following day again hiding in a barn. They must have been seen because they were arrested by police shortly afterwards.

Another chance soon offered. The Air Force officers were looked after by British army orderlies who lived in a nearby camp and entered the fort each day. From that camp other British soldiers went out on working parties in the countryside. An exchange with any of the orderlies provided an obvious chance for escape and four Air Force officers at different times managed to get away by this means, but all were recaptured within a short time.

ESCAPE
FROM
GERMANY

*Army
Officers'
Camps*

### Group Captain B. Paddon

After one such attempt, Squadron Leader, now Group Captain, B. Paddon, D.S.O., R.A.F., was sentenced to four months close arrest on a charge of insulting a German Flight Sergeant. By the intervention of the Protecting Power this sentence was quashed and a new trial was ordered for 3 February, 1942. This included a further charge of resisting the guard but the trial was postponed owing to inadequate preparation. The new date was fixed for 28 April but a further postponement was necessary due to a feigned illness on Paddon's part and a subsequent escape. He was transferred to the special camp at Colditz on 14 May and finally the Court Martial was fixed for 11 June at Thorn.

He left Colditz on 9 June under strong escort but took the precaution of taking with him escape equipment in the form of maps, money and forged papers. He arrived at the British Army camp at Thorn on 10 June and was placed in confinement. During that day, with a considerable amount of assistance from British Army prisoners he worked out a plan of escape. He had little time to spare as the Court Martial was due to start at 9 a.m. on the following day.

At 6.45 a.m. on 11 June he left the camp with a working party of British soldiers wearing a battle-dress over his own clothing. He had money, sketch maps of the area north of Thorn and forged papers representing him to be a Flemish worker. He was wearing R.A.F. trousers, a brown golfing jacket and a camp-made cap, the top of which was made from a French beret and the peak from a Belgian cap. He had also a brief case similar to those carried by most Germans, which contained sandwiches and an excellent set of forged documents.

The working party was taken about six miles south-east of Thorn and set to work on a German-occupied Polish farm. There were some twenty prisoners under one guard. Paddon waited until a British Sergeant signalled that all was clear then slipped into a barn where he stripped off the battle-dress. He walked off as a civilian and although there were a number of Germans about the farm they displayed no interest in him.

He made his way into the woods south of Thorn and walked south west and finally northwards keeping as far as possible in the woods. He emerged from the woods on the corner of an artillery range where a shoot was in progress. Crossing this and a road, soon he came to the marshalling yards between an inter-section of railways and passing through these went through Kleinnassau and across country to the river east of Thorn. He followed the tow-path for some miles then turned left over the main road to the railway which he followed to the way-side station of Weichsel where he arrived about 6.30 p.m., having covered some thirty miles on his circuitous route from his point of escape.

149

ESCAPE
FROM
GERMANY

*Army
Officers'
Camps*

By this time his feet were becoming very painful in his borrowed shoes. In a small restaurant he bought some beer and at 8.30 p.m. boarded a train for Bromberg. In the station he saw a military picket who appeared to pay particular attention to soldiers. Owing to the curfew in Poland he was unable to leave the station so bought a ticket to Gdynia and spent the night in the waiting-room.

Early next morning he travelled by train to Danzig. On arrival he purchased a meal in the station restaurant then travelled by train to Gdynia, arriving about 2 p.m. From the station he could see the harbour and observed only two converted merchantmen. In the Naval yard he saw a fair amount of activity and walked through the town to the seafront but did not inspect the docks closely. As Gdynia did not appear promising he returned to Danzig at 5 p.m., travelled by tram to Neufahrwasser and crossed the harbour on the ferry. He spent some time reconnoitring the Swedish ships lying in the ore-unloading basin then made his way to open country where he rested until dusk.

About 11.30 p.m. he returned to the docks and crawled down to the quay through the marshalling yards. There was only one sentry on about 500 yards of quay and he was able to cross it quite easily. He boarded a Swedish ship and made his way to a coal bunker which was nearly empty. At 9 a.m. next morning the hatches were removed and the ship was coaled. During this operation Paddon was fully employed trying to remain in shadow and to dodge the falling coal.

The ship was unloaded on 15 June and early next morning it was searched by German soldiers but as Paddon had built a hiding place behind the coal he was not discovered. The ship sailed at 9.15 a.m. and about two hours later he went up on deck but on seeing land only a few hundred yards away returned to the bunkers until about 6 p.m. then made his way to the bridge and reported as an escaped prisoner of war to the second mate who was in charge. The ship docked at Gavle about midnight on 18 June and Paddon was handed over to the Swedish Police. He was visited by the British Consul on 27 June being transferred to the British Legation at Stockholm two days later. After a short interval he was sent to the United Kingdom.

The Air Force officers were evacuated from the fort at Thorn in July, 1941, and transferred back to Spangenburg.

### Oflag XC—Lubeck

In July, 1941, a party of fifty Air Force officers was sent to Oflag XC from Barth. During the following three months this number was increased by

ESCAPE
FROM
GERMANY

*Army
Officers'
Camps*

new prisoners arriving from Dulag Luft. The camp at Lubeck, which was situated a short distance from that town, was administered and guarded by the German Army. Living conditions were extremely primitive and for the greater part of their stay there the prisoners were very short of food. Attempts at escape were made but none was successful. In October, 1941, the prisoners were transferred to Warburg, and Lubeck was not again occupied by Air Force prisoners until the last month of the war.

### Oflag VIB—Warburg

Oflag VIB was one of the largest Army officer camps in Germany and the one which received the largest number of Air Force officers during the period of their dispersal. It was situated about 3 miles from Warburg, which is approximately 20 miles north-west of Kassel. The camp stood on the side of a desolate slope astride a country road which served as its main artery. The huts were of wood with brick foundations, and the compound about a mile in circumference.

The main Air Force contingents were transferred there from Spangenburg and Lubeck in October, 1941, but by that time escape was already highly organised and although the Air Force officers played a full part, the story of escape in this camp belongs to the Army. Most of the Army officers had been captured in 1940 and their experience and skill were of the greatest value to their air-minded colleagues. Sappers and engineers taught pilots and aircrews much that they did not know about digging and shoring tunnels, surveying, mapping and forging, all of which was put to good use at a later date. In addition, Army officers who had made escapes earlier in the war passed on invaluable information.

Of the successful escapes made while the Air Force officers were accommodated in this camp, three were confined to Air Force personnel and the fourth was a joint Army-Air Force operation which was not only unique but one of the most daring of the war.

A successful tunnel was dug from one of the orderlies' huts by a mixed team of some twenty-five Canadian, British, Polish and Czech Air Force officers. Most of the earth from the tunnel was put between the ceiling and the roof of the hut, which was barely strong enough to hold it and made life almost unbearable for the occupants as so much dirt and dust leaked through on to beds, tables and utensils. The tunnel was about 200 feet long, 2 feet wide and 2 feet 6 inches high. Little shoring was needed because the earth was good hard clay. However, its designers allowed themselves the luxury of flooring it with boards taken from under the main dining-room floor. It took two months to dig and during that time the Germans failed to search the roof of the hut.

In April, 1942, the day arrived when the tunnel had gone the distance estimated as being necessary. Expert Army surveyors measured it and told

those engaged in its construction that it was long enough and indicated
roughly where the exit would be. That evening a Czech officer went down
to make the exit. After about four hours work, having fainted once
through lack of air, he dug his way through about 6 feet of hard clay only
to surface in the full glare of the flood-lights. Somehow the measurements
had gone wrong and the tunnel was too short by a few feet. This meant
that each escaper would have to cross a floodlit area before reaching the
darkness beyond the area illuminated by the lights. An order of exit had
been agreed upon and each man entered in turn. Several returned, however, maintaining that it was too risky to try. Five Air Force officers
escaped, but all were recaptured within two weeks.

The next escape was made in August, 1942, by one of the Air Force officers who had escaped through the tunnel. He was serving a term in the
cells in the camp and with the aid of razor blades, which had been conveyed to him concealed in bread, he managed to construct a trap door in
the corner of the wooden floor of his cell. Then he excavated a short tunnel. It was impossible for him to obtain maps or food so he decided to
make his attempt without.

At midnight on 17 August the Germans discovered another tunnel
which was being dug in the camp, and an alarm was given. Taking advantage of the ensuing confusion this officer hurriedly made a dummy which
he placed in his bed, left his clothing where the guard could see it, and, taking one blanket and wearing a sweater over his pyjamas, crawled through
his tunnel. The alarm had emptied the German compound and he made
his way to the road without difficulty. That night he put as much distance
as possible between himself and the camp, then hid during the daylight
hours of the following day.

He walked at night across country until he reached the Kassel–Frankfurt autobahn at a point about 90 miles south of Kassel. He crossed the
river Main over a bridge west of Frankfurt and at night attempted to steal
a German aircraft from a nearby aerodrome. As he was entering the cock-
pit he was seen and fired at, but ran into some woods and after a time
returned to the autobahn and walked along the edge of it. Suddenly he was
stopped by a policeman with a police dog, who shouted to another policeman who was approaching from the rear "I've got him!" The other policeman then approached, but while he was still a distance away the dog ran
towards him. The escaper took advantage of this and, jumping over a
small fence, hid in the woods bordering the autobahn, crossing a stream
many times in an endeavour to prevent the dog from trailing him. He
walked through the woods and later, while stealing vegetables from a garden, was caught by a policeman. He explained that he was a Polish worker,
but this story was not believed. As British aircraft were flying overhead at
the time the policeman expressed the opinion that he must be a member

151

ESCAPE
FROM
GERMANY

*Army
Officers'
Camps*

152

ESCAPE
FROM
GERMANY

*Army
Officers'
Camps*

of an aircraft which had been shot down in the area, but the escaper, a fluent German speaker, managed to convince him that this was not so. The policeman left him a few moments later when an aircraft crashed in flames a short distance away. He continued across country to Nuremberg, when he was seen by an anti-aircraft gun-crew during an air-raid. On the night of 2 September he was captured and taken later to the Gestapo Headquarters in Mannheim. Subsequently he was returned to the camp.

The other escape which was confined to the Air Force prisoners was undertaken by four officers, one of them a South African. Two of these had noticed that the guard on the main double gates went off duty at 7 p.m. and that there was no sentry on the gates until the night patrols came on duty at 9 p.m. The nearest guards to the gates during these two hours were in the watch-towers about 50 yards away on either side. These were armed as usual with rifles and machine guns and the towers were fitted with searchlights.

From their observations these officers thought it might be possible to crawl underneath the gates without being seen. In order to prove it the South African crawled up to the gate one night, loosened the wire on the bottom bar and measured the distance between it and the ground. He found that by bending up the barbed wire and scraping away a little of the gravel he could make room for a man to crawl underneath, lying flat. After this the four officers decided to make the attempt, and a large organisation was arranged to keep a check on German movements, to work a system of signals to let the men who were crawling know whether or not they were in danger, and to divert the attention of the guards in the towers who were within sight of the gate.

At 8.40 p.m. on 27 April, 1942, the South African began to crawl towards the gate followed at a three-minute interval by the others. Once beyond the line of the barracks their only cover was a shallow ditch which ran towards the gate at right angles from about 30 feet away, but even in the ditch they could be seen from two of the watch-towers. As they crawled down the ditch, pushing their packs in front of them and getting covered with mud, groups of their fellow prisoners spoke to the guards and started a fight. All four got underneath both gates and so well did the diversions work that the last man had time to bend the wire back into place and smooth over the ground before he received the signal to get away. As a result three Army officers were able to escape by the same method two nights later.

Outside the gate the four Air Force officers crawled to another ditch about six feet from the wire. Two of them were still in full view of the patrolling guards as they arrived on duty, but because the guards almost invariably looked inwards towards the camp as they walked along outside the fence they were not seen. It was almost dark then, but the moon was

shining and after about an hour's crawl among some piles of timber and a
few sheds, they reached a partly completed hut, where they took off their
camouflaged clothing. They then shook hands all round and set off in two
pairs. No one reached England, but the pair which headed for the Swiss
frontier 300 miles away, kept going for 17 days and covered 275 miles on
foot before being caught.

153

ESCAPE
FROM
GERMANY

*Army
Officers'
Camps*

One of the pair (not the South African) could speak Afrikaans and the
other a little French. They decided that if accosted by Germans they would
say they were Belgian workers going to whatever the next village on the
map happened to be. It was their intention, however, to walk only at night
and if possible never to be seen by anyone. At that time of the year this
meant spending approximately seventeen out of every twenty-four hours
either looking for or lying in hiding places. They also decided not to jump
trains or use any other form of transport, except as a last resort. Each prisoner carried approximately 15½ lb. of concentrated foods, with a little extra
dried fruit and some Horlicks and Ovaltine tablets. They estimated that
they would be able to last out 24 days on these rations. Except for a few
swedes picked up at one point of the trip, and only eaten with difficulty, a
10-oz. daily ration of food was never exceeded.

As neither intended to be seen clothes were a secondary consideration,
and they wore a mixture of Army and civilian garments common to many
foreign workers in Germany. They were well supplied with maps, and carried shaving, washing and boot-cleaning kit—a most important item.
Owing to the fact that only a small pack could be pushed under the gate,
they had no greatcoats, blankets or ground sheets.

On the first night out they were able to make fairly good time, travelling about 25 kms. They remained on a hill above the town during the day.
The cover was not good, but fortunately the day was fine and they were
able to get dry and scrape the mud from the ditch off themselves and their
clothing.

On the second evening they continued on the road south, but at about
8.30 p.m. a civilian on a bicycle overtook them, dismounted, and began
asking questions. The "Belgian worker" story seemed to work reasonably
well—at least as a delaying action—but he did not seem quite satisfied,
and continued walking with them and chatting, evidently intending to
make further enquiries at the next village. After about ten minutes they
branched off a small track to the left, leaving the civilian, and continued all
night across country in a south-easterly direction.

The next night they continued south-east across country, crossed the
Fulda river on a small road-bridge and reached the autobahn south of
Kassel. After travelling three or four miles down the autobahn, the feet of
one of them gave out completely, and they decided to stop and shelter in a
Dutch barn which was full of hay. They rested there the whole of the

ESCAPE
FROM
GERMANY

*Army
Officers'
Camps*

following day, during which several Germans came into the barn without seeing them.

By then they had discovered that the best way of travelling was to walk on the autobahn by night. Pedestrians and cyclists were forbidden, and once when a cyclist approached without lights, he sheered off when he saw them. The majority of the traffic, which was never considerable, consisted of heavy transport lorries often with one or two trailers attached. Whenever a vehicle approached the prisoners moved into the ditch or down an embankment and lay flat in the shadow. In this way they travelled 200 miles.

Throughout the trip they had an average of only three or four hours' sleep a day, as even when it was fine the first four or five hours after they halted were spent in violent shivering. It was often not until mid-day that they were warm enough to lie still. When they woke they found that their legs and feet were terribly stiff, and the first few hours of each night's march were an agony.

The best type of cover was a young plantation with thick undergrowth, but this was not always available. Some days they spent in ditches, covered with brown paper and dead grass, others in holes in the ground covered with rubbish, and yet others lying under piles of dead leaves. The greatest difficulty they found was to keep on at the end of a night's march until they reached safe cover, the temptation to "flop down" in the first spot which looked like a hiding place being almost irresistible. Both prisoners were often more or less "punch drunk" after the first week.

The eighth day was spent in a wood about a mile from the autobahn, and close to the town of Butsbach. When about to begin the usual evening "meal" at 7 p.m., a German N.C.O. and a girl came through the wood, presumably looking for a piece of thick cover such as the prisoners had selected, and almost walked on top of them. The N.C.O. was very surprised and at once suspicious. Putting business before pleasure, he began questioning them, and asked if they were Russians, a pardonable mistake, for in spite of the kit they carried neither prisoner had shaved since leaving the camp.

On being told the "Belgian worker" story he at once asked if they could speak French and began talking in fluent French himself. This immediately gave them away, and the N.C.O., now thoroughly excited, informed them that they were under arrest, and proceeded to try and march them off. Fortunately he was in walking-out uniform, and carried no small arms. The prisoners took to their heels, leaving the N.C.O. in a rage and shouting as only a German can, with the girl standing beside him. They found cover at the far end of the wood, and remained there safely until darkness fell.

By the fifteenth night they reached the point just outside Karlsruhe, where the autobahn forks, and took the branch which leads to Stuttgart. Both men were very exhausted. Almost the whole of the last 150 miles had been over dead flat country, and at even a small incline their breath came

155

ESCAPE
FROM
GERMANY

*Army
Officers'
Camps*

in short gasps and they could only walk at half the usual pace.

Unfortunately at this stage they began to forsake the good resolution never to move except in darkness to which they had so far rigidly adhered. The long evenings waiting for complete darkness to come became almost unbearable, and the temptation to push on a few extra miles after daylight was sometimes too great. They were both aware of a certain loss of judgment and agreed afterwards that by now they were affected mentally as well as physically.

On the seventeenth night there were thunderstorms and much rain. After passing through a small town on the way to Tuttlingen they took a wrong turning owing to a slight inaccuracy in the maps and the difficulty of finding signposts in the dark. The error was finally discovered, but of the eighteen miles covered that night only ten were in the right direction. A halt was made about two miles short of Wildberg.

The following day was perhaps the most miserable of the whole trip. Their bodies and clothes were soaked, and though the forest gave them security, the ground and trees were so wet that the only way to prevent shivering was to walk about. At this stage neither prisoner had either been warm or dry, or had any sleep for three days. Being near the limit of their endurance they decided that if they were to reach the frontier they must reach Nagold that night.

They approached the town of Wildberg stealthily. There were many civilians about, and soon they were on the outskirts of the town. Not until it was too late did they realise that with pedestrians all round them the only course was to walk through the town in broad daylight—the one thing which they had been trying to avoid doing for the past seventeen days.

Although both had shaved that afternoon, they could not help looking suspicious. Clothes had become soiled and worn, and one of them had very little seat left in his trousers. To the inhabitants of Wildberg many of whom were sitting around in the streets and smoking their evening pipe, the appearance of two such people at such a time, both carrying rucksacks, must have seemed peculiar. No one spoke but many stared. They reached the far side of the town and thought that possibly they were going to get away with it after all when a young policeman suddenly appeared and stopped them; he was joined by another who came up from behind on a bicycle. The police would not listen to any stories. Both were armed and resistance or flight were out of the question. This was on Thursday, 14 May. The escapers had averaged sixteen miles a night. Five days later they were returned to their camp.

Later these two prisoners made the following observations for the benefit of their colleagues:—

ESCAPE
FROM
GERMANY

*Army
Officers'
Camps*

(i) That two was the ideal number for a trip of this kind especially from the point of view of keeping up morale. When one was in a bad way or feeling particularly low the other was usually able to give help and encouragement. Loss of morale was due to:—

(*a*) Physical weakness, especially towards the end of the trip.

(*b*) The ever present feeling of being a hunted animal.

(*c*) increasing hunger with, occasionally, thirst.

(ii) One was a non-smoker and though the other carried cigarettes he had not the slightest inclination to use them. When he did try one he threw it away in disgust before it was half finished.

(iii) Although the packs were gradually becoming lighter this was never noticed; even on the last night's march they seemed to feel exactly the same weight as at the start.

(iv) Both prisoners complained of constipation and their blood became very bad. Small scratches turned into festering sores which took a long time to heal even under proper treatment. It was decided that in another attempt of this kind more dried fruit should be carried.

(v) On the trip one prisoner lost eighteen pounds in weight, the other ten pounds.

(vi) Heavy Army boots though previously worn-in and well greased, were most unsuitable. They bruised the Achilles' tendon and one prisoner had to cut away his boots at the back to relieve this.

(vii) The main reason for failure was the state of slight mental unbalance brought about by the cold and wet and the lack of suitable dry clothing. Both considered that if each had carried even a light ground-sheet and had rubber-soled shoes or light rubber-soled boots and better maps they would, despite the weather, have been able to reach the frontier.

## Operation Olympia

One of the most daring and the best organised of all escapes was known as "Operation Olympia" which took place on 30 August, 1942. The idea, which was conceived by a major and a captain, was to fuse all the lights around the perimeter fence, including the searchlights, and for numerous parties to climb the wire at several different places simultaneously with camp-made ladders. Realising that the scheme could be used by a large number of people the originators co-opted an Air Force and Naval Officer and laid plans to include from a hundred to one hundred and twenty prisoners. The scheme was proposed to the Escape Committee on 20 April.

According to the original plan the camp boundary lights were to be extinguished by throwing grappling-irons attached to a long cord over the electric light cables which ran round the camp just outside the fence. At a given signal the wires were to be pulled down and it was anticipated that all the lights would go out at once leaving the guards in complete darkness and considerable confusion while the ladders were placed against the fence. When this scheme was presented to the Escape Committee for the first time it was turned down as being too likely to cause casualties.

An Army electrician was next consulted and asked if he could find out some more certain method of extinguishing the lights. After two or three days he announced that he had discovered what he thought was a mains fuse box in the boot repairer's shop which was inside the camp. From this hut overhead cables ran directly to the Guardroom outside the fence. He considered that there was an even chance that should these wires be fused properly, the boundary lights and possibly the searchlights as well might be put out of action.

ESCAPE
FROM
GERMANY

*Army
Officers'
Camps*

As the whole scheme depended on the lights being put out at a given moment, it was decided to test the electrician's theory by fusing them for a very short time. The test worked perfectly, both the boundary and search-lights being put out without leaving any traces to arouse suspicion.

After this the Committee gave permission for preparations to be made. Because speed over the wire was vital it was decided to construct one ladder and to test it out in one of the barracks which was reserved for music practice. The ladder consisted of two parts, an ordinary ladder about twelve feet in length and two feet wide, and a solid extension about ten feet long and twenty inches wide which was fastened in such a way that when pushed to the top of the ladder it would tilt over to form a bridge over the wire fence. The ladder was bulky but when not in use its two parts were camouflaged as shelves in the music room and covered over with sheets of music. For the experiment two strong wires were stretched across the hut from wall to wall, six feet apart and ten feet high, to represent the double perimeter fence. There was just room under the roof for the first man climbing the ladder to push the extension up in front of him and tilt it over on to the second wire to form the bridge.

The camp was never completely free of Germans but with careful watching it was usually possible to practise the wire scaling two or three times before a warning was received. The ladder had then to be taken to pieces quickly and reassembled as shelves, while some member of the team played a popular tune on the piano and the rest joined in the singing until the German should pass the hut.

During the summer as much practice as possible was obtained and it was found that ten trained men with full packs could erect and climb over the ladder in from fifty to sixty seconds. Forty men who were to form the nucleus of twelve teams of one hundred and twenty in all were trained up to this standard, and it was hoped to operate the scheme in the autumn. However towards the end of August the Germans announced that the camp was soon to be moved. As a result it was decided that the scheme should be put into operation with the forty officers so far trained, of

158

ESCAPE
FROM
GERMANY

*N.C.O.s
in Army
Camps*

whom three belonged to the Air Force and two to the Navy, as soon as the moon and the weather were suitable. Before then some of the thirty-five Army prisoners were transferred to another camp and in order to keep four teams up to full strength some Air Force prisoners were hurriedly trained to take their places. Unfortunately, probably due to insufficient and hurried training, none of these substitutes got over the wire when the plan was put into effect.

It was decided to put the scheme into operation on the night of 30 August, between 10 and 11 o'clock. During the afternoon a team of carpenters built the additional three ladders needed. For security reasons this work had to be done between the ceiling and the roof of one of the huts and after completion the ladders were painted black and kept there until nightfall. As only four ladders were being used, and in order to make signalling easier, it was decided that they should all be placed close together against the same stretch of wire.

On the night chosen the four teams, with blackened faces and balaclava helmets, were concealed with their ladders in barracks close to the selected stretch of wire. After waiting about three-quarters of an hour the signal was received that the three guards had reached the extreme ends of their beat at the same time. This was "zero hour" and the lights were at once extinguished. The teams rushed out and all four ladders were erected and their extensions pushed out across the double fence. Two of the teams were completely successful, all ten men getting over very quickly. In the third team eight out of ten got over and in the fourth two got across before the signal to return was given by the controller.

Although there was a fair amount of shooting and plenty of shouting only one person out of the forty was injured and he received only a slight wound in the heel. Of the thirty prisoners who got over the wire seventeen managed to get clear of the camp area. Of these, three Army officers reached Holland where they were taken charge of by the Underground Movement, being eventually passed through Belgium and France to England. All the others were recaptured within a few days.

This camp was closed in September, 1942, the Air Force prisoners being transferred to Schubin.

## CHAPTER 16 · N.C.O.s IN ARMY CAMPS

When Barth became full, Air Force N.C.O.s were dispersed in Army camps throughout Germany, but unlike the officers, many of them remained in these camps throughout the war. Chief among these was Stalag VIIIB, later renamed Stalag 344, at Lamsdorf, near Breslau. When this camp became filled to capacity new prisoners were sent for a time to Stalag IXC, Bad

Sulza, and Stalag IIIE, Kirchhain. Towards the end of the war N.C.O.s were also sent to Stalag IVB, Mühlberg and Stalag Luft VII, Borkau.

### Stalag VIIIB—Lamsdorf

ESCAPE
FROM
GERMANY

N.C.O.s
in Army
Camps

Lamsdorf, which was about three miles from Anahof railway station in Upper Silesia, was a large base camp used mainly for other ranks of the British Army. It held approximately six thousand prisoners but its administration was responsible for another thirty thousand prisoners who were dispersed in working parties over a wide area in this industrial section of South-east Germany. The Air Force prisoners were kept in a compound by themselves.

The first Air Force prisoners reached this camp early in 1940 but these N.C.O.s were transferred to Barth when that camp was opened. When Barth became full early in 1941, batches of newly captured prisoners were transferred to Lamsdorf from Dulag Luft. Within a few months the Air Force compound contained about six hundred N.C.O.s and airmen. The majority of these were transferred to the Centre Compound at Sagan in May, 1942, but owing to insufficient accommodation there, further batches of new prisoners were housed at Lamsdorf from August, 1942, onwards. In the autumn of the following year the number was about two thousand, at which figure it remained until the camp was evacuated on 21 January, 1945, owing to the advance of the Russian Forces.

Although the Air Force N.C.O.s were not allowed to volunteer for working parties outside the camp, hundreds of them exchanged identities with Army prisoners and so got themselves transferred to the working parties which were not strictly guarded; once there they were able to acquire civilian clothes, maps, information and other escape aids through contact with Poles and in some cases the German civilian population. More Air Force prisoners made successful escapes from this camp than from any other in Germany, no less than eleven reaching the United Kingdom or the Allied lines.

Of the scores of failures one was particularly unfortunate. In April, 1941, two N.C.O.s, while members of a working party at Ratibor, walked off in their overalls intending to make for Prague where they had an address supplied by a Czech. They walked day and night, covering two hundred and fifty miles in nine days and a half. When they reached the outskirts of Prague one of them could go no further because of badly blistered feet. However they travelled by bus into the centre of the city and went straight to the address they had been given. The man whom they met there took them to his flat, and next day moved them to another address. Later a guide took them by train to Moravia and on foot to an inn on top of a hill near the town of Bystrice, where they were left to recover from the effects of their walk.

160

ESCAPE
FROM
GERMANY

*N.C.O.s
in Army
Camps*

After several weeks they learned that this inn was to be taken over by a Hitler Youth Hostel but the owner told them that they could remain there quite safely. Shortly afterwards, however, they had to move to another address for three weeks because of the activities of the Gestapo in the district. When they returned to the inn preparations were being made for their evacuation and they were told that they were to be taken back to Prague to be flown to the United Kingdom.

They left for Prague in mid-September and stayed there at the home of one of their helpers for three weeks. One night while they were asleep and their helper was at work members of the Gestapo entered at 3 a.m. and took them to their Headquarters for interrogation. They spent thirty-seven days in solitary confinement in a military prison at Prague, subsequently being placed together in a cell for three months. At the end of that time they were returned to the Air Force compound at Lamsdorf.

### Flying Officer E. D. Chisholm and Sergeant C. E. McDonald

The first successful Air Force escape from this camp was made by Warrant Officer, later Flying Officer, E. D. Chisholm, M.C., R.A.A.F., and Sergeant C. E. McDonald, M.M., R.C.A.F., in the summer of 1942. Each exchanged identities with an Army private and in due course they were sent on a working party to the Gleiwitz area. About 11 p.m. on 11 August, 1942, accompanied by another Air Force N.C.O. and a Polish Jew serving in the British Army, they got through a hole in the ceiling of the hut in which they were living and then down through the ceiling of a boiler-room. A key for the door of the latter had been made in the camp in preparation for the attempt. The gate in the perimeter fence surrounding the hut was unlocked and on a signal from watchers in the hut that the sentry patrolling outside the fence was at the opposite corner of the compound, they went through the gate. They walked south then east during the hours of darkness, hiding in woods during the day until after six days they made contact with some Poles near Gorki. With them they stayed for five weeks, then moved to another farm where they remained for a further month. At the end of that time the party was escorted to Warsaw. All four escapers stayed at different addresses, but Chisholm, McDonald and the Polish Jew, who acted as their interpreter, maintained contact with one another.

On 23 March, 1943, McDonald and two British soldiers who had also escaped from their working parties, were sent to Paris accompanied by a guide. They were provided with identity cards for Polish workmen to which their photographs and finger prints were added, and their guide had the necessary workers' passes and travel permits. They travelled by train via Cracow, Berlin and Metz arriving in Paris on 29 March. There they stayed at various addresses for about a month and were then escorted to St. Brieuc, but a scheme to get them across the Spanish frontier with a

161

ESCAPE
FROM
GERMANY

N.C.O.s
in Army
Camps

number of airmen who had evaded capture failed. They returned to Paris about 15 May. About a fortnight later, when the party was fourteen strong, they were taken to Pau and were escorted by Basque guides across the Spanish frontier after a most arduous journey over the Pyrenees. Reaching Spain just after daybreak on 3 June they gave themselves up to the Spanish Civil Guard and later were taken to Gibraltar.

It was arranged that Chisholm and the other R.A.F. prisoner who had been left in Warsaw should follow McDonald in two weeks' time but owing to the arrest of members of the organisation between Warsaw and Paris this became impossible. In October Chisholm met two Belgians who had escaped from Minsk and were endeavouring to return to Belgium. They agreed to take the two Air Force prisoners with them if the right papers could be found but the attempt to get Belgian identity cards took so long that the Belgians became impatient. One went to work in Warsaw and the other, having acquired a leave pass, went to Belgium. Shortly before Christmas Chisholm's Air Force colleague was arrested by the Germans.

By mid-March, 1944, the Belgian identity cards had been procured and all the arrangements completed. Meanwhile Chisholm had met two Dutch escapers and one of these accompanied him when he left Warsaw on 23 March on a military train for Berlin. They left Berlin at 11 p.m. on 24 March on a military train for Brussels. They experienced various difficulties with their papers, first at Venlo in Holland which caused them to return to Aachen, and then at Aachen itself where finally they received a frontier pass enabling them to travel to Brussels. There they made contact with the Belgian whom they had met in Warsaw and stayed at his house. Shortly afterwards they met a Pole who arranged to provide a guide to the French-Belgian frontier.

About 3 May they left Brussels with this guide and went via the outskirts of Roubaix to the French frontier. There they were held up for a week but then received French papers and travelled to Paris on 10 May. They were introduced to a man and stayed with his family on the outskirts until the outbreak of hostilities in Paris between the Free French Forces of the Interior and the Germans. Soon after the liberation of Paris they were returned to the United Kingdom.

### Pilot Officer H. L. Brooks

In May, 1942, Warrant Officer, later Pilot Officer H. L. Brooks, M.C., R.C.A.F., exchanged identities with a New Zealand Army private at Lamsdorf and in November was sent to work in a sawmill at Tost. Subsequently he was given a job as a lorry driver and left the mill daily to deliver lumber, which enabled him to get a good idea of the geography of the district and to make contact with various Poles.

162

ESCAPE
FROM
GERMANY

N.C.O.s
in Army
Camps

On 10 May, 1943, Brooks, accompanied by a British Army sergeant, sawed through the bars across the window of their room and climbed through. Walking by night along the highway and sleeping by day, they reached Czestochowa where they made contact with a Pole whose name had been supplied by a Polish airman before they left Lamsdorf. This man was a member of the Polish Underground Army and they remained with the partisans until the arrival of Russian troops in January, 1945. They were transferred to Odessa at the beginning of March and repatriated to the United Kingdom.

### Sergeant P. Bakalarski, and Sergeant W. Raginis

The next successful escape was made by Sergeant, later Warrant Officer P. Bakalarski, D.C.M., and Sergeant W. Raginis, both of the Polish Air Force serving with the Royal Air Force. At the beginning of 1943 they exchanged identities with Palestinian privates and were sent out on working parties in the area, eventually being sent to work in a coal mine at Jaworzne. The shifts were changed every fortnight and on 10 June, 1943, they were working on day shift. At 10 p.m. that night they cut a hole in the wire surrounding their camp and at 1 a.m. when the night shift returned from the mines and the barrack door was opened to let them in, the two escapers managed to slip out. It had been arranged that two Polish civilians who were to assist them should be waiting for them a short distance from the camp. Bakalarski got through the hole in the fence first and met his guide but they ran into a group of Gestapo who were waiting for Polish partisans who were hiding in the woods nearby. There was some shooting during which the guide was killed. Bakalarski evaded capture for two days, was then caught and taken back to the coal mine.

Raginis, who had been walking some distance behind Bakalarski, avoided the affray and was met by an unknown Pole who took him to a farm at Dabrowa where he stayed one night. Next day he was escorted by a guide to Szezakowa where he stayed for a few days with a Polish family. There he was provided with a railway uniform and travelling on a railway engine as assistant to the driver, crossed the new German frontier into Poland and went on to Cracow. He remained there for some time staying at various addresses.

Meanwhile Bakalarski had returned to work, and, about mid-July, while on night shift, he escaped again. Previously he had arranged with a member of the Polish Underground Movement that he should be met outside the mine by two men with bicycles. This time, he escaped by going down the mine as though to work and returning to the surface with four of the prisoners who were finishing the day shift. Normally the cage held only four and the guard at the top was unlikely to notice an extra man in the cage. The five prisoners were wearing civilian clothes issued to them

163

ESCAPE
FROM
GERMANY

*N.C.O.s
in Army
Camps*

for work in the mine, and when they reached the top, the guard took out the four others without noticing Bakalarski, and he walked behind whistling Polish tunes and talking loudly in Polish to other Poles in the vicinity. The four other prisoners were led to the shower room and Bakalarski walked through the gate with his miner's lamp in his hand just as though he were one of the civilian miners.

He walked down the road and met the two men who were waiting for him with the bicycles. One of them handed over his bicycle and the other led Bakalarski to his home about two miles from the mine. He remained there for four days hiding most of the time in a cornfield and for the next four days was hidden in a hayloft in another village in the district. The Germans were searching the area but the Polish organisation had warning of the search from Polish patriots. A week after his escape he was taken back to Jaworzno and hidden on the outskirts of the town for a further three days. At the end of that time he was taken to Czestochowa and given a railwayman's uniform and put on the engine of a goods train bound for Cracow. However he travelled only as far as Rudawa a few miles east of Krzeszowica, where he was sheltered for four days. On his first night there the Gestapo surrounded that village and an adjoining one. His host heard the Germans arriving and warned him so he hid in a potato field. About 25 July he was taken to Cracow where he met Raginis.

The two escapers remained in Cracow until 18 August being supplied with identity and work cards. In addition arrangements had been made with the Labour Office for them to be sent to work in Germany. Raginis was furnished with documents which gave his profession as a clerk who had received a university education, while Bakalarski was shown as a shop-keeper with a high school education. The story was that he had owned a shop in Cracow which had been taken over by the Germans and that he preferred going as a voluntary worker to Germany to remaining as an assistant in what had been his own business.

They left Cracow by train with a party of Polish civilians who had been conscripted for work in Germany. As alleged volunteers the two escapers were the only members of the party to whom a definite destination and definite employment had been assigned; this had been arranged with the Labour Office. They had been assigned to the station master in Sarrebourg. They travelled via Berlin and Saarbrucken where they bought their own tickets rather than go to the Labour Office which might have diverted them from Sarrebourg.

On arrival at Sarrebourg they reported to the Labour Office and police, and their employment was confirmed officially. A number of Poles had been working in the district for a long time but as it was so close to France there had been few new-comers. They were billeted in a camp where there were one hundred and fifty Polish and Russian women who were employed

164

ESCAPE
FROM
GERMANY

*N.C.O.s*
*in Army*
*Camps*

laying new and repairing old tracks on the railway. They were the only men there, all the male Poles being at work on farms, and were given light employment in the station master's garden and in the fields. They were under supervision all the time, working with a native of Lorraine to whom after two weeks they confided that they were escaped prisoners of war and asked for his help. They had passed out of the hands of the Polish Organisation when they were despatched to Sarrebourg. This man got in touch with a French organisation in Lorraine which undertook to help them.

Early on the morning of 14 September they left Sarrebourg with a railway worker who lived on the frontier and travelled to a small station, probably Hertzing. They were taken to a farm and then bicycled to the village of Foulcrey close to the frontier. The railwayman left them and they spent the day there. In the evening they were given directions about crossing the frontier, which they did while the German guard was changing, and walked to Igney. They had been told that they would be met outside this place but saw no one corresponding to the description of the man they had been told to expect. Failing to find their helper they went to a farmhouse where they were sheltered in a stable for the night by the owner. Next morning they again waited for their helper, who was to have provided them with French identity cards, but on the advice of the farmer they went to Luneville near the frontier where they found help. A few days later they travelled by train with an escort to Nancy, being supplied with false identity papers. After a few days they were escorted to Ruffec where they remained for about a week, being given new identity cards.

About 22 October Raginis and a New Zealand soldier, Driver F. C. Williamson who had also escaped from Lamsdorf, were taken by a Frenchman via Bordeaux to Toulouse where they met a Spanish guide. They travelled with him by train to Pamiers where they waited for Bakalarski, who arrived soon after with an R.A.F. sergeant who had evaded capture, escorted by a Frenchman.

At 6 a.m. on 25 October the party of four, accompanied by a guide, started off on their journey across the Pyrenees. It was raining when they set off and they walked until mid-day by which time Williamson was so exhausted that Raginis and the evader had to carry him. Bakalarski was sick and had pains in his legs. The guide had reckoned that they would reach the frontier of Andorra about 2 p.m. but at 6 p.m. it was still about five miles distant. By this time Williamson was very weak. The guide wanted to return to France but eventually agreed to go on with Raginis who was stronger than the others, and show him the road into Andorra. They went off, the guide taking Raginis as far as a lake about five miles north-west of L'Hospitalet. Unfortunately he directed him along the north side of the lake instead of along the east and as a result Raginis eventually found himself back in France.

165

ESCAPE
FROM
GERMANY

N.C.O.s
in Army
Camps

Reginis kept on walking until he got into a valley; the going was very bad in the deep snow. When it got dark he found it impossible to continue so spent the night in the snow. Next morning he resumed and after about five hours saw a small hut with smoke rising from the chimney. He thought he was in Andorra but for some reason unknown to himself decided to watch the door of the hut before approaching. About a quarter of an hour later he saw two Germans emerge from the hut and realised that he was in France again. He was too tired to return to the lake and pick up the road to Andorra again so worked his way round the hut and down-hill then followed the valley of the river Aston. He walked for two hours and reached a road-making party of Spaniards and Frenchmen at work beside the river. He went to their hut and being a fluent French speaker explained that he had just crossed into the Unoccupied Zone of France. He remained at this hut for three nights and three days as his hands and feet were swollen with frostbite.

When he had recovered sufficiently the workmen gave him some food and he walked to the outskirts of the town of Aston. He remained there in the woods for about a week observing the roads on which German patrols passed at regular intervals. At the end of that time he walked into Aston, stole an unattended bicycle, and cycled to Urs. He knew that a Spanish guide lived there as he had been with the party at the beginning of the journey and had handed over to the French guide who had left him at the lake. Raginis made contact with the Spaniard and explained what had happened. This man took him by train to Merins les-Vals and told him to follow the road, keeping to the fields and hills.

He started his second journey to the frontier about 3 November and after walking all day reached L'Hospitalet. There he began to climb the mountain at night and arrived in Andorra, about five miles south-east of Soldeu, after about five hours. Having discovered from a man on the road that he was in Andorra he followed the road as far as Escaldas. Shortly afterwards he met a Spaniard and was conducted across the Spanish fron-tier to Seo de Urgel eventually being taken to Gibraltar where he arrived on 27 November. A few days later he was returned to the United Kingdom.

Meanwhile Bakalarski, the evader and the New Zealander Williamson had been left alone because the guide did not return to them. It was snow-ing heavily, and on the mountains the snow lay more than knee-deep. They carried on for five hours and then Williamson died; they left him in the mountains, probably somewhere north of Pic de Rulle. They contin-ued walking and when it became dark lost the footprints of Raginis and the guide which they had been following. The sky cleared and it froze hard and their clothes, which had been wet, froze on them. They reached a rocky mountainside across which it took them about four hours to cover half a mile. Bakalarski was in front and when they reached a level stretch

166

ESCAPE
FROM
GERMANY

N.C.O.s
in Army
Camps

of snow he waited for his companion and when the latter reached him he lay down and fell asleep. Bakalarski discovered that the other had taken off his shoes and had been walking with them under his arm. He took off his companions socks, dried his feet and legs with a towel from his pack, and put a dry pair of socks and his shoes on his feet. This was very difficult as the man's legs seemed frozen stiff; his hands were also frostbitten. Bakalarski then smacked him all over until he revived, covered one of his hands with a handkerchief and the other with a sponge bag, then forced him to resume walking. They carried on all night.

At one stage they had to go back nearly two miles as they had lost their way. By this time there was no trace of the footprints of Raginis and the guide but they took the general direction the guide had indicated before leaving. It took them twelve hours to reach the top of the mountain, normally a climb of about an hour. When they reached the top, they looked at the evader's escape map and managed to locate south with the aid of the small compass which he carried, although it had been broken in one of his falls. They could see a lake on the top of the mountain which the guide had told them to look for.

After descending about half-way they could see Andorran mountain guards watching them through field glasses. Avoiding them they crossed the next mountain and followed the guide's footprints until they reached a road and eventually a cottage. They were directed to a second cottage where they were given hot milk and allowed to sleep in a hayloft. It was then 27 October, the crossing having taken two days and a night.

On the morning of 28 October they were visited by a man who spoke French and arrangements were made for them to be taken to Andorra where the evader was sent to hospital. Bakalarski was put into a hotel as there was no room in the hospital. Six days later they were taken across the Spanish frontier and later to Gibraltar, to be repatriated to the United Kingdom.

### Flight Lieutenant J. P. Dowd

The next successful Air Force escaper was Flight Sergeant, later Flight Lieutenant J. P. Dowd, D.C.M., R.A.F. On 22 June, 1943, he left the main camp for a working party at a sawmill at Grottkau, having exchanged identities with a soldier. During the next two months he made his preparations for escape and at 7 p.m. on 29 August walked out of his quarters, a building attached to the house occupied by the manager of the sawmill, while the guard was having supper. By arrangement he met a British Army sergeant who had escaped from the working party three days previously and was being sheltered by a German woman in the gate-house of the sawmill. The two escapers walked along the railway lines to Grottkau railway station.

167

ESCAPE
FROM
GERMANY

*N.C.O.s*
*in Army*
*Camps*

The Army sergeant bought two railway tickets for Brieg and on arrival there decided that as he had no papers he would not accompany Dowd but would go to an address in Czechoslovakia where he hoped to get shelter and help from a Czech woman.

Dowd who had good papers bought a railway ticket for Breslau and boarded the first train which turned out to be a special train carrying troops returning from the Russian front. Almost immediately afterwards the conductress asked him what he was doing on a military train. He explained that he was a foreign worker. Without asking to see his papers she told him that this was an express and demanded two marks additional fare. As she left him she shook her finger and said in German "Look out!" Dowd was standing in the corridor and was the only civilian. When a corporal of the Railway Police eventually came along and saw him he became furious, but a German Air Force N.C.O. who was standing nearby told him that Dowd had paid the additional fare to the conductress. The railway policeman passed on and Dowd arrived in Breslau about 10 p.m. without further incident. He travelled by train as a normal passenger to Stettin, arriving about 5.30 p.m. next day.

He left the railway station and walked round the town eventually meeting a man who called himself a Pole, whom he afterwards discovered to be a Polish Ukrainian. Dowd told him that he was a Swedish sailor, had missed his boat and wanted to meet some other Swedes. This man took him to a brothel for foreign workers near the harbour which was forbidden to Germans. Dowd, accompanied by the Pole, waited about near the brothel for several hours that evening and as they were leaving met two young Dutchmen whom they heard speaking English to a Swede. Thinking they were English Dowd asked them who they were and told them that he was an escaped British prisoner and that he wanted to get on board a Swedish ship. The two Dutchmen took him to a boarding house where one of them was living. On the way the Swede boarded a tram and Dowd did not see him again.

Next day the two Dutchmen took him to the harbour area, and in the afternoon they made a trip round it in a small pleasure steamer. On 1 September the Dutchman with whom he had been staying told him that he could not remain any longer as the owner of the house was returning that night. That day he had another trip round the harbour, this time alone. At night he returned to the brothel and met the two Dutchmen by arrangement. While he was in the brothel members of the Gestapo arrived and Dowd went upstairs to the room of a Polish girl. She spoke German and Dowd told her his true identity. At first she was very frightened but eventually hid him under the bed and sat on it. When the Gestapo men entered the room they merely looked around and went out. After they had gone the girl told Dowd to leave immediately but return next evening and meet

ESCAPE
FROM
GERMANY

N.C.O.s
in Army
Camps

her outside the door before the house closed saying she would try to find a pro-British Swede. After this Dowd met one of his Dutch friends outside and returned his passport which he had loaned him.

He went with the Dutchman to a camp for foreign workers and spent the night in his dormitory. There were three German A.R.P. watchers sleeping in the room. When they left next morning they informed the police at the nearby shipyard that there was one man too many in the room. Later two policemen visited the camp and asked Dowd what he was doing there. He told them that he was a Swedish seaman, that he had missed the tram the night before and now was going to his ship where he had to start work at 6 a.m. Fortunately he was wearing a small Swedish union badge which one of the Dutchmen had given him. One of the Germans recognised this and believed his story so he was told to get out of the camp and not to return.

Dowd left the camp and returned to the town and after another trip round the harbour spent the afternoon in a cinema. In the evening he returned to the brothel and persuaded a Dutchman whom he met there to tell two Swedish seamen who he was. They refused to help him. He saw the Polish girl again and she told him she had not been able to find a Swede to help him and could not help him herself. He spent that night in a small copse on the outskirts of the town.

He spent the next afternoon in a cinema and in the evening again tried the brothel but the Swedes he met either could not or would not enter into conversation with him. About 10 o'clock he went to the harbour and climbed the fence which enabled him to get alongside a small Swedish sailing and auxiliary motor ship. He was crossing the plank to the ship when a harbour policeman appeared. Dowd staggered, pretending to be drunk, and the policeman asked for his identity card. Dowd said in German, "I have twenty passes here," at the same time pulling out a packet of twenty French cigarettes. The policeman looked at the cigarettes and at Dowd and asked him who he was. Dowd replied that he was Swedish and belonged to a ship which he named, having seen her in the harbour. The policeman told him that he was in the wrong harbour, whereupon Dowd stated that he was sorry and offered him a cigarette. The policeman took the whole packet and showed him out through the main gate. Dowd walked right round the outside of the harbour to try to get in at the west side. There was a small waiting room used by passengers travelling on the ferry which crossed the harbour at this point. Two Danish ships were loading nearby and two searchlight beams were trained on the ships, lighting up the wire round the harbour just where he had hoped to climb over; in addition two harbour policemen were standing near these ships. Dowd lay down on a bench in the waiting-room and went to sleep hoping that the policemen would be gone by the time he awakened. At 6 o'clock next morning an old

169

ESCAPE
FROM
GERMANY

*N.C.O.s*
*in Army*
*Camps*

German workman woke him stating that the ferry was about to leave. He went on board and crossed the harbour, then walked back into the town. After a wash at a public washroom he went as usual to a restaurant for a coupon-free meal and to a cinema in the afternoon.

That evening he walked back towards the docks and on the way was stopped by five Danish seamen who asked him the way to the nearest restaurant. He took them in to a nearby inn and told them who he was. One of them spoke English and they agreed to take him back to their ship which was lying in the river Oder and would be sailing at 9.30 a.m. next day. The ship was moored in the river because her sailing had been delayed, due to riots in Denmark.

They walked to a point opposite the ship and the Danes signalled for a small boat. The Danish watchman from the ship arrived with the dinghy and said the German watchman was still on board. The Danes had half a bottle of schnapps and decided to make the German intoxicated. The whole party boarded the ship and found that the German was partly intoxicated already and gave him the schnapps. When his relief arrived on board about an hour later he left without counting the number of seamen on board. Dowd was in the forecastle with four of the five who had befriended him. Several of the crew knew that he was on board but none of the officers was informed.

At 9.15 a.m. next day the ship was searched by the Germans but as she had been searched before leaving the harbour they were not very thorough. Dowd was hidden under one of the bunks in the forecastle. The ship was bound for Riga in Latvia with stone chips, which were believed to be for making aerodrome runways in Russia. She sailed at the scheduled time and arrived in Riga on 8 September, where she remained for seven days. During the whole of this time Dowd remained hidden in the forecastle.

On 15 September the ship sailed and anchored off Gragar, Denmark, three days later. Five of the crew decided to desert and at 1 a.m. on 19 September they took one of the ship's lifeboats and with Dowd on board began rowing across to Limhaven, south-west of Malmo, Sweden. The crossing took five hours, the sailors rowing and Dowd acting as navigator, steering by the stars; they had taken a compass but when it was unwrapped it was found to be useless. They arrived in the harbour of Limhaven at daybreak on 20 September and a Swedish Customs Officer who met them telephoned the police who took them to the gaol in Malmo. Later that day Dowd was taken to the British Legation in Stockholm, being repatriated to the United Kingdom shortly afterwards.

### Flight Lieutenant A. F. McSweyn

Just before the transfer of the officers from Schubin to Sagan in April, 1943, Flight Lieutenant A. F. McSweyn, M.C., R.A.A.F., exchanged identities with an Army private who worked as an orderly. Upon arrival at Sagan the officer settled down to the second part of his plan—getting himself transferred to an Army camp.

ESCAPE
FROM
GERMANY

*N.C.O.s
in Army
Camps*

He worked as an orderly for nearly three months and whenever there was any particularly menial or unpleasant job to do he invariably volunteered, then after a few hours' work would choose a moment when there was a German in the vicinity, throw down his tools and refuse to do any more. In this way he became well known to the Germans as a nuisance and was frequently punished for refusing to obey orders. After a time the Senior British Officer, who knew the details of the plan, suggested to the German Commandant that, as this "orderly" would not work properly and appeared to be a trouble-maker, it would be better if he were transferred to another camp. In July the unruly "orderly" was transferred to Lamsdorf.

During the first week there he was content to study conditions and eventually went out of the camp with a working party to dig potatoes. As usual there were very few guards with the party and with very little preparation McSweyn was able to make an escape simply by eluding a guard and walking away. He reached Danzig where he was recaptured on board a Swedish ship after the Germans had used tear gas bombs which forced him to leave the coal bunker in which he was hiding. He was returned to Lamsdorf but his true identity was not discovered.

Shortly after his return he discovered that a tunnel had been completed and was ready for use. The organisers of the tunnel agreed that he should escape through it and it was decided that he should travel through Germany as a French workman medically unfit for further work in Germany. He spoke enough German for a foreigner but no French. It was decided therefore that Driver F. C. Williamson, a New Zealander, should accompany him as he spoke fluent German and had pre-war experience of German railways.

With the help of a British Army private McSweyn forged a medical certificate supposedly from the chief German doctor at Blechhammer, a nearby town, stating that he was suffering from tuberculosis of the larynx, was unfit for further duty, and was to be sent back to France to recuperate. In addition to this, Williamson and he each had a French identity card, leave pass, temporary identity card and a letter purporting to be from German Army officials stating that they should be permitted to travel to Marseilles and that this, the letter, should be accepted instead of their official documents which were unobtainable due to the bombing of the German offices in Berlin. Furthermore, Williamson had a document to the effect that he was entitled to return to France, having completed the requisite number of years' work in Germany and was accompanying McSweyn.

On 19 September, 1943, the two escapers entered the tunnel at 1 p.m. and a few minutes later emerged about thirty yards beyond the sentry

171

ESCAPE
FROM
GERMANY

*N.C.O.s*
*in Army*
*Camps*

patrolling the fence. As pre-arranged, at that moment a few of the prisoners inside the compound distracted the sentry's attention. Each escaper was dressed in civilian clothes, carried a small attaché case containing food and had plenty of German money. They walked to Lamsdorf railway station and purchased tickets to Breslau where they arrived without incident. There they changed to the Cracow-Berlin express but before reaching Berlin their papers were examined several times. They reached the Schlesischer Bahnhof Berlin at 10 p.m. and when they found that there were no further trains until next morning, spent the night at an hotel close to the station. At 10 o'clock next morning they boarded a train for Mannheim, passing through Erfurt, Gotha and Frankfurt; they arrived at Mannheim about 10 p.m. and walked across the station which was damaged very badly by bombing. They found it was impossible to obtain hotel accommodation and spent the night in a very crowded air-raid shelter.

At noon next day they left by train for Saarbrucken and on the journey met some Frenchmen from whom they learned about a French work camp at Forbach which was reputed to be very pro-British in its sympathies. They reached the camp that night and were told that they would be guided across the frontier in two days. However, an Italian who was to have acted as their guide refused eventually to do so and on 24 September a Frenchman in the camp undertook to escort them and took them to Metz where he spent two days trying to find a guide. During this time the escapers stayed at another working camp.

On the night of 26 September the two prisoners, the Frenchman and the guide, travelled by train to Moyeuvre-la-Grande, then walked about four miles and arrived at Auboue on the other side of the frontier. The border was marked by three barbed wire fences a few feet high and there were sentry boxes at intervals, but by careful timing they were able to cross without being seen. Their guide took them to a small hotel where they stayed overnight. Early next morning they were awakened and told that the Germans were carrying out one of their periodic searches of all houses in the village; they left the hotel immediately and travelled by bus to Longwy where they spent about two hours in a cafe awaiting a train. At the station they discovered that the German Field Police were checking all passengers going on to the platform, so they bribed a French railway official to take them round by the goods yard and they boarded the train from the wrong side.

The two escapers, accompanied by their helper from Forbach, travelled to Luneville where the Frenchman left them in a cafe and went in search of a friend. Some time later he returned with his friend and they stayed at his house for four days. By now they were in the hands of an organisation and on 30 September they were taken to Nancy. There they were given identity cards which stated that they were Frenchmen who had been bombed out

172

ESCAPE
FROM
GERMANY

*N.C.O.s*
*in Army*
*Camps*

of their homes at Nantes and that McSweyn was deaf and dumb. They were given food coupons and clothing cards. They stayed in Nancy until 4 October when the two escapers, accompanied by their helper from Forbach and another Frenchman, travelled to Lyons where they remained until 8 October.

On that day the two British prisoners travelled to Ruffec where they were met by a woman. They had learned that it was intended that they should cross into Spain by way of Andorra, but about that time Andorra became a defence zone and a special pass was required. It was not until 20 October that the pass was ready. During this time they were joined by Sergeants Bakalarski and Raginis and the R.A.F. Sergeant who had evaded capture whose story has already been told. These three and Williamson were sent on ahead of McSweyn, and Williamson died on the journey.

At the end of another week Captain Palm of the South African Air Force, also an escaper from Germany, and three R.A.F. evaders joined McSweyn and four or five days later their papers were ready. The party travelled by truck to Foix but found that this route had been discovered by the Germans and several people had been arrested. They returned to Toulouse where they remained for one day and then went back to Ruffec. During the next five days the organisation arranged a new route through Pau whence they travelled to Claron and Tardets-Sorholus; from there they walked to Agnos and Montory where the party was left with two guides. They were told that their journey was only about twelve miles and would be easy, so they did not take either food or drink.

At midnight they set off in pouring rain and walked until 4 a.m. when it began to freeze hard. One of the evaders had cramp in his heart and could not go on, so they waited with him until about 8 a.m. when they resumed. He was unable to walk by himself and McSweyn had to help him. About 3 p.m. it began to snow and within an hour-and-a-half it was well above their knees. When McSweyn was too tired to help the sick man further the two guides more or less carried him along. By this time another of the evaders was exhausted and kept lagging behind, but by taking his arm McSweyn was able to get him along. When they had crossed over the frontier the guides said they were lost and wanted to turn back. Fortunately they struck a valley with a stream running through it, which they followed, and saw in the distance a small hut. Every member of the party was exhausted and they had to help one another to reach it; when they arrived they discovered that there was no fuel with which to make a fire.

While they were in the hut two Spaniards arrived and were asked for help; they said they would send someone but went off and did not return. However, before leaving they said that there was a house about two miles down the valley. The three evaders decided to go on alone and Palm and McSweyn were left with the two guides, one of whom appeared to be

frozen stiff. They could not move his arms or legs. After working on him
for some time they managed to get him up but before the party had gone
five hundred yards he was dead. McSewyn tried to dig a hole in the
ground, wrapped his groundsheet round him and left him there. He caught
up with the others and they reached the other hut which they found
locked up; they broke in and lit a fire, then stripped off all their clothes and
dried them.

About 8'oclock next morning the party set off again, the guide now
stating that he knew where he was. The British prisoners doubted this but
followed him for about two miles downstream. Then the guide said that
he was going to go upstream but Palm and McSewyn refused to do this
and McSewyn took charge of the party. The first town they reached was
Uztarroz where they gave themselves up to the police. In due course they
were sent to Gibraltar and then repatriated to the United Kingdom.

### Warrant Officer W. G. Reed

In May, 1944, an Australian Warrant Officer W. G. Reed, D.C.M., R.A.A.F.,
was able to exchange identities with a British Army private and was sent as
a member of a working party to a coal-mine at Bethuen. He was accompanied on this working party by an Army private, a Jew with an excellent
knowledge of German. Reed was in possession of forged documents and
acquired civilian clothes after his arrival at Beuthen.

About 9:30 a.m. on 11 July, 1944, he and the army private left their
respective working places and changed their clothes underground. They
left the mine and walked into Beuthen, travelled by tram to Kattowitz and
from there by train through Gleiwitz to Breslau. Before reaching Breslau
their identity documents were examined but passed successfully. On
arrival they discovered that there were no more trains to Berlin that day so
they travelled via Frankfurt-on-Oder to Kustrin and on to Stettin.

On arrival they met two British soldiers also trying to escape but they
did not stay together. Reed and his companion went by tram to a suburb
and entered a wharf—where there was a Swedish ship—by climbing round
the wharf fence. They boarded the ship and hid in the engine room. They
were not discovered when the Germans carried out their search and the
boat sailed about 7'oclock on the morning of 15 July. The ship docked at
Solvesborg at midday next day and, after being interviewed by the Swedish
police, they were taken to Stockolm where they reported to the British
Legation. Soon afterwards they were returned to the United Kingdom.

### Warrant Officer G. T. Woodroffe

About July, 1942, Warrant Officer F. T. Woodroffe, M.M., R.N.Z.A.F.,
exchanged identities with an Australian Army private at Stalag Luft III,
Sagan. Originally the Australian had been in Lamsdorf where he had

173

ESCAPE
FROM
GERMANY

N.C.O.s
in Army
Camps

174

ESCAPE
FROM
GERMANY

N.C.O.s
in Army
Camps

exchanged identities with an Air Force N.C.O. and had been transferred to Sagan. The Air Force N.C.O. had escaped and upon recapture the exchange of identities had been discovered with the result that the Australian was to be returned to Lamsdorf. Instead, Woodroffe was escorted to Lamsdorf and became a member of various working parties attached to the main camp.

In preparation for his escape he obtained two suits of civilian clothes, civilian shoes and a suitcase. Eventually, while on a working party at Olbersdorf, he met a Palestinian Army private and they planned to escape together. Shortly afterwards each acquired a French travel permit, an identity card and a quantity of German money.

At 10.15 p.m. on 17 August, 1944, Woodroffe and his companion and two Army privates left the camp in pairs. Just as they got outside the camp walls the Palestinian realised that he had left behind his wallet which contained his identity card and travel permit. He put down his suitcase containing food and clothing and was about to crawl back into the camp when he was seen by a woman who raised the alarm. Woodroffe and the Palestinian hid until the first panic had died down and the two Army privates disappeared. Woodroffe and his companion walked to Rowersdorf where they spent the day of 18 August. On the following day they went to Zeigenhalse where their working party was employed and left a note for their fellow prisoners asking whether they could retrieve the Palestinian's identity papers. They waited in the woods until the evening of 21 August for a reply, then learned that in the first alarm following the escape the papers had been destroyed by their fellow prisoners. However they obtained a further supply of bread and cheese to replace the food that the Palestinian had lost. That night they walked to Neisse where Woodroffe bought two tickets for Breslau. They boarded the train about 11.15 p.m. and just as the train was leaving the station they experienced their first and only check of identity papers. The Palestinian, who was without papers, was arrested and taken off the train at Brieg.

On arrival at Breslau Woodroffe re-booked to Wismar and boarded what he believed to be the Berlin express. Unfortunately it did not go near Berlin but finally arrived at Halle about midnight. He went to the enquiry office on the station, produced his papers and said he was lost. He was told that there was no need to pay any excess fare and that he should travel on the Hanover express to Magdeburg. However, he went to sleep on the train and did not awaken until he arrived at Hanover. About 5 a.m. on 24 August he boarded the Hamburg train, changed at Ludwigslust and boarded a train to Wismar, arriving about 10.30 p.m.

On arrival he walked straight down to the wharves and stopped at an inn. After having a glass of beer he followed three Frenchmen out on to the road and told them that he wanted to board a Swedish ship. They said that

175

ESCAPE
FROM
GERMANY

*N.C.O.s*
*in Army*
*Camps*

it was quite useless to wait at Wismar as only fishing boats used the harbour. Feeling very disheartened Woodroffe started walking to Rostock but on the outskirts of Wismar overheard a Frenchman talking to a girl. He approached this man and asked him if he could help him. The Frenchman agreed to do so and took him to his apartment in the town where he remained for two days.

On the night of 25 August one of the Frenchman's friends took Woodroffe down to the docks and left him. The escaper strolled along the quayside and boarded the first ship that he saw flying the Swedish flag, then hid. Although there were several guards around the dock area he was not stopped. The ship was coaled on 27 August and that day the Germans came on board to make their routine search, but Woodroffe's hiding place was not discovered. The ship sailed that afternoon, then anchored in the harbour entrance because of a storm. That night mines were dropped, probably by R.A.F. aircraft, and the following day the ship sailed but stopped five hours later and waited, in company with seventeen others, for the mines to be swept. Finally the ship sailed at 1 p.m. on 28 August and arrived at Karlshamn, Sweden, twenty-four hours later; on 30 August the Swedish police took the escaper to Stockholm where he reported to the British Legation and was returned to the United Kingdom a few days later.

### Warrant Officer C. Rofe

Warrant Officer C. Rofe, M.M., R.A.F., exchanged identities with a Palestinian Army private in May, 1942, when he was about to be transferred to Stalag Luft III, Sagan, with a large number of Air Force N.C.O.s. He maintained this identity until August, 1944, then exchanged identities with yet another Palestinian and arranged that this man would resume his own identity within a few days.

On 20 August, 1944, Rofe and an Army corporal escaped from a working party at Schonberg where they were engaged in erecting wooden bungalows on the outskirts of the town. Normally they began work at 6 a.m. On this day, about a minute after that hour, they entered an empty bungalow and removed their overalls, then walked away from the site dressed in civilian clothes which they had been wearing underneath. The clothes, German money and forged documents were supplied to them by fellow prisoners.

They travelled by train to Beuthen where they arrived about half an hour later. While waiting there for a tram to Kattowitz they were approached by a member of the German Field Police who wanted to know the time. This man spoke broken German and after Rofe had answered him he stated that he was a Ukrainian. He was travelling to Myslowice and they travelled on the same tram discussing various topics.

The two escapers alighted from the tram at Kattowitz at 7.30 a.m. and

176

ESCAPE
FROM
GERMANY

*N.C.O.s*
*in Army*
*Camps*

went to the railway station. Producing their false identity papers at the booking office they bought third-class tickets to Zywice. The train left Kattowitz shortly after 8 o'clock and during the journey to Bielsko their papers were examined by the conductress. Some of the Germans travelling in the same compartment were not in possession of travel permits and the conductress showed them Rofe's papers explaining what was required.

They arrived at Bielsko about 10 a.m. and as an air-raid alarm was sounded soon afterwards went to an air-raid shelter. An hour later it was announced that the train to Zywice was about to depart and they boarded this. On arrival there about an hour later, they walked through the town to a wood on the eastern outskirts where they destroyed their false travel permits but retained their identity papers. They changed their shoes for boots which they had carried in parcels and walked east until evening, when they went to sleep in a wood.

They resumed walking east at 5 a.m. next day and crossed the new German–Polish frontier about twenty-four hours later, arriving eventually in Markow. They walked south-east across country and had to make many detours as German soldiers and Polish civilians were digging trenches in that area. They were given food by Poles at several villages on the way and continued walking by day, spending the nights in barns until the evening of 27 August when they were met by three armed Polish civilians near the river Poprad about five miles south of Stary Saez. After questioning the escapers these men stated that they were partisans and took the two escapers to their camp in the woods where they remained for four days. Six escaped Russian prisoners, Rofe and his companion were then escorted across the river and taken to another group of partisans who were encamped in a wood. They remained there for a further four days and were then escorted to a hill where they were to make contact with yet another partisan group. On the way they were joined by thirty escaped Russian prisoners but on arrival at the rendezvous were unable to find any partisans.

Rofe and his companion left the Russians and walked towards a hill named Helm about two miles east of Kaclawa. This whole area was being fortified and trenches were being dug by Polish women under the supervision of German guards. At the foot of the hill they were stopped by two German field police who examined their papers and packs. They discovered some chocolate and insisted upon buying two bars, paying them in Polish currency and allowing them to proceed. Next day they met again the party of Russians and in the evening the whole party went to a nearby village where the Russians had established contact with a helper. On arrival there Rofe and his companion were separated from the Russians and spent the next few days in various houses in the village and on the outskirts, eventually being moved south-eastwards. On the morning of 18

177

ESCAPE
FROM
GERMANY

*N.C.O.s
in Army
Camps*

September they met a patrol of Russian troops with whom they remained for eight days. In the interval they discovered that they were with four divisions who were cut off by the Germans, but the Russians fought their way back to their own lines and made contact with the main force. They remained with this Russian force, moving from village to village, until 24 November when they were taken by air to Moscow. Some time later they were returned to the United Kingdom.

### Leading Aircraftman J. G. Ward

Leading Aircraftman, later Warrant Officer J. G. Ward, M.C., R.A.F., was in charge of a working party of twenty British prisoners who were engaged in felling trees for the widening of a road on the outskirts of Lissa; there were two German guards with the party. On 17 April, 1941, Ward was wearing civilian clothes, which he had acquired previously, under his uniform. At approximately 2 p.m. he walked away from the working party unobserved and walked east through the woods. After travelling about two miles he discarded his uniform, burying it under a heap of fallen leaves, and continued walking east in the direction of Gostyn where he arrived about 20 April. During this time he walked across country at night avoiding all habitations and hid in the woods during the day.

On arrival at Gostyn he went to the railway marshalling yard at night with the intention of getting into a wagon of a train going east. While examining the labels on the side of a wagon by the aid of a match, he was caught by two members of the railway police. He was asked for his identity card and being unable to produce one was arrested and taken to the police station where he was searched and his prisoner of war identity disc discovered. On being interrogated he told the true story of his escape and requested that he be returned to the working party. He was informed that it would be necessary for him to be interviewed by the Captain the following day and that in all probability he would be shot.

Soon afterwards he was put into a small room at the rear of the police station and the door was locked. There was one window with strands of barbed wire across it, and during that night he broke the strands by bending them several times. When he had made a hole large enough he climbed through and walked across the yard. He discovered that this was surrounded by a wall about ten feet in height with broken glass set in cement on top, so he decided to attempt to get through the gate where there was a sentry. He looked around for a weapon and found a brick. It was very dark so he walked up to the guard quite openly and when he reached him hit him on the head with the brick, using all his strength. The German was wearing a forage cap and fell to the ground without making very much noise; Ward ran off.

After a few minutes he stopped running and got off the road, walking

178

ESCAPE
FROM
GERMANY

*Bad Sulza,*
*Kirchhain,*
*Muhlberg*

east across country. All his food, maps and compass, etc., had been taken from him at the police station. He hid during the hours of daylight and travelled across country at night until he reached Sieradz about 27 April. During this time he called at very small farms and was supplied with food and in many cases was given shelter during the day.

On arrival in Sieradz he met a man whom he told that he had escaped from a prisoner of war camp in Germany, and requested that he should be put in touch with the Polish Underground Movement. This man escorted him to a house where he was kept for three days. In the interval he was visited by another Pole who questioned him in order to establish his identity and about the end of April this man supplied him with a false identity card and a permit entitling him to travel to Lodz. The following day another Pole arrived at the house and escorted him there, travelling by train. On arrival he was taken to an address where he met the chief of the local Underground Movement. This man interrogated him about his identity, then escorted him to another address where he remained for about three weeks before being moved to Piotrkow where he stayed until the end of May. During this time he was supplied with new identity papers.

At the end of May, accompanied by a Pole, he travelled by bus to Warsaw where he stayed at a house for a month. It was the intention of the Underground Movement to send him to Russia but the outbreak of war between Germany and Russia on 21 June made this impossible.

From that date until about 18 January, 1945, he stayed at various addresses in Poland, chiefly at Warsaw. On that day he was at a house near Raszkow when Russian forces arrived in the area. Two days later an officer of the Russian Secret Police visited the house and interrogated him. Ward explained that he was an escaped British prisoner of war from Germany and was told to remain where he was until he should receive instructions.

Some days later he left the area as he had not received any further instructions and eventually reached Warsaw where he reported to the Russian Commander on 5 March. A few days later he joined a party of British and American prisoners who were being sent to Odessa. They arrived there on 16 March and later that day Ward was put on board a British repatriation ship and returned to the United Kingdom.

## CHAPTER 17 · BAD SULZA, KIRCHHAIN, MUHLBERG

### Stalag IXC, Bad Sulza

When the Air Force Compound at Lamsdorf became filled, about a hundred Air Force N.C.O.s were sent from Dulag Luft to Stalag IXC, Bad Sulza, near Mulhauzen in the summer of 1941, a camp which was used mainly for

Belgian and Serbian Army prisoners. Air Force prisoners were housed in a separate barrack and were not allowed to leave the compound on working parties. However, the fact that the other prisoners were taken out on working parties offered opportunities for exchange and many allied prisoners, particularly the Belgians and French were extremely helpful to the airmen.

179

ESCAPE
FROM
GERMANY

*Bad Sulza,
Kirchhain,
Muhlberg*

The first attempt was made on 14 August, 1941. Two Air Force N.C.O.s had procured civilian clothes, a map and compass from two Frenchmen who worked outside the camp and wire cutters from a Serb. At about 7.30 p.m. while the majority of the prisoners were watching a boxing match, they climbed over the perimeter fence at the point where it passed underneath one of the sentry towers. Unfortunately the gestures of three Serbian prisoners who happened to see them caused the guards to become suspicious, and as one of the prisoners was crawling along the bank of the stream just beyond the wire the guard opened fire and they were both caught a few moments later.

## Flight Lieutenant D. D. W. Nabarro

Another N.C.O. Sergeant, later Flight Lieutenant, D. D. W. Nabarro, D.C.M., R.A.F., prepared for escape by improving his French, obtaining a leather jacket and a pair of civilian trousers, and some German money. He arranged to go with a Belgian.

At 6.30 a.m. on 25 November, 1941, Nabarro and his Belgian companion walked to the compound gate and informed the guard on duty there that they were going to clean the Commandant's office which was outside the main fence. The guard allowed them to pass through without any fuss and the escapers had then only a single strand of barbed wire to negotiate which presented no difficulty. They went to a village nearby and took a train. The Belgian spoke German and throughout the journey bought the railway tickets without exciting comment. They changed at Naumberg, then travelled via Apolda, Kassel, Koblenz to Garolstein where they were caught leaving the station on the morning of 30 November. It was Sunday, which is observed strictly in this part of Germany, and their unusual appearance attracted attention. The station police asked for their papers but the forged documents for Belgian workers which they presented did not satisfy them. They were taken to a cell underneath the police station where they met a French prisoner of war who also had escaped.

All three escaped the following morning by going to the washing place, knocking the guard unconscious, and climbing out through the window. They ran across country due south for some miles, then hid. At night they started off by full moon and walked west to Prum where they arrived on 2 December. They hid in a wood, forded a river that evening and walked all night crossing the frontier into Luxembourg, near Trois Vierges, without realising it. They went on next day to Houffalise where they stayed for the

180

ESCAPE
FROM
GERMANY

*Bad Sulza,*
*Kirchhain,*
*Muhlberg*

night at a cafe. This was the first place they had sought assistance and the people were extremely sympathetic. The Belgian knew this part of the country and they went by tram to Bastogne and by train to Idbramont, staying the night at the Belgian's home. Next day Nabarro and the Frenchman travelled by train via Namur and Charleroi to Erquelines on the Belgian–French frontier. They walked over the frontier to Jeumont without being stopped. The Belgian's father had given them six hundred Belgian francs which enabled them to reach Paris by train, travelling via St. Quentin.

Nabarro went to Rouen to try to find a personal friend but without success. However he stayed one night with the parents of a Frenchman with whom he had been friendly in the camp, next day returning to Paris and staying the night with the brother of another Frenchman in the camp. Then he travelled to Nevers to find the Frenchman who had accompanied him as far as Paris. This man told him how to get across the demarcation line between German-occupied and Unoccupied France, but he was caught by the Germans just south of Nevers when he was crossing back to Occupied France by mistake, after having crossed once in the other direction. He told them that he was trying to get into the Occupied Zone and they sent him back to Unoccupied France. He thought this might be a trap so walked down the road towards Sancoine thinking that the Germans were watching him. The result was that he was captured by the French and sent to Toulouse, thence to St. Hippolyte on 18 December, 1941, and transferred to Fort de la Revere near Monte Carlo in March, 1942.

After several months of planning an escape was organised. The party consisted of three officers, another sergeant and Nabarro. From their room there was a coal-chute down into the kitchen which was locked, barred and wired. A key had been made for the lock and at 10.15 p.m. on 23 August, 1942, they opened the barred grille and crawled through the barbed wire into the kitchen which they knew to be empty. They broke three bars across the kitchen window and let themselves down into the moat by a rope they had made. From there they went through a sewer which led them beyond the bounds of the fort, having to cut another bar at the furthest end. This took them until just before midnight. A concert had been arranged to cover the noise they made but the escape was discovered within ten minutes. They saw the lights go up in the fort and ran as fast as they could towards Monte Carlo where they had the address of a helper. Owing to the alarm they missed the guides who had been sent to meet them. They reached a place they thought to be Monte Carlo but decided to wait until morning in order to determine their exact whereabouts. At daybreak they found that they were in Cap d'Ail and one of the party, who had a good identity card, went to Monte Carlo to establish contact with their helpers. In the afternoon they were picked up by members of the organisation and taken to Monte Carlo where they remained until 28 August.

181

ESCAPE
FROM
GERMANY

*Bad Sulza,*
*Kirchhain,*
*Muhlberg*

On that day they were taken to an address in Marseilles where they stayed until 19 September when they were taken to Perpignan and thence to Canep Plage. On the night of 20 September they were embarked on a ship from which they were transferred to a warship and taken to Gibraltar arriving on the afternoon of 24 September. Shortly afterwards they were returned to the United Kingdom.

The next escape from the camp was made on 21 January, 1942, by an N.C.O. who walked through the main gates disguised as a Belgian prisoner who, with five others, worked in the German camp. Once inside the German camp the escaper left the Belgians and went to a lavatory where he discarded his Belgian uniform. Under the uniform he had been wearing civilian clothes bought from a French prisoner. He had no identity papers, maps nor compass but was in possession of a quantity of Reichsmarks. A few minutes later he left the lavatory dressed as a civilian worker and went to a watermill close to the outer fence and pretended to carry out an inspection underneath it. This enabled him to get outside the fence about 9 a.m. and subsequently to walk away without arousing suspicion. He walked to Apolda and travelled as a fare-paying passenger to Erfurt, Kassel, Koblenz, Cologne and Werwitz.

He walked throughout that night and next day with the intention of reaching the German–Belgian frontier near Stavelot. On the evening of 23 January he hid in a wood as he had lost his bearings; next morning he resumed walking and arrived at Monschau, then realising that he had been walking in the wrong direction, checked his position by means of a map in the railway station. Shortly afterwards he bought a ticket and travelled by train to Werwitz, arriving about 8.30 a.m. He walked across the country, which was about two feet deep in snow, and because he was suffering from snow blindness and exhaustion, wandered around for the whole of that day and the following night. His next clear recollection is of asking at Weisnes railway station for a ticket to Brussels about 4 a.m. on 25 January. Realising what he was doing he rushed out of the railway station into the woods where he remained for the remainder of the night. He walked across country in daylight, resting in a wood until next morning, then continued to the German–Dutch frontier near Bernister. About 11 p.m. while watching a German frontier guard in bright moonlight he was fired upon by another guard and arrested a few moments later. He was not wounded but his feet were frost-bitten. He was not returned to Bad Sulza but was transferred to Warburg.

### Warrant Officer J. A. McCairns

Warrant Officer J. A. McCairns, D.F.C., M.M., R.A.F., escaped from the camp on the morning following the escape which has just been related. His preparations consisted of converting Royal Air Force clothing into

ESCAPE
FROM
GERMANY

*Bad Sulza,
Kirchhain,
Muhlberg*

civilian clothes and obtaining a civilian tie and cap. On 21 January, 1942, he took his equipment into the Belgian barracks and he and a Belgian who was to accompany him made their preparations in the barber's shop. A Frenchman acted as his coach and told him the route to follow and made him memorise it. After "lights out" the preparations were continued by candlelight until 3 a.m., then they rested.

The barrack doors were unlocked by the Germans about 6 a.m. and twenty minutes later McCairns and his Belgian companion walked out. Over his other clothes the British prisoner wore a Belgian greatcoat, khaki trousers and a balaclava helmet. As they passed the sentry on the gate they indicated that they were going to do cleaning. It was a cold morning and the sentry was not inquisitive. They entered the German administrative office outside the entrance of the camp, passed through it and up to the single-strand wire fence. McCairns removed the Belgian greatcoat, leaving it for another Belgian to collect, and a few moments later he and his companion climbed the fence.

They walked through Bad Sulza to Apolda which they reached about 8.30 a.m., having covered about seven miles in ninety minutes. They entered the station singly and bought tickets for Kassel. Although they travelled in the same carriage they avoided contact and arrived at their destination about 2.30 p.m. McCairns lost sight of his companion and later in the day travelled by train to Koblenz, arriving about 9.30 p.m. He spent that night on the outskirts of the town, returning next morning, when he saw his Belgian companion at the railway station. They talked for a few seconds and McCairns confirmed that he should take a ticket for Mainz. He travelled to Garolstein and St. Vith but jumped off the train before arriving at the latter as he had been advised that there was a special examination of identity papers there. There was a heavy snow-storm at the time and he reached a road, but finding progress impossible returned to the railway and walked on the sleepers. After a time the sleepers became invisible but he plodded on, eventually reaching a roughly-built shelter in a field where he rested until next morning.

From this point he continued by road and lost sight of the railway, finally reaching Weismes, whence he travelled to Malmedy by train. It was then about noon. He spent the next eight hours on the outskirts of the town sitting in a hollow in the snow beside some allotments where he was screened by a hedge. That evening he resumed walking and early next morning crossed the German–Belgian frontier, walking all night across fields through snow about a foot deep. At the time he was unaware that he had crossed the frontier but he had reached a church with a notice-board and upon striking a match saw a notice in French. He rested in a shed near the church until just after 7 a.m. when he approached a man and told him who he was, giving him a note which his fellow escaper from the camp had

written for him. He discovered that this church was just three hundred
yards inside Belgium. The Belgian took him into a house, dried his clothes,
fed him and gave him directions for the next stage of his journey.

183

ESCAPE
FROM
GERMANY

*Bad Sulza,*
*Kirchhain,*
*Muhlberg*

He left the farm about 9 a.m. and walked to Francorchamps where he
had an address supplied by his fellow escaper. Eventually he discovered
that he was in the hands of one of the underground organisations which
had helped so many Allied airmen to reach England and he stayed at various addresses in Belgium and France until he was eventually taken across
the frontier into Spain, and so to Gibraltar and the United Kingdom.

The Air Force N.C.O.s were transferred from Bad Sulza to the Centre
Compound at Sagan in May, 1942.

## Stalag III E, Kirchhain

In July, 1941, Stalag III E, a small camp formerly used for French prisoners
of war, was brought into use for Air Force N.C.O.s. It lay about one mile
north of the railway junction of Dobrilugk-Kirchhain where the main
lines from Berlin to Dresden and Halle to Cottsbus cross. The country was
fairly flat and wooded but being close to a river the lower part of the compound became flooded after heavy rain. The camp consisted of four brick
bungalows surrounded by a single barbed wire fence, the supporting
struts of which were sawn through at the base for two-thirds of their
thickness. The prisoners were forbidden to touch the fence and a warning
wire ran round the inside of the fence about three feet away from it. The
bungalows and a house which were used as the German Headquarters had
been a youth hostel and rifle club before the war. There was a rifle range
behind the German Headquarters outside the western end of the compound. The camp was opened in July, 1941, with a batch of about fifty
N.C.O.s who were transferred there from Dulag Luft. At intervals during
the following two months further batches of new prisoners arrived, and
the final strength was about one hundred and ninety men. The camp was
run by the German Army.

The first attempt at escape was made in early October, 1941, when a
number of prisoners discovered that if they made a hole through the west
wall of No. 4 barrack, which was made of cement blocks, it would lead into
the rifle range. Work was at once begun scraping away the mortar between
the blocks with an iron spike and during the final stages, on a sunny Saturday afternoon, community singing in the open air was organised by the
prisoners and the German administrative staff were invited to attend. The
invitation was accepted and the German Security Officer and a number of
the German N.C.O.s listened to the singing which ended only when a signal was received that the work on the hole had been completed.

About 10 o'clock that evening the loosened blocks were pushed out
into the rifle range and twelve of the forty occupants of No. 4 barrack

184

ESCAPE
FROM
GERMANY

*Bad Sulza,*
*Kirchhain,*
*Muhlberg*

crawled through. After, crawling along the rifle range to the southern end they scattered in various directions. The escapers had only a small quantity of bread because Red Cross food parcels had not yet arrived and the German rations were extremely meagre. Few had maps or compasses and none had any form of disguise. The Germans discovered the escape about three hours after the wall had been breached, when one of the escapers was caught walking through a nearby village whistling an English song. All the others were caught within five days.

The morning after the escape fifty or sixty guards were marched into the compound and drawn up in line before the barracks. All the prisoners were made to parade in front of them and the Germans were ordered to load their rifles and to place a round in the breech. After this had been done several sacks full of wooden clogs were carried into the compound and the prisoners were ordered to take off their boots and put on these clogs.

The prisoners were then formed up in single file and guards were posted at intervals of twenty paces around the field at the northern end of the compound. An officer with a pistol in his hand stood in the centre and the prisoners were ordered to march round the field in single file. The officer shouted in German that the first prisoner should march faster. This he was unable to do both because of the clogs and the effects of several weeks of semi-starvation. Thereupon one of the guards gripped him by the shoulders and forced him to walk faster by treading on his heels. The prisoner kicked off the clogs and attempted to walk in his bare feet, but the officer forced him to put the clogs on again. The marching was continued for two and three-quarter hours. Several prisoners who fainted were forced to continue to march supported on either side by other prisoners. Feeling ran high and the Germans began to threaten the men with rifle butts. Some of the more high spirited prisoners contemplated overpowering the guards but were deterred by seeing a machine-gun, which covered the field, mounted on the steps of the German Headquarters outside the compound.

While this march was in progress all the barracks were searched by the remainder of the guards. Some clothing was confiscated and bread, which some of the prisoners had saved, was strewn about the floors of the barracks. When the march was over the prisoners were herded into their respective barracks and were kept locked up for the next ten days. On the morning following this march one or two prisoners were late on parade. As a punishment all the occupants of their barrack were made to march round the field for one hour under the same conditions as before.

The construction of a tunnel had been suggested on a number of occasions, but because of the distance involved and the limited number of places from which a tunnel could be begun, the Committee decided that any attempt would need to be highly organised, employing almost every man in the camp. In December, 1941, a site under the floor of No. 2 barrack

which was raised about three feet above ground level and supported by
concrete pillars, was selected. There was a trap-door in the floor of which
the Germans appeared to be unaware. The tunnel was to run in an easterly
direction.

185

ESCAPE
FROM
GERMANY

*Bad Sulza,*
*Kirchhain,*
*Muhlberg*

The Germans had chiselled a number of peepholes through the outer
walls of the barracks below floor level through which they poked torches
to examine the ground underneath; but these inspections could not be
thorough because the line of vision was broken by the pillars supporting
the floor, and they were carried out only at irregular intervals. It was
decided to disperse the sand from the tunnel under the floor in such a way
that it could not be seen through the peepholes.

The Committee learned that two men, one British and the other Canadian, had mining experience and they were asked to undertake the design
and construction of the tunnel. In early January, 1942, work was begun by
sinking a vertical shaft about four feet square to a depth of six feet at a
point under the floor against the east wall; the shaft was shored. After the
shaft was completed the tunnel was started from just under the founda
tions of the barrack wall. Shoring was done with bed boards and the engineers worked by means of candles made with fats which the prisoners
saved from their rations. After the tunnel had gone about ten yards the air
became so foul that the candles would not stay alight. Air-holes had therefore to be bored through the roof of the tunnel and when work was finished each day a stone or brickbat was kicked into position to cover the
holes on the surface. These air-holes also served to keep the tunnel in the
right direction.

In early March, 1942, it was learned from one of the Germans that an
extensive search of the camp was to take place. The top of the vertical shaft
was covered with boards on which was laid a thick layer of sand and all
work ceased for a period of about ten days. In the interval the expected
search was carried out. It was very thorough and all hoards of chocolate,
dried fruits and other food which were discovered were confiscated, but
although an inspection under the floor of No. 2 barrack was made with
the aid of torches poked through the peepholes, the dispersal of the sand
was not noticed. The search coincided with the visit of an Inspecting General. All the prisoners were confined to barracks during his visit and while
he was walking across the compound with the Commandant he stopped
beside one of the bricks covering an air-hole of the tunnel. He was a restless man and it seemed certain that he would kick the brick, thus uncover-
ing the hole and leading to the discovery of the tunnel. He walked away,
however, to the relief of the anxious prisoners watching from the barrack-
room windows.

After the excitement following the search had subsided work was
resumed on the tunnel and continued at a steady rate until 1 May when it

186

ESCAPE
FROM
GERMANY

*Bad Sulza,
Kirchhain,
Muhlberg*

was learned from one of the Germans that the camp was to be evacuated within a week. At this time the tunnel was only half-completed. Tremendous efforts were made to complete it, but on 8 May the first hundred prisoners were transferred to the Centre Compound at Sagan, including four of the tunnel engineers and a member of the Escape Committee. At this time the tunnel was about twenty yards short of the perimeter fence. The final evacuation was scheduled for 12 May. Another "face worker" was recruited and he and the remaining two worked every possible moment of every day, while nearly every man remaining in the camp was called upon to form the human chain required to remove the sand from the tunnel face.

On the evening of 11 May the bottom of one of the poles supporting the perimeter fence was reached, but final stages were particularly difficult because the sentry patrolling the fence appeared to be suspicious, and work had to cease while he was within possible hearing distance. After the evening parade all those who wished to use the tunnel moved into No. 2 barrack. It was decided by a majority vote that the principal "face workers" should go first, followed by the Chief of the Escape Committee and his colleagues; the remaining places were decided by ballot.

Soon after dark the tunnel broke surface just outside the fence and the first two men crawled beyond the area illuminated by the boundary lights. There they lay down, watching the sentries who patrolled inside the compound after dark when the barracks were locked, and at a suitable moment they whispered to the next man that the way was clear. Then they crawled away and the third man crawled out and took their place. This procedure continued until fifty-two men had crawled clear, the last just as dawn was breaking. One man had a most interesting experience. As he lay in the tunnel with his head just above the ground level waiting for his signal, one of the sentries patrolling inside the compound peered in his direction. The escaper remained perfectly still and after a few seconds the sentry stooped down and lifted a small pebble which he threw at the escaper striking him on the head. Still the escaper did not move and the sentry shrugged his shoulders and continued his patrol.

About 5 a.m. the Germans entered the barracks to rouse the prisoners for departure. They asked for the Camp Leader, who also was the Head of the Escape Committee, but the prisoners said that they did not know where he was and in order to delay discovery refused to get out of bed. Eventually they were made to rise and the Germans at once realised that there were very few prisoners present. For an hour a thorough search of the camp was made but it was not until after 6 a.m., when the sentries took up their patrol outside the fence that the tunnel mouth was discovered; still they could not find the entrance and in the end a German entered the tunnel through the mouth and eventually reached the trap-door in the floor of No. 2 barrack.

187

ESCAPE
FROM
GERMANY

*Bad Sulza,
Kirchhain,
Muhlberg*

Meanwhile a search for the escaped men was organised within a radius of nearly a hundred miles. Troops, aircraft, Hitler Youth and Home Guard were employed and photographs and descriptions of all the prisoners were published in the Police Gazette; it is believed that the details of the escape were broadcast over the radio. Later officials arrived from Berlin to measure and photograph the tunnel. It was two hundred and twenty-seven feet in length, shored throughout with timber. The officials were impressed.

Some of the escapers were recaptured after a few hours and all were caught within ten days. Two Canadians who had travelled together were recaptured near Dresden; they had been sleeping in a wood near a railway siding and had removed their boots. They were awakened by a policeman who was holding a pistol and they stood up with their hands raised above their heads. One of them, Sgt. H. P. Calvert, R.A.F., who spoke only a few words of German, asked for permission to put on his boots. The policeman appeared not to understand and Calvert dropped one hand to point to his feet; the policeman shot him dead.

The remainder of those who had escaped were returned to the camp, and on 19 May all were transferred to the Centre Compound at Sagan.

### Stalag IVB, Muhlberg

Stalag IVB was situated on an open plain about two miles from Muhlberg on the east bank of the river Elbe. It was about forty miles north-east of Leipzig and a similar distance from Dresden. Opened in the summer of 1941, it was used as an army transit camp and a few months later housed one thousand five hundred prisoners. The majority of these were French, with a number of Belgians, Serbs and Russians.

In August, 1943, the first Air Force prisoners, seventy-four British N.C.O.s, were sent there from Dulag Luft and housed in a separate compound. A few days later they were joined by a Canadian Warrant Officer who had been transferred from Barth; he acted as the Compound Leader from then onwards, subsequently being appointed Camp Leader for the whole camp. With the fall of Italy, there was a large influx of British and American prisoners from that country including one hundred Air Force N.C.O.s and more than a thousand British airborne troops. The Germans regarded the latter as being in the same category as aircrew, and put them in the Air Force Compound. All soldiers below the rank of sergeant were at once transferred to working parties in subsidiary camps in the area, but airmen and airborne troops were confined to camp. From the time the Air Force Compound was opened until January, 1944, batches of new prisoners frequently arrived from Dulag Luft, the numbers being kept fairly constant at one thousand five hundred until the end of the war.

From the point of view of escape conditions for the Air Force were very

ESCAPE
FROM
GERMANY

*Bad Sulza,*
*Kirchhain,*
*Muhlberg*

like those at Lamsdorf; some airmen exchanged identities with Army privates and joined working parties, others managed to leave the main camp in the guise of French, Belgian, Serbian or Russian Army prisoners, who were not well guarded. Several partly successful escapes were made but only two men reached the United Kingdom.

### Flying Officer J. Branford and Sergeant J. L. N. Warren

On 30 April, 1944, Warrant Officer, later Flying Officer, J. Branford, M.B.E., R.A.F., and Sergeant J. L. N. Warren, B.E.M., R.C.A.F., were able to leave the main camp with the aid of French prisoners, posing as members of a fatigue party collecting coffee from the German canteen. Instead of returning to the camp they joined a football team of French prisoners which, accompanied by one aged guard, walked into Muhlberg to play against a team of French civilian workers. After the match the two escapers accompanied this second team to their encampment where they were given food. That night they made their way to a cemetery where two other escapers from the camp, a British paratrooper and an American airman, were hiding in the loft of a small building. The two soldiers had drawn the ladder up into the loft and as Branford and Warren failed to attract their attention they were forced to spend the night in a tool shed.

Early next morning they went into a nearby wood where they were found by the cemetery keeper, a Frenchman. He took them back to the tool shed and later in the day they joined the others in the loft. That evening two French escapers from the camp arrived. For the next three days the six men stayed in the loft, being supplied with food and additional equipment by two Frenchmen from the camp. A message was then received from the camp, stating that it was expected that the Germans would search the cemetery later that day and advising them to clear away all traces of their stay and leave immediately. That night they split into two parties and left the cemetery; Branford and Warren stayed together.

They walked across country and reached the railway near Haida, following it until they arrived on the outskirts of Elsterwerda where they made contact with a Frenchman whom they had heard about before leaving the camp. They remained in the woods in the vicinity for several days being cared for by their helper. During this time the four others who had been in the loft joined them. Nightly visits were made to the nearby railway marshalling yard in the hope of boarding a goods train going to Switzerland, but as they were running short of food this plan had to be abandoned and on the night of 9 May they boarded a train for Apeldoorn. The six escapers were locked in a goods wagon which was sealed by their French helper.

Three nights later the train crossed the Dutch frontier and was searched by Germans at Oldenzaal. But the sealed wagon was not touched, perhaps because of an air raid at the time. The train arrived at Hengelo the following day and the six men left the wagon, splitting into two parties as before. Branford and Warren called at a house and asked for help and in due course were taken in hand by the Dutch Underground Movement. Branford reached the Allied lines in September, 1944. Warren was recaptured by the Germans towards the end of August. He was in the hands of the Gestapo for many weeks and during this time met the American who had been recaptured in another part of Holland. While being taken back to Germany by train in December, Warren and a number of other Air Force prisoners escaped from the train before it left Holland by climbing through the carriage window. The German guards opened fire and at least one of the escapers was wounded. Warren, however, evaded capture and made contact again with members of the Dutch Underground Movement. He stayed at various addresses until his hiding place was over-run by the Allied forces on 16 April, 1945.

189

ESCAPE
FROM
GERMANY

*Oflag IVC,*
*Colditz*

### Stalag Luft VII, Bankau

This camp was situated near Kreuzburg in Silesia, about fifty miles east of Breslau. The first party of Air Force N.C.O.s arrived there in June, 1944, from Dulag Luft and were accommodated in small temporary wooden huts. Soon afterwards they were joined by a party of N C O s, formerly prisoners in Italian camps, who had been housed for some months at Stalag VIIA, Moosburg. Further parties of new prisoners arrived from Dulag Luft until January, 1945, when the number was over a thousand. As the war was so nearly over attempts at escape were few.

Some sporadic tunnelling was done, but without success. All the prisoners were evacuated to Stalag IIIA, Luckenwalde, on 19 January, 1945.


## CHAPTER 18 · OFLAG IVC, COLDITZ

There was one prison camp in Germany which differed from all others, and that was the officers' camp at Colditz. It was the escapers' gaol. To Colditz were sent not only officers of all three Services but officers of all allied nationalities, their common distinction being that they had persistently tried to escape or otherwise to undermine camp discipline. At Colditz they were regarded by the Germans as safe.

Colditz was a castle which had been built towards the end of the sixteenth century and had been used as a lunatic asylum since 1829. Like Spangenberg, it stood on top of a conical hill on the outskirts of a town to which it had given its name, about twenty-five miles south-east of Leipzig. The castle was four storeys high and contained two courtyards, one of which was occupied by the German Army officers and guards, the other by the prisoners. In the German courtyard were two main gates, one leading

to the town and the other into the castle park; the only gate from the prisoners' quarters led through an archway to the German courtyard and was
flanked by a guard room. A dry moat with a low outer wall surrounded the
castle and beyond this wall there was an almost perpendicular drop of
about thirty feet, then a ledge and a further drop of about twenty feet to
terraced gardens below. On the ledge stood a barbed wire fence about
eight feet high; the upper part of the terraced gardens was covered with
barbed wire entanglements and a second eight-foot barbed wire fence surrounded the bottom. There were eighteen sentry towers round the dry
moat, each fitted with a machine-gun and searchlight. Guards patrolled
the moat between the towers and two sentries were always on duty in the
prisoners' courtyard. Strong arc lamps lit up the greater part of the outer
walls of the castle during the night and the roofs of the prisoners' quarters
were covered thickly with barbed wire entanglements. The prisoners were
counted four times a day.

Within this stronghold lived some four hundred officers for the greater
part of the war. The first batch of British officers arrived in November,
1940, and within a short time their numbers had increased to seventy,
thirty belonging to the Army and the remainder about equally to the Navy
and Air Force. There were about twenty Army orderlies. This strength
remained more or less constant until June, 1943, when a further batch of
sixty-five Army officers arrived; the officers of other nationalities, except
those serving with the British forces, and a small de Gaullist faction, were
removed. During the next two years the only additions were a few British,
American, French and Polish officers, nearly all of whom had been connected with resistance movements in German-occupied countries.
Finally, in March, 1945, about twelve hundred French officers arrived from
a camp east of the Elbe.

In spite of its defences more persistent and skilful attempts at escape
were made at Colditz than at any other camp. For the first four years of the
war there was no prisoner there who did not spend the greater part of each
day performing some task connected with an escape plan. In general each
nationality worked as a group, but liaison was excellent and each group
helped the other. The British alone made more than sixty separate
attempts, three of which were successful.

Although the castle was built of stone on a foundation of rock, more
than thirty tunnels were begun; a brief description of two of them will
show the extraordinary ingenuity and tenacity required. The first major
tunnel was started in January, 1941. It took four months to build and ran
from the cellar under the canteen to the outer wall of the castle. The distance was only fifteen yards but it was through practically solid stone, a hole
having to be cut through the wall of the cellar and through the stone wall
of the castle. The stoutest implement used by the tunnellers was a table

191

ESCAPE
FROM
GERMANY

*Oflag IVC,
Colditz*

knife. The scheme involved a great deal of work which could be done only at night because the German Canteen staff were in the canteen during the day. Access to the cellar was through two locked doors for which master keys had been made. The tunnellers were locked into the cellar at night and released before morning by another prisoner. An attempt to escape through this tunnel was made by nine officers on 30 May, 1941. A German guard had been bribed to signal when it would be safe for them to emerge but he informed his superiors and all were caught as they left the tunnel.

In January, 1942, the Germans discovered a tunnel which had taken several months of dangerous and strenuous work to construct. The scheme was planned and worked by three officers assisted by a dozen others. The entrance was a hole, covered by a suitable trap-door, in the wall of a dormitory on the third floor of the castle which gave access to a hollow flying buttress. Ground level was reached by means of a rope ladder. A tunnel was dug from inside the base of the flying-buttress to a cellar under the building, then from the opposite wall of the cellar under the foundations. It had reached a point under the dry moat when it was discovered by the Germans, probably by the sound detector system which they had installed.

### Flight Lieutenant H. N. Fowler

On three occasions attempts were made by Army officers to walk through the gate leading from the prisoners' courtyard wearing some form of disguise, but all failed. In one instance after the attempt had been discovered and the alarm given, one of the guards who arrived on the scene shot one of the prisoners about two inches wide of the heart at point-blank range; fortunately he recovered. In October, 1942, however, a brilliant escape in disguise was achieved by six officers, two of whom, Flight Lieutenant H. N. Fowler, M.C., R.A.F., and a Dutch Naval Officer, reached England.

The German staff sergeant had an office within the building which housed the prisoners' sick quarters. It was decided to start a tunnel from this office as it was considered a most unlikely place for the Germans to search. The office had a lock of the cruciform type and was also padlocked on the outside, but suitable keys were made. Three British and three Dutch officers were engaged in the scheme and to build the tunnel one of them was locked in the office each night and let out in the morning after camouflaging the tunnel entrance. The tunnel ran to a clothing store which was outside the castle proper, but within the camp defences and the ring of sentries.

It was quite common for orderlies accompanied by German guards to be seen emerging from the clothing store with bundles of clothing. The six escapers were to pretend that they were such a party and for this purpose four were to dress as Polish orderlies, one as a German officer and one as a German N.C.O. The two German uniforms had to be perfect, as the party had to pass within one yard of a sentry in daylight. Besides uniforms the prisoners also made two boxes which looked like clothes chests in which to carry their civilian clothing. These were collapsible so that they could be pushed through the tunnel.

On 8 October all their preparations had been completed and after they had been counted at 8 p.m. the six escapers and two assistants hid under beds in the sick quarters while the Germans counted the prisoners there. The count over, the Germans went out locking the door leading to the courtyard in accordance with their normal practice. The eight prisoners then entered the German office and removed the last few inches of plaster at the end of the tunnel and cleared the way into the clothing store. When the collapsible boxes and clothing had been carried into the store, the two assistants boarded up the tunnel entrance, locked the office door and hid in the sick quarters until the outer door was unlocked next morning.

Once in the clothing store the six escapers plastered up the hole they had made and camouflaged it, then waited until morning. They intended to leave the store after 7 a.m. the hour at which the guards were relieved, so that the new sentry would not know whether or not anyone had gone to the store before he came on duty. The escapers donned their disguises as soon as it was daylight and about 7.30 a.m. the Dutchman, who was disguised as the German N.C.O., unlocked the door of the store from the inside and the party emerged in full view of the sentry who was standing near. He re-locked the door and the party passed through the first gate, the sentry saluting the bogus German officer, who was also a Dutchman. Two more sentries were passed and the second gate was negotiated in similar fashion. At the final gate the lock expert, the "German" N.C.O., discovered that he had not a key which fitted the lock. The six escapers were just about to drop all pretence and climb over it when a German guard arrived with a key and apologised for not being there before.

This gate was some distance from the castle and as soon as they were out of sight of the sentry who had unwittingly liberated them they headed for the woods. There they destroyed the German and Polish uniforms and donned their camp-made civilian clothing. Fowler's outfit consisted of a converted Naval jacket, R.A.F. trousers and a workman's peaked cap made from a R.A.F. officer's dress cap; he carried a small attache case containing shaving kit and tooth-brush. All the escapers had forged identity papers, Fowler's stating that he was a Belgian workman who was on fourteen days' leave with permission to travel on the railway. As an extra precaution he carried a document which stated that he had been granted permission to visit friends in the Swiss frontier zone; this he did not intend to show unless compelled by circumstances. His companion, the Dutch lock expert, had a genuine Dutch passport with a forged visa for the Swiss frontier area.

Soon after they reached the wood they split into three couples, each

1. *Above*: A Wellington of No. 301 (Polish) Squadron shot down off the German coast. The crew survived and were taken prisoner.
2. *Left*: An injured Flight Lieutenant Frank Day is helped ashore by Italian soldiers after spending two days in a dinghy off Crete. He was sent to Stalag Luft III.
3. *Below*: Officers at Dulag Luft in the summer of 1941. Aidan Crawley is standing on the extreme left.

F32 Stalag Luft 1

4. *Top*: Stalag Luft I, Barth
5. *Above*: The ice hockey match between Officers and SNCOs at Stalag Luft I in February 1942.
6. *Left*: Christmas 1942 at Colditz Castle.
7. *Right*: The prisoners' courtyard at Oflag IVC, Colditz Castle.

8. *Above*: General view of huts and compound at Stalag Luft III, Sagan.
9. *Below*: Sports Day at Stalag Luft III, August 1943.

10. *Right*: Prisoners at Stalag Luft III producing the regular news sheet.

11. *Above left*: Red Cross boxes provide material for the theatre set designers and workers.

12. *Above*: A theatre production in progress at Stalag Luft III.

13. *Left*: The prisoners' gardens at Stalag Luft III.

14. *Below*: Prisoners cooking in their hut at Stalag VIIIB, Lamsdorf.

**15.** *Above*: A plan of
the North Compound at
Stalag Luft III with the
direction of the four
tunnels marked.

**16.** *Below*: The
poignant entry in Frank
Day's YMCA diary noting
the names of his 50

colleagues murdered
after the Great Escape
from Stalag Luft III,
March 1944.

# To all Prisoners of War!

## The escape from prison camps is no longer a sport!

Germany has always kept to the Hague Convention and only punished recaptured prisoners of war with minor disciplinary punishment. Germany will still maintain these principles of international law.

But England has besides fighting at the front in an honest manner instituted an illegal warfare in non combat zones in the form of gangster commandos, terror bandits and sabotage troops even up to the frontiers of Germany.

They say in a captured secret and confidential English military pamphlet,

## THE HANDBOOK OF MODERN IRREGULAR WARFARE:

". . . the days when we could practise the rules of sportsmanship are over. For the time being, every soldier must be a potential gangster and must be prepared to adopt their methods whenever necessary."

"The sphere of operations should always include the enemy's own country, any occupied territory, and in certain circumstances, such neutral countries as he is using as a source of supply."

## England has with these instructions opened up a non military form of gangster war!

Germany is determined to safeguard her homeland, and especially her war industry and provisional centres for the fighting fronts. Therefore it has become necessary to create strictly forbidden zones, called death zones, in which all unauthorised trespassers will be immediately shot on sight.

Escaping prisoners of war, entering such death zones, will certainly lose their lives. They are therefore in constant danger of being mistaken for enemy agents or sabotage groups.

Urgent warning is given against making future escapes!

In plain English: Stay in the camp where you will be safe! Breaking out of it is now a damned dangerous act.

The chances of preserving your life are almost nil!

All police and military guards have been given the most strict orders to shoot on sight all suspected persons.

## Escaping from prison camps has ceased to be a sport!

**17.** *Above*: A warning to the prisoners posted by the Germans. (ADM 1/15107)
**18.** *Left*: A prisoner on the Long March captures the ordeal.

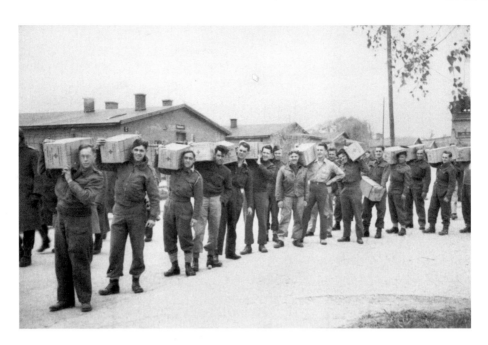

**19.** *Above*: Prisoners liberated at Stalag 7A, Moosburg collect Red Cross food parcels.

**20.** *Below*: Liberated allied POWs wait at a Belgian airfield to board Short Stirlings of No. 299 Squadron for repatriation.

consisting of one Englishman and one Dutchman, and started off in different directions. One pair was heading for Danzig, the second via Ulm to Switzerland, and the third, which included Fowler, via Stuttgart to Switzerland. It was essential that they should get well away from the camp and reach a railway station before the alarm was given, and to help them the prisoners in the camp behaved in a particularly rowdy manner at the 8.30 a.m. parade so that the Germans postponed it for an hour, as was their habit in such circumstances.

193

ESCAPE
FROM
GERMANY

*Oflag IVC,*
*Colditz*

Fowler and his companion walked hard for about twenty miles along the road through Rocklitz and reached Penig railway station about 4 p.m. On the way they had stopped for a drink at two inns and as they aroused no suspicion their self-confidence was increased considerably. From Penig they travelled by train as normal passengers via Zwickau to Plauen. In the train they spoke only when necessary and then in German. They arrived at Plauen at 9 p.m. and spent five hours in the waiting room waiting for the next train to Stuttgart. When it did arrive it took them only to Hof and stopped. They were told that another train would arrive in half-an-hour but when finally it arrived it was six hours late and very overcrowded. They did not reach Stuttgart until 8.30 p.m.

By then both were extremely tired and as it was evident that they could not reach the frontier that night they decided to risk sleeping in a small hotel so as to be fresh for the twenty-mile walk which they expected next day. They selected a small hotel at Muhringen, in the south-east quarter of Stuttgart, and told their previously prepared stories to the proprietor. He appeared to be satisfied and did not ask to see their identity papers. He showed them a very poor room with no blankets on the beds which they accepted. Having satisfied themselves that there was an easy way out through the window should the necessity arise, they slept.

Next morning they left the hotel and bought a map of the Swiss frontier area in a shop, then travelled by train from Vaihingen to Tuttlingen. Once again, at Herrenberg, the train stopped and went no further so they spent all day in a nearby wood waiting for the next one. On arrival at Tuttlingen they decided to walk to the frontier as they believed that all the area ten miles north of it was patrolled and that travelling in this zone by train would be inadvisable. All the way from Tuttlingen to Helsingen they used only the by-roads. The only incident was at Ehringen where they were stopped by an S.S. policeman who examined their identity documents. He allowed them to proceed and it was apparent that the forged visa on the Dutchman's genuine passport had impressed him considerably.

They reached a certain wood between Helsingen and Singen by nightfall and waited until 11 p.m. before skirting around it and attempting to cross the frontier. Presently they discovered that they had not gone far enough and after some searching sighted the correct wood about half a mile to the east.

Upon reaching the southern end of it they waited and watched. The night was still and as they had been making a tremendous noise with their boots they removed them. Soon afterwards they saw a patrol car with its engine off coasting along the road they were watching. They were able to hear but not see the sentries on the road so they crossed over immediately after the patrol car had passed. A hundred yards further on they passed over the frontier and heading due south soon struck a fringe of trees which led them to a Swiss Customs House. They entered and declared their identities at 1.30 a.m. on 13 September. Both were repatriated to England. The four others who had participated in the escape were recaptured within twenty miles of Colditz.

Five attempts were made by individual officers to leave the camp by hiding in German vehicles. One was discovered while the van was being driven through the German courtyard; another who was hidden in a packing case, was detected at the local railway station because of the weight of the box; the other three succeeded in getting clear of the camp area. One was caught in Vienna after six days, and the second was free for ten days before being recaptured at Hanover; the fate of the third officer is unknown.

### Flight Lieutenant H. D. Wardle

The majority of schemes, apart from tunnels, were a combination of wall scaling and wire cutting; of twelve attempts of this type one was completely successful, all four members of the party reaching Switzerland. Lieutenant Commander W. L. Stephens, D.S.C., R.N.V.R., Major R. B. Littledale, D.S.O., K.R.R.C., Captain P. R. Reid, M.C., R.A.S.C., and Flight Lieutenant H. D. Wardle, M.C., R.A.F., escaped from the camp on the night of 14–15 October, 1942. The kitchen in which the prisoners' food was cooked had a window which overlooked a flat roof over a boiler house in the German courtyard. This window, which had iron bars fitted across the outside, was in full view of the windows of the German quarters and was within the view of a sentry for part of his beat; it was lit up at night by one of the floodlights. The plan of escape was to climb through the kitchen window on to the flat roof, then drop to the ground within the German courtyard while the sentry's back was turned and enter a carpenters' workshop by unlocking the door. It was hoped that a way out would be found on the other side of the workshop, and that by descending the three terraces of the old moat it would be possible to get on to a road leading out of the castle grounds. It was known that the road ran past the German married quarters and that there were iron gates at the end set in a high wall with barbed wire on top.

On the four nights before the escape the kitchen was entered through a

195

ESCAPE
FROM
GERMANY

*Oflag IVC,
Colditz*

window in the prisoners' courtyard while the attention of the two sentries on duty was distracted by other prisoners. The escapers cut the rivet heads of the transverse bars across the window overlooking the German court-yard. It was found that the rivets had been hot-sweated and the bars could only be loosened by a screw-press manufactured by the prisoners. This applied very strong pressure forcing the rivets out of the bars. This work had to be done very silently and without trace.

On the evening of 14 October the four escapers again entered the kitchen. Each carried an attaché case containing civilian clothes and shaving kit. Shortly after nine o'clock Reid and Wardle removed the loosened iron bars, climbed on to the flat roof and dropped to the ground, a distance of about ten feet. It had been arranged that the signal for them to proceed should be given by accordion music, but for some reason it never came and they waited for two hours in a convenient doorway. Finally they went ahead, crossed the sentry's beat while his back was towards them, and crept along the side of the German Headquarters building. At one point a German passed within a yard of Reid who was lying flat on the grass beside the path but he was not noticed.

At the end of the Headquarters building, near the carpenters' work-shop, they found a cellar in which they rested. Shortly afterwards Stephens and Littledale joined them. Although they had been provided with keys which should have unlocked the door of the workshop, this was found to be impossible. However a way was found through an extremely narrow flue running at ground level from the cellar to the outer side of the castle. Iron bars were fitted across the flue but one of these was loosened and all four got through in an hour. Three terraces, each about ten feet above the other, were next descended with the help of a sheet although the top ter-race was within a few yards of sleeping Germans, and the bottom one some ten yards from the dog kennels. Twice during the descent an Alsatian dog barked furiously but no action was taken by the Germans.

When all four had reached the lowest of the terraces they walked along the road between the German married quarters and then scaled the gate in the wall at the further end. At this point, as arranged previously, the party split; Reid and Wardle forming one pair and Stephens and Littledale the other. It was then about 4 a.m. on 15 October. Each pair travelled on foot and by train towards the same sector of the Swiss frontier, following dif-ferent routes.

Wardle and Reid walked to Penig which they reached during the after-noon of 16 October. They walked mainly by night and across country, hid-ing in the woods during the day. From Penig they travelled by train as fare-paying passengers passing through Zwickau, Munich, Rottwell, Augs-burg and Ulm to Tuttlingen where they arrived in the late afternoon of the following day. The journey was uneventful except for one examination of their identity papers on the express between Zwickau and Munich.

After leaving the station at Tuttlingen they walked south-west, slept in a wood from midnight until about 7 o'clock next morning, and then with the help of a map of the Swiss frontier and a compass, through Benningen and Helsingen into the hills near Singen. About 6 p.m. they began a reconnaissance in daylight to find a certain fork in the road, one prong of which led to the part of the frontier which they intended to cross. Unfortunately their arrival at this point coincided with the passing of a German cyclist patrol and it was necessary to continue walking towards Singen for the sake of appearances. At the main road junction they were stopped by a German sentry who demanded their papers and asked questions, but their explanations were satisfactory and they continued on their way. Out of sight of the sentry they broke off the road northwards and in a wide circle returned to the original point from which their reconnaissance had begun.

Knowing their position they then took a road through the woods. After crossing a railway they entered a wood in sight of a road and after careful scrutiny, for it was nearly dark, spotted the sentry post which was the landmark they had been seeking. The sentry post was about three hundred yards east of the edge of the wood and by placing themselves midway between they took a compass bearing of magnetic south which pointed to the left hand edge of dark low woods about one thousand yards across open fields. This was the exact spot they had decided upon before leaving Colditz.

The moon was behind cloud and visibility was restricted to about two hundred yards. They crossed the road quietly and ran in a crouching position across the fields for about five hundred yards. Knowing that they were then in Switzerland they continued at walking pace on the magnetic south bearing which took them straight to Ramsden across open country, and at about 8 p.m. they gave themselves up to the Swiss police. Stephens and Littledale arrived in the same village about thirty-six hours later. All four officers were repatriated to the United Kingdom.

In the previous month, September, 1942, an Air Force officer had escaped alone. As a security measure all British officers had been ordered to pack their surplus clothes in tea chests which the Red Cross had used for certain types of food. The chests were to be stored on the third floor of the German Headquarters building. This officer, wearing camp-made civilian clothes and in possession of forged identity documents and German money, had himself nailed up in one of these chests which was then removed to the store with the others. He had with him a long blanket rope and a quantity of food. That night he forced his way out of the box and lowered himself from the window of the store to the ground, a distance of sixty feet. He was in the German part of the castle and was able to leave without being seen.

197

ESCAPE
FROM
GERMANY

*Oflag IVC,*
*Colditz*

During the next ten days he travelled to Frankfurt-am-Oder on foot, by bicycle and by train. He was caught, but his interrogator, a German Army Sergeant, left the room for a few moments and he re-escaped through the window. He met some Poles in Frankfurt who hid him for a time and gave him food. Later he made his way to Danzig where he was arrested in the harbour area by Harbour Police. In due course he was returned to Colditz.

A rather similar method was adopted by two other British officers, one Army the other Air Force, in January, 1944. Their attempt was timed at dusk just before the perimeter lights were switched on. Both were dressed in civilian clothes and had false identity papers and German money. They carried one brief-case containing food and a change of socks. As silence was essential they wore socks over their shoes and in order to render themselves less visible had dark balaclava helmets covering their heads. Two of the bars on the outside of one of the windows in the outer castle wall had been cut and a sixty foot blanket rope had been fastened to a sturdy support within the room; to the other end were tied the brief-case and another, shorter, rope. The Army officer, who was to go first had a pair of wire cutters tied to his leg.

The success of the scheme depended upon perfect timing and a number of colleagues were stationed at vantage points on higher storeys to report on the movements of the sentries. Upon receipt of the signal that all was clear the bars across the window were bent and the first escaper was pushed out feet first. He clambered down the wall with the aid of the blanket rope followed quickly by the second man. After gaining the terrace about twenty-five feet below, they ran to the balustrade, threw the remainder of the rope over it and then clambered another twenty feet down into the terraced garden. There they lay flat against the base of the wall while their comrades hauled up the long rope. After a few moments they dashed across the strip of garden to the first wire fence and whilst the Army officer cut through this his companion watched the sentries. He saw that one of them was standing on the first terrace they had crossed and was looking up at the window they had climbed through a few moments previously.

At the sound of the first cut on the wire the German turned round and looked in their direction, then looked back at the window. He heard the second and third cuts but failed to locate the source of the noise. Another sentry near the fence appeared not to hear anything unusual and continued to pace his beat. The officer who had cut the fence crawled through the gap he had made, then fastened one end of the short rope and dropped over to the lower part of the terraced gardens. The second man followed through the gap and while trying to patch the hole he heard the German whose suspicions had been aroused shout "Hullo," whereupon he dropped down and joined his colleague.

198

ESCAPE
FROM
GERMANY

*Train
Jumping*

This part of the gardens was a steep slope covered in barbed wire entanglements and they made their way along the base of the wall as quickly and silently as they could. After covering about twenty yards and tearing their clothes, they came to the final fence through which they again cut and passed through to freedom., Two days later they were recaptured at Rheins, about twenty-five miles from the Dutch frontier, after an examination of their papers by the civil police.

The last attempt to escape from this camp was made on 25 September, 1944, by the Army officer who was shot in the chest during a previous attempt. On this occasion he tried to climb over the barbed wire fence surrounding the exercise ground in the castle park in daylight. One of the guards shot him and he died shortly afterwards. Soon after this, as in other camps in Germany, attempts to escape were abandoned.

## CHAPTER 19 · TRAIN JUMPING

As the reader will have gathered, most Air Force prisoners made several train journeys during their captivity. The Germans continually underestimated the number of Air Force prisoners they were likely to hold and no sooner had they segregated them at one camp than that camp overflowed and they had to disperse them again among the Army. For an airman to spend more than six months in one compound was the exception rather than the rule until the last two years of the war.

Train journeys were always an event. It was not only the change in scenery and surroundings which was exciting, but the fact that in a remote way a prisoner again felt himself a citizen of the world. He would pass through crowds which contained women and children, and perhaps stand next to some woman in a corridor; he would see refreshment rooms, catch a glimpse of streets and traffic and shop windows; occasionally he might march through a town. Even curtained windows, with the suggestion of bright wallpaper and warmth within, were exhilarating. But train journeys were also an opportunity for escape. In a train the first and greatest obstacle, barbed wire, had been left behind, and the mere fact that prisoners were on the move meant that the routine for guarding them had been broken and that some unexpected chance might occur.

The trains in which prisoners travelled varied from third class passenger coaches to cattle trucks many of which bore the familiar marks "Chevaux 8, Hommes 40," though in practice the Germans usually exceeded the forty men. Coach windows were nailed down and the vents in cattle trucks covered with wire. The doors were locked and were seldom opened for any purpose more often than once in six hours, and were sometimes kept shut for as long as two days and two nights. Normally the proportion of guards was one to every four prisoners and in passenger trains two guards sat in each compartment; in cattle trucks the prisoners were sometimes left alone. As the guards were liable to severe sentences should anyone escape they were often nervous and inclined to shoot on the slightest provocation.

199

ESCAPE
FROM
GERMANY

*Train
Jumping*

Nevertheless even under threat of court martial, guards were fallible. For some reason the nailing of carriage windows was nearly always primitive and there was seldom much difficulty in getting one open. Sometimes one or both guards would fall asleep so soundly that it was possible for a prisoner to drop out of the compartment in which they were sitting. More often it was possible to loosen the window of the lavatory during a number of visits, and after opening it noiselessly to drop out while the guard stood outside. Of course the number of occasions during a night when the train was going slowly enough for this to be safe was few and there was always the risk of a guard at another window on the train seeing something. However despite all precautions someone escaped on almost every journey made by passenger train.

One of the first of these was made on a journey from Dulag Luft to Barth in February, 1941. Four officers managed to open the carriage window and to jump off whilst the train was travelling at approximately thirty miles per hour in the neighbourhood of Prenzlau. One of them struck a signal-post and injured an already badly damaged knee. The four walked along the railway track for several hours then separated into two pairs. One pair was recaptured shortly afterwards and the other, by walking and travelling on goods trains, reached the northern outskirts of Berlin then began walking west by night. A few days later suffering from hunger, privation and extreme fatigue they were caught.

A most courageous attempt was made on the journey from Dulag Luft to Barth in October, 1941, when two officers, an Australian and a South African, found themselves in a compartment without a guard. They managed to open the window and choosing a moment when the train was slowing down, jumped out. However the train must still have been travelling at about thirty miles per hour because they landed heavily and were injured. Both lost consciousness but the Australian picked himself up after a few moments and made off. His companion, who had landed a short distance away, had broken his skull and lay with his neck across the line for approximately half an hour. Fortunately no other train passed and he was picked up by a German. Later an operation was performed on his skull and he was presented with a piece of bone as a souvenir. The Australian kept going for five days, at the end of which time he was in a third-class passenger train in France in a state of delirium due to hunger and cold. Afterwards he was told that he had proclaimed his identity so often and so loudly that it was impossible for the French not to hand him over to the Germans.

On the journey from Sagan to Heydekrug in June, 1943, an N.C.O. escaped by climbing through the lavatory window at Gniezno, twenty-five miles east of Posen, where it had stopped. He ran into the marshalling yard and hid in the brake-compartment of a goods train which was bound for Posen. During the next two days he travelled in the brake compartments of various other goods trains endeavouring to reach Danzig but he was caught by a farmer while walking across a field.

In March, 1944, the same N.C.O. escaped in a similar way while being transferred from Barth to Heydekrug, on this occasion leaving the train just as it was moving after having stopped near Konigsberg. He met some French prisoners near Konigsberg and asked for help which was given in the form of civilian clothes and false identity papers. Eight days later he travelled to Danzig and again received help from some Frenchmen. A week later he made his way into Danzig docks through a gap in the fence and while attempting to board a ship under cover of a cloud of steam was seen by the German guard. He managed to evade capture but was caught later when looking for another ship in the harbour.

The fact that when the German Army were handling prisoners they often made officer prisoners travel in cattle trucks, inclined the German Air Force to insist upon using passenger coaches. Sometimes, however, cattle trucks were preferable. For German troops they were equipped with benches and in winter with an oil stove, and under these conditions prisoners were comparatively comfortable. The benches made it impossible to cram more than thirty-five men into a wagon and by using the benches and the floor it was possible for most of the prisoners to lie at full length. Normally, however, the trucks were bare and frequently filthy, and on numerous occasions between forty and fifty prisoners were herded into each so that there was barely room for each man to sit on the floor. Sometimes the doors were kept locked for twenty-four or thirty-six hours at a time and men suffered not only from thirst and cramp but from the lack of sanitation. It would have been difficult to say whether hot or cold weather was worse, but prisoners who passed through the camps at Salonika, where more than half of them caught dysentery, and then travelled in mid-summer in cattle trucks to Germany will not readily forget the experience.

Nevertheless as already stated cattle trucks frequently offered better opportunities for escape than passenger coaches. Even when guards were present the noise and overcrowding were such that they had the utmost difficulty in seeing or hearing what went on. The usual method of escaping from a cattle truck was to saw through the floor-boards or through the end walls. It was difficult to carry out such an operation with a small hacksaw blade but many men carried these concealed in their clothing and providing that the journey lasted for longer than two hours the task could be accomplished. Sometimes table-knife saws had been smuggled through the searches and these were more effective. Once the hole had been made men could climb through and by hauling themselves along the chassis could sit on the buffers between trucks or on the axles ready to drop off when the train should go slowly.

201

ESCAPE
FROM
GERMANY

*Train
Jumping*

Six officers escaped from cattle trucks on the journey between Lubeck and Warburg in October, 1941. There were about thirty prisoners in the truck with three German guards who were stationed near the sliding doors. After a few hours, under cover of playing cards, one of them cut through two of the floor planks at the end of the wagon with a knife-saw making an opening large enough to climb through. The noise had been covered by the rattling of the train.

The work took two hours and at the end of that time the officer who had made the hole went through, clinging on to the chassis of the truck underneath the floor. His companions passed him his food and clothes then he moved on to the buffers between this wagon and the next. As he did so a shot rang out which amazed him as he could not understand how he could have been seen. However he did not waste time and dived on to the sloping railway embankment. In his hurry he did not stop to consider whether or not there was a fence at the bottom, but he was fortunate and went straight through a gap which may have been a gate. He got up and ran across the field and as he did so heard two more shots which caused him to trip and fall. Scrambling to his feet he ran a few more yards then fell into a stream. Picking himself up he ran on for about an hour until he was exhausted. As he discovered later, his panic was quite unnecessary as the guards were not firing at him but at two other prisoners who had attempted to escape from another part of the train at the same time.

He walked for two days and nights eventually being caught by a railway worker who took him to a village garrison which consisted of an N.C.O. and about six men. The N.C.O. was a little tin god, being treated with the utmost reverence by his men. The escaper was questioned and searched without incident until they came across a small microphone concealed in the seam of his greatcoat. He was asked what it was and when he refused to answer they began cutting his coat to discover for themselves. The escaper then produced it and thinking he might get some fun out of them said as he laid it down on the table "Eine kleine bombe." This disturbed the Germans and the N.C.O. picked it up carefully and touched one of the terminals. Immediately the prisoner ducked behind one of the other men and in a flash the room was deserted and he found himself standing rather foolishly looking at the little gadget on the table. Presently a hand came round the door with a gun in it, followed by a German face and a voice which gave him to understand that he was going to be taught a lesson. He was searched again in a rather different manner then taken to a cellar under a school where a man had recently been kept for some months without being allowed out for any purpose. It was filthy. Next day he was taken to the camp at Warburg.

### Squadron Leader R. Bushell

The others who were to follow this officer through the hole in the wagon floor realised that he had not been seen as he emerged and followed in a more leisurely fashion. Among these was Squadron Leader Bushell and a Czech officer. Once again Bushell had made the more careful plans and once again was successful except at the very last stage. He and his companion, having managed to conceal suitable clothing under their uniforms, travelled as civilians and went by train to the Czech frontier. They had forged papers and at the Czech border the Czech officer took control and they reached Prague successfully. They stayed there for some weeks whilst Czech Underground Movement tried to arrange their departure first into Italy then Yugoslavia. While these preparations were still under way the Gauleiter Heydrich was murdered and both Bushell and his companion were caught in the house to house search which followed.

The two other officers who escaped from that train reached Stettin where one of them boarded a ship. However it proved to be a prison ship and he and his companion were detained in it until they were returned to the camp.

There were other methods of escaping from cattle trucks. On 19 June, 1941, while being taken from Wolfsberg to Litzmanstadt five N.C.O.s escaped. The plan was made on the journey, two of the prisoners persuading some of their colleagues to crowd round the three German guards at a given signal. At dusk conditions were suitable, with woods near the railway track and the train travelling at about thirty miles an hour. While their companions in the wagon crowded round the guards two prisoners pressed the iron bar on the door on the other side of the wagon out of its socket with a penknife. The bar made a lot of noise as it swung down on the outside of the door and this attracted the attention of the guards, but the five escapers pulled open the door and jumped off within a few seconds.

Just as the last man was about to jump one of the guards raised his rifle when about two yards away from him, but the rifle was knocked up by two other N.C.O.s. The guard fired and the bullet went through the roof of the wagon. The five men had landed within about one hundred yards and were fired on by guards in the train which came to a standstill a few moments later. However they ran into the woods and hid successfully. For the next ten days they walked south-west and south towards Switzerland being guided by the stars at night, hiding in woods during the day. They lived on raw potatoes and as a result suffered from dysentery. At the end of this period they reached the Danube valley where they were able to steal chickens from the farmyards at night, cooking them in the woods. About

203

ESCAPE
FROM
GERMANY

*Train
Jumping*

29 June one of them decided to leave the rest as he felt that with dysentery and blistered feet he was holding them back. At that time they were observing an aerodrome near Regensburg. After doing so for a day they decided to cross the Danube to the aerodrome.

The remaining four found a canoe and on reaching what they thought was the opposite bank allowed the canoe to drift and then discovered that they were on an island. The main stream was too fast for them to swim so they swam back to the east bank and observed the aerodrome for another day, then walked from Regensburg at night to the aerodrome. They crawled past the sentries and reached a group of aircraft which were picketed near the hangars. A guard was patrolling the aircraft and using a torch freely. They discovered that the aircraft had engine and cock-pit covers and came to the conclusion that it would be impossible to remove these and to start the engines without immediate discovery so left the aerodrome. For the next two nights they walked south along the railway track trying without success to board goods trains. On 1 July they decided to split into two parties. One pair continued to walk south along the railway track at night and on two occasions burgled houses in order to obtain food. Early in the morning of 7 July one of this pair left his hiding place in the wood and approached a workman in a nearby quarry whom he asked for matches. Conversation ensued and the quarryman became suspicious but supplied the matches. About half an hour later a policeman accompanied by the quarryman came to their hiding place and arrested them. The other pair were also caught.

### Captain R. B. Palm

Although not made from a train, the story of the escape of Captain R. B. Palm, D.S.O., S.A.A.F., has a place here for it was essentially an escape in transit. In September, 1943, he and a large number of Air Force prisoners were transferred from Italian prison camps to Germany. En route they were lodged for a few days at Stalag VIIA near Moosburg, an army camp housing French and Russian prisoners.

A few days after his arrival Palm, who had made several attempts to escape in Italy, learned from a Frenchman that if he remained in the camp long enough it would be possible to get out. The idea was that he should join one of the Russian working parties in the guise of a Russian, but before the exchange could be effected the Germans warned the Air Force officers to prepare to move that afternoon. Palm therefore approached an American Air Force officer who was not interested in escaping at that time and he agreed to leave the camp in Palm's name. The Germans had no nominal roll and appeared to be concerned only about numbers. The Air Force officers, including the American who was impersonating Palm, were moved on 23 September.

204

ESCAPE
FROM
GERMANY

*Train
Jumping*

Owing to incessant rain and the shortage of German guards working parties were temporarily stopped, so Palm with a Greek officer serving with the British Forces who could speak excellent French, devised another scheme. They were to hang under a tractor drawn trailer which left the camp for the railway station to fetch parcels for the prisoners. The driver of the tractor, a prisoner, told them that the Germans made a point of looking underneath but that it was worth taking a chance.

On 29 September, 1943, the two officers hung under the trailer and left the camp successfully. On arrival at the station the trailer was drawn up close to some railway wagons and they dropped off, crawled underneath the wagons and walked away on the opposite side. By selling food to Frenchmen in the camp they had acquired two hundred Reichsmarks. After leaving the goods yard they went to a wood and hid until dark then walked in a northerly direction in order to skirt the prison camp, intending eventually to make their way to Munich having learned from Frenchmen in the camp that they would be likely to obtain assistance from Frenchmen there.

They met a German officer on a bicycle and the Greek aroused his suspicions by trying to hide behind a small bush. They tried to persuade the German that they were French workers employed at a nearby farm but he expressed his intention of escorting them to the camp in order to check their identities. They were discussing the point when two German soldiers appeared, obviously dressed for an evening out and much against their will these were ordered by the officer to escort the two prisoners back to the camp. They were trying to persuade the German soldiers to allow them to go when they were overtaken by another officer on a bicycle who was on his way to the camp. The two soldiers induced him to undertake the mission of escorting them. This officer was foolish enough to walk ahead of the prisoners leading his bicycle, remonstrating with them all the time about being out after the curfew limit for French workers. The prisoners kept saying "Yes, yes" and when passing a pond of muddy water Palm saw an opportunity and picking him up from behind pushed him and his bicycle into the pond. The two escapers ran away and the German fired several shots but none went near them.

They followed the Isar river, walking by night and hiding by day and skirting Freising reached Munich on 4 October. They had been told by Frenchmen at their camp to make for a certain café and ask for a certain Frenchman. As soon as they arrived there they met the man in question and he arranged for them to stay in a barracks for French workers. They were given work suits and placed on the work-roll.

It was arranged that they should go each night to the marshalling yard at Laime to ascertain whether any goods trains were leaving for France. Presently a Frenchman volunteered to put them into beer barrels which he

205

ESCAPE
FROM
GERMANY

*Stalag Luft
III, Sagan*

East Compound,
04/42–03/43

was loading into a goods train. On 23 October this was accomplished successfully and they left, each in an empty beer barrel, on a train for Strasbourg. When the barrels had been loaded into the wagon the door was sealed by the Germans but the train did not move for two days. During this time they had no food and only a little water. The two officers remained in the train until 3 a.m. on 27 October when the truck was shunted into the marshalling yard at Strasbourg and they climbed out.

Their helpers had told them to attempt to persuade one of the bargees at Vendenhaim, about ten miles north-west of Strasbourg, to take them on board a barge for France. They attempted this but no one would take the risk. The next night they began to walk along the canal, their route being Waltenheim, Saverne and through the canal tunnel east of Sarrebourg. While walking through the tunnel they had to cover approximately twenty-five miles in one night as they had been informed that it would be impossible to hide before reaching No. 3 lock.

Next night they continued via Hertzing to south of Rochineou where they reached a point about two miles from the frontier. They rested there for the following day then crossed the frontier during the night. They reached a village and learned from their map that they were in France. Presently they approached a farm east of Luneville where they were given food and shelter and told how to get in touch with a helper in Luneville. They did so and from then onwards their journey was arranged by the French Underground Movement. They were provided with identity cards and moved to Nancy, Paris, Rouffec and Pau. There they met Flight Lieutenant McSweyn and Palm travelled across the Pyrenees to Spain with his party. The Greek officer followed later.

## CHAPTER 20 · STALAG LUFT III, SAGAN
### *EAST COMPOUND, APRIL, 1942–MARCH, 1943*

In April, 1942, Goering's much vaunted camp, known as Stalag Luft III, was opened at Sagan in Lower Silesia, about eighty miles south-east of Berlin. It was intended to house all air force prisoners, and by the end of the summer of 1942 all but a few had been concentrated there; but as the numbers being shot down always exceeded German expectations, other camps had soon to be built or re-opened. Stalag Luft III, however, remained the chief camp for British and American Air Force officers until January, 1945. From its original two compounds, housing about 2,500 officers and N.C.O.s, it grew to six compounds, housing some 10,000 officers and about 300 orderlies. Air Force N.C.O.s were evacuated in the summer of 1943 and thereafter had a separate history.

Sagan is a historic place. It was the seat of a Duke of Courland in the

206

ESCAPE
FROM
GERMANY

*Stalag Luft
III, Sagan*
East Compound,
04/42–03/43

days when Courland was a Russian province, and the site of a battle where the Russians defeated Frederick the Great. During Napoleon's reign it came into the hands of a French family, and a Duc de Sagan was still the owner of the chateau, which was built in French eighteenth century style, when the war broke out in 1939. The Germans respected his title to ownership but requisitioned the property during the war.

Round the chateau had grown up a small and rather uninteresting town, important mainly as a railway junction. The surrounding country is dead flat, the horizon broken only by pinewoods. It is perhaps the ugliest part of the North German plain and produces little but wheat and timber. South of the town of Sagan is a forest of fir which runs unbroken for between twenty and thirty miles towards the Czechoslovakian frontier and spreads about the same distance east and west. It was on the northern edge of this forest that Goering's camp was situated. A great clearing had been made in the trees, and over the tree-stumps wooden huts had been erected.

Had the numbers in the compounds at Sagan ever been kept down to the level intended, the camp might have passed ordinary military standards. But rooms intended to hold six officers almost invariably had to house ten and sometimes twelve; and in barracks which might reasonably have held between eighty and a hundred N.C.O.s there were normally twice that number.

Wooden hutments are the same the world over. Pre-fabricated, erected in sections but united by the tarred felt over their roofs, they were divided into rooms if intended for officers, and divided in half if intended for N.C.O.s. Each barrack measured 160 feet by 40 feet and officers' rooms were normally 16 feet square. In the early compounds each barrack contained a small auxiliary kitchen in which tinned food could be heated and water boiled, and a primitive night urinal, but there was neither running water nor drainage. The walls were double with a three-inch space between them; and the floors, also double, were of wood laid on low piles about a foot clear of the ground. At first a wooden skirting round the outside of the barracks closed this gap and prevented the icy winds from making life unbearable in the winter; it also enabled prisoners to get under the floors of their barracks without being seen from outside and for this reason the skirtings were removed after a few months.

Into these huts in April and May of 1942 came Air Force prisoners from Barth and Army camps all over Germany, until by the middle of that summer there were more than 500 officers and one thousand N.C.O.s in what were known as the East and Centre Compounds. At the outset the German Air Force guards made an attempt at greater friendliness than had been apparent in Army camps, but though interpreters called prisoners "old boy" and German officers were profuse in their assurances that they wished to make prison life civilised, their sense of chivalry was governed mainly by circumstances. The equipment in the camps never even reached the standards the Germans themselves laid down, and tables and benches were always so short that had not prisoners made their own chairs from Red Cross packing-cases they would soon have had to sit in relays. Drainage and sanitation were primitive; yet when an American Colonel, who had learned the rudiments of sanitation at Annapolis, put forward plans for their improvement it was only with difficulty that the Germans were persuaded to agree. On the other hand the shortage of materials in Germany was no doubt a real difficulty, and perhaps prisoners were lucky to get as much as they did.

207

ESCAPE
FROM
GERMANY

*Stalag Luft
III, Sagan*
East Compound,
04/42–03/43

If any spur had been needed to induce prisoners to escape from the compounds at Sagan, the bleakness of the surroundings would have provided it. The areas inside the barbed wire were covered with tree stumps and were without a blade of grass; and the soil, which was mainly pine needles on top and sand underneath, crumbled into dust in summer and in winter became mud. Outside the wire a monotonous and unbroken vista of fir trees was all that prisoners could see.

The defences of the camp have been described; even during the first few days, while parties of prisoners were manning winches to remove the tree stumps, attempts to overcome them were made. Within a week of his arrival from Barth, Wing Commander Day, the Senior British Officer and two others, tried to walk out of the gate disguised as Germans. Their papers were not in order and they were caught. A day or two later an officer who was serving a term in the camp gaol for an attempt to escape from a previous camp, stole a key from a door and altered it with a nail file to fit the lock of his cell. While another prisoner in the gaol diverted the guard's attention, he opened his cell door, jumped through an open window and climbed over the nearby perimeter fence. Travelling partly by goods trains which he boarded in marshalling yards and partly on a stolen bicycle, he reached Zulichau on the Polish frontier in five days. Here he was seen and arrested while climbing into a train going to Warsaw where he had hoped to obtain assistance. He was returned to Sagan and sentenced to a term in the cells. While serving this sentence he and another officer in the gaol obtained two hacksaw blades from British orderlies. They started to cut the bars of their cell window but were caught.

Proposals for tunnels came from almost every barrack, but Lieut.-Commander Buckley, who had come with Wing Commander Day from Barth and who had again been put in charge of the organisation of escape, had decided that only three should be allowed. They were to be dug from three different barracks with all possible precautions.

At Barth the level of water had been so close to the surface that all tunnels had to be shallow. At Sagan the sand under the top went to a depth of seventy-eight feet before it reached water, but at a depth of between four

ESCAPE
FROM
GERMANY

*Stalag Luft
III, Sagan*
East Compound,
04/42–03/43

and six feet there was an admixture of clay which was firm enough to allow tunnels to be driven through it without support. As, however, ground microphones were already in operation, it was decided to dig below the clay at a depth of twelve to fifteen feet, and to shore the tunnels solidly with wood.

The policy of restricting the number of tunnels became increasingly difficult to enforce, for two reasons. The new prisoners who arrived almost every week felt that they were being excluded or made to take a place too far back in the queue; and the difficulty of hiding the bright yellow sand which came out of the tunnels made it impossible to conceal from the Germans that tunnelling was in progress, and so destroyed the argument in favour of limiting their number. If the Germans knew that tunnels were being dug, then it was argued, it would be better to dig as many as possible in the hope that one would get through.

When, through carelessness, one of the three deep tunnels was discovered after it had gone about eighty feet, the policy was changed and a large number of shallow tunnels were allowed to start in the hope that even if the Germans did find the sand they would have difficulty in finding all the entrances.

As a result, during the summer of 1942, between thirty and forty tunnels were begun from the various barracks in the East compound at Sagan. Yet all except one were unsuccessful. This was due mainly to the distance from the barracks to the wire, which was never less than sixty yards, and to the fact that all the entrances to the tunnels were underneath barracks and little effort was made to find new ways of disguising them. It was also quite impossible to hide the great quantity of bright yellow sand which was excavated.

The "ferrets" who had learned the first principles of escape detection at Barth, accompanied the prisoners to Sagan, so that most of the devices for hiding sand were already known. To begin with, prisoners hid it in the roofs of the barracks or under the floors, taking great care to cover it with the pine needle mould which formed the normal surface. But a roof collapsed, and the Germans were quick to notice when the space between the ground and a barrack floor was filling up; and although a good deal of sand could be dispersed on bare patches of ground in the open and trodden down, care was still needed because the excavated sand was so conspicuous.

As one tunnel after another was discovered, the experts were forced to think again, and to concentrate on ways and means of completing one or two tunnels and, in particular, on devising new and more ingenious entrances. Experiments in starting a tunnel out in the open were made and it was one of these that eventually succeeded.

A plague of wasps and flies, due to bad drainage, had made life so unbearable in the East compound that the Germans were persuaded to allow the prisoners to dig several new drains. The drains were very narrow, about 18 inches wide, but ran directly from the latrines towards the wire ending in a sump not more than twenty yards from the perimeter fence. Three of the prisoners who had been building the drains conceived the idea of hiding in one of them after the camp had been closed at night, and then digging their way straight out like moles, cutting their way about three feet under the surface and pushing the earth back behind them as they went. It was a dangerous plan because they would be completely closed in after the first few yards and could only keep themselves alive by narrow air holes which they would have to bore through the ground above them.

209

ESCAPE
FROM
GERMANY

*Stalag Luft
III, Sagan*
East Compound,
04/42–03/43

When they had made their preparations one of the prisoners built a dam across a drain and then, under cover of the digging operations, tunnelled several feet while his friends dispersed the sand on the heaps which were being piled up from a new drain alongside. When the tunnel was long enough to hold all three men they crawled in and their friends sealed up the opening. It was then seven o'clock in the evening. The camp was closed at ten and as there had been no sign that the Germans suspected anything everyone hoped that the three would dig their way out before morning.

When morning came, however, early risers noticed three or four thin wisps of steam rising from the ground in a line from the point where the tunnel began. It was plain that the men were still there, and that they were still breathing; and as the last air-hole was near the fence it was also plain that they had not much farther to go. Word was quickly sent round the camp warning people what had happened and cautioning them not to show signs that they had noticed anything unusual, and men were detailed to keep watch through the day for any signal of distress. None came, however, and the steam was still visible when the camp was once more locked for the night. At 11 p.m. that evening the first man broke surface near a tree on the edge of the road beyond the wire and all three crept out without the sentry noticing them and reached the wood on the other side of the road. They were at large for five days, being caught on a boat on which they were sailing down the river Oder.

The success of the "mole" led to other attempts of the same kind, so that the Germans became alarmed and to prevent tunnels of this kind their Chief Security Officer, whose name was Peschel, decided to dig a ditch eight feet deep by three feet wide round the whole camp. Knowing that "moles" had to be dug quickly and could not go deep because of the danger of falls and suffocation, he calculated that this would put an end to them. After platoons of German soldiers had spent one of the hottest fortnights of the war in arduous digging, the ditch, which later became known as "Peschel's folly," was completed. Within a week it was itself used as cover for a further "mole" which very nearly succeeded.

ESCAPE
FROM
GERMANY

*Stalag Luft
III, Sagan*
East Compound,
04/42–03/43

Being deep and narrow it was impossible for German guards in the towers to see the bottom of the ditch, and as it was not more than thirty-five feet from the outside of the wire, three more prisoners calculated that if they could get into it unobserved they could dig themselves out in a single night. The ditch itself was beyond the warning wire but a narrow open culvert led into it at right angles across the perimeter path. The prisoners judged that there was just room for a man to drop into the culvert as he walked round the path, and then slide into the ditch.

A large-scale diversion was therefore organised. It was a fine evening towards the end of July and the guards in the watch towers must have noticed rather more prisoners than usual strolling round the perimeter path in groups of two and three. On a tree-stump not far from the culvert they must also have seen a prisoner practising on a saxophone. This was not unusual as saxophones made so much noise in a barrack that the players were often banished to far corners of the camp.

But on the evening in question both the strollers and the saxophonist were playing a double role. The duty of the saxophonist was to watch the guards in the towers on either side of the culvert and to continue playing unless both were looking away. The strollers were to provide a screen behind which the prisoners were to disappear. It was quite common for groups of prisoners taking exercise to get bunched together, and each time they neared the culvert three rows of three men closed to within a few yards of each other, with the prisoner who was trying to escape on the outside of the middle row. For an hour about half the camp walked round and round, and by the end of that time all three prisoners were lying safely at the bottom of the ditch. The saxophonist was almost exhausted but he had been silent just often enough for each of the three men to drop into the culvert.

They dug through the night without being discovered, but next morning once again three small columns of steam were seen rising, from the ground just short of the wire. The officers were still not outside and this time the steam was so obvious that it seemed as if it must give them away. But after a little while one of them emerged in a state of exhaustion and the attempt was over. They had a partial revenge however. Before the end of the summer platoons of German soldiers again marched into the compound armed with spades, but this time their job was not to dig the ditch but to fill it in. Security Officer Peschel had seen his folly.

Meanwhile the general policy towards tunnels had been changed. As all shallow tunnels had been discovered it was decided once more to concentrate on the one deep tunnel which had survived. Should the prisoners get restless they were to be allowed to build one or two further shallow tunnels, but in the eyes of the Committee these were treated only as "blinds."

For some time this policy worked well. In spite of a fall which half buried the chief engineer and necessitated a fresh beginning, the deep tunnel progressed satisfactorily. One of its special features was a dummy entrance. After sinking the shaft and tunnelling about twenty feet the tunnel apparently came to an end in an unfinished condition. But a trap had been made in the floor and a further shaft sunk, and the tunnel continued at a lower level. The idea was that if the entrance was discovered by the Germans, they would think that the tunnel had not gone very far and merely fill in the first section leaving the deep and real tunnel undiscovered. A new entrance could then be dug to join up with the tunnel proper. This is exactly what happened and this tunnel eventually became the largest operation of its kind yet undertaken by prisoners, and the experience it afforded was the basis of later successes.

211

ESCAPE
FROM
GERMANY

*Stalag Luft
III, Sagan*
East Compound,
04/42–03/43

From the barrack the tunnel ran to the camp kitchen which was about seventy feet closer to the wire and underneath the concrete kitchen floor a shaft was bored upwards and a chamber constructed in which an air pump was installed. After the tunnel had been in progress for three months it was decided to extend it backwards to another barrack so that in the concluding stages sand could be packed into this extension, and no trace of the tunnel be seen above ground. This backward extension was dug from both barracks at once and after a junction had been made the back entrance was blocked up. As sand could now be disposed of underground, work went on day and night.

There was no reason to believe that the Germans had any knowledge of the backward extension of the tunnel but soon after night work had begun their searches were intensified. Nothing was discovered and work went on, though now by night only. In September their searches became even more drastic. At four hours' notice the prisoners were turned out of the barrack under which the entrance to the extension lay and the Germans went to work thoroughly. The floor was taken up and all the excavated sand which had been packed underneath it was cleared away until the original layer of pine needle earth was laid bare. In that earth the filled in shaft must have been clearly visible, a yellow square on a black background, for the prisoners had been in too much of a hurry to match the earth when filling in the shaft. The Germans then excavated to a depth of five feet and found the tunnel level. Their adventures, however, were not over. "Charlie" and another "ferret" went into the tunnel and were unable to find any exit. Once more platoons of Germans were brought into the camp and the whole course of the tunnel was traced by holes dug from above. It was nearly four hundred feet long. The tunnel was then filled' with water and much of it collapsed, but not until the Germans had taken photographs of its interior for their museum.

Meanwhile, throughout this summer, numerous individual attempts at escape were made. Every form of transport which came into the camp, including the dung cart, was boarded at some time or another by a prisoner

212

ESCAPE
FROM
GERMANY

*Stalag Luft
III, Sagan*
East Compound,
04/42–03/43

attempting to go out through the gate. The stench and steam from the dung nearly suffocated the prisoner who hid in it and he had to climb out, and suffocation also betrayed a prisoner who had been dumped by the main gate of the camp in a bag of laundry. Successful escapes were made in disguise and by cutting the wire.

It had been noticed by an American, a member of the Eagle squadron, that the guard towers were set back level with the outside edge of the double wire fence; he thought therefore that there might be a blind spot right underneath the inside of the fence exactly between the two towers where the posts holding the wire would form a solid screen as the guards in the towers looked along them. Fortunately an opportunity to test this theory occurred. The construction of a new compound for officers was begun at Sagan that summer and prisoners used to go and help pull up tree stumps in order that the compound should be more habitable when it was opened. During one of these expeditions Lieut. Commander Buckley climbed into one of the new guard towers and looked along the line of posts which had just been erected to take the wire fence. He found that about twenty-five yards from the tower the line of posts did form a solid screen for about ten yards, and he could not see anyone standing or lying close underneath them.

A British officer joined the American and the attempt was planned. The problem was to cross the dead ground between the warning wire and the perimeter fence without being seen by the guards in the towers or any other German, and then, after having cut the wire, to get away unobserved from the other side.

Daylight was chosen for this operation because the difficulty of reaching the wire at night in face of the searchlights had already proved very great. An Army orderly had crawled for forty-five minutes towards the wire and been picked up by a dog when still some yards from it. In daylight, however, all prisoners were allowed up to the warning wire and it was a question of diverting the attention of the guards for a few seconds while the escapists stepped over the warning wire, walked up to the fence and lay down. Even then, of course, there was still considerable risk, for when lying down the prisoners would be visible to the guard in one tower on the far side of the compound, and to the guard at the gate. They gambled on the fact that most guards confined their attention to the area immediately around them.

The scheme was carried out during the early part of an afternoon in September when the camp was clear of all Germans except the N.C.O. who looked after the compound kitchen. Buckley took up a position where he could command a view of all the sentry boxes and also the guard at the main gate. At a signal from him a prisoner engaged the attention of the sentry at the gate by playing an accordion in front of him; another prisoner spoke to the guard in one of the nearby towers and asked whether he would arrange for an interview between the Senior Officer and the Camp Commandant; Buckley himself engaged the guard in the second tower in conversation and a further diversion was created by other prisoners walking backwards and forwards in front of him in groups of four and five. The guard in the third tower was asked by another prisoner for permission to cross the warning rail to retrieve a football, and a boxing match had been arranged in front of the fourth tower in which there was to be a knock-out followed by a lot of cheering and splashing of water over the victim's face.

213

ESCAPE
FROM
GERMANY

*Stalag Luft
III, Sagan*
East Compound,
04/42–03/43

Whilst these diversions were in operation the two escapers stepped over the warning rail, walked up to the perimeter fence and lay down close to it. While the American kept watch the British officer proceeded to cut through the wire with wire cutters which had been made in the camp, propping up the coils on forked sticks as he went. Owing to the quantity of coiled wire between the double fence it was considered most unlikely that any sentry would be able to see them once they were in the middle and this proved to be the case. It was known that it would take a considerable time to cut through and it had been arranged that when the last strand had been parted the escaper would raise his left thumb over his left shoulder and the first person to notice it from those little groups which were walking backwards and forwards was to blow his nose as loudly as possible. At this sign Buckley was to give the signal for the synchronised diversions to be repeated, the first sentry being told that the British officer did not want an interview with the Commandant after all, the second being engaged in conversation again by Buckley, the third being pleaded with again for permission to retrieve the football and another knock-out with much cheering and more water splashing being arranged for the diversion of the fourth.

At the end of exactly eight minutes the signal was given and the diversions were successfully repeated. The two escapers crawled through the gap they had made and reaching the middle of the road beyond the wire stood up unnoticed. They had made themselves imitations of French uniforms because Frenchmen from a nearby camp often walked up and down this road in the afternoon and the escapers hoped to be mistaken for two of them. They dusted their clothing and sauntered down the road passing one sentry who looked at them suspiciously but made no attempt to stop them. When out of sight they hid for the rest of that day.

Shortly afterwards the guards in the towers were changed and as the new guards marched by they noticed the hole in the wire and raised the alarm. Dogs were set on at once but although the prisoners were not far away they were unable to pick up the scent. The escapers travelled on foot at night only for two nights, stole two overcoats and then boarded a goods train at Furth. They jumped off near Berlin but were caught because all

ESCAPE
FROM
GERMANY

*Stalag Luft
III, Sagan*
East Compound,
04/42–03/43

civilians were being stopped and interrogated after an escape by a number of Russians in that area. They were questioned by the Gestapo, mistaken for Russians and beaten up. Eventually they convinced the authorities that they were escaped British prisoners and were returned to Sagan. After this escape the sentry towers were extended so that they projected right over the double wire fence and additional guards were put on patrol outside the wire between the towers.

Although the Germans had discovered the hole in the wire within a quarter of an hour of the escape, they had no idea how many men had gone out and three other officers immediately "went to ground" in the camp. Like all previous "ghosts" their object was to make the Germans think they had already escaped and so have plenty of time to make their plans and to get away without the Germans being aware of the time of their departure. All three officers were well known to the "ferrets" so that they had to spend their time in a tunnel or remain constantly on the watch to avoid being seen. As "snap" roll calls were sometimes held at night they had to be prepared to get out of their beds and hide at a moment's notice. After five weeks of this sort of existence, one of the prisoners was recognised by a German. He managed to evade capture but his presence in the camp convinced the "ferret" that the other two missing prisoners were there also, and though no definite search was made, watchfulness increased. Shortly afterwards one of the three was surprised by a "ferret" in a barrack and after an exciting chase was caught. The other two determined to make their attempt at once.

As the East compound opened into another which was heavily guarded, there was no sentry on the gate at night. The two prisoners had examined the shadows cast by the posts of the gate in the searchlights and had come to the conclusion that it would be possible to cut through the wire on one side of it. This would bring them into the outer compound. Besides containing the "cooler" which had a permanent staff of three German soldiers, this compound was guarded by another double gate at which a sentry was permanently on duty. To the left of this gate, however, there was a vegetable garden which at that time of the year was thick with tomato plants. These tomatoes grew to within a few feet of the wire fence.

Once inside the outer compound the prisoners planned a long crawl across the open until they could gain the shelter of a barrack which was used as a store, from where they could walk under cover to the edge of the vegetable garden. They then planned to crawl through the tomatoes and cut their way through the wire about twenty yards to the left of the sentry on the main gate. They had to risk the presence of the German dog patrol, and at both points where they intended to cut the wire they would be under fire from at least two machine guns from guard towers if they were seen. They chose a moonless night and made their attempt. Everything went without a hitch and they were clear of both compounds within half an hour of leaving their barracks. Once again, however, both prisoners were recaptured within a week.

Of the two escapes in disguise, the first was made in the summer of 1942 by the Chief Education Officer of the compound, who was also the camp interpreter. It had been noticed that a German medical orderly came into the camp at times when few other Germans were there. A medical pass was obtained and forged, and it was then proposed to the British interpreter that after the orderly had come into the camp he should be detained by cups of coffee and conversation, and the interpreter should walk out in his place. The interpreter, who had not been thinking about escape for many months, jumped at the chance.

An excellent uniform was made, and one of the medical students of the camp who spoke good German was enlisted to go down to the gate with the "orderly" and carry on a conversation in German with him in front of the guard on the gate before the "orderly" attempted to go through. Security was excellent, and only a few prisoners realised what was happening when the medical student and his "German" companion came down the centre aisle of the camp. The student was carrying an enamel medical bowl and a sheaf of papers about which he was talking volubly. A few yards from the gate, the pair stopped and stood talking for three or four minutes, the student emphasising the urgency of a certain case in the camp, and the "orderly" being sympathetic. In the end the "orderly" asked if he could take the papers, and after doing so, turned and walked towards the gate. He had his pass in his inside pocket, but the guard, who was already holding the gate open for him, hardly bothered to look at it, and the "orderly" walked down into the outer compound. He repeated his success at the next gate and after throwing away his uniform in the woods caught a train as a civilian. He then probed the north German ports from Danzig to Stralsund for several days attempting to find a Swedish ship. In the end he was caught on the way to Berlin, from where he had made up his mind to try for Switzerland.

The other escape in disguise came even nearer to success. A Dutch officer in the R.A.F. who had been at a German university and spoke perfect German, had been watching the movements of the "ferrets" at night. He noticed that when they came into the compound they came alone, let themselves in and out through the gate, and when walking about shone their torches on the ground as a signal to the men in the watch-towers. Often they disappeared into the compound kitchen for an hour or more at a time.

The uniform of a "ferret" being easy to copy, the Dutchman decided to try and let himself out of the compound in disguise and to bluff his way through the second gate. His first need was a key. The gate of the compound was secured with a padlock of a fairly simple type, and as parties of

215

ESCAPE
FROM
GERMANY

*Stalag Luft
III, Sagan*
East Compound,
04/42–03/43

ESCAPE
FROM
GERMANY

*Stalag Luft
III, Sagan*
East Compound,
04/42–03/43

prisoners often went through the gate to shower baths, there was no doubt little difficulty in taking an impression of the keyhole. A sketch of the key face was made by one of the prisoners who was frequently escorted through the gate alone on his way to the parcel store, and who often saw it.

A comparison with the padlocks inside the compound was made, and one of the same type was found on a fusebox in one of the barracks. A genuine key to fit this padlock was obtained from the prisoners' own stores, but though this key fitted it would not open it. The padlock of the fusebox was then dismantled and an examination of the mechanism showed that all the wards preventing the bolt from sliding were held into position by a single spring. By slightly altering the key face and always inverting the padlock when opening it, a master key was produced which would unlock the padlock on the gate.

A torch was secured by bribery, and with overalls made from sheets and dyed blue and the rest of the uniform drawn from stock, the Dutchman had only to wait for an evening when a "ferret" came in at a suitable time and went to the kitchen, and he could make his attempt. The time was important because he had to be out of the camp before midnight to catch the train he wanted.

The Dutchman changed his room so that he could be near the gate and also get out of a window which could not be seen from the watch-towers, and special signals were arranged between barracks so that he should know when the moment arrived. One night, when he was playing poker, a friend came in and quietly gave him the signal. He finished the hand he was playing and then left the table to put on his clothes. A few moments later he was in the compound walking towards the gate, shining his torch on the ground.

When he reached the gate the searchlights were full on him. He put in his key and found that it opened the padlock at once. He walked unhurriedly through, and turned to lock the gate again. Those who were watching him noticed that it took him a few seconds longer to do this than it had to open it, but he was soon out of their sight on his way through the outer compound. As no alarm was given within the next half hour they knew he had succeeded.

However, the key which had worked so well to open the padlock had refused to lock it, and a little later when the real "ferret" went out and found the padlock open, he at once gave the alarm. But by then the Dutchman was many miles away.

On reaching the gate leading from the Vorlager into the German compound the Dutchman had produced his forged pay-book and was allowed to pass through. Once there he climbed over the fence behind the guard-room and crossing the road discarded his "ferret's" uniform. Now dressed as a civilian he entered Sagan railway goods yard and jumped on to a

goods train that was pulling out. Travelling on various trains eventually he
reached Neudingen and then started walking towards the Swiss frontier
dressed as a hiker. On the way a member of the S.S. on a motor-cycle
stopped and asked him where he was going and when he mentioned a village nearer the frontier gave him a lift for many miles and recommended
to him a good place for his holiday. They talked cheerfully on the way and
after bidding each other goodbye the Dutchman continued on foot. Some
hours later he walked along a road which was within a few yards of the
frontier for a mile without being challenged; he arrived at the point where
he intended to cross then hid until it was dark. Crawling up a bushy slope
to the frontier he was heard and attacked by patrol dogs and captured. He
insisted that he was a Dutch workman but this was not believed nor was
his confession that he was an escaped British prisoner. He was beaten
severely in the police cells but eventually his identity was established.
While being taken back to Sagan he slipped away from his guards during
an air raid at Leipzig. However he got only as far as an air-raid shelter
where he was recaptured during a police check. He was returned to Sagan
but far from being discouraged he attempted to escape from the camp
gaol and was again recaptured. He was sent to the special camp for invet-
erate escapers at Colditz.

In the autumn of 1942 escape activity was interrupted by two events. In
September one hundred officers were sent to Schubin followed by a similar number in November, and about this time the Germans announced that
the new North Compound would be ready for occupation in the spring
and those who had remained in the East Compound would be transferred
there. A few determined attempts before this happened were made.

A daring attempt to cut the wire took place on 30 November. Two officers crawled across the compound and climbed the unlighted and unpa-
trolled fence separating the East and Centre Compounds, then crawled
across the latter, using blankets as camouflage and began to cut through
the wire between the Centre Compound and the German compound. Just
before they finished, the patrolling guard outside the wire saw them and
they were arrested.

Four days later two other prisoners hid in a latrine near the wire when
the barracks were locked up for the night and crawled to the fence, using
white sheets for camouflage as it had been snowing. Just as they got outside the perimeter fence by cutting through it they were caught by a
patrolling guard. After serving their sentences they attempted to repeat
their performance, having bribed a sentry who was patrolling the wire to
turn a blind eye while they cut through the fence. However they were seen
by another sentry in the glare of a searchlight and arrested.

In early March, 1943, a Polish officer serving in the R.A.F. who bore a
very strong resemblance to a German interpreter impersonated him and

217

ESCAPE
FROM
GERMANY

*Stalag Luft
III, Sagan*
East Compound,
04/42–03/43

218

ESCAPE
FROM
GERMANY

*Stalag*
*Luft III*
Centre
Compound

passed through both compounds gates into the German Compound. The German interpreter was off duty at the time but as the impersonator was walking past the guardroom on his way out of the camp a friend of the impersonator came up and talked to him. The conversation was too much for the prisoner and he was discovered.

In March, 1943, before the North Compound was completed, parties of prisoners from the East Compound were taken there each morning under escort to help prepare it for occupation. Officers had to give parole, but N.C.O.s were not allowed to as the perimeter fence of the North Compound was not guarded in any way and only one sentry accompanied each party. Two officers decided to exchange identities with N.C.O.s and one day when work ceased for the mid-day meal they slipped away and climbed the fence. They covered a considerable distance during the next two days but were recaptured and returned to the camp.

## CHAPTER 21 · STALAG LUFT III
### *CENTRE COMPOUND*

When the camp at Sagan was first opened the N.C.O.s were housed between the East Compound and the German headquarters; their compound was known as the Centre Compound. It was a little larger than the East Compound but although the lay-out and defences were similar the accommodation was inferior. Instead of containing rooms the barracks were divided in half, and although they were not intended to hold more than a hundred men each it was not long before they were holding a hundred and sixty.

The first prisoners to reach the Compound were the N.C.O.s and airmen who were transferred from Barth in April, 1942. Within the next few weeks batches of N.C.O.s and airmen were transferred from Kirchhain, Lamsdorf and Bad Sulza and until October, 1942, parties of new N.C.O. prisoners continued to arrive from Dulag Luft. By this time the barracks were very over-crowded and one hundred and fifty volunteers were transferred to Barth, which was re-opened. This left approximately one thousand eight hundred N.C.O.s and airmen at Sagan. In April, 1943, all Polish and Czech N.C.O.s serving in the R.A.F., and all American N.C.O.s, a total of about eighty men, were transferred compulsorily to Barth.

During the fifteen months they spent in this compound the majority of N.C.O.s showed little interest in escape. In the main this was due to the fact that most of them had previously been in Army camps where there were no facilities for sport or entertainment. Those things were available at Sagan, and for a time even the keenest escapers took real pleasure in them. Nevertheless there were always a few enthusiasts who persisted in

219

ESCAPE
FROM
GERMANY

*Stalag
Luft III*

Centre
Compound

attempting to escape. To begin with they concentrated on tunnels; eighteen were started and two were within a few feet of the perimeter fence before being discovered, probably through the ground microphones which the Germans had installed.

When an Escape Committee was formed in the autumn of 1942 it was decided that only one tunnel should be built at a time, and in the spring of 1943 a voluntary organisation known as "Tally Ho" was formed which undertook disposal of sand and security, but no tunnel succeeded.

As tunnelling proved abortive the enthusiasts tried other methods. A daring attempt was made by two Warrant Officers shortly before Christmas, 1942. The Germans wanted to cover the dead ground between the warning wire and the perimeter fence with bright yellow sand and for this purpose dug several pits in that area. When the sand had been excavated the pits were filled with ashes, empty food cans and other rubbish and finally covered with sand.

One of the Warrant Officers noticed that one of these pits, which was about four feet deep, was being dug half way between two sentry towers and decided that if he could get into it unobserved he should be able to dig a "mole" tunnel to a point beyond the fence. He estimated that the "mole" would have to be about thirty feet long and that he could dig it within a few hours. Because the "ferrets" were working in the pit during the day and no prisoner was allowed within a hundred yards of it after dark, the only way to reach the pit was to crawl across the compound as soon as it was dark, and complete the "mole" before dawn.

A friend joined him in the scheme and equipped with some French money, a map, compass, concentrated food, a three-foot length of broom shaft with which to make air-holes while in the "mole", and a spade fitted with a short handle which had been stolen from the Germans, they hoped for a misty evening. Both wore khaki battle dress to match the sand and balaclava helmets. Just before seven o'clock in the evening they left their barrack and after receiving a signal that the compound was clear of Germans, they made their way between the rows of barracks to the point from which they intended to start their crawl to the pit. The temperature was below freezing and as they waited in the shadows watching the searchlights sweeping the ground in front of them it seemed impossible that a man could cover more than a few yards without being seen, for there was not even a blade of grass to afford cover. However, slight undulations in the ground cast long shadows, and by crawling towards one of the lights they hoped that their shadows would not appear unduly large.

Soon after seven o'clock the two escapers saw the sentries change and the first man began to crawl flat, on elbows and toes, towards the pit, hoping to cover some distance before the eyes of the sentries became accustomed to the pattern of shadows cast by the ground. He covered about ten

220

ESCAPE
FROM
GERMANY

*Stalag
Luft III*
Centre
Compound

yards before the beam of one of the searchlights swept towards him, then lay quite still until it had passed. His friend, who was watching him, said afterwards that at that moment he felt quite sick and waited for the sound of the machine gun which he knew must come.

The first man continued to crawl, moving an inch at a time, and reached the pit shortly after nine o'clock. It had taken two hours to cover a distance of approximately one hundred yards. At once he began to excavate the "mole" about two feet and a half below the surface. No shoring was necessary because the area between the warning rail and the fence was covered with the stumps of small fir trees which had been cut down when the compound was constructed and the roots served to bind the sand. When his companion failed to arrive after some minutes had elapsed he became worried. Then suddenly he heard a dull thud behind him as he worked in the "mole", and on emerging was delighted to find his friend. He had dropped the pole for making air-holes while crawling and had gone back again and searched until he found it.

The "mole" had progressed about twelve feet and both men were resting in the pit before finally sealing themselves in when suddenly an Alsatian dog appeared and stood looking down at them. It made no sound and after a few seconds went away. They remained quite still for some moments and were just beginning to hope that all was well when the dog reappeared and a few seconds later a torch was shone into the pit and the two escapers were ordered out at pistol point and marched off to the camp gaol. Subsequently it was learned that the dog patrol had entered the compound an hour earlier than usual because one of the sentries had seen a prisoner running from one barrack to another after the doors had been locked and had reported the incident to the guardroom.

For some unknown reason the Germans did not fill in the pit but contented themselves with collapsing the tunnel and levelling the surface. Accordingly about two months later two other N.C.O.s attempted to carry out the same scheme but they were seen before reaching the pit and one of them, Sergeant Joyce, A.E., R.A.F., was wounded seriously by machine-gun fire from one of the sentry towers. He died some weeks later.

Three N.C.O.s got away from the camp by walking through the gates in disguise. The first of these escapes was carried out in July, 1942, by a Warrant Officer who was similar in appearance and build to a German Corporal who was in charge of the issue of stores. The Warrant Officer managed to borrow the Corporal's pay-book and gate pass and to have copies made; as it was summer most of the Germans wore off-white fatigue jackets while on duty and one of these was made from German towels; a camp-made German Air Force field-service cap, badges of rank, leather belt and pistol holster completed the uniform.

A day was chosen when the German Corporal was on leave, and the

221

ESCAPE
FROM
GERMANY

*Stalag
Luft III*

Centre
Compound

prisoner donned his disguise and walked from the equipment store to the gate carrying a fourteen-pound German jam tin which had been converted into a bucket. This contained a few new scrubbing brushes and floorcloths, under which was concealed the escaper's food and a camp-made civilian cap. He wore a camp-made civilian jacket under his fatigue jacket.

As he approached the compound gate the sentry opened it, merely glancing at his pass as he went by. He walked across the Vorlager, the compound which housed the camp stores, coal dump and sick quarters, and exactly the same thing happened at the gate leading into the German compound. Although this escaper was able to speak German fluently he was not called upon to utter a word at either gate. After passing through the second gate he spent the following five or six hours in the German compound, mostly in an air raid shelter and in lavatories, and when it was dark left through a wicket gate at the side of the German Officers' Mess. He was recaptured a few days later because of the inadequacy of his identity papers.

Just after Christmas, 1942, the same prisoner and a companion, also a German speaker, left the compound at night disguised as two of the German guards who were in the compound theatre at that time watching a stage performance given by the prisoners. They produced forged passes to the sentry at the gate and told him that they did not like the show. Both escapers were disguised as Corporals and they rated the sentry for having been some distance from the gate when they arrived. With many apologies for having kept them waiting the sentry unlocked the gate and they passed through.

At the second gate the sentry on duty asked for their numbers. This took them by surprise as they did not know that the German Security Officer had just introduced a system whereby each German entering the compounds was issued with a number. But they cursed the sentry so thoroughly for keeping them waiting while he unlocked the gate that he let them pass without further question. They left the German compound by the gate near the Officers' Mess and, after altering their disguises to that of foreign workers, walked to Sagan railway station. They travelled by train to Bayreuth, where they were caught two days later through a check of documents as they left the station.

About five months later the third escape of this type was made. Once a week a party of about eighty Germans used the prisoners' shower-baths in the Vorlager. Normally the party entered the Vorlager about 8.30 a.m. and left about 9.30 a.m. The Escape Committee decided that it might be possible for an escaper disguised as a German to join this party as it re-assembled before being marched into the German compound. Roll-call was at 9 a.m. and it was decided that the escaper should go with the party which attended the camp dentist immediately afterwards and escape from the dentist's waiting room, which was in one of the buildings close to the shower-baths.

ESCAPE
FROM
GERMANY

*Stalag
Luft III*
Centre
Compound

Although it was May and quite warm, it was arranged that for several weeks all prisoners attending sick and dental parades would wear their greatcoats so that the escaper could wear his two disguises under a greatcoat when leaving the compound. A lock-pick had been made and tested on the waiting room door. After one false start due to the dental parade being late the plan was carried out. With two layers of disguise bulking large under his greatcoat the escaper went out with the dental party. A few seconds after the medical orderly had locked the door of the waiting room the lock-pick unlocked it. While another prisoner watched the German in the surgery, the escaper took off his greatcoat, put on his German Air Force field-service cap and with towel, soap and an empty food tin in his hand walked out into the corridor. Seconds later the door was relocked.

The timing of the whole operation was perfect. As the escaper reached the outer door of the building he saw the Germans who had been lolling about outside the shower-baths begin to fall in. He ran the intervening distance of fifty yards and fell in with them. The Germans began to sort themselves into files of three and the escaper manoeuvred himself into the centre file about two-thirds of the way from the head of the column. A German Senior N.C.O. counted the party, then walked back to the beginning looking very puzzled and made a re-count. Discipline was lax and the Germans were carrying on conversations so that each time the Senior N.C.O. came near him the escaper addressed a few remarks to one of the Germans standing beside him. After the re-count the N.C.O. in charge of the party shrugged his shoulders and gave the order to march. The gate leading into the German compound was opened by the sentry and the party marched through singing lustily "Deutschland uber Alles"—in which the escaper joined.

The escaper entered a barrack, walked along the corridor and out at the far end, and then made his way to a lavatory where he remained for about two hours. When he came out he picked up a length of planking which was lying near by, and walked through the German camp carrying it on his shoulder, eventually reaching a shed with a hayloft in which he intended to hide until the evening. Two Germans were tidying-up outside the shed, and with a curt "Good morning," he began to do the same, working a few yards away. Shortly afterwards the Germans ceased work and left the shed. After a suitable interval the escaper climbed the ladder to the hayloft and hid. From this position he was able to see the greater part of the camp.

He saw at once that a towel was hanging outside a particular window of one of the barracks in the compound, which indicated that his absence from the dental party had been covered, and when after evening roll-call the towel was still in position he knew that there would be no search for him that night. At dusk he left the hayloft and spent the next few hours in various lavatories in the German camp, finally reaching one near the southern fence. Soon after midnight he buried his German jacket and cap in the cess-pool, left the building in his civilian disguise and climbed over the single nine-foot high barbed wire fence.

223

ESCAPE
FROM
GERMANY

*Stalag
Luft III*

Centre
Compound

He headed for Warsaw, hoping to get help from the Polish Underground, but was caught by a German farmer in occupied Poland. The camp authorities were unaware that anyone had escaped until informed by the Gestapo that a prisoner had been recaptured. They never knew how the escape had been made.

A few days later one of the cleverest escapes of the whole war was made by the Warrant Officer who had already escaped twice disguised as a German. His plan was to disguise himself as a German electrician, carry out tests on the telephone wires which ran along the top of the perimeter fence, and in doing so cross the fence and walk off. His equipment consisted of a dark blue boiler suit, German Air Force field-service cap and leather belt, and an imitation electrician's meter for testing wiring, several spurious identity documents and a quantity of concentrated food, and a civilian coat which he wore under the overalls.

An elaborate system of signals was arranged and shortly before three o'clock on the selected day the escaper, having put on his disguises, made his way to the compound theatre and borrowed the ladder used for the stage. He carried this to the warning fence opposite the place where telephone wires from the German compound crossed the barbed-wire and called out in German to the guard in the tower explaining that he was going to test the telephone wires. The guard waved to the man in the other tower covering this zone, then indicated that it was safe to cross the strip of ground between the warning fence and the wire.

The escaper stepped over the warning fence and propped the ladder against the wire, then produced his dummy test meter and made a show of testing the telephone wires. After a few moments he informed the guard in the tower that the fault must be further over, climbed down the ladder and walked to where a plank was lying near the fence a few yards away. He carried this up the ladder and placed it across the top of the double fence. Unfortunately the plank was too short and it fell down on top of the barbed-wire entanglements between the fences. Unperturbed, the escaper climbed down the ladder, swearing volubly in German, recovered the plank and replaced it where it had been lying, then walked to another part of the compound and found a longer plank with which he returned. He climbed the ladder and placed the plank firmly across the gap between the fences.

After clambering on to the plank he resumed testing the telephone wires, finally reaching the end of the plank furthest from the prisoners' compound. At this stage the sentry patrolling outside the fence stopped opposite him and enquired what he was doing. Not satisfied with the reply

224

ESCAPE
FROM
GERMANY

*Oflag XXIB,
Schubin*

he demanded to see the escaper's identity papers. The escaper produced his false camp pass and told the guard to mind his own business, with the result that he resumed patrolling his beat.

A few moments later the escaper deliberately dropped his test meter among the barbed-wire entanglements but close to the German side of the fence. Swearing profusely, in German, he climbed down the fence within the German compound and recovered the test meter. After examining this he grumbled to the guard in the sentry tower, who had watched the whole proceedings with a bored air, about the amount which he would have stopped from his pay because the meter was damaged. He was about to walk away, but after a brilliantly acted momentary hesitation he removed the plank which spanned the fence and laid it on the ground a few yards from the fence within the German compound. This done he walked off through the German camp. His colleagues persuaded a German N.C.O. to fetch the ladder back to the theatre, alleging that it had been removed by one of his staff. Travelling by train the Warrant Officer reached Stettin, but while looking for a neutral ship was picked up on the fifth night after his escape.

Meanwhile the evacuation of the compound had started and by the end of June all the N.C.O.s with the exception of fifty who had volunteered to remain as orderlies for the American officers who were coming into the compound, had been transferred to the new Air Force camp at Heydekrug. An officer from the East Compound was able to exchange identities with an N.C.O. who had elected to remain, and he accompanied the N.C.O.s to their new camp.

About mid-July all the American officers at Sagan were transferred to this compound and a few British officers were transferred from the East Compound to help them settle in. New American prisoners arrived steadily throughout the summer. The small British contingent remained in the compound for three months and during that time one of them was able to emulate the Warrant Officer's feat which has just been described. He noticed that the Germans were carrying out modifications to the fence between the compound and the German camp and decided to impersonate them during the luncheon hour. He was completely successful but had the bad luck to run into a "ferret" who recognised him as he crossed the German compound.

## CHAPTER 22 · OFLAG XXIB, SCHUBIN

Schubin (Szubin) is a small market town in Poland lying about twenty miles south of Bromberg (Brydogoloz) and about one hundred and fifty miles due west of Warsaw. It is in the centre of a great undulating agricultural plain which is almost entirely under the plough. From 1939 until

1945 it was in the newly created German province of Warthegau.

225

ESCAPE
FROM
GERMANY

*Oflag XXIB,
Schubin*

On the outskirts of the town about two miles from the railway station stood a large girls' school consisting of a main building, a chapel, a modern sanatorium, a small brick bungalow, a special bath house, a stable and quite extensive grounds. The grounds included a playing field and two large vegetable gardens with a greenhouse and potting sheds. Secondary schools were closed by the Germans in that part of Poland which they annexed and this particular school became a camp for prisoners of war in 1940. The main building, which was white, was of a good period and behind it stood the sanatorium also well built and well equipped. The grounds sloped up behind these buildings, the playing field having been levelled and fringed with trees. A grove of chestnut trees surrounded the carriage way behind the main school building. To house the prisoners twelve brick barracks had been built in the grounds, six below the playing fields and six above on the steep part of the slope. Round them and also enclosing the main school buildings were the usual barbed wire fences and sentry towers.

When the first Air Force prisoners arrived at the camp in September, 1942, from Warburg and Sagan they were pleasantly surprised by their surroundings. The trees and flowers around the sanatorium, the little bungalow which was to house the Senior British officer and his staff, the well-kept vegetable gardens and the haphazard location of buildings which still suggested an estate rather than a prison camp, created a feeling almost of homeliness. Beyond the wire instead of a monotonous vista of pine trees, fields stretched away into the distance and all the business of farming could be watched every day.

The pleasantness of these surroundings was offset by the accommodation. The brick barracks were little more than barns with raftered roofs and no ceilings. There were no partitions, but at either end, in the centre of the floor, stood a brick or tiled stove. There were no other fixtures but each pair of prisoners was given a double-decked bed and a cupboard, and two benches and a table were provided for every twelve men. The prisoners arranged this furniture in such a way that small cubicles were formed along each side of the barrack, but a prisoner lying on a top bunk looked from one end of a barrack to another and conversation was carried on in a mass of cross-talk. Nevertheless, partly because of the discomfort but more because the camp offered so many opportunities for escape, morale was extremely high. Even though forced to change their barracks almost weekly carrying their belongings through the snow and in spite of a severe winter, prisoners at Schubin were more consistently cheerful than in most camps.

From the point of view of escape the camp was almost ideal. It had not been designed for any military purpose and not only were many of the buildings so placed that they created blind spots which were hidden completely from the guards in the sentry towers but the many large trees and steep banks also provided excellent cover. The compound was small, many of the barracks being only seventy feet from the perimeter fence—a much shorter distance than in most Air Force camps and the soil was well drained so that tunnels could be built at any level.

Almost as important as the topography was the fact that the camp was guarded and administered by the German Army. Some German Army camps were controlled efficiently but before the arrival of Air Force prisoners the Schubin camp had housed French Army prisoners and discipline had become lax.

The German Security Officer could not have been less suitable. Formerly a Professor of English at a German university he was an attractive character with a large red face and deep husky voice. He treated the whole business of war as an absurd episode in which the one thing that mattered was to preserve a sense of humour. Obviously he was lazy and it was easy to picture him in better times seated in an armchair wreathed in pipe-smoke having long and rather irrelevant discussions with his pupils. He was one of the few German officers among prison camp staffs who was not afraid of his superiors and towards the prisoners was always mildly apologetic.

Some of his colleagues were of very different type. A renegade Czech named Simms, a Captain, performed the duties of Camp Adjutant and was assisted by a fat little Lieutenant who had been a grocer before the war. Simms was irascible, anti-British and vindictive; the grocer was noisy and totally incompetent. Had Simms thought a little less of inflicting discomfort on the prisoners and little more of his duties the story of Schubin might have been different. As it was he added spice to every attempt to defeat the enemy.

The German Air Force guards who escorted the prisoners to the camp attempted to warn those responsible for security of the capacity of the captives for contriving means of escape. Jealousy between the Services was such that they were not allowed to enter the camp, but eventually Glemnitz the chief "ferret" at Sagan managed to talk his way in and did his best. His efforts caused great offence, however, and he was ordered to leave immediately. As he passed out through the gates he had to pass the prisoners who were waiting to go in and he told some of them what had happened. He made a bet that there would be a mass escape within a month and said that it would serve the Army right. It was no fault of his that he did not win his money.

But more important than either topography or the character of the Germans was the fact that the camp was in Poland. The courage of the Poles in this last war has become proverbial but it was nowhere shown more plainly than in their attitude towards prisoners of war. The Germans were ruthless and any Pole caught helping prisoners was shot. Neverthe-less of the dozens of Poles with whom the prisoners at Schubin came into contact only one proved unreliable. All the others, including many women, helped in every way they could.

227

ESCAPE
FROM
GERMANY

*Oflag XXIB,
Schubin*

Almost every day Polish workmen entered the camp to light stoves, repair buildings, or do some other work and through them contact was established not only with the Polish Underground Movement but with many individual families in the neighbourhood who were prepared to take great risks to assist prisoners to escape. It is not surprising therefore that to veteran escapers the camp seemed a paradise or that many others who previously had not thought seriously of escape should feel that the chances were so good that they must make an attempt.

During the first few weeks conditions for escape were unbelievably good, but unfortunately the prisoners, half of whom had come from the army camp at Warburg and half from Sagan, failed to establish a proper organisation, and one attempt after another miscarried.

The first successes were achieved by the orderlies, a hundred of whom had accompanied the officers when they were transferred to this camp. Eighty-five of these were Army N.C.O.s and other ranks from Warburg, and fifteen were Air Force N.C.O.s from Sagan who had volunteered for this work in the hope of being able to escape. All the orderlies were housed in the stable, which had been converted into a barracks. Small parties were allowed outside the camp accompanied by guards to take swill to the pig-sties, or collect fuel, and larger parties, more heavily guarded, went into the town of Schubin once or twice a week to fetch bread and Red Cross parcels from the railway station. In late October, 1942, a British Army cor-poral slipped away while on a visit to the piggery and rode off on a bicycle; unfortunately he was recaptured shortly afterwards as he rode through the town of Schubin. A few days later a Warrant Officer of the R.A.F. broke away from a party which was collecting bread from the railway, but he, too, was recaptured within a few minutes.

In November a further party of approximately one hundred officers which included Wing Commander Day and Lieutenant Commander Buckley, was transferred from Sagan. Their arrival brought about a great change. Day took charge of the camp as Senior British Officer and Buckley at once established an Escape Organisation on the model of the one he had built up at Sagan. A new Escape Committee was formed which decided that as many escape attempts as possible should be made at once before all the opportunities due to German laxity should vanish. Owing to the size of the camp, tunnels offered the best opportunity, and three were begun at once. Working at great speed it was possible to construct a tunnel which would reach beyond the fence within a few days. It was worth taking risks with security therefore, in the hope of completing the job in between

228

ESCAPE
FROM
GERMANY

*Oflag XXIB,*
*Schubin*

routine searches. As it turned out, although one tunnel reached some feet beyond the wire, all three were discovered.

The "blitz" having failed the policy was changed with the approach of winter. Long-term tunnels were planned, to be dug with the maximum security, for use in the spring. The entrances of two of these tunnels were at the western end of the camp, one in a latrine and the other in a barrack. The third was in a latrine in the centre of the camp, the tunnel running northwards up the slope. Later a fourth tunnel from the centre of the camp running south was also started. The utmost care was taken to conceal entrances and no risks whatever were allowed in the disposal of the excavated earth so that progress was slow.

### Sergeant Wareing

Meanwhile there were a number of individual attempts. On 16 December, 1942, Sergeant P. T. Wareing, D.C.M., R.A.F., left the camp as a member of a party of orderlies engaged in collecting bread from the railway. The bread arrived at a railway siding at Schubin in a closed wagon. The orderlies were taken to the station in a lorry, which was backed up to it. The bread then was loaded on to the lorry, and during this operation one of the other members of the working party dropped a loaf on the line. Wareing went to pick it up, squeezed between the lorry and the wagon, got underneath the latter and ran across two sets of lines and two platforms. The German driver of the lorry had left the wagon with Wareing, but he got back into the cab of the lorry and started the engine; the other guards were in the wagon and could not see him. The time was about 5.30 p.m. and it was almost dark. Wareing's clothing consisted of faded and dirty Army officers trousers, a R.A.F. tunic which he had altered to look like a civilian jacket, and a cloth cap. He was in possession of a certain amount of food, maps and a compass.

From the railway station he ran south-east across marshy country past the village of Blumenthal into the woods. Then he turned north-east and after passing another prisoner of war camp skirted the north-east side of Netzwalde and joined the main road to Bromberg, which he reached after losing his way the following afternoon.

In Bromberg he stole an old bicycle standing at the curb in one of the main streets then cycled along the Danzig road, heading toward Graudenz. The bicycle was not very serviceable, and he walked and cycled alternately. There were signposts all the way and a moon in the early part of the night. Just north of Grippe he turned off the Danzig road and crossed the Vistula by what appeared to be a temporary wooden bridge. There were German traffic policemen and machine-gun posts at both ends of the bridge, and sentries at intervals of about one hundred yards. The bridge was about half a mile long. He passed these defences without incident and reached Graudenz about 8 a.m. on 18 December.

229

ESCAPE
FROM
GERMANY

*Oflag XXIB,
Schubin*

In the camp he had learned that British soldiers had boarded ships for Sweden at Graudenz, but although he walked north along the river for a considerable distance he saw only river steamers and barges, and no facilities for larger boats. Returning to Graudenz he cycled up to the railway station, which he entered by a porters' entrance at about 11 a.m. He was unable to see any notices indicating that passenger trains left that station for Danzig nor any goods trains which appeared to be going there. However, he did not risk examining the goods trains too closely and did not go into the main booking-hall. On leaving the station he saw a German leave a new bicycle against the wall so he took this, leaving his old one in its place, then cycled back through Graudenz and re-crossed the bridge over the Vistula. One of the guards stopped two Germans in uniform and turned one back, and while he was doing this Wareing rode round the group and crossed the bridge without being challenged.

He rested under a bridge just north-west of Michelau and had some food. He set off again about 2 p.m., rejoined the main road to Danzig and cycled through Neunburg and Mewe. At one stage he found a large can of milk standing by the roadside and helped himself. Reaching Mewe about dusk he was in a very exhausted condition, and slept in a haystack north of the town from about 5 p.m. until 3 a.m. on 19 December, when he set off, continuing along the main road. He talked to a British soldier who was working with German civilians on the road and obtained from him the information that the docks were in the centre of Danzig. He passed through Proust and entered Danzig at Peterehagen. He walked about for several hours searching for the docks, and with difficulty got into the harbour. He followed a smallish inlet for some time, but saw no large ships, and finding that he could not get any further turned back. On return to Danzig he met a Pole, who promised to show him the docks, but merely took him back to where he had been.

In the evening he left Danzig on the east side and walked along a road parallel to the river which he hoped to cross. There were no free ferries, however, and he had no money, having forgotten to place this in his pocket before leaving the camp. He slept in an unfurnished house from about 9 p.m. until 3 o'clock next morning. During this time a man, probably from a neighbouring farm, entered the house flashing a torch, but Wareing left by one door as he entered another, and was not seen.

In the morning he cycled east for about six or seven miles, but was unable to reach the sea. He returned to Danzig at about 7.30 a.m., and succeeded in getting into part of the harbour. A policeman approached and he made a detour, eventually getting close to the ships. He saw three or four flying Swedish flags and two flying the Blue Peter. In order to avoid the sentries posted on the quay beside the ships he hid himself and the bicycle in stacks of timber beside some railway lines. From this hiding place he watched the boats for about an hour during which time one sailed.

Just as the guards were being changed Wareing left his hiding place, and when the guards who were relieved passed he walked in the direction of the ships. He walked slowly to the last ship which was loading coal. As he approached, the guard on the gangway turned and strolled away, whereupon Wareing walked up the gangway and got into the main forward hold into which coal was being loaded. He entered by way of the hatch which was not then being used and climbed down the side of the hold, dropping on to the coal. Going right forward and hiding against the side, he moved later on to the back. He entered the hold at about 9.30 a.m. and remained there all day. When the hold was about three-quarters full about a dozen Russians and two or three Germans entered to trim the coal. The escaper hid behind a pillar and was seen by several of the Russians, so he addressed one of then, saying "Angliski pilot." This man told his companion, and none of them said anything. By this time it was dark and the Russians were working by flood-light. Between 10 and 11 p.m. the Russians were taken away and Wareing forced a trap door into the trimming bunker. There was no one there and he dug a hole in the coal at the side of the ship and concealed himself.

The Germans searched the ship next morning, and one entered the trimming bunker flashing a torch, but Wareing was not discovered. The boat sailed at about 9 o'clock on 21 December. Wareing remained in hiding for three and half days altogether, spending each night beside a boiler. He left his hiding place in the early hours of the morning of 23 December and was seen by one of the crew. He was told that the ship would reach Halmstad about 2 p.m. On arrival there he was handed over to the Swedish police, and was taken to the British Legation at Stockholm a few days later. Shortly afterwards he was repatriated to the United Kingdom.

\*    \*    \*    \*    \*

Two officers exchanged identities with orderlies and made an unsuccessful attempt to get away from a party which was fetching coal, but the orderlies were so well known to the Germans that this became impossible. To walk through the gate in disguise was equally difficult, first because the uniform of the German army was green and almost impossible to counterfeit, secondly because the area around the gate for some forty yards was out of bounds to all prisoners. The only way to surmount these difficulties appeared to be by boarding some form of transport.

The first attempt of this description was made in December, 1942. A film van with a canvas hood had arrived in the camp and stood empty outside the door of the main school building for some hours. The doors were locked and Germans were always sufficiently near to make tampering with

231

ESCAPE
FROM
GERMANY

*Oflag XXIB,
Schubin*

the van difficult. In despair of finding a safer way an officer decided to climb on to the van and lie on the hood hoping to be driven out unobserved. The guard and the driver had their attention diverted for a moment and the prisoner climbed up. The lorry was tall and the hood sagged just enough to prevent him being seen by those standing at the side of the vehicle; those standing a yard or two away could see him easily. He lay still hoping for the best. It was dark when the film show was over and the driver and guards packed the van, climbed in and drove down to the gate, which was brightly lit by an arc lamp high over the centre. To the prisoners who were watching the man on the roof was in full view, but although the guards at the gate looked inside and underneath the lorry most carefully, not one of them thought of looking on the roof. The lorry drove off into the night, and shortly afterwards the escaper slid down to freedom. He was caught the following evening on Bromberg aerodrome attempting to steal an aircraft.

The second escape through the gate needed more careful planning. Officer prisoners were provided with sheets and the sheets were washed in the local town. A laundry van came right into the camp every week and the laundry was loaded from a shed. The officer in charge of the laundry planned to have himself concealed and driven out in the van. Several times preparations were made, but it was impossible to put the plan into effect either because of the failure of the guard to take long enough over his cup of tea or some other accident. Eventually, however, the prisoner succeeded in getting into the lorry unobserved, was covered with laundry and driven out of the camp. He too was caught soon afterwards hovering around an aerodrome. The third escape through the gate was timed to coincide with the tunnel, which was successful. A Polish Flight Lieutenant who had been the main liaison between the prisoners and the Poles outside had arranged hiding places for himself and a friend and wanted twenty-four hours' start before the mass escape occurred. Accordingly he entered into an arrangement with the Polish driver of one of the tanks used for emptying the cesspools. These tanks were long and tubular, sealed by round bulkheads on top, and looked rather like small petrol wagons. Without hesitation the driver agreed to enlarge the bulkhead sufficiently to allow a man to climb into it, to clean the tank and to drive two men out in it. In order to make success certain he brought the tank into the camp, and having parked it in a place out of sight of any German guards, carried out a dress rehearsal.

The prisoners intending to escape climbed into the tank and sat on a small stool. They found that there was just room for them but discovered that although the tank had been cleaned carefully the fumes were overpowering. However this difficulty was overcome by the construction of special gauze masks which were treated with strong disinfectant.

On 3 March, 1943, two days before the tunnel was due to be used, the

232

ESCAPE
FROM
GERMANY

*Oflag XXIB,
Schubin*

tank was deliberately left overnight in the camp. The next day a second similar tank was driven in and after doing its rounds of the cesspools was substituted for the one which had been left. Meanwhile the two escapers had climbed into this and were driven through the gates and out to their pre-arranged rendezvous. The next day the tunnel was used and the Germans naturally assumed that the two officers concerned had gone out with the others. Their true method of escape was never discovered. However, like those who had escaped through the tunnel, they were recaptured eventually.

*     *     *     *     *

Meanwhile progress was being made with tunnels and although more than one was discovered when the thaw set in unexpectedly early in January, two new ones went quickly ahead. One of these was successful. At the eastern end of the camp the latrine was the closest building to the fence. The building was divided into two by a brick wall. Below the floor of one half was a sump and below the other a great pit. The dividing wall was carried down between them. A hole was knocked into the dividing wall large enough to allow a man's shoulders to slip through and a brick panel was made to fit it. Through this hole, at one side of the sump, a large chamber of approximately 500 cubic feet was excavated, the earth being thrown through the hole in the wall into the cesspool. From that chamber the tunnel itself was dug.

The tunnel was intended to come out in the corner of a shallow potato ditch which began five yards beyond the fence and led directly away from it. The distance from the chamber to the proposed exit was about one hundred and thirty feet. Work in the tunnel was started in the beginning of January, 1943. Twenty-four officers and four N.C.O.s worked in three shifts. The first digging, the second dispersing the earth, the third going in after the earth had been removed and shoring the tunnel with boards taken from beds and tidying-up generally. The earth was disposed of mostly in the cesspool which was so full of semi-liquid refuse that it could absorb a great quantity. Complaints were received from the driver of the tank, a Pole, that after pumping out the refuse his tank was half-filled with sand, but this never reached German ears. The rest of the earth was disposed of in the open. When there was fresh snow this was difficult and the earth had sometimes to be sprinkled openly on the paths as though to make them less slippery. After the thaw, with the playing-field a quagmire and the vegetable gardens ready to be dug, dispersal was a relatively simple matter. Prisoners were not locked in their barracks until 7 p.m. and as in January and February it was dark from 5.30 p.m. onwards almost anything could be done with safety. During that period the only guards in the camp were two ancient infantrymen who wandered slowly and harmlessly around the compound and were easily trailed. There were too many trees, buildings and banks to make searchlights any real danger. At one time the Germans became a little apprehensive that something might be going on and threatened to lock the prisoners in their barracks at 5 p.m. daily, but this was resisted successfully on health grounds.

233

ESCAPE
FROM
GERMANY

*Oflag XXIB,
Schubin*

Every evening groups of prisoners could dimly be seen walking up and down the dark side of the football field or digging methodically in the gardens. At given signals kitbags full of earth were carried out and dumped in front of them to be trampled or dug into the ground. To avoid the ground microphones the tunnel had to go deep but it was soon learned that these microphones were far too sensitive and that the noise of prisoners walking around the perimeter of the camp or skating on the flooded football field made it impossible for other sounds to be detected clearly. By the end of February the tunnel passed under the fence at a depth of fifteen feet and from that point it rose steeply in the five yards between the fence and the potato ditch. It was shored with boarding throughout and was about two feet and a half square. There was just room for a man dressed in a greatcoat and pushing a small pack in front of him to get through.

By 3 March, 1943, the tunnel was ready for use and all those who had taken part in the digging and four others chosen by the Escape Committee made their preparations. They were better equipped than Air Force prisoners had ever been before. Owing to the help of the Poles a great deal of information and material had been acquired. Civilian workers' passes, clothes, maps and plans of the locality, all were available and all those who intended to travel by train had proper identity cards, in most cases bearing their own photographs. The taking of these photographs had been arranged by a Polish girl, a friend of a Polish officer serving in the Royal Air Force, who sent a camera into the camp by one of the many Polish workers and then had the films developed and printed outside. Food had been saved through the winter and all had as much as they felt they could or need carry.

The escape was planned for the night of 5 March, 1943. As the barracks were locked at 7 o'clock it was necessary for all the thirty-two prisoners who were going to escape to be under the latrine before that hour. Sixteen were to lie head to toe in the tunnel itself, the other sixteen to wait in the chamber which was just large enough to hold them. The prisoners went down in ones and twos and by 6.30 p.m. the last man in the draw had been pushed through the small brick trap door and squeezed into the chamber. The brick panel was then replaced, the latrine seat put back and the latrine deserted. About three feet of earth remained to be dug out in order to reach the surface and space for this earth had been left on the floor of the tunnel itself.

Due to excellent survey work the tunnel came out exactly where it was

234

ESCAPE
FROM
GERMANY

*Oflag XXIB,*
*Schubin*

intended and the first two men left at 10 p.m. Some difficulty was experienced by those who followed because as each man went out he kicked back a certain amount of earth and the tunnel began to narrow just at the point where it curved upwards. More than one prisoner was stuck temporarily with his head only two or three feet from the fresh air and had to dig himself clear, passing the earth back to the man behind him. One rather fat officer took forty minutes to clear himself and was so exhausted afterwards that he failed to get far.

As each man put his head above the ground, he was able to see the guard patrolling the brilliantly lit fence only five yards away. It seemed impossible that he would not see or hear something. However, after watching him for a few seconds, each escaper became assured that the bright lights made all else inky black and that the guard's attention, such as it was, was concentrated on the inside of the camp. To each the noise which he made as he got out of the tunnel and crawled along the ditch seemed deafening, but only once did the guard stop and peer in the direction of the tunnel exit. If he had heard a noise he did not take the trouble to walk a few paces necessary to discover what it was.

By midnight the last of the escapers had crawled away and the tunnel lay empty and open. Three changes of guard took place but even with the coming of daylight no one noticed anything although the tracks of the men who had crawled across the stubble in the neighbouring field were visible. There was great excitement in the camp and to one Wing Commander the temptation of an open tunnel, even though it meant emerging a few feet from a German in broad daylight, was too good to be missed. Parade was not until 8 o'clock and a little before 7 he and three other officers wandered down to the latrine. The trap was removed and the Wing Commander lowered into the chamber and a few moments later early risers saw first a head and then a body emerge from the ground just outside the wire. The guard still walked his beat and did not look round. The Wing Commander stood up looking very much like a Polish workman, brushed the sand from his clothes and strolled away to temporary freedom.

In the camp itself pandemonium soon broke loose. The testy little Czech Simms took the parade and at first when he realised that so many prisoners were missing he thought that the British were playing a joke. Then the guard patrolling outside the fence discovered the tunnel mouth. No German dared go down the tunnel and a Russian prisoner with a rope round his waist was sent in head first, in due course arriving under the latrine seat. At 11 o'clock that morning bus loads of special S.S. troops began to arrive outside the camp. As the Commandant had placed special patrols on the road to search all persons and vehicles going past, some confusion followed. The camp guards made a gallant attempt to board and search the buses but were soon retreating in disorder. After some

235

ESCAPE
FROM
GERMANY

*Oflag XXIB,
Schubin*

hours of talk, parades and inspections of the tunnel exit, the S.S. formed up outside the gate and marched slowly into the camp in single file. The prisoners were delighted and lined the route cheering.

The S.S. turned them out of their barracks and made some attempt at a personal search. As they appeared not to know what they expected to find this proved abortive. In one barrack there was a barrel of beer in the passage and many of the S.S. troops asked how much it cost per glass and were charged fifty pfennings. German money, of course, was illegal for prisoners and most valuable. Later one of the officers of the S.S. used the barrel as a seat not knowing that in a false bottom beneath the beer were most of the papers and maps of the forging and map departments. A good deal of chocolate and other items were sold for high prices. Several hours were then spent by the prisoners on the football field while their barracks were searched but as far as is known nothing was either found or taken away.

Of the thirty-three escapers none reached England. Lieutenant Commander Buckley, the first and perhaps the greatest organiser of escape in Air Force camps in Germany, reached Denmark with a prisoner who was a Dane serving in the R.A.F., but it is believed that they were drowned whilst attempting to cross to Sweden in a canoe. Of the others, two reached the Ruhr, a third got to Hanover and a fourth was caught near Innsbruck, all having travelled by train. Two Polish officers reached Warsaw and spent some weeks there in hiding before being caught by the Gestapo. They were threatened with death but were eventually sent to Sagan.

Although the final result was disappointing the escape had several satisfactory features. Three of the prisoners who travelled by train passed five examinations with their forged papers and a fourth, seven. In several cases the examiners were members of the Gestapo and experts in the matter of identity cards. Even better was the general disturbance in the German High Command. Mass escape was always a question for the High Command and on this occasion, according to the Germans themselves, three hundred thousand troops and police covering the whole of the province of Warthegau and all frontier areas were turned out for the search. More than one prisoner had the satisfaction of seeing lines of the German Home Guard combing the fields sixty or seventy miles away from Schubin as he passed them comfortably in a train. In all frontier zones the Railway Police were doubled and special patrols were placed on all main roads and bridges. The Home Guard in Warthegau was on full-time duty for a week during a period when they were badly needed in the fields.

Meanwhile the Gestapo had taken over the administration of the camp. The Commandant was superseded by the head of the local Criminal Police, every member of the German administration was interrogated and all the officers were court martialled. Some prisoners returning from their escape had the satisfying experience of seeing the officers who had been bullying them for so many months standing rigidly at attention in front of their new civilian chief and being dressed down like schoolboys. The results of the court martial are not known but the Commandant was replaced within a fortnight and when the prisoners left Schubin about a month later the other officers were awaiting sentence.

The reign of the Gestapo lasted a month, after which camp life returned to normal. A second tunnel was at once completed. It was one hundred and ten feet long and sixty feet beyond the perimeter fence. All preparations were made for an even larger mass escape and then, for the only time in over three months, the security system broke down. On 26 March the last load of sand had to be disposed of and one of the tunnel leaders was throwing it out of a window on to a bank behind his barrack when he saw a German sentry outside the fence watching him; a watcher had failed to give warning. The Germans who had already made several searches stopped at nothing and eventually discovered the entrance, and Russians were ordered to fill in the tunnel. However two prisoners were not defeated. They managed to crawl into the tunnel just before the Russians broke into it with their spades. One or two prisoners who were watching saw a Russian suddenly stop digging and a broad smile break over his face. A moment later he continued and exposed the tunnel but by then the two British prisoners had passed along it and were beyond the fence. The Germans put guards on the tunnel and a triple cordon of sentries round that side of the camp that night. The two prisoners broke out and by crawling flat on their stomachs covered about a hundred yards in two hours, but they were picked up by the triple cordon of which they had not been aware.

Even then the game was not finished. It was known that the camp was soon to be evacuated and the mere fact that two men had emerged from the tunnel gave an opportunity to others to pretend that they had escaped in the hope that they could hide until the camp was deserted. Four "ghosts" joined four who had been living underground since the first tunnel and as no other tunnels were available they led a hectic life during the next five weeks, sleeping underneath beds at night and finally taking up their quarters in the attic of the sanatorium. During this time the camp was being evacuated in batches of two hundred and it looked as if their plan would succeed. By sheer bad luck, the day before the final batch was due to leave the camp, a chimney sweep arrived to clean the sanatorium chimneys and found them in the attic. He was a Pole and was bribed heavily to say nothing but many of his compatriots had been shot after the previous escape and not unnaturally he was afraid. He reported the "ghosts" to the police in the village who in turn informed the camp authorities, they were found just in time to be sent to Sagan.

\*   \*   \*   \*   \*

237

ESCAPE
FROM
GERMANY

*Stalag Luft
III, Sagan*

East Compound,
04/43–01/45

During the evacuation one officer escaped in a packing case which he had made with wood from the top of a greenhouse. The packing case was so made that one side of it fastened on the inside. A great deal of heavy luggage was being taken each day from the barracks to the camp luggage store, and this particular packing case was filled with clogs and various items of equipment and sent to the store where it was searched and put behind the counter. At mid-day the escaper went into the store with a number of other prisoners who were handing in their belongings and hid behind a pile of old palliasses. When the guards left the store to go for their mid-day meal he pulled away some boards which divided the hut and got into the luggage store, afterwards replacing the boards. He found his special packing case, emptied the contents behind some other packing cases in a corner, and shut himself in it.

About two hours later this packing case was loaded on a lorry and although the escaper had intended to get out of it on the way to the railway station, he was unable to do so because heavy packages had been piled on top. The case was put down in the station yard and he tried the hinged side which unfortunately sprung open and he could not close it again. However, he beckoned to a Russian prisoner of war and by sign language made him understand what was wanted, whereupon the Russian banged it shut. The escaper had seen that his position was in a shed and near the shed door.

When he heard the lorry drive away he got out of the case and hid behind some luggage until dark. The shed door was locked and a guard was stationed outside. He decided to wait until daylight when he hoped that the guard would be removed, but he was unable to leave the shed until the next night when he opened the door with a skeleton key. He walked out of the railway yard at about 10 p.m. and made his way towards Bromberg aerodrome intending to steal an aircraft. Whilst hiding during the next day in a hole near the railway line he was caught by a German and taken to the aerodrome, eventually being returned to Schubin.

## CHAPTER 23 · STALAG LUFT III, SAGAN
### *EAST COMPOUND, APRIL, 1943–JANUARY, 1945*

As they had expected, the prisoners who returned to Sagan from Schubin went into the East Compound. They found about twenty prisoners awaiting them who had been left to prepare for their arrival. These officers had been alone in the compound without parades or other disturbances for more than a week and felt that they had been given a holiday rare in prison life. The rest of the officers who had remained at Sagan, their numbers

238

ESCAPE
FROM
GERMANY

*Stalag Luft
III, Sagan*
East Compound,
04/43–01/45

augmented by British and American officers who had become prisoners during the autumn and winter, had been moved to the new North Compound on 27 March, 1943. As this compound was not quite full a few of the older prisoners who returned from Schubin were allowed to transfer to it.

The East and North Compound were about half a mile apart and out of sight of each other. Between them lay the Centre Compound, the compound which housed the German guards and camp Headquarters, a road and a narrow strip of trees. Some contact between the compounds was maintained but combined escape efforts were not possible, and their histories are separate.

The Escape Committee which had functioned at Schubin continued almost unchanged in the East Compound but as Buckley did not return, a Wing Commander became chief executive. In order to help morale and encourage new prisoners several tunnels were permitted to start, but the "ferrets" had dug inspection trenches beneath every barrack which made examination of the area so easy that there was little hope of success unless some new means of hiding tunnel entrances and disposing of the excavated sand could be invented. Again the prisoners won the battle of wits and two tunnels were completed within a year.

### The Trojan Horse

One of the most remarkable of all escapes was achieved with a device known as the "Trojan Horse." Flight Lieutenant E. E. Williams, M.C., R.A.F., suggested constructing a hollow vaulting horse and using it daily out in the open on a spot close to the warning rail. He and an accomplice were to wedge themselves inside the horse whilst it was being carried out, and then, day by day while the vaulting was going on, they would sink a shaft and dig a tunnel. The sand from the tunnel was to be put into small sacks which would be hung on a bar inside the horse and dispersed after the horse had been carried indoors. Williams was to be helped by Lieutenant R. M. C. Codner, M.C., Royal Artillery, who had been captured while working with the Air Force. Later they were joined by Flight Lieutenant O. S. L. Philpot, M.C., D.F.C., R.A.F.

When the idea was first mooted the Escape Committee was sceptical. Although the distance from the vaulting ground to the outside of the wire was only about 100 feet, it was plain that so little sand could be carried away each day that it would take many weeks and perhaps months to build the tunnel. Bad weather had also to be reckoned with and it seemed too much to hope that the Germans would not notice anything for so long a period. But there was nothing to be lost in trying, and the plan had the great advantage of providing an entirely new kind of entry to a tunnel. As the ground chosen was sandy and was constantly churned up by people playing games, there would be no difficulty in hiding the trap, and provided it was strong and did not give when trodden on, there was at least a chance that it would never be discovered. Williams was given permission to go ahead and all possible help was provided.

The carpenters made an excellent vaulting horse out of three-ply packing cases, with a pad along the top made of sacking stuffed with wood shavings. It was light, strong, and thoroughly serviceable. Inside the frame there were sufficient cross-pieces to allow two, and occasionally three men to wedge themselves in, and a bar which could hold all the sacks that it would be possible to lift. There were holes in the sides of the horse through which two long poles could be pushed so that four men could carry it.

The operation began on 8 July, 1943. The horse was kept in the canteen, which was in the main kitchen building and nearer the wire than any barrack. From there it was carried daily by four men to a spot not more than five yards from the warning wire just inside the perimeter track. The Germans had inspected the horse and knew that it was quite light, so that however many men were concealed inside it the carriers had to appear to be doing their job easily; they therefore usually held the bars with one hand only. There were three steps leading down from the canteen building to the ground and as these were in full view not only of the watch-towers but of the woods outside where the "ferrets" were often known to spy, it was necessary to keep the horse close to the ground when going up and down them so that no one could see underneath. Sometimes a "ferret" was actually sitting on the steps as the horse was being carried in and out, and to those carriers who felt themselves staggering under the weight of two men and twelve or even eighteen sacks of sand, it seemed a miracle that they never spotted anything.

Once the horse was in position on the vaulting ground the procedure was comparatively simple. A system of signals by tapping on the side of the horse told those underneath when the Germans were near, and a prisoner always stood by the horse to act as instructor and give such signals in case of emergency. Day after day parties of prisoners, many of whom had done no gymnastics for years, performed neck rolls, "scissors" and handstands in relays for two or three hours on end. The Germans, who loved athletics, approved this new and harmless activity, and more than once "Charlie" and "ferrets" walked up and talked to the vaulters and encouraged them. When tired of vaulting the prisoners did other forms of physical exercise near the horse until the signal was received that digging for that shift was over.

Underneath the horse the tunnel progressed slowly but steadily. The trap door was of wood set about two feet below the surface; above it the much trodden sand was indistinguishable from the rest of the surface of the vaulting ground. At the start of each shift this sand was removed, the trap lifted and the digger, in the shelter of the horse, went down into the

239

ESCAPE
FROM
GERMANY

*Stalag Luft
III, Sagan*
East Compound,
04/43–01/45

240

ESCAPE
FROM
GERMANY

*Stalag Luft
III, Sagan*
East Compound,
04/43–01/45

shaft and into the tunnel. The shaft was about three feet deep and just wide enough for a man to crouch and get into the tunnel opening. To minimise the amount of sand which had to be carried away the tunnel was kept as narrow as possible and was little more than eighteen inches square. This was shored solidly with wood for the first few yards until it had passed under the perimeter track and thereafter only where the sand showed signs of crumbling.

Air holes were always a source of risk because steam might be seen rising from them or a dog might put his foot in one; the tunnel was therefore driven almost to the wire before a hole was made. Because of foul air only one man worked in the tunnel at a time but after it had gone about forty feet two men went down, one of whom stayed at the bottom of the shaft pulling the sand back in a metal wash-basin to which ropes had been attached.

As always, dispersal of the sand was a most difficult matter. Some space was found under the floor of the canteen and under the passage of the kitchen, two places normally not searched by the Germans. Some was put in the roof of the canteen building and small quantities were carried away from the kitchen in potato boxes or underneath vegetables and dispersed in gardens. However, long before the tunnel was finished the Germans had discovered sand in all these places but because other tunnels from under barracks were discovered at the same time their suspicions were never directed to the vaulting horse. That an operation carried out daily under the eyes of the guards in two sentry towers and in full view of all "ferrets" and other Germans patrolling the camp was a real source of danger did not occur to them. After the tunnel had been going for some weeks Williams, its chief architect, became ill through working under such conditions and was threatened with an operation. He insisted on carrying on and by the end of the second week in October the tunnel was ready, being nearly one hundred feet in length. It was planned that the exit should be in a shallow ditch just beyond the patch on which the sentries outside the wire patrolled their beat but on the near side of the road running along this side of the compound. In these circumstances it was necessary for those escaping from the tunnel to cross the road and reach the wood on the other side unobserved; naturally they waited for a night when there was no moon.

At 1 p.m. on 29 October Codner went down ready to escape and was sealed into the tunnel; he had to dig away the last foot or two of earth and make final preparations. The count at the evening parade was successfully falsified and afterwards Williams, Philpot and another prisoner who was to close the trap once they were in the tunnel, were carried out in the horse. Just before 5 o'clock the three escapers were sealed in and after a final display of vaulting the horse was carried into the canteen for the last time.

The three escapers waited until it was nearly dark but broke surface

241

ESCAPE
FROM
GERMANY

*Stalag Luft
III, Sagan*

East Compound,
04/43–01/45

just before the night patrol arrived on duty. The exit was about a foot short of where they had intended and actually broke the edge of the path on which the sentry must walk. Fortunately the patrol was late that night and with the help of black clothing and face masks all three got out of the tunnel and into the wood without being seen. Once in the woods they discarded their black clothing and set out as prearranged. Codner and Williams who were travelling together aimed to get to Stettin and Philpot planned the longer journey to Danzig.

William's disguise consisted of an Imperial Airways raincoat, a converted Marine's uniform, black shoes and a beret made from a German blanket. He carried a small leather attache case containing escape food, shaving kit and a black roll-collar sweater for his role as a Swedish sailor. During the journey through the tunnel until reaching the woods outside the camp, he wore woollen combinations dyed black with a black hood for his head: his jacket and raincoat were contained in a long sausage-shaped bag also black. Codner wore a converted Naval tunic, converted battle dress trousers, brown shoes, civilian shirt, collar and tie, R.A.F. officer's raincoat and a camp-made beret. He carried a camp-made canvas valise containing washing, shaving and boot cleaning materials, food and spare socks; he wore black overalls until clear of the tunnel exit. Each was in possession of appropriate forged identity documents and in addition Williams carried two letters written in French addressed to himself in his assumed identity and a photograph of a girl inscribed "A mon cher Marcel —Jeanne".

It had been arranged that the tunnel should be used at 6 p.m. in order that Williams and Codner could travel on the Frankfurt train which was due to leave Sagan at 7 o'clock. Actually they emerged at five minutes past six and after adjusting their disguise walked to the railway station where Codner bought two tickets to Frankfurt-on-Oder. In the booking-hall of the station Williams came face to face with a German doctor who had been treating him in the camp's sick quarters only two days previously, but fortunately he had removed his rather heavy moustache and was not recognised. They boarded the train and the journey was uneventful, the train being extremely crowded and quite dark. They arrived at Frankfurt-on-Oder at 8.50 p.m., and tried to get accommodation at four hotels but all were full so they walked out of the town and spent the night in a drain. It was dry and sheltered but extremely cold. They had intended to spend all their nights under cover and had not taken enough warm clothing.

They left their hiding place before dawn on 30 October and walked about the streets until it was light, then had coffee in the station waiting room, Codner bought tickets to Kustrin, his own identity card being sufficient for the two tickets. They left about 8.50 a.m. and arrived at Kustrin about an hour later without experiencing any identity check. There they

ESCAPE
FROM
GERMANY

*Stalag Luft
III, Sagan*
East Compound,
04/43–01/45

walked into a park where they tidied up and had some food. At mid-day they had a coupon-free meal at a cafe then went to a cinema. About 5 p.m. they travelled by slow train to Stettin arriving at 8 p.m. They tried several hotels but all were full so they walked into the suburbs looking for a place to sleep. After some time they reached a path which led to the back gardens of a row of houses; each house had an air-raid shelter dug in the garden and choosing the most comfortable they spent a cold but secure night.

They left before dawn next morning and cleaned up in a washroom in the town. They had not been able to shave since leaving the camp but looked sufficiently respectable to book a room at an hotel about 9.30 a.m. where they had to produce identity cards and complete registration forms. They stated they were French draughtsmen on their way to Anklam to work at an aircraft factory and managed to book for two nights explaining that they were visiting a director of the concern at Stettin and he would not see them that day, Sunday. They shaved then went out to look at the docks.

During the following few days they stayed at various hotels, fearing to remain in one for more than two nights as they believed that a longer stay must be notified to the police. Several visits were made to the docks and Reiherwerder coaling station, about two miles distant, in an endeavour to find a Swedish ship. They saw one but when they returned that evening and climbed over the dock fence with the intention of trying to get on board and hide they found that she had sailed. Each afternoon was spent in a cinema, a safe place in which to while away the hours until it should be time to start their nightly rounds of the cafes frequented by Frenchmen. They hoped to find a French worker who would assist them to get out of Germany.

One encounter with a Frenchman almost cost them their liberty. This man was most anxious to help but was so furtive in his manner and so obviously a conspirator that he was rather a liability than an asset. He took them to another cafe, seated them at a table and told the waitress in a loud voice that they were Swedes and if any more Swedes came in they were to be shown to that table, then walked out. A few moments later a German woman went across to the two Britishers and began to talk in Swedish. Williams mumbled something unintelligible and walked out while Codner tried to explain that Williams was Swedish and he was French, then he too left the cafe.

On 4 November they met two Frenchmen who themselves were trying to escape and at first had thought that the British prisoners were Gestapo agents. Through them they met another Frenchman who told them he was leaving for Denmark the next night, however he did not think there would be room for the two Britishers.

On 5 November the outlook began to appear rather grim—as the escapers had stayed at all the available hotels they could find except one, which they had been warned about as the proprietor spoke fluent French.

They decided to return to the air-raid shelter where they had spent the
first night feeling that the word was going round among the French and
that they should be successful in the end. About 10.30 p.m. they met a
Frenchman at a cafe who on hearing that they had no bed insisted on taking
them back to his camp. They hesitated, knowing that the punishment for
the French would be severe if they were discovered, but this man insisted
and they returned with him to his camp several miles outside Stettin.

243

ESCAPE
FROM
GERMANY

*Stalag Luft
III, Sagan*
East Compound,
04/43–01/45

At 7.30 a.m. next morning one of the other contacts, a Frenchman,
arrived there, having walked several miles in order to tell them that he had
found a Danish sailor who would help them. They hurried down to the
docks where they met the sailor who said he would take them on board.
This was the same ship in which the Frenchman was going to Denmark.
They walked on to the docks using this Frenchman's pass and found him
already on board; he had told his helpers that the British prisoners were in
Stettin. Once on board they were hidden in a tiny compartment in the
forecastle until the ship had been searched. After the search, which had
been carried out with the help of dogs, they were put into another compartment where they remained until clear of Swinemunde; then they were
given food in the forecastle where they spent the night.

The ship whose route was Stettin, Copenhagen, Oslo, Goteburg,
docked at Copenhagen about noon on 7 November. They were taken
ashore by the sailor they had met at Stettin and hidden in an apartment
some distance from the town. About mid-day on 10 November the ship
sailed for Oslo. The escapers were put into a small compartment where
they remained for the rest of the day and night during which time they
were very ill. They remained below deck until just after mid-day on 11
November when they were taken to see the ship's officer who told them he
had arranged for them to go ashore with the Swedish pilot whom they
were dropping at Stomstad; this was considered safer than taking them to
Goteburg. They were put ashore at 5 p.m. and taken to the police station
where they had a bath and a meal and spent the night in a cell. Next day
they were taken to Goteburg where they met the British Consul and later
that day they were sent to the British Legation at Stockholm. A few weeks
later they were repatriated to the United Kingdom.

Meanwhile Philpot who had made the longer journey to Danzig had
reached Sweden nine days earlier than Williams and Codner. He was posing as a quisling Norwegian (hoping that he would never meet a Norwegian as he was ignorant of the language) on an exchange from Norway to
a Margarine Marketing Union in Berlin and doing a tour of all branches
and factories in Germany. He had an excellent set of documents to support this story. His outfit was essentially respectable as he considered that
once he started looking like a tramp he would be ruined. He had a Hom-
burg hat, R.A.F. officers' raincoat and gloves, new shoes, a pair of Naval Air

244

ESCAPE
FROM
GERMANY

*Stalag Luft
III, Sagan*
East Compound,
04/43–01/45

Arm trousers and a nondescript black civilian jacket. He carried a small vulcanite suitcase containing primarily the means to keep looking well shaved and smart and secondarily some concentrated food disguised as margarine produce. He had a pipe to cover any linguistic lapses and to give an excuse for not speaking clearly. He wore a Hitler moustache.

As Philpot queued up for his ticket at Sagan railway station he saw Codner just ahead of him and although all three prisoners travelled to Frankfurt-on-Oder in the same train Philpot did not see the others after leaving Sagan. He left the train at Frankfurt-on-Oder and as there was no further connection that night walked down one of the main streets of the town and slept beside some water, possibly the Oder. In the early morning he returned to Frankfurt and had a wash and then left on the 6.56 a.m. slow train for Kustrin which started and arrived late. During this part of the journey he was left alone with a little old man who was quite pardonably confused as to which station he should get out, Kustrin-Neustadt or one of the other Kustrins. Philpot found that it was very difficult to understand this man and soon told him that he was a Norwegian, whereupon the German became very friendly and said his son had been in the German Navy off Norway for some time. At Kustrin he left his fellow traveller and after a time walked about in the town and sat in a park. At 10.30 a.m. he boarded the Konigsberg express which was punctual but crowded and spent the journey to Dirschau in the gangway of a third-class coach. There were few incidents and he maintained a superior aloof attitude which at one stage of this part of his journey was rather impaired by his going to sleep on his case, falling off and saying "Damn" to the general amusement of surrounding soldiers and civilians.

After he had passed Scheidemuhl he experienced his first and only train identity check. A plain clothes member of the Criminal Police asked most politely for his identity card and studied it with very little concern. When he asked about the "Norwegian's" movements, Philpot explained that the Dresden police had insisted on keeping his Norwegian passport for the time being and had issued this identity card for travelling. The policeman then enquired whether the other would be returning from Danzig soon and Philpot said he would. The policeman ended by saying that if the Dresden police had stamped the photograph on the identity card it then would be quite correct but it was sufficiently in order, then went away. The photograph, incidentally, was not of Philpot but of another officer.

At Dirschau he changed to a fast train going to Danzig from Breslau. He had been afraid to take this from the Sagan area believing that it passed through Posen which was regarded by the Escape Committee as a dangerous place. He arrived in Danzig about 5 p.m., twenty-three hours after emerging from the tunnel. After a beer in the refreshment room in the station he travelled by tram to the docks to reconnoitre, but in the gathering darkness he could see little.

He went to an hotel close to the railway station and asked for a room. His reception was unfriendly but Philpot concluded that this may have been the reception clerk's normal attitude. He stated that there were no rooms available but after reconsideration said there was a bed in the same room as another man. He asked for Philpot's travel permit and Philpot had to explain that his identity card was perfectly good authority; to add colour he also showed his police permit and the clerk was satisfied.

ESCAPE
FROM
GERMANY

*Stalag Luft
III, Sagan*
East Compound,
04/43–01/45

This occasion and the train check near Scheidemuhl were the only occasions during the whole escape when he had to show any papers whatsoever. He had to complete a registration form in the hotel stating who he was, nationality and last address, none of which were at all difficult as he had taken care in the preparation of his story.

He went to his room, had a bath in a private bathroom adjoining, hurried to bed and was asleep before the other man arrived. Having no pyjamas and possessing rather odd equipment generally he was afraid of arousing this man's suspicions, however he arrived in the room late and to Philpot's great relief left at 7.45 next morning. When he had gone Philpot got up, avoided breakfast because he had no food coupons, paid his bill and left. He travelled round the harbour on a ferry which made a round trip of the whole dock area and saw a Swedish ship being loaded with coal in the Swedish dock. The ferry took him quite close and he was able to plan a method of approaching this ship along the dock.

Returning to the dock area late that evening he made an attempt to get on board the Swedish ship. Finding there was no one near the Swedish dock he climbed down on to the stage and walked along just above water level below the lip of the dock round past a barbed wire fence extension. He could see that the gangway of the Swedish ship was guarded by a sentry who had a beat of about ten paces in front of it. As he got on to a vertical steel ladder running up the side of the dock a small boat, apparently containing harbour officials or police, approached, and Philpot crawled swiftly up on to the dock just as one of the sentries from a nearby gate approached flashing his torch. However the sentry went to one side of a large sand-box and he to the other. After the sentry had spoken to those in the boat the disturbance died down and Philpot decided to proceed further.

All this time he was intending to reach the mooring cables of the ship. As he crawled towards them two other guards approached with torches but he lay quite still near the railway track and they walked by the width of the track away. After this he reached the cables and climbed up one of them but this was a bad error as it was secured to the far side of the ship being drawn tightly round the stern plating affording no hand-hold up by the vessel. He knocked on a port-hole without result so returned to the

246

ESCAPE
FROM
GERMANY

*Stalag Luft
III, Sagan*
East Compound,
04/43–01/45

quay. After a rest he hauled himself up the next cable which went directly through a large hole in the plating to the deck. He scrambled through this and as there was no shouting or excitement concluded that he had not been seen. During the whole evening the fairly strong deck lights lighted the area and the loading of the ship with coal was taking place with a powerful searchlight following the grab. As he could see no promising hiding place on deck and it seemed senseless to remain there too long, he crawled midships and entered a door which led to a passage in which there was a small galley. He drank a sort of chocolate drink which he found simmering on the fire, then searched further and eventually stowed away in a coal bunker, later moving to a hiding place in the engine-room.

The ship cast off at 7.45 a.m. on 2 November and when well out to sea he disclosed his presence to a member of the crew who took him to the Captain. He was entertained as a guest on board and at midnight on 3 November the ship docked at Sodertalje where he spent the night in a police cell. Next day he was taken to Stockholm where he reported to the British Legation, being repatriated to the United Kingdom some time later.

Shortly after this success two officers escaped from the East Compound in disguise. They had worked for some time in the book store in the Vorlager and had established a close liaison with the German Corporal Hesse. The book store was close to the small enclosure where the Russian prisoners were housed and it had been possible to observe Russian movements. There were approximately a hundred and twenty Russians and they used to go out of the Vorlager daily to do various jobs. With the help of Hesse, who was one of the interpreters who had to watch the gate of the Vorlager, these two prisoners learned that the Russians were the only people who were not given numbers when they passed through the Vorlager gate and sometimes were scarcely even counted, simply having to show a pass. A pass was obtained, forged copies made, and two Russian uniforms acquired.

In order to ensure that the Germans would not notice that two extra "Russians" had gone through the gate until some time after their departure, it was necessary for the two escapers to make sure of being out first in the early morning. In order to do this it was necessary that they should hide overnight in the Vorlager. Fortunately the book store itself was the best place for this purpose. Compounds frequently exchanged books and sackloads of books were often taken from the East Compound to the book store on a hand-wagon which was pushed by the prisoners themselves. The prisoners loaded the cart under the supervision of a German N.C.O. whose attention could easily be distracted. On 19 November the two officers were tied into sacks and loaded into the cart together with sacks containing books. They passed through the compound gate and having been unloaded in the book store were released and hidden. Next morning there were few Germans about in the Vorlager and as soon as the Russian barracks

247

ESCAPE
FROM
GERMANY

*Stalag Luft
III, Sagan*
East Compound,
04/43–01/45

were opened and the Russians had begun to move about freely the two British prisoners climbed out of the window of the book store and walked up to the gate leading out of the Vorlager. Their Russian disguise was excellent and with a superficial glance at their passes they were allowed to pass through. They crossed the German compound and hid their Russian uniforms in a wood, then walked to Sagan railway station disguised as French workers and travelled by train to Leipzig. During the journey an identity check was carried out and they were arrested as foreign workers travelling in suspicious circumstances owing to a minute error on their identity cards. Having persuaded the police that they were escaped British prisoners they were returned to the camp.

The "Trojan Horse" had shown that when its entrance was sufficiently well disguised, a tunnel could still succeed from this compound. Shortly after news had been received that Williams, Codner and Philpot had reached England a group of prisoners suggested that the daily roll-call which took place on the football field and lasted from ten to twenty minutes, provided the cover that was needed.

For these roll calls the prisoners formed up in squadrons about a hundred strong standing in three ranks. In this compound the squadrons were drawn up in an "L", one leg of which ran parallel to the perimeter fence and close to the warning rail. The counting was done by two German N.C.O.s, one of whom walked in front of the prisoners and the other behind them. There were a number of guards placed at strategic points but there was seldom more than one guard patrolling to the rear of the prisoners. The distance from the rear rank of the prisoners to the outside of the perimeter fence was less than one hundred feet. The prisoners were directly under the observation of the guards in the watch towers, but as the ranks stood close together these could not see much that went on in the middle. As soon as each squadron had been counted the prisoners broke ranks and became a huddled group.

The plan suggested was that during roll-call a trap should be sunk in the centre of one of the squadrons and a tunnel started. The Committee approved the plan and a team of five officers worked on it in relays. No other tunnels were being built and in order that the word "tunnel" should not be used in conversation for security reasons it was given the name of "Margaret."

At first work could only be done during a roll-call. The wooden trap to cover the vertical shaft was made and carried on parade under a greatcoat. This needed a great deal of care as the Germans were always suspicious of any half-hidden bulky objects. During that parade a cube of earth measuring two feet in all directions had to be dug away, the trap laid down and the earth replaced. This was accomplished successfully and during every subsequent parade this trap was raised and more of the vertical shaft dug

ESCAPE
FROM
GERMANY

*Stalag Luft
III, Sagan*
East Compound,
04/43–01/45

out. Like the tunnel from under the "Trojan Horse" this tunnel was to be shallow. When the vertical shaft had been sunk four feet and enough room at the bottom had been cleared for two men to manoeuvre, they were able to enter it during the morning parade and stay there until the late afternoon, working throughout the day with the trap closed down above them.

The plan worked without a hitch. In order to make sure that the men who had been working throughout the day should emerge in time to be counted, their squadron had to appear on afternoon parade early, but in order that this should not appear suspicious two or three other squadrons accompanied them. After the diggers had returned to the surface and the trap had been replaced, other members of the squadron stamped about until the earth covering it became indistinguishable from the surrounding area. As the excavated sand was removed in small quantities its dispersal was comparatively simple. The tunnel was being dug in the winter and, as all prisoners wore greatcoats, the small sacks into which the sand was packed were hitched on to slings which hung from the shoulders underneath the greatcoats without attracting attention. Subsequently it was buried in different parts of the compound.

A danger which had to be guarded against was bad weather, when the Germans might decide to hold roll-calls inside the barracks. Normally prisoners were only too anxious to agree to this and on days when the weather looked bad no work on the tunnel would be started. But if the weather broke late in the afternoon the Escape Committee was in a difficulty. A man was in "Margaret" and had to be brought to the surface before nightfall or he would be left below without food or drink and in bitter cold until morning. By then he might not be in a condition to answer signals and even when brought to the surface might need treatment which it would be impossible to hide and which might jeopardise the whole scheme. The only way to overcome this was by organising rugby football practices. As the entrance to the tunnel was on the football pitch there was no difficulty. During practices it was quite usual to hold a scrum for a long period in the same place and as the Germans understood very little about the game it was possible to add a few men to either side. All that was necessary was to hold an enlarged scrum over the trap which enabled the man to be brought to the surface without anyone seeing him. As a precaution rugby practices were often held even in the worst weather and soon it ceased to excite the comments of the Germans who had long since become accustomed to the Briton's passion for sport.

Having been begun in January "Margaret" was almost complete by the middle of March and everything was ready for the team of five men to go out. However on 23 March the mass escape by tunnel from the North Compound took place and the reprisals taken by the Germans altered the position. The men who had dug "Margaret" decided that, with the war far

249

ESCAPE
FROM
GERMANY

*Stalag Luft
III, Sagan*
North Compound

advanced and the German break-up on the Eastern front daily becoming more evident, it was foolish to risk being shot in cold blood for the sake of attempting to reach England a few months before the end of the war. Although "Margaret" was brought to a state of completion so that it could be used at any moment, plans for its use were suspended temporarily. After a few weeks, when the first shock of the murder of the escapers from the North Compound had worn off, the will to escape began to reassert itself. News reached the camp that American and British Army prisoners who had escaped during May from camps elsewhere in Germany had been treated normally, and when a little later a prisoner from the North Compound and two American prisoners from the Centre Compound were caught making attempts and received nothing more than the usual disciplinary action, prisoners became reassured.

Only one of the original team which had dug the tunnel wished still to escape and three other prisoners were selected to accompany him. Their attempt was timed for about 12 June, a moonless period. On 6 June came the invasion of France. News of this was received by the prisoners over the German wireless, the loud speaker of which was on the kitchen building and could be heard all over the compound. Its effect perhaps can best be judged by the behaviour of one of the oldest and most respectable inmates of the compound, a bearded and philosophical Lieutenant-Commander of the Fleet Air Arm, who leapt into the air and then ran screaming round the compound at full speed; occasionally the word "invasion" was heard coming from his lips.

At once all thought of immediate escape was postponed. The mere fact that the invasion had succeeded in establishing a bridgehead suggested a supremacy which meant the end of the war within a few months. After waiting so long for freedom it seemed more foolish than ever to take unnecessary chances. With the end of the battle of Caen and the American break-through at Avranches the end seemed in sight. Mr. Churchill's words confirmed the belief of every prisoner that before the leaves of autumn fell they would be at home. "Margaret" therefore remained a secret, a useful means of exit in any emergency during the process of release. It was never used.

## CHAPTER 24 · STALAG LUFT III, SAGAN
### *NORTH COMPOUND*

For prisoners moving camp was a mixed blessing. Like men in a ship, however uncomfortable their surroundings they made niches for themselves with whatever equipment was at hand and created at least an illusion of homeliness. After hours and weeks spent in building armchairs,

ESCAPE
FROM
GERMANY

*Stalag Luft
III, Sagan*
North Compound

book-shelves, tables or more complicated utensils such as coffee percolators or double-boilers, it was something of a wrench to pack up suddenly and leave the fruits of so much labour behind. On the other hand a move meant a change of scenery and new faces, perhaps new and inexperienced German Staff, and occasionally some new comforts and improvements. Although, therefore, most people grumbled at the prospect of a move, many were glad of the change when it came.

The North Compound at Sagan had held great promise from every point of view for many months before it was opened. It was larger than either of the older compounds, being almost a mile in circumference, and the barracks contained not only the kitchens, but wash-rooms and lavatories with plugs that flushed. In all previous compounds the wash-houses and earth latrines had been in separate buildings to reach which prisoners had to cross long distances in all weathers.

The German Commandant, Baron Von Lindeiner, considered it a luxury camp. With typical German optimism he really hoped that the prisoners would be so pleased with their new surroundings that they would give up all ideas of escape and settle down comfortably for the rest of the war. He had some excuse. He gave leave for them to construct their own special theatre with an auditorium for 350 people and a stage to be thoroughly equipped by the Y.M.C.A., and against the advice of his security officers he also allowed the groves of pine trees within the compound to remain standing.

It was also unusual that plenty of warning of the impending move had been given to the prisoners. For at least eight months before the camp was opened, British prisoners had been clearing tree stumps for the sports ground and doing other jobs which they knew would never be done unless they did them for themselves. They had taken advantage of the opportunity not only to make a preliminary survey of the camp but to ensure that all vital equipment, including the radio was so carefully concealed that when the move took place on 1 April, 1943, the only piece of contraband equipment which was lost was an old German table-knife which had been converted into a saw, which the owner had made no attempt to hide.

Once installed in the new camp prisoners worked with new energy. The clearing of the sports field was soon finished and the building of the theatre was completed within nine months. A new educational programme was begun and several officers achieved considerable academic honours before the year was out. But the greatest zeal of all was put into escape.

The main lines of escape policy had been laid down long before the new compound had been occupied. Tunnels were still the surest way of bringing about a mass escape, and taught by experience in the East compound, the Committee had resolved to subordinate all other considerations to security. So many tunnels had been betrayed by the Germans discovering some of the sand which had been taken out of them and then searching relentlessly until they found the entrance that, unless a tunnel could be completed without the Germans being aware that it was being dug, there seemed very little hope of success.

251

ESCAPE
FROM
GERMANY

*Stalag Luft III, Sagan*
North Compound

Under Bushell's leadership four important decisions had been taken. First of all tunnels were to be carried out as camp operations under the direct control of the Committee. Previously the Escape Committee had allowed "private enterprise" tunnels to be run by self-appointed teams after their plans had been approved. In the new compound the Committee was itself to appoint the organisers of tunnels and would not only approve the plans but keep a general control of operations. No private tunnels were to be allowed.

Secondly, it was decided to start three large tunnels in different parts of the camp simultaneously. Experience had shown that it was about thirty to one against any tunnel succeeding, but three tunnels of more elaborate construction and larger dimensions than before were dug at the same time, there was at least the chance that the Germans would be so impressed by the size and quality of any one they discovered, that they would not believe it possible that two, let alone three tunnels of such proportions could be built in one compound at the same time.

Thirdly, the direction of the tunnels had been fixed. To the East lay the German camp, where the risks of capture were obviously too great, and to the South the distance under the sports ground was too long. The shortest distance lay to the West and it was decided to build two tunnels in that direction, one from a barrack on the outside and one from a barrack more towards the centre of the camp. The third tunnel was to be built in a northerly direction from a barrack on the North edge of the compound.

Lastly—and this was perhaps most important of all—it was decided that if at any time during the course of operations the suspicions of the Germans were aroused, work should be stopped immediately and not begun again until their apprehensions had died down. In the past too many tunnels had been sacrificed by being dug to a definite date; in the North compound, time was to be a secondary consideration and, however long it took, one tunnel was to be finished. It would then be used when the best opportunity occurred. To prevent the use of the word tunnel in conversation all three were given names; they were to be called Tom, Dick and Harry.

During the first fortnight of occupation the organisation of escape seemed to some prisoners to have broken down. As had been shown this was far from true but at the opening of any new compound there was so much traffic through the gate that both German and British control had to be relaxed. German civilian workmen were still putting the finishing touches to many buildings, trees were still being felled or lopped and trunks and branches taken through the gate in cart-loads. Visits of German officers

252

ESCAPE
FROM
GERMANY

*Stalag Luft
III, Sagan*
North Compound

and other members of the camp staff were much more frequent than usual and British prisoners were continually coming and going, collecting furniture or making representations about equipment in the Vorlager. As a result tools could be stolen, passes filched from workmen's coats.

Meanwhile, long-term preparations went steadily ahead. The day after the camp had been occupied, notices were posted in every barrack inviting those who wished to take part in various kinds of sport to put their names on a list. It had already been made known secretly that these lists were to register volunteers for the escape organisation, and about two-thirds of the camp applied. As sport on such a scale was impossible and such long lists might have aroused suspicion, they were at once re-sorted by the camp adjutant in a special file under educational headings. Under "History" for instance, came those who were to disperse sand from tunnels, under "German" those who were to be contacts, under "Rugger" those who were to dig, and so on.

Next an accurate survey of the whole camp was made by the mapping department. All distances between buildings, and the wire and even beyond as far as the edge of the woods were measured, and these and all "blind" spots were charted. Based on this chart, sites for the entrances to the tunnels and places where sand could be dispersed were chosen, and during the first two or three weeks, when there was too much movement to begin tunnelling in earnest, all the other preparations were made. Tools and machinery such as the air pump and airlines were constructed in parts and hidden, and teams for digging and dispersing were chosen and their equipment made. The methods of dispersal were also decided.

With all this activity going on security was vital. In addition to the normal "duty pilot" and "stooge system", the North compound was divided into two zones. The zone to the east was the safe zone, because, although nearer the German compound, no escaping operations were to take place in it and Germans could do little harm while they remained there. The zone to the west was the danger zone and if any "ferret" or other inquisitive German crossed the line, all escape operations were immediately suspended. As the barracks were not locked until 10 p.m. a special system of signals by torch and runner was devised to cover the hours of darkness. These precautions were so successful that although the Germans eventually discovered one tunnel no prisoner was ever caught doing anything connected with escape and no important piece of escape equipment was found by the Germans in a search.

Although tunnelling dominated operations, other forms of escape were not neglected. An attempt in disguise took place on 10 April when two officers wearing Russian uniforms, with civilian clothes underneath, joined a party of Russians who had been engaged on clearing trees from the sports field. As the party moved towards the gate one of the escapers

253

ESCAPE
FROM
GERMANY

*Stalag Luft
III, Sagan*
North Compound

heard a sentry in a watch-tower shout "There are two British prisoners among the Russians." He broke away and ran back to his barrack but his companion carried on and when the guard stopped him at the gate, the Russians swore that he was one of them. He got through but was recognised immediately afterwards by a guard and arrested.

The first mass escape was the result of a particularly bold piece of bluff. It had been noticed that the precautions at the gate were not as strict as they had been in the East Compound, and that anyone with a pass could get through without much questioning. It was decided therefore to try and get hold of the pass used by German soldiers who accompanied prisoners out of the camp and to use it on a large scale. Bribery produced a pass, which was soon forged and early in May the plans were laid.

The presence of lice in any prisoner of war camp was not unusual, but was one of the things which always galvanised the German authorities into rapid action. Lice carry typhus, and a typhus epidemic cannot be contained by barbed wire; the Escape Committee decided that lice should be found in the camp and that a series of de-lousing parties should be organised. These parties would have to go out of the gate and then turn right along the road for a few hundred yards to reach the compound in which stood the hospital. On the left of the road was a pine wood leading down to the railway lines and the station.

The plan was that once a few genuine de-lousing parties had gone out of the gate a party of the same size, accompanied by a prisoner disguised as a German guard and carrying a forged pass, should follow and once through the gates and on to the road should disappear into the woods. It was important to make sure that as few Germans as possible were about at the time, and that no German detailed to accompany a real de-lousing party should be waiting about for that purpose.

On the day chosen lice were duly discovered and de-lousing parties immediately organised; and in order to be rid of German escorts for long enough to carry out the scheme, a verbal arrangement was made between the British and German adjutants that after the last morning party had returned about 12.30 p.m. no further parties would leave the camp until 2.30 p.m. This arrangement, being verbal and unofficial was not communicated to the guardroom, and the prisoners gambled on the hope that the new guard, which took over at 2 p.m. would know nothing about it and would not be surprised if de-lousing parties appeared at any time.

One further precaution had to be taken. The road along which the party would have to walk was within sight of the guards in the sentry towers, and if they should happen to look behind them they would see the prisoners disappearing into the wood; it was necessary to cause some diversion to keep their attention on the compound. A decoy party of senior officers, also accompanied by a prisoner in German uniform with a

ESCAPE
FROM
GERMANY

*Stalag Luft
III, Sagan*
North Compound

forged pass, was therefore detailed to follow immediately after the main party ostensibly to attend a conference with the German Camp Commandant. It was calculated that their presence at the gate would occupy the attention of the guards in the towers for long enough to enable the first party to disappear and should they be able to pass through successfully, they too would take their chance of being able to escape into the wood.

Three officers, two Belgian and the other Dutch, all of whom spoke fluent German were chosen to act as the German guards. The uniforms were made in the compound on what were by now standard lines and they carried genuine pistol holsters acquired by bribery which were filled with blocks of wood. The other officers to take part in the escape were chosen by the Head of the Escape Committee because it was unlikely that it would be long before the Germans discovered their departure, and it was necessary for most of the prisoners to travel on the very first trains out of Sagan station; a knowledge of some foreign language was therefore important.

At a few minutes past 2 o'clock in the afternoon of the selected day, just after the German guards had been changed, the main party of twenty-seven escapers began to assemble at the main gate accompanied by two of the "guards." Each man wore civilian clothes under his uniform or great-coat and a few minutes were spent while the two "guards" made them stand in threes for counting. While this was happening the second party, consisting of six senior officers, was paraded behind the main party by the other "guard." The German who was guarding the gate was within a few yards of the prisoners, waiting without particular interest for them to pass through. The main party moved off and when it reached the gate the "guard" who was in front showed his pass. The sentry glanced at it and opened the gate without comment. Having seen the party pass through the compound gate the guard at the second gate was even more perfunctory and the whole party passed out of the camp without question and turned right along the road.

Meanwhile the second party had arrived at the compound gate and they in turn were passed through. When they reached the second gate however the sentry, not recognising the German "guard" personally as one of the N.C.O.s of the camp, took him into the guardroom to ask him some questions. The other six prisoners stood by the gate watching the main party down the road.

When the main party had marched about half the distance between the compound and the gate leading into the Vorlager it was halted. The "guard" in charge of the party once again counted the prisoners ostentatiously and while doing so observed that the second party had been held up. Without hesitation he marched his party off the road along a track leading into the woods and when it had gone a few yards into the trees dispersed it. The plan had worked perfectly, the guards in the towers had watched the second party and no one saw the main party disappear.

255

ESCAPE
FROM
GERMANY

*Stalag Luft
III, Sagan*
North Compound

Meanwhile in the guardroom the Guard Commander telephoned the German Officers' Mess to make enquiries. The Security Officer at once became suspicious because he knew that no meeting between the Commandant and the senior officers had been arranged, and he and several of his staff hurried up to the guardroom. Realising that they were about to be arrested, one or two of the party managed to throw their forged papers back into the compound over the wire before being taken into the guardroom, where they were stripped and searched.

The German Security Officer was delighted at having caught all the senior officers red-handed, and one of them agreed with him when in great good humour he said that it really was useless for prisoners to try to escape because his security measures were so efficient. At that moment the telephone bell rang. Realising that the second part had been a fake, one of the German guards had telephoned to discover whether the first de-lousing party had arrived at the de-lousing shed, and the reply was being given. The Security Officer's face changed from incredulity to horror and from horror to fury as he realised what had taken place, and at that moment the Camp Commandant himself came into the guardroom. Both lost their tempers at once and picked on one of the senior officers as the ring leader, telling him that his days were numbered. All were then sent to the "cooler" for a sentence of ten days.

None of those who escaped reached home. Most were caught in the woods or at the railway station, and one or two managed to remain at large for a day or two. One prisoner walked the sixty miles south-west into Czechoslovakia.

The whole of the area was forest, and he covered the distance in a week. Once across the Czechoslovakian frontier he decided to try and obtain help and made himself known to some Czechs in an inn. At once they took charge of him and he remained in Czechoslovakia for three weeks while the Czech Underground Movement tried to get the necessary papers to enable him to reach Switzerland. They were unable to do this, but they gave him new clothes and bought a railway ticket to a place near the southern end of the Czech-German frontier. He crossed into Germany on foot, then travelling by train, made his way to within about forty miles of Lake Constance. He continued on foot aiming for a part of the frontier near Bregenz, of which he had a detailed map. There is a loop in the Rhine at that point and an island between the bed of the old Rhine and the course of the new. This is, in fact, Swiss territory, the frontier being along the old river bed, which is comparatively dry. It was here that he aimed to cross but he missed it and came upon the frontier rather sooner than he expected. Here he made the mistake so many others had done before him. Instead of treating the last mile or two like a deer-stalk, he walked boldly along a path and in the darkness walked straight into a guard, who arrested him. He was within a few yards of Switzerland.

The perimeter fence was climbed on two occasions. Soon after the compound was opened an officer managed to get up to the wire under a sentry box and climbed over without being seen. He was caught almost immediately. Shortly after the mass escape through the gate another officer bribed a sentry to allow him to climb the wire, and on 12 July he and a Norwegian climbed over the fence while the attention of the sentries was distracted. But the sentry who had been bribed fired a warning shot, and the two escapers were caught shortly afterwards in the woods.

Another officer had bad luck trying to reach Switzerland. The guard on the compound gate was a new man, unfamiliar with prisoners, his fellow guards and procedure. The escaper, who spoke fluent German, put on a German uniform over civilian clothes and on 14 July walked to the compound gate, where he told this particular guard that he was a member of the camp security staff and demanded to be allowed through. The guard opened the gate, and the escaper having disposed of his German uniform in the woods, walked to Sagan railway station. He travelled by train to Strasbourg, and visited an address which had been supplied to him by the Escape Committee. Unfortunately he was unable to obtain help there so travelled by train to Mulhouse, where he visited another address similarly supplied, with the same result. He met a French prisoner of war to whom he told his story, and was advised to try and reach Switzerland via Weil. He travelled there by train, but as he was unable to show any papers permitting him to cross the frontier he was arrested and accused of being a spy. Eventually he had to confess his true identity.

The final attempt to escape through the gate of this compound in disguise was made by a Norwegian sergeant serving in the Royal Air Force. He passed through the compound gate in the guise of a "ferret" under which he wore a civilian suit. He intended to travel as a Danish worker being transferred to Flensburg. He was a fluent German speaker, and was able to bluff the guard on the gate, explaining that his gate pass had no photograph because he was a new arrival. A German N.C.O. who overheard this discussion followed him and arrested him on the road outside the camp.

## CHAPTER 25 · TOM, DICK AND HARRY

By 11 April, 1943, the sites for the traps of the three major tunnels had been chosen and work begun. For security reasons the tunnels were known as "Tom," "Dick" and "Harry." The traps which disguised the entrances of these tunnels were amongst the most ingenious ever constructed. In each

257

ESCAPE
FROM
GERMANY

*Tom, Dick
and Harry*

barrack the floors of the wash-rooms and lavatories were concrete and the few feet around the stoves in each room were tiled and laid on brick foundations, which went straight down into the ground. This meant that when a "ferret" went underneath a hut to search for a tunnel he could neither see nor penetrate into the section which these foundation walls enclosed. If the entrance shaft of a tunnel was within such a section the only way that the trap could be discovered was on the surface, and so long as the trap was made carefully enough discovery was extremely difficult. The work of making all the traps was entrusted to a group of Polish officers serving in the Royal Air Force who were expert engineers. Tools of all kinds, including the stone-masons' chisels, had been stolen, and cement was never a difficult commodity to acquire because frequently it was used for repair work in some part of the compound.

The tunnel known as "Tom" was dug from hut No. 123, and the site which was chosen for the trap was in the concrete floor of a small passage next to the kitchen. Its construction involved cutting out a square of concrete just large enough to allow a man's shoulders to go through and replacing it with another square of concrete which could be lifted out when necessary. This was a delicate task because not only must the square be cut with the minimum of noise, but it had to be done neatly, leaving the edges as smooth as possible. Furthermore, the square which was to replace it had to fit as tightly as possible and be sufficiently solid not to sound hollow if trodden on or tapped. Lastly, when in position, it had to be concealed in such a way that no cracks would be visible. The new trap was made first, a square of concrete in a wooden frame. When it was ready the floor was cut and the new square inserted at once. The cracks were concealed by cement covered with ordinary floor dust, and the original concrete slab from the floor was broken up and powdered. To lift the trap all that was necessary was to insert a knife blade in the new cement covering the cracks and raise the blades of thin sheet wire which lay along the sides of the wooden frame under the cement and which when erect served as handles. When it was finished, even those who watched this trap being made could not tell exactly where it was in the floor when they returned to open it. Nevertheless because it was a straight cut in a cement floor it was the most precarious of the three traps. Should any German prod the floor sedulously with a skewer or a pick there was always a chance that he might land in the crack and discover it.

The tunnel dug from hut No. 122 was known as "Dick" and, like "Tom," it ran in a westerly direction. The entrance was also cut through a concrete floor, but the trap was a very different type. Each barrack had a wash-room, and in the centre of the floor was a drain sump a little over eighteen inches square and some two feet deep. It had a wooden grating and into two sides of it ran the two drains from the wash-bowls on either side of the

258

ESCAPE
FROM
GERMANY

*Tom, Dick
and Harry*

room. The waste pipe ran from the third side of the sump, which was normally three-parts full of dirty water, and therefore offered an almost perfect disguise. The trap was made by emptying the sump and removing the whole of the side which had no pipes, replacing it by a reinforced concrete slab which could slide up or down. When fitted, the bottom and the sides were made watertight by using blue clay mixed with a small quantity of cement. When the sump was filled again with water, detection by the Germans was made virtually impossible. The alterations were completed in one operation in half a day.

The third tunnel, which was to run in a northerly direction, started from hut No. 104, and yet another trap was invented. In one of the corners of every officer's room was a small iron stove standing on a tiled floor about four feet square. Each stove had an iron chimney-pipe leading to a brick chimney in the wall. The floor in the remainder of the room was wooden planking, with the result that there was a crack in the floor where the planking met the framework which encased the tiles. The tiles lay flush with the floor on a solid foundation enclosed by brick walls, which went approximately three feet down into the sand. The area between the sand and the underside of the tiles was filled with rubble and concrete. In this case the whole tiled section of the floor in a room used temporarily by the Germans as a store was converted into a hinged trap door. In order to do this the stove had first to be moved and an extension made to its chimney so that it could be used even when not standing on the tiles. All the tiles were lifted separately, cleaned and re-set in cement in a wooden tray, which was hinged along one side so that when the stove was removed the whole section could be lifted. The removal of the tiles was a delicate task because they were broken easily, and scraping off the old concrete made a lot of noise. Having decided how far the noise would carry and set their watch accordingly, the team of engineers set to work on the trap on 4 May. The first afternoon only three tiles were lifted and scraped. Next day, however, using a pickaxe instead of a cold-chisel, they lifted nearly half of the hundred tiles, scraped them and put them back in a bed of sand. By brushing grey dust over the sand the floor looked almost exactly the same as before. While the tiles were being lifted the carpenters were making the wooden frame for the trapdoor. This had to be very strong as the weight of the tiles was considerable. In order to make the cement grip, small nails were driven into the bottom of the frame and wire coiled round them. When the tiles had been cleaned they were bedded in the frame in cement. This was completed on the fourth day and the work was left to set.

Four days later when the cement had hardened an inspection was carried out. Some of the tiles had cracked and it was decided that if more tiles could be found and a second trap made, the job would be perfect. Such care over the making of a tunnel entrance had never been taken before and

259

ESCAPE
FROM
GERMANY

*Tom, Dick
and Harry*

it illustrates how minutely security was being watched. Some good tiles were found under another stove and a few were brought from the East Compound by the German N.C.O. in charge of the kitchen as a result of a special request. In order to prevent noise and to save time it was decided to make a new trap and to move it bodily when replacing the other one. Moving anything as large as a four foot square without discovery was not easy, but it was done by using it as a carrying tray. Two poles were placed underneath it and a pile of old crates on top, the whole then being carried across to the kitchen building as if to collect vegetables and dumped in the room where the new tiles had been placed. The new trap was made in seven hours and replaced the same day. Four days later inspection showed that the work was perfect. The wooden frame was hinged at the back and along the sides lay two very thin but strong pieces of sheet metal which were fastened at one end only, enabling them to be lifted into a vertical position. The sheet metal had holes through which handles could be inserted. The cracks between the frame and the floor were sealed with a thin layer of cement, and just before the cement dried the sheet wire was pulled through it, making a cut so fine that detection was practically impossible. By inserting a knife blade through this cut, however, it was possible to raise first the blades of sheet metal, then the trap without difficulty.

With the traps for all three tunnels completed a highly dangerous phase of the great tunnelling operation was finished. The second phase was the construction of the vertical shafts and the chambers at their base for storing sand. Until such chambers existed the traps had to be kept open all the time when digging was in progress and the sand dispersed on the surface immediately it came up, factors which added greatly to the risk of discovery. Owing to the microphone around the perimeter fence all three tunnels were to be dug to a depth of twenty-five feet and the vertical shafts were sunk to this depth before lateral shafts could be begun. As the construction of all three shafts was similar a description of "Harry" will serve for the other two.

Underneath the tiled floor which had been made into a trap lay more than two feet of solid concrete and blue-brick which had to be chipped away before the sand could be reached. Despite the tests for noise which had been made, this was a nerve-racking operation and to those using the pickaxes the sound seemed deafening, but on the third day the sand was reached, the hole squared and electric cables led to its edge. From then onwards the operation followed an established pattern. The shaft was dug two feet square, the sand being put into large metal jugs which the Germans provided for carrying water. As the shaft became deeper the jugs were raised and lowered on ropes. This was not without risk because when full, each jug weighed more than thirty pounds and should a rope break the jug must land on someone's head.

At a depth of five feet digging was stopped and the first section of wooden shoring was put into place. This consisted of four stout wooden posts—the uprights of the two-tier camp beds—fastened together with cross-pieces and then lined solidly with boards. When a section of shoring was complete it looked like the inside of a packing case standing on its end with both ends removed. All three shafts had five such wooden sections, the uprights of each being dove-tailed to those of the one above it. As each section was put into place a small cavity about six inches square was excavated behind one side of it to carry the air pipe-line because no deep tunnel could be dug without fresh air. At the same time a ladder was fixed on the inside of the shoring, section by section.

Wood for the shafts and for the shoring of the tunnel came from two sources. Each barrack had a double wooden floor, the upper half of which consisted of planks nailed longitudinally in two sections, the lower of boards about two feet six inches long and from four to eight inches wide which lay loose across beams with a lining of tarred paper on top of them. Each barrack had several hundred such boards under its floor and many square yards of tarred paper. The second source was the beds. These were made entirely of wood either in two or three tiers and consisted of uprights which supported bed frames about six feet long and three feet wide. Across the base of each frame lay boards about three feet long and anything from five to eight inches broad on top of which was placed the mattress. The beds contained the largest boards and the best timber, and this was used only for special work such as vertical shafts or underground chambers. The lower floor boards were used for lining the tunnels. Should any large number of bed-boards have disappeared the Germans would have scented danger at once, but as a general levy of one board from each of the two thousand beds in the compound provided enough timber for one tunnel, and as the boards were used for many domestic purposes, the timber was not missed. When uprights were needed and complete beds disappeared, prisoners made hammocks out of string.

The most difficult of all the tasks was the construction of the chambers at the foot of each shaft. Actually three chambers were required in each tunnel, one to house the air-pump, a second for storing sand until it could be dispersed, and a third for use as a workshop. The pump chamber was the smallest because the man who operated the pump did so from a sitting position and the pump itself could be housed in a horizontal cavity two feet square. Where the man sat a little cabin about four feet square was built. The sand storage chamber was the size of an ordinary double-tiered bed five feet six inches high, two feet nine inches wide and six feet long, sufficiently large to hold the sand excavated from about twenty feet of tunnel. The workshop was of the same height and width but only three feet long, a kind of blister to the tunnel itself in which there was just room

261

ESCAPE
FROM
GERMANY

*Tom, Dick
and Harry*

for a man to stand and work. When completed and fitted with hooks and gadgets and lit by electricity the chambers appeared as palaces to those who worked in them.

Foul air being one of the great difficulties in the early stages of a tunnel it might have seemed natural to build the pump chamber first, but as the excavation of each chamber made the likelihood of a fall of sand greater, it was necessary to build the largest (the sand-storage chamber) first and to excavate every foot of it with the utmost care. After each six inches of a chamber had been dug it was shored with a frame consisting of a floor board, uprights and a cross-piece at the top. When two frames were in position roofing boards were laid above the cross-pieces and then as further frames were inserted more roofing boards were pushed into position. When four frames were in position the lining boards at the sides were put into position and sand packed tightly behind them. When the chamber was complete there was still a gap between the roof boards and the sand above it which might at any moment cause a serious fall because the roof was always cut in a shallow arch. This space had also to be packed and in order to do it one of the lining boards of the vertical shaft had to be removed and sand poured through the hole. A gadget rather like a large-sized croupier's rake was used to push the sand in over the roof boarding.

During the construction of the workshop in "Harry", a disaster occurred which might have proved fatal. Just as the very last roofing board was being placed into position the two officers engaged in the work heard a very faint sound in the sand above them. Like lightning they were out of the chamber and up the shaft. Only a week or two previously these two officers, when working in the shaft of "Dick" had heard this same sound. On that occasion they had climbed the ladder a few seconds before the entire shaft had been filled in by a fall. After waiting a few minutes they returned to the bottom of "Harry's" shaft to find that the whole of both the newly dug chambers and the bottom of the shaft itself had been filled in. The sand had poured like a cascade through the gap left by the board they were sliding into position. Having cleared a way through the sand to allow them to examine the damage they found to their surprise that instead of having fallen in a mass the fall had hollowed out a "chimney" which ran above the roof of the chamber diagonally towards the vertical shaft. By climbing this and tapping the wall they found that it rang hollow near the top and after removing a lining board they found the top of the "chimney." This fall, therefore, was less troublesome than it might have been because all that had to be done was to haul the sand from the bottom of the shaft and pour it down the "chimney" until it was full.

Once the dispersal chamber and the workshop had been completed there was more air at the bottom of the shaft and work was less exacting. The pump chamber was built without incident. The pump itself was taken

262

ESCAPE
FROM
GERMANY

*Tom, Dick
and Harry*

underground in sections and assembled in the chamber. In addition to having double the normal capacity it had a special valve which allowed fresh air to circulate through the pipes and into the tunnel when the trap was closed, a very important innovation. The pipe for the fresh air had been carried down behind the lining of the shaft as already described and the air itself was drawn through one of the perforated bricks which formed part of the foundation wall of the barrack. The foul air was expelled through another channel which had been cut through the brick foundations into the chimney. This was important because there was no danger of the foul air from the tunnel, which always smelled very strongly being detected either by a dog or a German. From the pump the main air pipe-line for the tunnel was laid under the floor. As soon as all the air apparatus was installed a test was carried out with smoke. A smouldering rag was placed on the end of the pipe where it was attached to the perforated brick and the pump was operated. The smoke was drawn into the pump, passed through the system and emerged through the chimney. During the test the pipes were examined for escaping smoke and found to be satisfactory. The only modification necessary was a silencer. It was found that when the pump was operating the noise of the valves striking their seatings could be heard outside the barrack through the perforated brick. This might have been noticed by a dog or a "ferret" had he stood near or sat against the wall. The silencer consisted of a wooden box about two feet long lined with blanket and paper wrappings and fitted with four baffle plates which were also lined and padded. The baffle plates were simply small pieces of padded board jutting out from the sides of the box attached to either side a few inches apart, their ends over-lapping. When the air was drawn through the box therefore it had to wind its way past these plates which deadened the sound. This silencer was fitted on to the air intake at the bottom of the shaft.

The vertical shafts and chambers of all three tunnels had been completed by the end of May and a considerable length of tunnel in "Tom" and "Dick" already had been dug. There was nothing unusual in the digging except that greater care than ever was taken in maintaining direction and in avoiding the danger of falls. Time being no object each tunnel was dug frame by frame, roofing and sides being shored and the floor laid before the next section was excavated. After each tunnel was about twenty feet in length a railway system was installed.

The lines for the railway consisted of wooden battens taken from the wall of the barracks. The battens were intended to join the wooden sections of the walls and were about two inches broad, half an inch thick and eight feet long. In order to get them into the tunnel it was necessary to cut them in halves. The gauge of the track was twelve and a half inches and the "lines" were laid by nailing the battens on to the floorboards, a special gauge measure being used to ensure accuracy.

263

ESCAPE
FROM
GERMANY

*Tom, Dick
and Harry*

The trolleys were masterpieces. In long tunnels the crawl to the workings face was exhausting because being slightly less than two feet square the diggers had to drag themselves along on their stomachs. The trolleys therefore were designed not only to carry sand from the working face to the storage chamber but to transport workers as well. The wood for the trolleys was taken from barrack stools and benches and was well seasoned. They consisted of an oblong hollow frame on four wheels on to which two movable boxes were fitted. When the trolleys were used for transporting men the boxes were removed and one man was able to lie flat on the frame. It was not comfortable and there was so little room that if a man raised his head he would bump it on the roof of the tunnel, but to those who had been used to crawling such a means of transport was a godsend. The first man had to propel himself along by pushing with his hands, those following were pulled along by a rope made of plaited string. The axles for the trolleys were made from metal tubing which had previously formed a guard-rail to the cooking stove and these were set in roller-bearings made of hard wood. The wheels were made of beech to the pattern of railway wheels, built in two halves and rimmed with tin. When complete the trolleys were two feet six inches long, twelve inches wide and eight inches high. They could convey two hundred pounds of sand and were so strong that although running repairs sometimes were carried out underground, the same trolleys were used until the tunnel was completed.

In addition to their normal functions, trolleys provided a means of signalling. Rather surprisingly sound does not carry very far in a tunnel and if a man was more than sixty feet away from his neighbour, he could not hear what he was saying. Two sharp tugs on a rope meant that a trolley was ready to be hauled and varying numbers of tugs meant other things.

While the three tunnels were being dug slowly but surely during the summer months rumours had spread that another new compound was to be constructed to the west just where "Tom" and "Dick" were intended to break surface. When the Germans began to cut away the trees there it was plain that the rumour was true and it became necessary to modify the tunnelling campaign. The Germans were known to be suspicious, of the barrack from which "Tom" was being built and as this trap was by far the most vulnerable it was decided to try and complete "Tom" at once. "Harry" was closed down for the moment and "Dick" which was already seventy feet long was to be used for the dispersal of the sand excavated from "Tom." Clearly there was no chance of finishing "Dick" before the new West Compound would be completed.

All three digging teams therefore were switched to "Tom" to work in relays and the sand from the next fifty feet of "Tom" went straight into "Dick" until only twenty feet of tunnel, the shaft and dispersal chambers

264

ESCAPE
FROM
GERMANY

*Tom, Dick
and Harry*

remained. However, the extra speed with which "Tom" had been dug had meant some lessening of security and somehow the Germans noticed something. After a week of high-pressure digging the Escape Intelligence Section informed the diggers that the Germans were convinced that a tunnel was being dug on the west side of the camp but that they were not yet sure where. A race then began, the diggers in "Tom" trying to complete the tunnel before the German Security Department decided from which of the barracks it started. With the tunnel two hundred and eight-five feet long the diggers were beyond the original fringe of trees and needed only another ten feet before making a vertical shaft to the surface. However, at that point the Germans decided that the tunnel was being dug from hut No. 123 and began a series of very thorough searches. Still they failed to find the trap until one day by pure chance some workmen who were laying a drainpipe outside the entrance to the hut left a pickaxe lying about. One of the "ferrets" who had been searching picked it up, wandered into the hut and started tapping the concrete floor. The point of the pick landed right on the edge of the trap where the cracks had been re-cemented and a chip flew off. "Tom" was discovered.

"Tom's" life however did not end at once. Having found the tunnel the Germans had to find how to destroy it. Its construction was far more formidable than anything they had met before. To have filled it with water would have achieved nothing; to have dug it up would have occupied a large number of men for a great many days or even weeks; therefore they decided to blow it up. For this purpose they sent a sapper from one of the nearby Army units and whilst waiting for his arrival "Tom" became a celebrity. Officials arrived from Berlin, photographers took a series of photographs and the Commandant and his staff seemed to take a pride in showing what a wonderful tunnel their prisoners had built.

The sapper arrived and for three days laid charges in the tunnel. He was a man of uncouth appearance and did not inspire confidence in the prisoners. When the moment came for the explosion they stood at a safe distance hoping that something would go wrong; their hopes were realised. When the plunger was pressed not only did sections of earth fly into the air, but large pieces of the concrete floor of the barrack went straight through the roof and the chimney near the vertical shaft sank suddenly about six inches. There was much applause from the prisoners and in due course the Germans had to repair thirty-six square feet of roof and lay a completely new concrete floor in the room where the trap had been. The sapper had used a hundred pounds of dynamite without making any additional exit to the tunnel other than the narrow shaft eighteen inches square. An elementary knowledge of his trade might have told him what would happen.

Even that was not the end. The tunnel had passed under one of the main drains in the camp which served not only the prisoners' but the German compound as well. As a result of the explosion this was broken at a point about twenty feet below the surface just outside the perimeter fence and the Germans had to dig to repair it. They began digging close to one of the watch-towers and after they had excavated about ten feet, the tower with the guard inside it subsided slowly and came to rest at a precarious angle. As a wag amongst the prisoners remarked: "The third and last Reich indeed was slipping."

265

ESCAPE
FROM
GERMANY

*Tom, Dick
and Harry*

The discovery of "Tom" was due to misfortune. It was true that the vibration detector system under which the tunnel had passed was known to have registered an unusual volume of sound for some time, but had the "ferret's" pickaxe not landed in the crack in the concrete floor it was more than probable that the entrance would not have been discovered and that the Germans, as on other occasions, would have found some other explanation for the vibration and given up the search. It is quite certain that apart from the microphone no evidence whatever had been found to show that a tunnel was being dug, yet in the four and half months from the commencement of the tunnel campaign more than one hundred and sixty-six tons of sand had been excavated from three tunnels and hidden in a compound only a mile in circumference which was constantly patrolled and inspected by Germans. The organisation which achieved this was under the command of a Lieutenant-Commander of the Fleet Air Arm.

The sand from previous tunnels had usually been put underneath the barracks, the floors of which were raised from a few inches to as much as two feet above the ground. Skirting boards round the outside of the barrack screened the gap from view so that prisoners could work under the huts without being seen by the guards in the towers. Nevertheless, however carefully the sand was mixed with soil or covered over with the dry earth underneath the huts, it was invariably detected either because of the rise in the level of the soil underneath the barracks or because the Germans scraped away the top soil and found the camouflaged sand itself. In the North compound, therefore, it was decided that the ground underneath the barracks was to be left undisturbed at all costs. This alone, it was calculated, would incline the Germans to believe that no tunnel was being built. The alternative method of dispersal was to dump the excavated sand at various points in the open. This was considered possible not only because sufficient trees had been left standing to make it comparatively easy to conceal movements from the guards in the towers but also because there were a large number of blind spots hidden from the view of any watch-tower, enabling work to be done whenever Germans inside the compound were sufficiently far away. In addition the excavations necessary for digging barrack foundations, drains, the cesspool and other purposes connected with the building of the compound had left innumerable sandy patches where newly excavated sand could be dumped and disguised.

Despite these advantages the dispersal of so much sand was no simple matter. As has been explained previously the Germans had built several observation posts in the woods beyond the perimeter fence from which "ferrets" kept observation with field glasses and Germans of all kinds were constantly moving about in the compound. Prisoners carrying sand had therefore to disguise their movements sufficiently well to deceive those watching from the woods, and the security system had to ensure not only that no traces remained but that no prisoner engaged in this work should be confronted by a German. However well disguised the method of carrying sand might be, the risk of an accident was too great to be taken.

The security was covered by a system of "duty pilots" and "stooges" which has already been described. In addition a special watch was kept on the observation posts in the woods in an endeavour to ensure that no German should enter one unobserved. As far as possible sand was moved only during the mid-day meal period and from 7 p.m. to 9 p.m. when there were few Germans in the compound.

At first the sand was carried in bags slung across the back of the carriers neck and hanging on his chest underneath the battle-dress blouse, but this method proved unsatisfactory. Not only had the packs to be lifted off before they could be unloaded but they hung at an awkward height for filling. At the end of April a method was adopted which had been used successfully in the East Compound in the summer of 1942. German face towels, which were issued to all prisoners and were about the size of a dish-cloth, were made into narrow sacks about twenty inches long with a diameter rather larger at the top than at the bottom. These sacks were hung on an adjustable sling. Each sack was slit up the side for several inches near the bottom and fitted with three metal eyes and button-holes. The slit was closed by securing the eyes in the holes by a long pin which was attached to the top of the sack by a string. Simply by pulling on the string it was possible to open the slit. The slings were worn across the back of the neck so that the sacks hung inside the trousers legs above the knee. The pockets of the trousers were slit so that the carrier could get at the strings to release the pins without anyone being aware of what he was doing. Each sack carried approximately eight pounds of sand.

In loading the sacks speed and cleanliness were vital. When digging was in progress the prisoners who carried the sacks had to work fast to keep up with excavation and in any case the time during which the camp was free of "ferrets" was so limited that it was necessary to work at top speed. Before dispersal began on any particular day the sacks were hung on hooks on the wall in the room where the tunnel entrance was situated and as the carriers entered they took their slings and adjusted them to the correct length, stood over the tunnel entrance, held the sacks open for the tunnellers to fill them, fastened their belts and walked off. By this method as many as four carriers could be loaded per minute. More than one tunnel had been discovered in the past by fresh sand being found in the cracks of the floor so that elaborate precautions for cleanliness had to be taken. Blankets were spread on the floor round the tunnel entrance and funnels were constructed so that sand could be poured from jugs into the sacks without any being spilt. Kitbags were kept in readiness so that everything connected with the work could be placed into them and dropped down the vertical shaft in case of emergency. In less than two minutes all traces could be removed once the alarm signal had been received.

267

ESCAPE
FROM
GERMANY

*Tom, Dick
and Harry*

Concealment depended largely on the skill of each carrier in disguising the bulges inside the legs of his trousers and in walking naturally despite his encumbrance. Because of the slightly straddled gait which most carriers assumed in the early days, they were known as "penguins". Although the name stuck it was not long before they ceased to deserve it. Because he could be issued with out-size trousers a tall man had comparatively little difficulty and often it was difficult to tell even at a distance of a few feet whether or not he was loaded. For small men it was more difficult but all carriers were constantly walking in full view of the guards in the towers and none was suspected.

Although most of the sand was dispersed in this way other methods were used. A team of South African officers invented a scheme for carrying sand inside the trousers themselves. Two pairs of trousers were worn, the inner ones being fastened tightly round the ankles with a release device similar to that on the sacks. The sand was poured inside the inner trousers and packed itself tightly round the carriers' legs. By this method about thirty pounds of sand could be carried on a single journey but this advantage was off-set by the fact that loading was much slower because the sand had to be shaken into place all round each of the carriers legs and because it was much more difficult for the carrier to walk naturally. On balance the slings were the simpler method and the use of trousers was confined to the South African team. In fine weather prisoners frequently took their blankets out into the compound and lay on them to sun-bathe. By laying a blanket out on the floor, pouring some sand on to it and then rolling it up it was fairly simple to carry the blanket under one arm and then to spread it out with the sand underneath on the spot chosen to sun-bathe. The carrier could then lie "down and spread out the sand at his leisure. Another method was to fill the sleeves of greatcoats with sand, tying up the ends with string. The carrier would fold his arms inside the coat and sling it over his shoulders.

The number of prisoners employed in the disposal of sand varied from two hundred to two hundred and fifty. Five different teams each composed of twenty-five men, one British, one Dominion, one American, one

268

ESCAPE
FROM
GERMANY

*Tom, Dick
and Harry*

Polish, and one of other Allied officers, operated the sack method, fifteen South Africans made up the sixth team which worked with two pairs of trousers. A separate team composed of thirty (later increased to fifty) American prisoners supervised the camouflage of the sand when it had been deposited on the selected dumps. Another team of about thirty British officers staged diversions in the form of games or physical exercises to provide cover for traffic or for the operations on the dumps. In addition a few skilled sempsters were employed continually on the maintenance of sacks and trousers.

The routeing of such a large number of men, most of whom had at some time to pass through a single room, was a delicate matter because a stream of prisoners going to or from a particular place always aroused German suspicion unless there was an accepted reason for it. Various methods of controlling the traffic were devised. Men were directed to go to the operative barrack from certain directions and at certain intervals and advantage was taken of every legitimate occasion of mass movement such as a parade or a queue for hot water at the compound kitchen. As an example, after twenty-eight officers had escaped by walking through the gate in June the Germans ordered four parades a day. For a parade all officers streamed out of the huts on to the sports ground and large numbers of prisoners were on the move for four or five minutes. As soon as the signal was given for parade, carriers were directed through the operational hut to rooms in other huts nearer their particular dumps where the sand was left in boxes under the beds during parade. The Escape Intelligence system was so good that the chances of an unheralded search of any barrack could be ignored. Later the sand was carried to the dumps from many different directions when the compound was free of Germans. When the weather was suitable loads were carried in the sleeves of greatcoats on to the parade which was always a deliberately slovenly affair, then carried back to different barracks afterwards to await dispersal.

As mentioned previously there were many places which were suitable for the dumping of sand. In addition to the natural dumps such as sand heaps thrown up by drains or other legitimate excavations, there were patches of sand and gravel which had been exposed when tree stumps had been pulled up, several small clearances where prisoners played deck-tennis or some other game, and gardens. However, the sand which came out of tunnels was bright yellow and after it had been dumped could not be left lying as it was. The "ferrets" had developed a quick eye for anything that looked like new sand and all dumps had to be able to survive close inspection. New sand had either to be mixed thoroughly with what was already there so that it became indistinguishable or it had to be covered completely. Gardens were also used. Most of these were along the sides of the barrack just under the window and many of them were hidden from

the guards in the towers. By digging a fairly deep trench, laying sand at the
bottom, then replacing the top soil and either sowing it with vegetable seed
or marking it as sown with labels, many tons of sand could be hidden with
absolute security. Other blind spots were also used. The peat which had
been formed by the pine trees was excellent cover. It was cut out in sods, the
underneath half being scraped away and used for soil in gardens, the top
half being replaced after sand had been packed in at the bottom. At every
dump there was a special supervisor to ensure that no carrier did his work
superficially.

269

ESCAPE
FROM
GERMANY

*Tom, Dick
and Harry*

In August the dispersal system was modified. In summer the compound was the scene of so much casual activity that it was thought possible to extend dispersal operations to places under the eye of the guards in
the towers which had previously not been used. Instead of each carrier
being responsible both for dumping and concealing his load of sand it was
arranged that a man should be waiting for him at the dump whose job it
would be to camouflage the load. This new system required a very extensive organisation but it had three advantages; it was possible to make use
of pieces of ground which were not suitable for dumping on a large scale;
it completely broke up any streams of carrier traffic; and each carrier
spent less time in disposing of his load. The danger was lack of supervision, but by this time carriers had become so experienced that close supervision was less necessary and no mistakes were made.

The amount of work done by the dispersal organisation can best be
given in figures. Sand which came out of the tunnels was frequently weighed
on an accurate set of German scales and it was found that twenty cubic
feet weighed one ton. This of course made no allowance for compression
but it was found in practice that in a tunnel the cross section was rather
less than four square feet. Three and a half feet of tunnel length produced
one ton of sand for dispersal. The vertical shafts and chambers at the bottom of the three tunnels each produced twelve tons of sand and between
April and September, when "Tom" was discovered, three hundred and
ninety feet of tunnel proper had been dug producing one hundred and
thirty tons. (The extra tonnage came from falls and other soil irregularities in the digging and from chambers which were dug every hundred feet
in the lateral shafts.) Therefore one hundred and sixty-six tons of sand
was disposed of in these four and a half months. Since the average load
carried was approximately sixteen pounds this meant in round figures,
some eighteen thousand individual journeys on the part of the carriers
and corresponded to rather more than three feet of tunnel per day.
Remembering that there were only three hours a day in which work was
possible and that at this period the prisoners, although adequately fed for
bare existence could not have been described as physically fit, this was a
creditable performance. The record rate of dispersal was three thousand

six hundred pounds of sand— a ton and a half—in one hour.

As soon as it became known that the Germans suspected the existence of "Tom" efforts were made to mislead them. The chief "ferret" was not popular with his subordinates and it was thought that if a sufficient number of Germans could be convinced that a tunnel was not being constructed, it might be possible to make him appear ridiculous and so induce him to relax his efforts. Accordingly several open shafts were dug quickly underneath different barracks and sand from "Tom" was dumped in large quantities in boxes in one particular hut. The idea was to make the Germans think that in order not to disappoint the chief "ferret" the prisoners had dug several tunnel entrances for him to find so that he could save his face. To improve the joke several officers, carrying empty boxes which might be supposed to be going to be filled with sand, followed the chief "ferret" around the compound in order to irritate him and on one occasion every man in the compound took an empty box with him on parade. The ruse certainly succeeded in annoying the "ferret" and one prisoner carrying an empty box was arrested and sent to the "cooler". However, before it could be known whether or not his belief in the existence of a tunnel had been shaken, the chance blow with the pickaxe had been struck and "Tom" had been discovered.

Two days after the discovery of "Tom" work was resumed on "Harry." It was known that the Germans were greatly impressed with the size of "Tom" and it was thought they could have no idea that any other tunnel was in existence. However, the Germans were adept at bolting the stable door after the horse had gone and for the first few weeks after any escape they took extra precautions. Though they had little idea what they were looking for the "ferrets" spent so much time in the compound that work became virtually impossible and after four days, during which the dispersal of sand had been very difficult, it was decided to cease all tunnel operations for an indefinite period and to start again only when German suspicions had been finally lulled.

The winter passed comparatively quietly. The prisoners' calculations about German suspicion proved correct and within a few weeks it was learned that the German Security Department was confident that the will to tunnel had been broken in the compound and that no further trouble on that account was likely.

In these circumstances it would have been possible to re-start digging "Harry" before Christmas, but as this would have meant its completion some weeks before winter was over it was decided to wait. Many people needed a rest, and except for those who were able to travel by train escape during the winter months was very difficult. Even when properly clad and carrying adequate food, to have to spend many nights in the open during hard frost was a severe test; for prisoners who were undernourished it almost destroyed any chance of getting out of Germany. It was decided therefore not to begin work on "Harry" again until after the New Year. The Germans knew from experience that the main escape seasons began with the spring and were likely to remain off their guard until the thaw set in. The intention was to complete the tunnel during the last few weeks of winter and to have it ready for operation before the recognised "Escape Season" arrived and well before the Germans would be expecting attempts on a large scale.

271

ESCAPE
FROM
GERMANY

*Tom, Dick
and Harry*

Between October and January a few attempts were made to walk out of the camp in disguise or to cut the wire and this encouraged the Germans to think that escape was contemplated only by a few desperate individuals. These attempts have been described already and none succeeded. Football, ice-hockey, the theatre, debates and a full educational programme were the order of the day and although the winter itself was one of the worst of the war with only a short period of frost and many weeks of gales and rain, the spirits of the prisoners were maintained by the progress of the campaign in Italy. Slow though this appeared to be when watched day by day on a map from behind barbed wire, it was the first break in the "Fortress of Europe" of which Hitler had boasted for so long and gave the prisoners the feeling that the ring round the Nazis had begun finally to close in. The arrival of several Air Force officers who had been imprisoned in Italian camps was also a tonic for those who had been prisoners for a long time. Many of these men had spent weeks or months at liberty in the mountains of Italy trying to penetrate the lines or reach Switzerland and their periods of freedom and the stories they had to tell put fresh heart into all.

On 10 January work was resumed on "Harry." It was not without excitement that the small team of expert engineers and carpenters assembled by the entrance. When digging had ceased the tunnel was already one hundred and fifteen feet long and the first chamber had just been completed. They felt that it was going to be interesting to see how the wooden shoring had stood up to the winter weather and how solid the construction of the tunnel as a whole had been.

The trap had been so securely sealed that it took the engineers two hours to open it. Down they went and finding the tunnel intact they subjected it to a thorough examination. Every frame was tested and those which needed repair or replacement were marked with white chalk, but it was found that only four frames had become loosened. However, the air system had become damaged. The kit-bags used in the construction of the pump were rotten and when they had been replaced and a test carried out it was found that a section of the pipe had become choked with sand and that there were so many leaks in the remainder of it that the whole had to be re-laid. This was difficult because the weight of sand on the shoring

272

ESCAPE
FROM
GERMANY

*Tom, Dick
and Harry*

made the lifting of the floor boards in the tunnel impossible. Holes had to be drilled in every few boards, the boards sawn in half and lifted out in two sections. It was then possible to remove a section of pipe from underneath and insert a new one; this operation took four days.

Meanwhile one major alteration of plans had to be made. As it was now mid-winter and the ground was covered with snow the sand from the tunnel could no longer be dispersed over the surface of the compound. The decision not to disturb the ground underneath the barracks was upheld and alternative places sought. The solution was found in the theatre which occupied an entire barrack and had been built by the prisoners themselves during the previous summer. Although theatrical equipment was on parole such a parole could not be held to apply to everything done in or under the building; those who had constructed it remembered that there was some space under the tiered seats of the auditorium and on investigation it was calculated that this would be large enough to take all the remaining sand from "Harry." As a stream of prisoners to the theatre would have been much more noticeable than their movements to the different dumps scattered over the compound, it was decided that dispersal of sand would take place only after dark. Movement between barracks was allowed until 10 p.m. and this gave the sand-carriers at least four hours daily in which to operate.

The whole organisation of sand dispersal therefore was altered and simplified. Instead of covering the whole compound the dispersal security system was concentrated on certain fixed routes to the theatre and a special system guarded the hut from which the tunnel began. Since the discovery of "Tom" a special security patrol usually consisting of one "ferret" had been instituted from 6 p.m. onwards and a special "contact" was detailed to look after him each evening and to keep him fully occupied.

The method of carrying sand was also altered. As the sand was brought back from the working face in the tunnel it was loaded directly into kit-bags at the bottom of the vertical shaft. When half-filled each kit-bag weighed between eighty and a hundred pounds and after being hauled to the surface they were taken to another barrack nearby where a room was set aside for loading the carriers. These men still wore slings across their shoulders but the sacks were of a larger size, each holding about thirty-five pounds instead of the former eight and without any opening at the bottom. In the loading room the sand was transferred from the kit-bags to the carriers' sacks. Each carrier, wearing a greatcoat, then went by an allotted route to the theatre and dumped his load through the trap in the floor of the auditorium.

The carriers were chosen for their height because tall men wore long greatcoats and could hide their bags more easily. Under the auditorium floor worked another party which had been chosen for exactly the opposite reason. There was not much room and a small man could move about more easily. To have spread the sand in the uneven space formed by the auditorium would have been slow and awkward and in order to overcome this, the men working there dug special trenches to give them greater freedom of movement. Special movement control officers were stationed at various points between the tunnel entrance and the loading room, along the routes to the theatre and in the theatre itself; any one of whom could order work to stop in case of emergency.

273

ESCAPE
FROM
GERMANY

*Tom, Dick
and Harry*

The loading room was the most vulnerable point because there was no means of disguising what was taking place and if a "ferret" should walk in discovery was inevitable. However "ferrets", particularly when they were alone, were not in the habit of walking into prisoners' rooms in a haphazard manner. However tough a man might be, it was not easy for him to enter rooms where he was sure of a hostile reception day after day and year after year. On the other hand, once a "ferret" discovered a room in which he received a welcome, a cup of tea and a cigarette, it was not very long before he found his way there regularly.

Some points on the routes from the loading room to the theatre were open to view from the watch-towers and carriers could be caught in the searchlights. As these were concentrated mainly on the area near the fences there was very little danger of figures seen only in a passing beam of light arousing any suspicion but when snow was on the ground and there was a full moon visibility was so good that work had to be suspended. An unexpected difficulty against which special precautions had to be taken was the smell of the freshly dug sand. This had always been noticeable when a tunnel was opened but it was found that it hung in the loading room as well. In order to neutralise it a tin of particularly strong tobacco was kept smouldering in the corridor.

The number of officers employed in this method of sand dispersal was about eighty, of whom thirty-five were carriers, twelve worked below the theatre floor, fifteen transported the kit-bags from the shaft to the loading room and the remainder were traffic controllers, loaders, messengers and maintenance men.

On 15 January, four days after it had been re-opened, work was restarted on the tunnel. The estimated distance to the trees beyond the perimeter fence was a further two hundred and twenty feet; two more staging posts or "half-way houses" as they were called, had also to be dug and then a vertical shaft twenty-five feet high to the surface. "Half-way houses" got their name from an earlier tunnel when the description had been accurate and consisted of a sort of blister or all round enlargement of the tunnel about eight feet long, three feet wide and rather more than three feet high. They were useful for many reasons. When a tunnel was more than one hundred feet long the time taken to haul the trolley from

274

ESCAPE
FROM
GERMANY

*Tom, Dick
and Harry*

the working face to the base of the vertical shaft and back again was considerable and the length of rope required became more and more cumbersome. With a staging post large enough to accommodate a man, a changeover could be made and a new section of the railway operated. Such a post could also be used to house equipment, to carry out running repairs to trolleys, and generally to allow diggers to get the sand out of their eyes, light a cigarette and do the things which it was impossible to do in the narrow confines of the tunnel itself.

Work both in the tunnel and on the surface went smoothly until the end of January when the full moon made dispersal difficult and slowed down operations. A further slight delay was caused by a fault in direction. One day the surveyors noticed that the tunnel appeared to be turning to the right and on taking a bearing discovered that it was a foot out of line. Owing to the fact that no shoring could be removed without the risk of a fall this error had to be cured gradually and the tunnel was not straightened finally until the curve had travelled a lateral distance of four feet. The tunnel then went ahead in the right direction on a course parallel to the original. At this point the prisoners had a stroke of luck. Shortage of cable had limited the electric lighting of the tunnel to one lamp at the base of the vertical shaft but owing to the quickness of a Canadian officer this was now improved. Returning from a visit to the camp gaol, where he had been serving a sentence, the Canadian saw a German laying a new overhead electric cable into the compound and as he passed noticed a large coil of insulated electric wire lying at the base of a pole. As the workman was at the top of the pole and there were no guards near enough to interfere the Canadian lifted the coil of wire and disappeared into a barrack. The workman protested loudly but was so frightened at having lost his wire that he failed to report it, an omission which cost him dearly later on. When examined the coil was found to contain just over eight hundred feet of wire insulated with a red plastic substance which was quite impervious to moisture. No better wire to light a tunnel could be imagined and from this time onwards there was one lamp in each "half-way house" and another at the working face. As the current for the compound was turned on for the greater part of each twenty-four hours in winter this made work much easier.

The February moon period came and went without incident and a day or two later the tunnel passed the two hundred foot mark and the second "half-way house" was begun. Progress was well up to expectations when towards the end of February it was learned that the senior and most dangerous ferret was to go on a fortnight's leave on 1 March. It was decided that if it was humanly possible the tunnel would be finished before he returned in order that the trap could be sealed until the time arrived for the tunnel to be used. No sooner had this decision been taken than a calamity befell the prisoners. On 1 March, without any warning twenty prisoners including one of the chief tunnel engineers, the tunnel security officer and the officer in charge of sand dispersal were called out of the ranks at morning parade and told that they were leaving the compound at

once and being sent to the new one which had just been built at Belaria three miles away. To make matters worse they were not even allowed to return to their barracks to collect their belongings but were held in the very barrack from which the tunnel was being dug while their kit was brought to them and they were searched. A whole day out of the fourteen in which the tunnel was to be finished therefore was wasted.

Instead of dampening the spirits of those who remained, the loss of so many experts acted as a spur. So far as could be ascertained their transfer was not connected with any particular suspicions on the part of the Germans but in order to make doubly sure from then on until the tunnel was finished every man worked as though his life depended upon it. Many persuaded themselves that if only the tunnel could be finished before the chief "ferret" returned from his leave the gods would be on their side. During the fortnight these men thought tunnels, dreamed tunnels and even with caution, talked tunnels. There appeared to be no time to think or do anything else. The results surpassed expectations. On 3 March twelve feet of tunnel was dug, shored and the sand dispersed. Next day that record was beaten and fourteen feet of completed tunnel was constructed, a record which lasted until the end of the war. On the tenth day the length of the tunnel was three hundred and twenty-six feet and the work on the last "half-way house" begun. This meant that in nine days one hundred and twelve feet of tunnel had been dug and shored and four days were left to complete the last "half-way house" and dig the vertical shaft. At the time this seemed out of the question but the prisoners went on trying. Although it was longer than its predecessors by two feet the last "half-way house" was completed in one day. This left three days for the construction of the vertical shaft.

The vertical exit shaft was more difficult to dig than the entrance for the simple reason that the digger had to work upwards and all the sand he cut fell on top of him. This made it not merely unpleasant but dangerous work. While the last "half-way house" was being completed the carpenters were busy constructing special shoring for the shaft and a special shield under which the diggers were to work. The shield consisted of a frame of three boards, each of which could be moved in turn. The digger held the shield above his head and while standing under two of the boards, removed the third and dug through the gap. Then he would replace the board, remove another one and so on. The effort of holding up the shield at the same time as digging was very tiring.

The night before work was begun on the vertical shaft the prisoners

276

ESCAPE
FROM
GERMANY

*Tom, Dick
and Harry*

had a stroke of luck. There was a fall just at the end of the tunnel and after the sand, which had poured through on to the floor, had been cleared away it was discovered that there was a hollow beyond the last frame rising in a dome over the roof of the tunnel to a height of four feet. This made the construction of the first section of the exit shaft much easier and the posts and lining for the base were erected to a height of three feet without any digging whatever. The sections above were difficult, however, because it was necessary to cut into the dome caused by the fall and this caused further falls. The shield served a double purpose, for in addition to preventing sand falling on to the digger it acted as a tipper from which the sand was diverted on to the roof of the tunnel, thus helping to fill in the gap. As frame after frame of the shaft was erected, the apex of the fall moved more and more over the centre of the shaft until it became stable at a height of about twelve feet. The roof of the last "half-way house" at the end of the tunnel had then to be strengthened to take the weight of loose sand which was being poured on to it, but by the end of the second day the top of the fall had been passed and the whole cavity filled in.

The second day was decisive. At the end of it the diggers knew that the unbelievable had been achieved and that the tunnel would be completed within the fourteen days scheduled and before the chief "ferret" should return from his leave. Although no one realised at the time that they were going down for the final working shift, some premonition of it must have been felt for as the team gathered round the trap they were unusually silent. The engineer in charge of the project has stated:—

> "Many of us felt that we had nearly come to the end of a job that had been our whole existence. We had spent more than a third of our conscious time down this hole out of the last ten weeks and some of us nearer half our time; when we were not actually working all our thoughts seemed to be taken up with the tunnel's needs. Even in bed it was on our minds. We had lived 'Harry', slept 'Harry' and eaten 'Harry', for sand seemed invariably to be in one's hair, one's ears, one's eyes and somehow to find its way into one's food.
>
> "As shift boss I knew the idiosyncracies of every member of the team. We were an international shift composed of men from England, Ireland, Scotland, Wales, France, Denmark, Norway, South Africa, Canada, Australia, New Zealand and the Argentine. They had pulled together as a team proverbially should. Even when feeling ill or hungry they had turned up for work day after day with nothing worse than a crack at me for always picking on them when there was dirty work to do. Oddly enough it was with a feeling of sorrow that we went below to complete the final stages."

What was true of the engineer's team was true of every man who had been employed in whatever capacity. In a sense digging was the easiest task because it was exciting. Carrying sand, and above all keeping watch, were often boring and in time became drudgery, and if any were to be selected for special praise it should be those who were responsible for security, on which all else depended.

The ladder was fitted in sections to the side of the shaft and at the end of the second day's work the shaft was nineteen feet high. In the evening the second engineer went down to test the distance between the top of the shaft and the surface. This was done with an old fencing foil which was pushed through the earth slowly until it ceased to meet with any resistance. It was dark and there was no chance of it being seen. The second engineer had not been gone more than twenty minutes when he reappeared at the entrance to the tunnel in a state of great excitement and reported that he was amazed to find that the shaft was within nine inches of the surface. Should one more frame have been put into the shaft before the test had been carried out it would have broken surface unintentionally. The shield was put on top of the shaft and packed tightly with sand in case anyone stepped on the ground at that point, and at 9.45 p.m. on 14 March the last shift returned to the surface and the man in charge of the trap sealed it to await the day for the tunnel to be used.

When completed "Harry" was three hundred and thirty-six feet long, the entrance shaft was twenty-eight feet deep and the exit shaft twenty feet high. No doubt the discrepancy was due partly to the lower level of the ground outside the camp where the tunnel emerged and also to the fact that the level of the tunnel had risen one or two feet during its building. Since the resumption of work on 10 January eighty tons of sand had been taken out representing approximately two hundred and thirty feet of tunnel. Counting the blank days when no movement of sand was possible this gave an average of three and a half feet of tunnel dug each day, a slight improvement on the rate of progress maintained the previous summer. The greatest amount of sand dispersed in one evening under the theatre was just under four tons. This meant that ninety-eight kit-bags half-full, representing thirteen feet of tunnel, had been hauled up from the shaft. On this particular evening the "ferret" who was on patrol spent two hours in a "contact's" room which was actually in the barrack from which the tunnel started.

## CHAPTER 26 · ESCAPE

The day after the tunnel had been completed and sealed, a conference was held to consider dates for the escape. The weather was all-important. To be ideal the night needed to be moonless, with a strong wind to cover up the noise of twigs snapping, not too cold, and without too much snow on the ground. It was hoped also that the weather would synchronise with the tour of duty of a particular "ferret" who could be counted on to go to one room and stay there for the evening. The nearest moonless nights were 23, 24 or 25 March and the 24th was provisionally chosen for two reasons: it was the night when there was no moon at all and it was a Friday, which meant that on the following day Saturday's trains would be running, whereas had the 25th been chosen, prisoners would have been handicapped by a Sunday train service. No irrevocable decision was taken, and if the weather was wholly unsuitable the Committee reserved the option to postpone the escape for another month. But the tunnel engineers were very much averse to this being done because the trap was beginning to show signs of wear, and the longer it was left the greater the chances of detection.

Even with a tunnel ready and waiting, escape was not quite so simple as might be imagined. Had all those who were to go out been experienced diggers there would not have been much difficulty, but tunnels were usually dark and cramped places in which men who went down for the first time were sometimes overcome by claustrophobia. Even if no one panicked, the fact that those who were going to escape would all be carrying a certain amount of kit was bound to make their journey down the tunnel difficult. Nothing was easier than for a clumsy man to dislodge a frame and cause a fall which might hold up operations for several hours.

Careful organisation was therefore necessary. "Harry" had one great advantage in that its entrance was in a barrack, and those who were to use the tunnel could therefore be assembled in the rooms of the barrack itself instead of having to lie head-to-toe throughout the length of the tunnel, or be packed like sardines into the chambers at the base of the shaft as had been the case on previous occasions. But the problems which remained to be decided were the priority of those who were to go out, the equipment they were to take, how their arrival at the barrack should be regulated, and how they should be passed through the tunnel and out at the other end with the least possible delay and with the least possible risk of any Germans seeing them when they emerged.

About six hundred people had taken some part in the building of the tunnel and all of them were considered eligible for a place in the escape. In addition, room was to be found for members of the camp administrative staff and for those who organised the camp entertainment. For though none of these officers had taken part in the digging of the tunnel, in their different ways they had performed work just as essential, and it was felt only fair that their public spirit should not be allowed to bar them from an escape in which they would certainly have taken part had their duties not prevented them.

On the day chosen darkness fell at about 9 p.m. camp time and dawn broke at about 5.30 a.m., so that there were about eight and a half hours during which the escape could be made. From previous experience it was known that if everything worked perfectly, one man could get away every one or two minutes; but when a large number of inexperienced people were using a tunnel there were invariably hitches of some kind, and if an average of one man out every three or four minutes was maintained throughout the night, the Committee knew that they would be doing well. To prepare for the best, however, two hundred people were to be ready.

Accordingly, with eight nominees from the camp entertainment and administrative staffs, five hundred and ten names were put into the hat for a draw. As some people had worked far longer and harder than others, the Escape Committee decided on certain priorities. The first thirty places were reserved for those who, in the opinion of the Committee had the best chances of reaching England. Nearly all of them were German speakers intending to travel by train, and it was important for them to be out of the tunnel as early as possible, for not many trains ran after midnight. Forty of the key workers of the Escape Organisation were then selected, and twenty of their names were drawn out; after that, the names of the thirty next most important workers were, and following them the remaining twenty key workers drew their places. The first hundred names therefore were specially selected. The second hundred were drawn from all the remaining names on the list. Finally the list had to be revised so that every twentieth man was an experienced tunnel worker. This was necessary in order that there should be someone to haul the men through the tunnel on the trolleys. So much could go wrong in this operation that unless experts were there the whole operation might be jeopardised. Once these alterations were made, the order of going out was announced.

Almost all the special equipment was ready some time before the tunnel was complete, but the dates on forged papers could not be filled in until the last moment and the final preparation of the food to be carried had to wait as long as possible. In the first fortnight in March, one hundred and eighty pounds of special escape "fudge" was produced and packed into four-ounce cocoa tins for distribution. Each tin held enough food for two days. When everything was ready, an inspection was carried out. Suitcases were limited to a size which made passage through the tunnel easy, and every man's method of packing his food round his body was examined to make sure that he would not be too bulky. Those who were taking blankets had to roll them in lengths not longer than fifteen inches, tie them at the ends and attach a loop of string so that the roll could hang round their necks without fouling the wheels as they lay horizontal on the trolleys.

The collection of more than two hundred extra people in a single barrack, needed careful planning. The Germans were always on the look out for any unusual traffic, and as this traffic would be going only one way it was vital that it should not be noticed. In order to make doubly sure, a special survey of the normal flow of traffic during the evening hours was carried out some days beforehand, and graphs were produced. On the night of the escape all movement in the compound after a certain hour was controlled and no man left his barrack without leave. Every man who was going to escape had been given a definite time at which to leave his own barrack and was then routed to various control posts before finally reaching Barrack Nos. 109 or 110 where the final traffic controls were stationed. From there each escapist was routed to a particular room in Barrack 104. So successful was this arrangement that one of the things that puzzled the Germans most after the tunnel had broken was how so many people had been congregated in one barrack without the guards in the towers having noticed anything. The chief "ferret" believed that a tunnel from another barrack must have been specially constructed and spent some days in a futile search for it.

The final preparations in the tunnel itself were as thorough as the rest of the organisation. First some new and stronger rope had to be found for the trolleys. Very opportunely, about four hundred feet of manilla rope an inch thick was brought into the camp a week before the tunnel was due to break. It was intended for a boxing ring, but as it was not supplied on parole it was immediately taken for the tunnel. In the tunnel itself solid platforms had to be fitted to the trolleys so that the coats and equipment of those going out should not fall through the frames and interfere with the wheels. Then the first and last fifty feet of the railway lines had to be covered with strips of blanket so as to deaden the noise of the trolleys which might otherwise have been heard at either the entrance or the exit. The electric light cables had to be tapped and extra bulbs placed in the tunnel, both to give confidence to those who were new to it, and to make it easier to do any repairs in case of an accident. Two blankets were hung across the end of the last half-way house to prevent the light from the tunnel being reflected up the exit shafts, and a further blanket was folded on the floor of the exit shaft to deaden the noise of any earth which might be kicked down by those going out at the top. A special wooden shovel was made for the cutting of the exit so that there should be no danger of noise if a stone was struck or if the shovel itself was dropped. All these things were done on the afternoon of the day on which the escape was made.

On 23 March the two hundred men who had drawn places to go out were briefed in batches of twenty on the use of the tunnel. First they were told how to lie on the trolleys, for as the platform overlapped the ends of the trolleys by nearly a foot, it was only too easy for a man lying down in the tunnel to overbalance and lift either the front of the rear wheels off the track. Since there was no room to manoeuvre in the tunnel this meant he would have to drag the trolley back to the entrance, put the trolley back on the lines and then try again, and so cause considerable delay. Each man was told to lie flat, and above all to keep his head down and not to look where the trolley was going, for by raising their heads they ran the risk of knocking one of the roof boards out of place and of causing a fall. Very careful instructions about how to carry suitcases were given and each man was told exactly how to crawl through the half-way house and change trolleys without getting entangled in the rope coiled on the floor.

The exact procedure in the tunnel was also carefully explained. Two of the chief engineers were to go down first and cut the last nine inches of earth away from the top of the shaft. They were to be the first two men away. Behind them, in the last half-way house, were to await the next four men on the list. The fifth man sat behind them to haul the trolleys from the centre half-way house, and the twentieth man would take his place when he took his turn in the escape queue. That man would haul twenty, and his successor twenty, and so on.

In the centre half-way house there was to be one man lying on the trolley in the tunnel waiting to be hauled; a second man waiting his turn and a third hauling trolleys from the first half-way house. In the first half-way house that order was repeated and at the base of the shaft there was one man lying on the trolley in the tunnel, a second waiting his turn, and the control officer who was the third one of the chief engineers but was not himself going out on the escape. He was to stand on the ladder and direct operations both above and below.

In the passage of the barrack itself sat the surface control officer who was in touch with the chief engineer at the bottom of the shaft, and who had two runners to fetch the escapists from their rooms as their turns came. Ten other officers were stationed as sentries at various windows of the barrack to report any movement of Germans. After midnight the lights in the camp were always turned out by the prisoners, and all the shutters were thrown open. In case the Germans should see an unusual number of people in any one room, all those who were going to escape had orders to take up their positions on the floor of the passage.

Even at the exit of the tunnel, prisoners were to remain under control. As in the tunnel, the first officer out was to act as a traffic controller for the next twenty. He was to lie on a blanket beside the hole, facing the camp so that he could watch the sentries on their beats, and he was not to allow anybody to leave the tunnel unless the sentries were far enough away. For a signal he was to keep one hand on the head of the man waiting to come out of the tunnel, and the man was not to move until he took his hand away. Once out of the tunnel prisoners were still to be kept under control until they were well into the wood. The second man out was to take with him a rope which was fastened to the ladder at the top of the shaft, and to tie it to a tree about thirty yards away. Each man who came out afterwards was to put one hand on this rope and then crawl along it till he reached the end. If the controller at the tunnel mouth wished to warn the man on the rope to lie still, he was to give the rope a series of sharp tugs; as soon as it was all clear again he gave one pull and the man on the rope would carry on.

Even at the end of the rope the escapists were still not free to go as they pleased. Behind the tree to which the rope was tied stood an officer who was responsible for the control of ten others until they were outside the immediate neighbourhood of the tunnel. As each member of his party arrived he detailed them to stand behind one of the nearby trees and wait till all ten were in position and he gave the order to move. The prisoner behind the tree kept his hand on the rope so that he could be warned of any danger, and if he considered it necessary, he had the authority to move off with however many men had already arrived at the rope end. Each party of ten left the woods by a pre-arranged route.

As the day of 24 March dawned the prisoners saw that there had been some snow in the night but it was not considered enough to make going impossible, and the weather was unsettled enough to promise wind in the evening. A conference was called at 11.30 a.m. and the decision to use the tunnel that day was taken within ten minutes. Within another five minutes every man in the camp knew, and the atmosphere became so electric that many feared it would convey itself to the Germans. From mid-day until evening roll-call at 5.30 p.m. a team worked in the tunnel putting the finishing touches. The Forgery Department worked solidly all day, filling in the dates of all the four hundred and fifty forged papers, and every escapist checked his equipment.

Evening roll-call passed without incident, and as there was still work to be done in the tunnel, a small shift went down again immediately afterwards. One of their last tasks was to install the extra lights, and when they saw the tunnel properly illuminated for the first time one of them remarked that it looked like Broadway; all felt proud of having built it. By 8.30 p.m. when the first two men were due down, it only remained to fix the new ropes to the trolleys and by 9 p.m. all those who were supposed to be in the tunnel were in their places; an extra man was at the air pump to provide air until the shaft itself was opened.

Zero hour was 9.30 p.m. As it approached, the barrack became very quiet, what talking there was being in whispers. When 10 o'clock came and there had still been no movement in the tunnel men became anxious, and the control officer at the bottom of the shaft was asked what was the matter; but he could not discover for the nearest man was at the end of one hundred feet of tunnel and speech was impossible. A few minutes later he suddenly felt cold air coming up the entrance shaft from the tunnel itself, and he knew at once that the break had been made, and passed the information

to those in the barrack. The excitement was tremendous, but there was
still no movement in the tunnel and everyone waited to know whether it
had broken surface as planned or whether modifications in the plans for
leaving would be necessary. As it turned out, the tunnel came out just
where it had been intended within the fringe of the wood; but as luck
would have it there were no trees between the tunnel mouth and the guard
towers immediately behind it, and great caution had to be taken by those
coming out of the shaft.

At 10.30 p.m. the man on the trolley at the base of the entrance shaft
was suddenly pulled away and the escape began. The first delay came with
the third man down. The control officer had inspected all suitcases but
one, the owner of which promised that it would be of a correct size. On
turning to greet the third man, however, the control officer found himself
confronted not with a suitcase but with a small trunk. The officer in question was Flight Lieutenant Walenn who besides being a man of much gentleness and charm, had been in command of the forgery department for
many years, and he had worked so hard and so brilliantly, that the control
officer had not the heart to send him back. Walenn was confident that he
could manage; but to make sure the control officer sent the trunk alone on
the trolley and made Walenn follow it on a separate journey. Both he and
his trunk successfully emerged, Walenn never to be seen again by most of
his friends.

Walenn's trunk was a portent. It had been expected that the first thirty
men who were travelling by train and carrying suitcases would take some
time to pass through the tunnel, but owing to the fact that some had
brought different suitcases from the ones that had been inspected, and
that others forgot the instructions they had been given, the rate of departure for the first hour or two was only one man every twelve minutes.
Then at 11.45 p.m. came a most unwelcome interruption. On any other
occasion a British raid on Berlin would have been greeted with cheers, but
on this particular night it meant that all the lights in the camp went out
and that the tunnel was plunged in darkness in the middle of operations.
The emergency had been foreseen and margarine lamps were ready; but
before they could be passed down and placed in the half-way house thirty-
five minutes had been lost. When the escape was resumed it was possible to
make up some of this time because the camp boundary lights had also gone
out and the officer controlling the tunnel mouth was able to work in almost
complete darkness and to allow people to leave more quickly than before.

Some time after 1 a.m. the last of the "suitcase brigade" had been
passed through, and those with blankets began to follow. It had been
hoped that men carrying neatly rolled blankets would go quickly; but
once again many had failed to follow their instructions and either the rolls
were too large or the men got excited in the tunnel and lifted their heads or

fell off the trolley. At the last moment one man had thought that it was simpler to carry his food, rolled in the blanket and arrived at the top of the shaft with a roll which would not even fit into the tunnel so that the whole thing had to be repacked; another decided to take so much food that, as the controller remarked, he arrived looking like a large edition of Falstaff. He stuck in the tunnel no less than three times, and it was not until he was forced to remove his surplus food under threat of being sent back to the surface that he was finally passed through. Owing to all these delays, the rate of departure, far from having increased, had dropped to one man every fourteen minutes, and the control officer, who had gone up to the surface for a breather, gave the order that no more blankets were to be taken into the tunnel. The prisoners were so impatient to get away that they accepted it cheerfully, but even with this modification it had already become clear that at least half of those who had drawn places would not be able to go, and many were ordered to bed. They lay awake eating as much of their escape rations as they could, and giving the rest away. Shortly afterwards further delays were caused by two shoring frames being knocked out of place. Two hauliers crawled down the tunnel and cleared away the sand with wonderful speed, but fifty minutes had been lost. Thereafter the rate of departure increased to one man every ten minutes.

At 4 a.m. the last change of guard occurred among the sentries patrolling the wire, and at 5 a.m. the team which was to close the exit, in the faint hope that it might never be discovered and that the tunnel might be used again, stood by. At the same time number 87 on the list was told he was the last man to be allowed to go through. At 4.55 a.m. exactly, just as this last man was disappearing down the entrance shaft, there came the sound for which all had been waiting subconsciously throughout the night, that of a rifle-shot. For two or three seconds there was dead silence. Then followed a spate of orders. The watchers at the windows were told to report all movements of Germans, and everyone in the barrack to destroy all their papers and to hide what other gear they could. The control officer went down the shaft to call the men back from the tunnel. As he went he heard from a watcher that a party of German guards had just left the guard-room and was running along the wire towards the tunnel mouth. The last shred of doubt that the tunnel had been discovered disappeared.

At the bottom of the shaft the control officer looked up the tunnel and saw a man lying on the trolley in the first half-way house. He began to pull him back. The man on the trolley, thinking no doubt that someone was making a mistake, resisted and hung on to the wheels. The control officer shouted in vain and then pulled so hard that the rope broke. This penetrated the consciousness of the man on the trolley, who saw the control officer's signals and began to propel himself back as fast as possible. Without a rope the trolley was useless, and it was hurled to one side at the shaft

bottom. Looking down the tunnel again the control officer saw a body
crawling through. The prisoner arrived, pouring with sweat, having
crawled two hundred feet with heavy escape clothing on. He gasped out
that the "ferrets" were just behind him, and disappeared up the shaft.
Looking through again the control officer saw another body crawling
through which was clearly not a "ferret" because of the way in which it was
dressed. He too arrived pouring with sweat and saying that the "ferrets"
were behind him. The seventh man who returned in this way, stating that
the "ferrets" were behind him, was the man who had been at the bottom of
the exit shaft when the rifle-shot was heard. This time his statement was
believed and the trap was closed down.

Meanwhile watchers had reported that a small party of four or five
prisoners appeared to have been led off from the woods to the guardroom, escorted by Germans armed with tommy-guns. It was impossible to
see who they were. The hut itself was full of smoke from papers which
were being burnt on the floor, and muffled sounds came from those who
were stuffing themselves with escape food.

At 5.30 a.m. a single German guard, armed with a revolver and leading
an Alsatian dog, came into the hut. He was an inoffensive little man who
plainly had not the smallest idea what to do. He contented himself with
taking all overcoats down from the pegs and putting them in a heap in the
passage. The dog thereupon lay down on the heap and went to sleep, and
his master settled down on the box beside him.

For the next hour no action appeared to be taken by the Germans and,
though it was against orders, a few men climbed through the windows of
the barrack and got back to their own huts. At 6.30 a.m. a German riot
squad in steel helmets and armed with tommy-guns and heavy machine-
guns entered the compound. They immediately mounted the four
machine-guns round the barrack and covered it. Immediately afterwards
came the Commandant and his party, including the chief ferret. There was
a short conference and the doors of the huts were thrown open and the
prisoners ordered out.

The Commandant and his staff were plainly in a state of great agitation. All had drawn revolvers and the Commandant was so angry that he
could hardly speak coherently and was bright red in the face. By contrast
his security officer was dead white and his hands were shaking so much
that some of the prisoners were afraid his revolver would go off by mistake. Even more uncomfortable was the chief "ferret" whose face, perhaps
by way of compromise, was mottled. All however were in a dangerous
mood, and the Commandant had already been heard telling the Germans
that if there was any trouble at all from the prisoners he himself would
personally shoot two of them.

As the prisoners came out of the barrack it had begun to snow. They were lined up in two ranks, made to strip completely and then searched. One or two who could not get their clothes off quickly enough to please the Germans were at once sent to the "cooler". At 8.30 a.m. a photographic check of the whole camp was made and it was only then that the Germans realised how many of the prisoners had escaped. From that moment the Commandant and most of his staff knew that they were bound to be court-martialled.

While these events were taking place there was one amusing incident. The chief "ferret" of the East Compound, "Charlie" Pilz, had gone down the tunnel from its mouth and had reached the trap which was closed above him. Hearing this, the German adjutant, a fussy little man who had been a history professor, went off to get the British adjutant, who was in bed in another barrack, to ask him to open the trap. The British officer in question was a large man, full of bluster, and made the most of the situation. At first he argued, then very slowly he got out of bed and dressed. Just as he was leaving the hut he stopped and strolled back down the barracks, telling the German to wait while he fetched his coat. The German adjutant meanwhile had been in a great state of agitation, saying plaintively that one of his guards was suffocating and that they really must hurry. When they finally arrived at Barrack 104, the German found that he had lost his dignity to no purpose; another prisoner had already opened the trap, and Pilz was there greeting him with a broad smile.

For a fortnight no one in the camp was allowed into Hut 104, but the prisoners enjoyed the perplexities of the Germans who, on dismantling the tunnel, were puzzled to know where so much electric cable had come from and how so many people had been hidden in one hut unnoticed. An additional diversion was provided by the procession of distinguished visitors who came to see the tunnel and to study the photographs which had been taken. This time, however, the Commandant was not heard to boast what a magnificent tunnel his prisoners had built.

Finally, the Germans were faced with the problem of how to destroy "Harry." With the memory of the blowing up of "Tom" fresh in their minds, they decided to fill in the tunnel proper with sewage and the entrance shaft with sand up to the last two or three feet, and then with solid concrete. When this had been done parties of prisoners were allowed back into Hut 104, to collect their personal belongings, including mattresses and blankets, and as a result a great deal of escape material which had been hidden on the morning of discovery was recovered. The Germans, having searched the whole of the rest of the camp, had forgotten to search the very block in which the escape took place.

The tunnel was found by chance. The arrangements at the tunnel mouth had worked perfectly and as every twentieth man emerged he had taken the place of the controller lying by the edge of the hole and directed the flow of prisoners. Apart from the changes of guards every two hours, and the regular approach of the patrol on his beat outside the wire, there were no interruptions, and had the arrangements inside the tunnel worked as smoothly many more prisoners would have escaped.

Nevertheless, there had been some anxious moments. Just before the change of guard was due at 4 a.m. the controller whose number was 60 took over. After he had brought his first two men up, the new guard party, which had to pass within seven or eight yards of the hole, appeared on his left, and he lay still. The guards straggled past him without looking up, but as they relieved the men in the towers individually, Germans kept coming back singly along the track for the next twenty minutes or so. In that time only two more men were brought out.

Then, at 4.30 a.m. a crisis occurred. The German guard in the tower immediately opposite the tunnel mouth and only about fifteen yards away suddenly called to one of the sentries who was patrolling the wire. The sentry climbed up into the tower and the man who had called him came down and strolled across the road straight towards the hole. The controller thought that he had suspected something and that the game was up. The German came on towards him and then, when within about four feet, suddenly turned aside and relieved nature. The tunnel mouth, with a man's head just below the surface and the controller with his hand upon that head and his face buried in the ground, were almost within touching distance, and the broad tracks in the snow made by the men who had crawled along the leading string were only too visible. Yet the man saw nothing and when he had finished turned round and strolled back to his tower, and the sentry came down and resumed his beat.

As five o'clock approached and the first glimmerings of dawn began to show the leader of the last ten was at his tree with the first of his group near him behind another, and a third man out of the tunnel and crawling up the leading string. As the fourth of the group came out, the controller noticed the patrolling sentry coming towards him. He was some distance away, but for some reason he was walking wide of his beat instead of close to the wire. If he kept on in that way he was bound to walk right on to the tunnel mouth. The controller pulled the leading string sharply twice and the third man of the group, who was still moving along it, lay still. The controller himself and the man who had just come out lay prone. The sentry came on. When within a few feet of them he had still seen nothing, and for a moment it seemed possible that he would walk by. His left foot landed within a few inches of the mouth of the tunnel and with his next stride he missed treading on one of the prone bodies by an even narrower margin. Then suddenly he noticed something.

With a grunt he swung round and brought his rifle to the ready. He saw the man lying beside the leading string and lifted his rifle. At that moment the leader of the last group emerged from behind the tree waving his arms and crying in German "Don't shoot!" The German was completely taken aback, and aiming wildly somewhere between the two figures, let off his rifle. The man by the leading string leapt to his feet at once and ran crouching into the wood, followed by the second member of his group, who until then had stayed behind the tree. The leader, who was still covered by the guard, came forward with his hands up, and then the two men by the tunnel mouth stood up.

For a second the guard seemed stupefied, and then at last came to his senses. He pulled out his torch, shone it down the hole, and saw the man who was waiting his turn, the eightieth man on the list. He blew his whistle, ordered the man out of the tunnel and then covering the four, marched them off towards the guard room. In the German compound the four prisoners met the Commandant. Both they and he knew that this escape meant a court martial and the loss of his job, if not a severe sentence. Normally he was a polite man, but on this occasion he was plainly out of control, and after shouting abuse, told the prisoners that he would hand them all over to the Gestapo to be shot. The prisoners did not answer, and were taken to the cells.

As far as is known, it was pure chance that the sentry who discovered the tunnel chose to walk along the edge of the wood instead of beside the wire. If he had maintained his normal beat it is almost certain that all eighty-seven men who were scheduled to escape would have got out, and that the tunnel would not have been discovered until next morning. In that case many of those who were recaptured quickly would have got further on their way and perhaps one or two more would have reached England.

\*   \*   \*   \*   \*

Of the seventy-six prisoners who escaped three reached England, fifty were recaptured and shot, five were sent to the concentration camp at Sachsenhausen, three to the air force camp at Barth, and the remainder were returned to Sagan.

The first to reach England were Sergeant P. Bergsland and Pilot Officer J. E. Muller, two Norwegians of the R.A.F., who travelled to Stettin by train and there got into touch with the French workers, who eventually put them on board a ship to Sweden. Their adventures were not unlike those of Codner and Williams, who had taken the same route and need not be described in detail. They reached Stockholm on 30 March and England soon afterwards.

## Flight Lieutenant B. Van Der Stok

Flight Lieutenant B. Van Der Stok, M.B.E., a Dutchman serving in the Royal Air Force, had a more arduous journey and eventually reached Gibraltar on 8 July. The start of his journey is interesting for the picture it gives of the scene on Sagan railway station while the escapers were catching their trains. He was number eighteen in the tunnel and was wearing a Naval jacket and trousers with an Australian greatcoat which had been converted to look like a civilian overcoat and beret. On the way to Sagan railway station he was accosted by a German civilian who asked what he was doing in the woods. He was posing as a Dutch worker so told this to the German and said he was afraid that the police might arrest him for being out of doors during an air-raid. The German said "It is all right if you are with me." He escorted the Dutchman to the station, where he had to wait for three hours because trains were delayed by the air-raid on Berlin.

At the station one of the German girl censors from the camp spoke to another escaper. She was suspicious of him and got a Captain of the German Military Police to examine his papers. While this was being done she asked the Dutchman a number of questions, but he was able to satisfy her. The train for Breslau arrived at 3.30 a.m., and the Dutchman travelled second-class, arriving at 5 a.m. There was no check of identity documents; he saw eight of his fellow escapers during the journey.

From Breslau, Van Der Stok went to Holland, where he obtained help from friends and was provided with an escort into Belgium. In Brussels he was put into the hands of one of the Underground Organisations and sent by train to Toulouse, where he was joined by several evaders. Although their guide was shot by the Germans when returning to a farmhouse to pick them up, another guide was supplied by the Maquis and all reached Spain, later being escorted to Gibraltar.

\* \* \* \* \*

Very little was known in the camp of the progress of those who had escaped until some of them returned at the end of the first week in April and managed to smuggle notes out of their cells giving the names of others who had been seen in various prisons. Meanwhile, however, a team of Gestapo and S.S. men had arrived in the compound and carried out investigations which resulted in the court martial of many of the German staff. On 26 March the Camp Commandant, Lt. Col. von Lindeiner, was relieved of his post.

Early in April the new Commandant summoned the Senior Officer of each British compound separately to his office, where he made the following announcement in German:—

"I have been instructed by my higher authority to communicate to you this report—

'The Senior British Officer is to be informed that as a result of a tunnel from which seventy-six officers escaped from Stalag Luft III, North Compound, forty-one of these officers have been shot whilst resisting arrest or attempting further escape after arrest.' "

Asked how many had been wounded, the Commandant, who appeared to be ill at ease, said: "My higher authority only permits me to read this report and not to answer questions, or to give any further information." Asked again how many had been wounded, the Commandant replied that he thought none had been wounded.

A few days later a list of those who had been shot was pinned up on the North Compound notice board. It gave forty-seven names, to which three were added later. Shortly afterwards some of the personal belongings of those who had been shot were returned and towards the end of April fifty cremation urns were brought into the compound, each of which bore the name of one of the officers who had been shot.

The prisoners who were murdered were:—

| | |
|---|---|
| Flight Lieutenant H. Birkland | R.C.A.F. |
| Flight Lieutenant E. G. Brettall, D.F.C. | R.A.F. |
| Flight Lieutenant L. C. Bull, D.F.C. | R.A.F. |
| Squadron Leader R. J. Bushell | R.A.F. |
| Flight Lieutenant M. J. Casey | R.A.F. |
| Squadron Leader J. Catanach, D.F.C. | R.A.A.F. |
| Flight Lieutenant A. C. Christiansen | R.N.Z.A.F. |
| Flight Lieutenant D. H. Cochran | R.A.F. |
| Squadron Leader I. K. P. Cross, D.F.C. | R.A.F. |
| Sergeant H. Espelid | R. Norwegian A.F. |
| Flight Lieutenant B. H. Evans | R.A.F. |
| 2nd Lieutenant N. Fuglesang | R. Norwegian A.F. |
| Lieutenant J. S. Gouws | S.A.A.F. |
| Flight Lieutenant W. J. Grisman | R.A.F. |
| Flight Lieutenant A. D. M. Gunn | R.A.F. |
| Warrant Officer A. H. Hake | R.A.A.F. |
| Flight Lieutenant C. P. Hall | R.A.F. |
| Flight Lieutenant A. R. H. Hayter | R.A.F. |
| Flight Lieutenant E. S. Humphreys | R.A.F. |
| Flying Officer G. A. Kidder | R.C.A.F. |
| Flight Lieutenant R. V. Kierath | R.A.A.F. |
| Flight Lieutenant A. Kiewnarski (Pole) | R.A.F. |
| Squadron Leader T. G. Kirby-Green | R.A.F. |

| | |
|---|---|
| Flying Officer W. Kolanowski (Pole) | R.A.F. |
| Flight Lieutenant S. Z. Krol (Pole) | R.A.F. |
| Flight Lieutenant P. W. Langford | R.C.A.F. |
| Flight Lieutenant T. B. Leigh | R.A.F. |
| Flight Lieutenant J. L. R. Long | R.A.F. |
| Flight Lieutenant R. Marcinkus (Lithuanian) | R.A.F. |
| 2nd Lieutenant S. C. A. N. McGarr | S.A.A.F. |
| Flight Lieutenant G. E. McGill | R.C.A.F. |
| Flight Lieutenant H. J. Milford | RAF. |
| Flying Officer J. P. Mondschein (Pole) | R.A.F. |
| Flying Officer K. Pawluk (Pole) | R.A.F. |
| Flying Officer H. A. Picard (Belgian) | R.A.F. |
| Flying Officer P. P. J. Pohe | R.N.Z.A.F. |
| Lieutenant B. W. H. Scheidhauer | Free French A.F. |
| Warrant Officer E. Scantziklas | R. Hellenic A.F. |
| Lieutenant R. J. Stevens | S.A.A.F. |
| Flying Officer R. C. Stewart | R.A.F. |
| Flight Lieutenant J. C. Stower | R.A.F. |
| Flight Lieutenant D. O. Street | R.A.F. |
| Flight Lieutenant G. D. Swain | R.A.F. |
| Flight Lieutenant P. Tobolski (Pole) | R.A.F. |
| Flight Lieutenant A. Valenta (Czech) | R.A.F. |
| Flight Lieutenant G. W. Walenn | R.A.F. |
| Flight Lieutenant J. C. Wernham | R.C.A.F |
| Flight Lieutenant G. W. Wiley | R.C.A.F. |
| Squadron Leader J. E. A. Williams, D.F.C. | R.A.F. |
| Flight Lieutenant J. F. Williams | R.A.F. |

During the summer, permission was obtained to build a stone memorial in the woods outside the compound in which the urns could be kept and on which the names of the officers were engraved. This memorial was carefully tended by the prisoners while they remained at Sagan, but when a British officer returned in February, 1946, he found that as the war had swept over the area someone had looted it. Some of the urns were missing and ashes were scattered over the ground. Later, when the German population was driven out, and the Poles occupied Sagan, the memorial was once again properly tended.

The murders had a profound effect on the prisoners left in the camp. Everyone knew at once the German statement that the men had been shot while resisting arrest was a lie, because not one prisoner in a thousand would have done such a thing. None of the escaped men carried arms, and all were too well versed in the rules of escape to have provoked attack once they had been caught. It was one more sign that the Nazis were getting desperate and to bitter resentment at the fate of so many friends was added an anxiety that the rules of war governing prisoners might be abandoned altogether. That the Nazis would be in any way deterred by fear of reprisals on German prisoners, of which by 1944 there were a far greater number, seemed most improbable.

But although the general enthusiasm for escape had been impaired, the resentment of many prisoners soon turned to defiance, and a group of enthusiasts was soon planning another mass escape from North compound. In the middle of April, only a few days after the news of the murders had been confirmed, a meeting of the heads of the old escape departments was held and it was unanimously decided to build another tunnel, on the same lines as "Harry," the entrance to which should be under the auditorium of the theatre. It was an indication of the mood of the camp that other reasons besides escape had to be advanced in justification of the idea, and it was suggested that a tunnel would be useful to send out scouts if the war came to an end suddenly, would provide storage space for food if rations ran low, and would be an ideal place to hide some prisoners if the compound was evacuated on the approach of the Russians.

The main opposition to "George," as the tunnel was called, came not unnaturally from the theatre players, who on two occasions threatened to strike if the tunnel started and who obstructed the building of it as much as possible. More general opposition throughout the compound also made it difficult to collect the bed boards, tins, string and other material required.

All these difficulties were eventually overcome and the tunnel was started in May, 1944. A new trap was made in the third row from the front of the theatre and a large chamber was built almost directly underneath, which included a pump room and workshop. The tunnel itself ran under the stage towards the East boundary and needed to be 300 feet long to reach the wood.

The dispersal of sand was comparatively easy as it was packed under the floor boards of the theatre. The tunnel itself was of the same dimensions as "Harry" but the air pump, electric system and trolleys were much improved, the air pump in particular being such a masterpiece of carpentering skill that it could be worked slowly with one hand without fatigue and yet give ample air to the face. Shifts of diggers and sand-dispersers carried on even during theatre shows. The shifts would go down half an hour before the curtain went up and watchers were placed at various points in the auditorium and communicated to the workers by pieces of wire through the floor. The presence of Germans in the theatre did not stop work.

By November about two hundred feet of tunnel had been dug, but it was then decided that the war had reached a stage which made escaping hardly worthwhile. Large quantities of food were therefore stored in the tunnel and under the theatre. Finally in January, 1945, it was decided to use the tunnel for hiding officers if the camp moved.

Enough food, water, mattresses and blankets to last seven officers for a week was put down and the air conditioning system was reversed so that air could be drawn in even if the theatre was burned down. On the night of 27 January, 1945, when the prisoners were ordered to march, seven officers went down this tunnel and the trap was sealed. Later, however, the Senior British Officer ordered these seven prisoners to come up from the tunnel and march with the rest of the compound. As the camp was occupied by Russian troops ten days later, this party would have reached home some months before the end of the war.

## CHAPTER 28 · MURDER

What happened to the fifty officers who were murdered has been pieced together partly from the evidence of those who were returned to Sagan and partly as a result of the indefatigable efforts of the Provost Marshal of the Royal Air Force and his department who, from the moment the murders were known, determined to try to bring to justice some of those who had been directly concerned. Under the personal direction of the Provost Marshal enquiries were begun in collaboration with the Judge Advocate General's War Crimes Section, Military Intelligence, United States Army War Crimes Liaison and the Czech and French War Crimes Commissions. When the war came to an end, a Royal Air Force Police investigation team consisting of five officers, sixteen N.C.O.s and sixteen interpreters undertook a search through Czechoslovakia, Poland, Denmark, France, Holland and the three Western Zones of Germany. The co-operation of the Russians was also sought. After sixty thousand Germans had been interrogated the search was narrowed down to three hundred and nineteen people, twenty-five of whom were brought to England for interrogation.

In November, 1947, eighteen men were brought to trial at Hamburg, under the proceedings against War Criminals instituted by the United Nations. After a trial lasting three weeks, fourteen were sentenced to death by hanging, two to imprisonment for life and two to imprisonment for ten years. Two others who would have been brought to trial committed suicide after arrest and the death of a third has been established. A further two men were executed by order of the Czechoslovakian Government, after conviction for other war crimes and still another is held in custody by the Czechs pending trial for war crimes against Czech Nationals. Thus twenty-four of those concerned in the murders have been accounted for.

Enquiries are continuing in Germany. Twenty-eight other men are known to have been directly concerned with the murders, and will, if caught, be brought to trial. Several are believed to be in the Russian Zone. It is believed that the Poles have executed two more of the wanted men.

Early in March, 1944, a new order, which did *not* apply to the British and Americans, had been issued by the Gestapo that prisoners of war who escaped and were recaptured were not to be returned to prison camps but were to be shot. The International Red Cross were to be told that they had escaped and had not been recaptured. A hint of this order had been given at Stalag Luft III by "Charlie" Pilz, who had told the Escape Intelligence Officer of the East Compound that "a very serious" order had been issued and that prisoners would soon get "very bad news." But there was no corroboration, and as it was in "Charlie's" interest to frighten the prisoners the matter was dismissed by the Escape Organisation.

The mass escape took place at a time when, owing to reverses on every front, the German High Command was extremely nervous of an uprising among the millions of foreign workers in Germany and the occupied territories and there is little doubt that when they heard of it, the German Staff believed there was a link between the prisoners and the various underground movements. It is clear from the interrogations of those who survived that the fact that as many as twelve men were heading for Czechoslovakia, which neither bordered on a neutral country nor had a port from which neutral ships sailed, confirmed these suspicions in the minds of the German police.

Hitler himself had always been sensitive about the danger from foreign workers, and either because the general staff were afraid to conceal an escape which, on their hypothesis, might have dangerous repercussions inside Germany, or as a matter of routine, the news of it reached him. He at once called a conference at which Himmler, Goering and Keitel were present when he is believed to have stormed at Keitel for letting the prisoners escape and to have ordered those who were recaptured to be shot as an example. An argument then followed because Stalag III was a German Air Force camp, but Goering apparently won it by pointing out that for inspection purposes it came under Keitel. Goering is reported to have said that the constant escapes were "a bad show" and Himmler complained that he had to mobilise about sixty thousand additional members of the Home Guard as a result.

An account of this conference was given by Keitel to Major-General Westhoff who was then in charge of the Prisoner of War Inspectorate and was later captured by the British. After saying that he had been reproved by Goering in the presence of Himmler for having let the prisoners escape, Keitel went on: "These escapes must stop. We must set an example. We shall take very severe measures. I can only tell you that the men who have escaped will be shot—probably, the majority of them are dead already."

After General Von Graevenitz, who was also present, protested that escape was not a dishonourable offence, Keitel said: "I don't care a damn. We discussed it in the Fuhrer's presence and it cannot be altered."

Some of the written orders for the murders were signed by Himmler, some by Kaltenbrunner, and in every case the shooting was done by the Gestapo. Westhoff stated that he had never received any reports suggesting that the prisoners had committed sabotage or espionage, nor is there any evidence that any of them resisted arrest.

Though the majority of the prisoners were caught within fifty miles of Sagan, others scattered to all corners of Germany. Four were caught at Danzig, twelve on the frontiers of Czechoslovakia, two on the Swiss frontier, three at Flensberg on the Danish frontier, one near Frankfurt-on-Main and two at Saarbrucken. The procedure in almost every case seems to have been the same. The prisoners, all of whom were in civilian clothes, were put in civilian gaols where they were interrogated by members of the Gestapo. Many were threatened and told they would be shot, or that they would not see their wives again, and although some of the interrogators were polite some were menacing, flourishing their whips and coming close to the prisoners and shouting in their faces. Most prisoners were asked what had been their number in the order of exit from the tunnel, who had ordered them to escape, where they had got their papers and clothes from, where they were going, whether they had friends in Czechoslovakia and how the tunnel had been constructed. Almost all the prisoners refused to answer the questions except to point out that their clothes were converted uniforms. When this statement was challenged one prisoner suggested the Germans bring in someone who knew about clothes to pass judgment. A middle-aged stenographer from the next room was called in and after running her fingers over them said that they were not proper civilian clothes as the seams were where they should be on uniforms. The prisoners were told that as they were dressed as civilians they would be treated as civilians, but this was a threat which had often been used before. On the other hand the fact that they remained in the control of the civil police was unusual, and to the more experienced of the prisoners alarming.

Of the seventy-three who were recaptured, thirty-five were collected at Gorlitz, a town about sixty miles south of Sagan and a district headquarters of the Gestapo, and housed in the civil gaol. They remained there for several days, being taken out singly to be interrogated at the Gestapo headquarters in the town. When they returned to the gaol they were sometimes put in the same cell as before and sometimes in a different one; but they were never told why.

The reports of the survivors are very brief, but give something of the atmosphere at Gorlitz.

"The next morning we were loaded into a lorry and, accompanied by two car loads of guards, were taken to Gorlitz and placed in cells. After two days we were taken out for interrogation. I was asked the ordinary routine questions, with the exception of one, which was to ask me why we were going to concentrate in Prague. Since I knew nothing about going to Prague, I could not answer.

"I remained at Gorlitz for eleven or twelve days. From about 30 March, a guard would go into different cells and call out names. These men would then be taken away and we did not see them again. We thought that they were being taken out for further interrogation and, when they did not return, that they had been sent back to camp."

A Flight Lieutenant wrote:—

"Next morning we were taken out and interrogated by an interpreter and the civilian Head of the Criminal Investigation Bureau. A female typist typed our statements. They asked why I was wearing civilian clothes, where I was going, what papers I had, how I got out of camp, and so on. I answered in a very simple manner, pretending to be a simple sort of man. All through the interview their attitude was very threatening and I could see they meant business."

A Scotsman was even more laconic:—

"I was carrying false papers and wearing civilian clothes. I was recaptured by members of the Home Guard who made a half-hearted attempt to beat me up. I was taken to the prison at Gorlitz, where I was interrogated by members of the Gestapo. I was able to eat my false papers and sew R.A.F. buttons on to my greatcoat; this may have been the reason why I was not shot."

When prisoners were together they could usually keep up their spirits, but at Gorlitz the atmosphere was charged with foreboding. The Gestapo guards were thugs to a man and one of the prisoners who had been in the Czech intelligence service during the early years of the war and knew their methods feared the worst. Food consisted only of bread and watery soup and all the prisoners were hungry.

As the first party of five were being taken away on 30 March, one of the prisoners in another cell went to the lavatory and saw one of them hand-cuffed to a very tall broad-shouldered civilian who had a battered pugilis-tic type of face. They were taken away in three ordinary cars accompanied by ten members of the Gestapo in civilian dress. Prominent among them was a very large middle-aged man. This was Scharpwinkel who later organised the Gestapo as a fighting unit to hold out to the last man in Breslau and who, as head of the Breslau Gestapo, was responsible for carrying out

the Gorlitz murders. Later he fell into Russian hands. On 31 March and 6
April two further parties were removed from the cells in a similar fashion
and on 13 April the last of the prisoners who had remained alone at Gorlitz disappeared.

It was learned later that detailed instructions for the murders were sent
by teleprinter from Gestapo Headquarters in Berlin to the prisons in
which the escapers were held. According to these instructions the prisoners were to be driven to isolated places, made to get out of the cars, told
either to relieve nature by the road-side or just ordered to walk away from
the car, and then to be shot in the back to give the impression that they had
been running away.

These orders were not always exactly carried out. The four escapers
who were caught near Flensburg were held in the ordinary civil gaol. One
day they were collected by the Gestapo and driven off in two cars, one
prisoner being in the first and three in the second. When the first car
reached the selected spot the prisoner was taken out, his handcuffs were
removed and before his comrades arrived he was shot by rifle fire in the
back, being killed instantly. A few minutes later the second car drove up.
The three prisoners, still handcuffed with their hands behind their backs,
were ordered into the field where they saw the body of their friend lying.
They were shot simultaneously in the back by three Gestapo men. One,
who was not killed instantaneously, was shot again in the head. After the
murders the bodies were placed side by side near the hedge along the road
and the Gestapo agents proceeded to Kiel where they made arrangements
with an undertaker for the removal of the bodies to Kiel Crematorium.

When the report of these murders reached Gestapo Headquarters it
was realised at once that orders had not been strictly carried out and that
conflicting evidence might be given to the protecting power. The men who
had done the shooting were therefore made to re-enact the whole scene,
driving out to the woods, stopping and firing their rounds, the difference
being that on this occasion the cars arrived together and the imaginary
prisoners were all shot at once. This farce of pretending that the men had
been shot while trying to escape was also carried through at Gorlitz where
some of the bodies of those who had been shot in the gaol were sent away
to Breslau and Liegnitz to be cremated so as to make it appear that the
shooting had been dispersed over a wide area. In one instance the shooting was formal. Six prisoners were lined up and told they were going to be
shot, and the Gestapo agent, in making his report afterwards, remarked
that he was amazed at their outward calm. But to the protecting power the
same story was told in every case: the prisoners had been shot trying to
resist capture.

On 12 June, 1944, the Germans sent a note to the protecting power stating that mass escapes were a danger to public security in Germany and

therefore that special orders to guards were necessary in such cases. Weapons, the note continued, had to be used against fifty prisoners who had escaped from Stalag Luft III and clarification of the cases would take time. The urns containing the ashes of twenty-nine of those shot had been returned to the camp.

However, the Swiss Camp Inspector had already visited Sagan in April and heard the evidence of those who had been at Gorlitz, and on 23 June Mr. Eden, the Foreign Secretary, made a statement in the House of Commons which exposed the German explanation as a lie. Soon afterwards the Germans refused to furnish any more information to the Swiss. By 14 July the last of the fifty urns containing the ashes of the murdered men had arrived in the camp and it was seen that in accordance with the order made earlier in the year all except three of the prisoners who were not British had been executed. Those three were required for further interrogation about their alleged connection with French and Czechoslovakian resistance groups.

Eight of the escapers were neither shot nor returned to Sagan. Five of them, including Wing Commander Day, were sent to Sachsenhausen Concentration Camp. When interviewed by the Gestapo officials in Berlin, Day was told that he and his friends had been giving a lot of trouble and that he was going to be put in a place where he would cause no more bother. He took this to mean that he was going to be shot, but on finding himself at Sachsenhausen soon escaped again with two of his Royal Air Force colleagues. The other three prisoners, who were caught in Czechoslovakia and interrogated at Prague, were sent to Stalag Luft I at Barth. All eight survived the war.

## CHAPTER 29 · COURT MARTIAL

Meanwhile the trials of the German Commandant, Lt.-Col. von Lindeiner, his chief security officer, Captain Broili, and nine other members of the German staff at Stalag Luft III were taking place before courts martial in Breslau. Documents relating to the trials were later captured in Berlin and a translation made. Some of the evidence throws an interesting light on the attitude of the Germans towards prisoners in 1944. Extracts from the summary of evidence against von Lindeiner read:—

"On the night of 24/25 March, 1944, there was a mass escape of English Officer prisoners of war, from the northern compound of Air Force Prisoner of War Camp No. 3 in Sagan, by means of a tunnel 96 metres long, 7½ metres deep and 65 centimetres high and broad, which had been dug by

299

ESCAPE
FROM
GERMANY

*Court
Martial*

the prisoners in about a year's working time, the exit being outside the camp fence. A sentry who was patrolling outside the camp between two watch towers noticed moving shadows in the wood about 5.15 a.m. His immediate action led to the seizure of four prisoners. Seventy-six Englishmen had already come through. The discovery of the flight prevented the escape of a further 120 prisoners. The Prisoners' Committee organising the flight had reckoned on the escape of 200 persons from this tunnel. The extensive search which the police headquarters in Breslau began immediately after the announcement of the flight resulted in the arrest of 73 escaping prisoners; so that, from the total of 80 escapers, only three escaped arrest.

"The non-discovery of the big tunnel, which had been made during many months of working time and was lined with wood and provided with a lighting system, the successful mass escape itself and the fact that the escapers were well provided for in the matter of clothing and with forged passes either as a foreign civilian worker or as a German soldier, led to an enquiry into all the conditions of the Prisoner of War Camp at Sagan by a military court. The enquiry was carried out by a Field Court in conjunction with a Special Commission of the Criminal Police headquarters in Breslau. ...."

Later the report continues:—

"One means for discovering the tunnelling work of prisoners is the so-called listening system, the principle of which is as follows:—

"Outside the fence of the camp are microphones at a distance of about 30 metres apart and built into the earth to a depth of three metres. The microphones contain a very sensitive swinging pin, which is set in motion by the slightest disturbances in the ground. The movements are recorded on a membrane and then converted into sound. The noise thus caused goes through each microphone by a cable into the central listening post. There the sounds pass through an amplifier into the individual listening rooms and are made quite plain by a loudspeaker. When a sound is located by a microphone—better named the listening head—an indication of the sound follows. The listening head is undoubtedly sensitive, *e.g.* movements of trains on the railway not far from the camp or movements of motors on the roads outside the camp can be heard. These noises, however, are distinguishable from tunnelling noises. These come over a loudspeaker in the form of scraping noises. The noises that are identified by the listeners are advised every day to the guards. Thus the guards received valuable information about the preparation of prisoners for escape.

"In Sagan the listening apparatus for the East and Middle Compounds were put into use in the summer of 1942. The listening apparatus for the

North Compound from which the mass escape took place in March, was ready for use in January, 1943. Microphones 53 and 54, which were placed outside Barrack 104, had constantly registered loud noises since May, 1943, which appeared in the monthly reports as on a particularly thick sound band. The searches which were made following on this evidence did not lead to the discovery of the tunnel. It was finally assumed that the noises came from workers in the coal dumps in the vicinity of the microphones. But it was overlooked that the listening system recorded noises also at night, when no work was in progress in the coal dumps. This superficial decision on the part of the Guard is even less understandable since a mass escape tunnel from Barrack 123 was discovered in September, 1943, with the help of the listening apparatus. It should have been the duty of the Guard to take particular notice of the noises which came month by month from the same place and with the same strength, and not to relax their efforts to find the tunnel. If the warning through the listening system had been regarded by the Group Defence with the necessary seriousness, the escape tunnel must have been discovered in time. Finally, the Guard were in the best position to know, from their experience, that the prisoners were always tunnelling, for this escape tunnel was the hundredth attempt in Sagan camp.

"In such a situation it appears little short of grotesque that on 19 December, 1943, on the instructions of the defendant Colonel von Lindeiner, and with the knowledge and consent of the Chief Guard Officer, the complete listening apparatus should be put out of action. The reason for this was the extension of the system to two new compounds and the proposed reorganisation of the whole scheme for this purpose. There is no doubt that the rebuilding was judicious and necessary. But the responsible authorities incurred the greatest blame in that they kept the system idle for over three months and thus denied themselves an important aid to the prevention of escapes. On 24 March, 1944, the day of the mass escape, the complete apparatus was still out of action.

"The admission of Colonel von Lindeiner that he had purposely laid on the work for the winter months because from experience the prisoners did no tunnelling at this time of year does not in any way excuse his methods. The facts about the tunnel that was discovered in Sagan prove that the tunnel work was broken off only by the heaviest frost. The mild winter of 1943/44 had in no way disturbed the prisoners at their tunnelling. . . .

"Every prisoner of war receives every week the contents of a 5-kg. parcel containing food and useful articles from the Red Cross of his country via the International Red Cross in Geneva. At this time there were in Sagan up to 150,000 such parcels. Their distribution was carried out by the Parcel Control provided by the Group Guard. Each parcel contained, among other things, ten air-tight tins with various contents.

"According to High Command Order No. 199, tins which had come in Red Cross parcels or privately could not be handed out to the prisoners but only their contents. Further High Command Order of 17 August, 1943, adds thereto: 'The keeping of food gifts in open tins is forbidden. The Camp can demand for this purpose up to two plates for each Prisoner of War who receives gifts.' In Sagan camp these orders have been continually disobeyed. Each prisoner was handed all the packages from Red Cross parcels. In this way, with an average strength of 5,000 men, 50,000 air-tight tins found their way into the hands of the prisoners. Nevertheless, every tin should have been pierced before being handed out, in order to make them unsuitable for preserving food and putting by provisions for escape. The perforation was done by the prisoners of war who were employed in the Parcel Control. It is plain to what extent the latter, profiting by the deficiencies in the Parcel Control, brought unperforated tins into the camp. The unlimited issue of air-tight tins offered countless possibilities to technically gifted prisoners for making the equipment useful for escape. The Escape Museum in Sagan provides plenty of exhibits...

"The provision of extra plates to facilitate the storage of food, as laid down in High Command Order of 17 August, 1943, was not carried out. It must not be overlooked that the emptying of 50,000 tins weekly, even when the work was carried out by prisoners of war, provided considerably extra work for the German Control personnel. But the work had to be done, because there was the clear order and the fact of the conversion of tins for escape purposes was known. An entirely false concern for the imprisoned 'terror airmen' was the real basis for this disobedience. The Commandant and the Guard did not think they could ask the prisoners to hand over the contents of the tins in view of the shortage of china and tin containers...

"On arrival at the camp every prisoner received, in addition to a bed and a paliasse, knife, fork, spoon, dish, one coffee cup, two blankets, three articles of bed linen and one towel. In the period 15 January, 1943, to 19 April, 1944, Group Administration advised the loss of the following public property:—

1,699 blankets. 192 bed covers. 161 pillow cases. 165 sheets. 3,424 towels. 655 paliasses. 1,212 bolsters. 34 single chairs. 10 single tables. 52 tables for two men. 76 benches. 90 double beds. 246 water-cans. 1,219 knives. 582 forks. 408 spoons. 69 lamps. 30 shovels.

In spite of payment of damages in money by the prisoners the fact remains that the overtaxed state of the German linen industry could not cope with such a strain. While German families who had lost all could only receive replacement for their lost possessions in the most needy circumstances

302

ESCAPE
FROM
GERMANY

*Court*
*Martial*

owing to the shortage of linen articles and household goods, the imprisoned 'terror airmen' lived among the things entrusted to them in almost devilish ways and with them constantly continued the war against the Reich behind the barbed wire, and with success. There is no doubt that the prisoners purposely destroyed part of the things merely with the idea of causing damage to the Reich...

"Although according to existing rules, the camp language was German, the first accused had, since the commencement of his employment in Sagan, used only English in his personal dealings with the prisoners. The talks with senior Englishmen and Americans, which took place once a week, were carried out in English. The accused had constantly greeted prisoners with a hand-shake, and, in three instances, had sent birthday greetings to senior prisoners and their adjutants and provided them with wine.

"The atmosphere of a prisoner of war camp is made by the personality of the Commandant alone. The tolerance, politeness and consideration of the first accused were certainly diplomatic moves designed to gain influence over the prisoners and to find out their views, to gain an advantage in dealings with the Protecting Power and to prevent serious offences against the good order and discipline of the camp. But the accused forgot that his behaviour must cause misunderstanding in the Officer Corps and particularly among his men and lead him to be regarded as Anglophile. Further he forgot that his approaches to the Englishmen not only made no impression, owing to their mentality, but were explained simply as German weakness. But above all, he forgot the misery and suffering that the 'terror airmen' had brought to German men and German cities, and that therefore no good German should shake hands with such enemies and give them presents."

A section of the evidence against Captain Broili deals with photographs taken in the camp:—

"In December, 1943, the third accused, Captain Pieber asked the second accused (Captain Broili) if there were any reason why he should not lend his Contax camera to the prisoners in the North Camp for a few hours for the purpose of taking pictures of scenes from a play produced by the Englishmen. The accused raised no objection. Thus the Englishmen were in the undisturbed possession of a Contax for half a day. At this time dozens of forged identity card photographs of prisoners of war, for escape purposes, had fallen into the hands of the Guard, particularly the second accused. It had been forbidden for a long time to give prisoners photo-graphs which they could possibly misuse. They could be given only group photographs which were so small that, according to normal standards, the

303

ESCAPE
FROM
GERMANY

*Court
Martial*

use or conversion of the single photographs for a forged pass was out of the question. Larger individual photographs, which prisoners still had in their possession, were confiscated when they were found during barrack inspections. The Guard inspectors had also found in the camp unexposed films of English manufacture which fitted the German Contax exactly. It was clear that these films must have been smuggled into the camp with the help of German personnel. It is not necessary to possess long years of experience as an officer of the Guard at a prisoner of war camp to realise that the possession of a photo-apparatus must help the prisoners forward considerably with their preparations for escape. It is beyond comprehension that the second accused did not clearly realise that it was simplicity itself for the prisoners, among whom were specialists from every technical department, to take out Captain Pieber's film from the Contax, take unlimited forbidden exposures with their own film and then re-insert the old film and prepare it for taking permitted photographs. Development and enlargement of the Contax photographs was done either with the help of picked German soldiers or by the prisoners in their own photo-laboratory. After the untrustworthy element had been removed from the Parcel Control a complete chemical photography laboratory was confiscated from a private parcel from England."

Among the evidence against the N.C.O.s appears the following:—

"In January, 1944, the eleventh accused, Oberfreiter Lubos was employed on wiring duties in the prisoner of war camp. He brought three 200 metre drums of cable into the camp. The prisoners crowded round him. One offered him cigarettes which he accepted and asked for some red cable, at the same time promising him more cigarettes. The accused refused this offer but left the drum of cable lying by a telegraph pole and gave no further thought to it in the course of his work. He did not need the third drum for his work. When the accused left the camp, after finishing the wiring job, the prisoners had taken the third drum. Later the cable was found in the escape tunnel used as lighting cable. There is definite suspicion that Lubos had purposely left the cable for the prisoners and received a corresponding consideration for it. But if the statement of the accused is accepted as the truth, he is guilty of dereliction of duty and by reason of the fact that every German soldier in the course of his duty is the superior of the prisoners, of not reporting a punishable offence."

All the accused were sentenced to terms of imprisonment. But all the sentences were cut short by the end of the war, and the Commandant and several other members of his staff were then brought to England for interrogation.

## CHAPTER 30 · STALAG LUFT VI, HEYDEKRUG

ESCAPE
FROM
GERMANY

*Stalag
Luft VI,
Heydekrug*

Stalag Luft VI, the main camp in Germany for Air Force N.C.O.s, lay about two miles south-east of the small town of Heydekrug, about half-way between Tilsit and Memel and close to the Lithuanian frontier. The camp was built on sand. The surrounding country was flat, swampy and wooded, the majority of roads being cart tracks and the principal means of communication the single-track railway between Tilsit and Memel. It was impossible to imagine a more isolated spot and the prisoners felt cut off from civilisation. To add to their discomfort a strong wind blew at all seasons with the result that fine sand found its way everywhere and irritated men's eyes.

The camp was divided into three compounds known as "A", "E" and "K", each of which held about two thousand men. "A" Compound was opened in early June, 1943, when a batch of new prisoners was transferred from Dulag Luft. In that same month nearly all the N.C.O.s from the Centre Compound at Sagan also arrived in batches of approximately two hundred, and further parties came from Dulag Luft until October, 1943, when the compound was overcrowded. "K" Compound was then brought into use and a small number of the prisoners from "A" Compound were transferred to it, followed almost immediately by the N.C.O.s who came from Barth. New prisoners continued to arrive and by February, 1944, this compound was also full. By then "E" Compound was ready and further new arrivals were housed there. The majority of these new prisoners were American N.C.O.s and in March, 1944, "E" Compound was given over wholly to Americans, all the non-American prisoners being transferred to "A" Compound. There were a certain number of wooden huts but the main buildings were single-storey brick barracks divided into nine rooms, each holding fifty men.

Apart from the buildings the compounds at Heydekrug were very like those at Sagan and Barth. The camp had been built under the supervision of the German Security Officer from Sagan who remained as Chief Security Officer for the N.C.O.s; the defences were therefore of the same pattern. One minor innovation had unexpected results. Almost immediately after their arrival from Sagan thirteen prisoners in "A" Compound were compelled to live in one half of one of the wooden barracks. All these men had bad records from the German point of view, the majority having made several attempts to escape and the remainder having acquired a reputation as trouble-makers because of their anti-German attitude. For a time they were under special surveillance and whenever there was any friction between the prisoners and the Germans the culprit was always sought in the "black room" which was the name given to the quarters occupied by the thirteen. Although this was inconvenient it had the great advantage that a number of men who were keen to escape lived together and were able to make their plans and preparations much more openly than would have been possible in a normal barrack-room. After a few months the Germans were forced by lack of space to put a further thirteen men, all new prisoners, into this room, and soon afterwards the special observation ceased.

305

ESCAPE
FROM
GERMANY

*Stalag
Luft VI,
Heydekrug*

A more effective change was the introduction from October, 1943, onwards, of between ten and twenty unarmed German guards into each compound from 9 a.m. until 5 p.m. daily. Those men were in addition to the normal "ferrets," and were told to look out for any suspicious activity.

The extent to which the organisation of escape at Heydekrug differed from that at other Air Force camps has already been described in the first part of this book. Based on voluntary effort, it resulted in one of the most intensive and ambitious campaigns waged by prisoners. The Escape Committee lived in "A" Compound, where the main activity took place, and all operations in the camp were controlled and co-ordinated from there. As usual, tunnels were the most popular method to begin with and within a few hours of the arrival of the first party from Sagan, the sole member of the Escape Committee who had arrived was besieged by groups of enthusiasts who clamoured for permission to begin tunnels from every conceivable vantage point in the compound. But because of the difficulty of hiding the sand, and also because it was felt that the discovery by the Germans of one tunnel after another would make the Escape Organisation the laughing stock of those prisoners who were not interested in escape but whose co-operation was essential to success, it had been decided by the Escape Committee before anyone left Sagan that only one tunnel should be built at a time. This decision was upheld, and soon after all the N.C.O.s from Sagan had arrived the Escape Committee considered all the proposals which had been made, examined the sites and finally decided that work should begin on a tunnel from the west wash-house, the joint proposal of an officer who had exchanged identities with an N.C.O. at Sagan, and an N.C.O.

Work started on the entrance to the tunnel early in July, 1943. This was under one of three laundry coppers in a small room having a concrete floor. In order to make the entrance the copper was removed from its frame and the bottom of the fire-box, an iron plate, was broken out in one piece. A hole then was cut through the concrete floor, slightly smaller than the outside dimensions of the fire-box, and a concrete slab made and fitted into the hole. This could be removed easily by means of pieces of wire passed through loops made by two nails embedded in the slab and the trapdoor then was covered with ash which hid the nails.

The next stage was the sinking of a vertical shaft to a depth of about eight feet, followed by the excavation of a chamber for the air-pump. This chamber was well below the concrete floor of the wash-house, so that

306

ESCAPE
FROM
GERMANY

*Stalag
Luft VI,
Heydekrug*

tapping would not sound hollow, and was shored and roofed with bed boards. A normal air-pump, made from a canvas kit-bag, was installed and work was started on the lateral shaft.

The arrangements for getting in and out of this tunnel were excellent. While work was in progress the copper and fire-box were empty but in position and the bottom plate of the fire-box and the trapdoor were removed. At the end of a shift, or when a signal was received that a German was approaching the wash-house, the copper was removed from its frame by two men who were always on duty for that purpose and the workers climbed out. They wore the minimum of clothing and passed into the shower-room, in the same building, where they washed the sand off their bodies in a few seconds. As soon as the last man stepped through the frame of the copper, the trapdoor, a fire-box plate and copper were replaced and while one of the two attendants transferred a few shovelfuls of burning fuel from one of the other fire-boxes to the empty fire-box, the other man poured a few bucketfuls of warm water into the empty copper. This occupied only a few seconds and a pail of water thrown on the floor removed all trace of fresh sand. These precautions were scrupulously observed the whole of the time the tunnel was under construction.

During the excavation of the first few feet of the lateral shaft the sand was pushed back by hand into a small storage chamber. Afterwards wooden sledges, which were hauled by ropes, were used for transporting the sand from the working face. Owing to the position of drain pipes between the wash-house and the perimeter fence, the tunnel could not be constructed in a straight line and men were stationed at all bends to prevent the sledges or haulage ropes from damaging the sides of the tunnel. It was not possible to tunnel beneath the drains as the water-level was only six feet below the surface; the tunnel was constructed just above that level. The system of shoring was a box-section every two feet and a half, with a complete roof of boarding fitted in. The timber was bed boards collected from all prisoners in the compound, and light was provided by duck lamps with cloth wicks floating in German margarine.

The sand which was excavated was disposed of in the interval between the afternoon parade, which took place at 5 p.m. and 9 p.m. when all the prisoners were locked in their barracks. It was hauled up from the storage chamber in partly filled kit-bags and then carried through the shower-room and dumped in the cesspool under the same building. The floor of the lavatory consisted of loose planking laid on joints which it was quite easy to lift and a different plank was lifted each day so that the sand was spread over as wide an area as possible. This was important because after the cesspool had been emptied the "ferrets" always inspected it for signs of extra sand.

Work continued steadily for about six weeks, direction being main-

307

ESCAPE
FROM
GERMANY

*Stalag
Luft VI,
Heydekrug*

tained with the aid of a compass. At the end of that time the tunnel was about one hundred and forty-five feet long and was judged to be approximately forty feet beyond the perimeter fence. The Escape Committee had intended that the exit should be beyond the first trees of the wood which bordered the compound, a distance of about another thirty feet, but owing to the intensive searches which the Criminal Police were making in the compound at this time, a number of the prisoners who were to escape through the tunnel agitated for its immediate use.

The Escape Committee insisted on their plan as they considered the risk of discovery through searches remote and the distance which had been reached beyond the fence insufficient to ensure that escapers would get away without being seen by the guards in the towers or the patrolling sentry. The engineer of the tunnel supported them but the two proposers of the scheme opposed it and were supported by many of the intending escapers, some of whom threatened to use the tunnel as it was despite the Committee's ruling.

The Committee decided to attempt to persuade these men to agree to wait for another week and they arranged a meeting of the fifty selected escapers on the morning of 29 August. The head of the Committee addressed the meeting and stated that information had been received from reliable sources that no further large-scale searches would take place for some considerable time and emphasised the risks of discovery while leaving the tunnel. He asked everyone to agree to wait for a further week while the last thirty feet was dug so that the exit would be within the wood. One of the proposers of the project then stated his point of view which was that the tunnel should be used at once. He contended that as the tunnel was well beyond the fence, the risk of discovery before it could be used should not be increased by further delay. There was strong support for both points of view and the chairman of the Committee decided to settle the matter by vote. The result was a majority of one vote in favour of using the tunnel at once; one man did not vote. Immediately afterwards the order in which the escapers were to leave the tunnel was decided according to the amount of work which each man had done.

At about 7 p.m. that day the fifty men began to enter the tunnel and when the last man had gone through the entrance the trapdoor was replaced and ash was scattered over it. The plate was put back in the bottom of the fire-box which then was filled with partly burned fuel, and finally the copper was restored to its frame and filled with water.

At approximately 10 p.m., when it was dark, the men in the tunnel broke through to the surface. Thereafter at intervals, when the guard patrolling outside the wire was some distance away, escapers crawled to the edge of the wood. Eight of them reached the trees without incident but the ninth man, who did not take sufficient care, was seen by the guard.

ESCAPE
FROM
GERMANY

*Stalag
Luft VI,
Heydekrug*

Some shots were fired but no one was hit. The forty-one men still in the tunnel were trapped as the entrance had been sealed, but they buried all their forged documents and maps. Within a few minutes a large number of guards arrived in the compound and surrounded the wash-house, and others went to the tunnel exit where they arrested a few of the men nearest the surface. The German Security Officer and the Camp Commandant went to the wash-house where they tried without success to find the tunnel entrance. It was not until the escapers themselves tried to move the trap door from below that it was discovered. They were arrested as they emerged and after being searched and questioned about the number of men in the tunnel, were marched off to the camp gaol. The Germans were told that the sentry had seen the first man out and that no one had escaped.

The eight men who had reached the cover of the wood walked across country avoiding all habitations. Most of them crossed the Lithuanian frontier about six miles away, but all were recaptured within fourteen days and returned to the camp.

On the morning following the escape the German Security Officer ordered a special parade of all the prisoners in the compound and special precautions were taken in counting them. Nevertheless, due to the activities of the Escape Organisation, the final figure was in excess of the correct number. That evening, at about 8 o'clock, all the prisoners were paraded in the compound and surrounded by a large number of guards. The prisoners then were passed in single file through a structure similar to a sheep-pen and counted by several Germans who were working independently. The Escape Organisation encouraged the mass of prisoners to do everything possible to upset the count and to treat the whole thing as a huge joke. Within a short time the prisoners who had been counted and those who were waiting had lighted bonfires of waste paper and were dancing around them like dervishes. Those who were passing through the "sheep-pen" imitated the bleating of sheep while others kept up a continual din of cat-calling and gibing. Some who had been counted joined those who were waiting, despite all the German precautions to prevent this, and were counted a second time. The parade lasted until 11 p.m. when the Germans gave it up in disgust with a count of seventeen men too many.

Next morning another special parade was ordered. This time all the prisoners' identity cards were carried into the compound and placed on tables in the centre of the parade ground. The prisoners were called by name and checked with the photographs on the cards. At first only one prisoner at a time was allowed to approach each table, but gradually crowds gathered in front of each table and edged closer and closer. Eventually the Germans discovered that a complete box containing between three and four hundred identity cards was missing. A search was made at once but the box had been well hidden. The Germans tried to establish the identities of the men whose cards were missing but this was prevented by prisoners who had been identified already going forward a second time. By this means the absence of those who had escaped was covered and not until they were recaptured did the Germans know how many men were missing.

309

ESCAPE
FROM
GERMANY

*Stalag
Luft VI,
Heydekrug*

Shortly afterwards the Criminal Police arrived in the camp and all the prisoners were transferred to another compound. Both they and the barracks they had left were then searched. After this the prisoners were passed back into the compound in single file, being checked with their identity cards and having their finger-prints taken. The individuals whose identity cards were missing were photographed and new identity cards were issued; even then many substitutions were effected.

Many other tunnels were started but only one survived the early stages of construction. The tunnel was started from under the barrack nearest the south and west fences of "K" Compound and ran direct to the west fence, which separated the compound from the Vorlager, a distance of about twenty yards. The whole of this section was well shored. From there the tunnel turned south and ran beneath the double fence and as this could not be walked upon comparatively little shoring was necessary. The distance from the bend in the tunnel to the south fence was approximately eighty yards and the tunnel was nearing completion when a "ferret" saw a prisoner jumping on the floor of the barrack-room from which the tunnel started. The prisoner was forcing the wooden trapdoor into place. Next day a search was made and the tunnel was discovered.

The first individual attempt to escape from Heydekrug was made in June, 1943, during the period when the various batches of prisoners were being transferred from Sagan. A number of crates and packing cases containing sports gear, theatre scenery, costumes and books were due to arrive from Sagan. Arrangements had been made with the Germans that these should be placed in a barn outside the camp near the German quarters, where they could be sorted before being sent into the compound; it was also agreed that what was not required immediately could remain there. A prisoner suggested that a packing case be made in the camp, that he be sealed into it and that the case be then substituted for one of those outside the camp. The plan was approved and on 20 June the escaper was placed in the crate and the top fastened. The prisoners who were dealing with the boxes which had arrived from Sagan loaded a similar crate on to the lorry which the Germans had supplied and in due course the lorry arrived in the compound. Some members of the Escape Organisation began to unload the boxes from the lorry while others engaged the driver and guard in conversation. After a few of the packing cases had been removed from the lorry, the box containing the escaper was placed on it, and a little later the driver was told that the boxes which remained on the lorry contained theatre equipment which had been sent into the compound by mistake.

ESCAPE
FROM
GERMANY

*Stalag
Luft VI,
Heydekrug*

He was asked to take them back to the barn.

When the lorry arrived back at the barn the prisoners there unloaded the boxes and put the one containing the escaper in a previously selected position. The escaper remained in the packing-case until evening when he released himself and left the barn at about 11 o'clock. He walked to the outskirts of Memel where he was caught by a farmer and a policeman on the morning of 22 June. He was returned to the camp.

Next day the same scheme was repeated on behalf of two of the escaper's friends. They were taken to the barn without incident but a little later in the day one of the Germans on duty sat on the crate containing one of them. He felt the heat of this man's breath through a small hole and investigated, with the result that he was discovered. The guards who were present were furious and smashed their rifle butts through other packing-cases in the barn. The second man escaped injury but was discovered.

There were several unsuccessful attempts to board transport going through the gate and then, in September, an unexpected opportunity occurred to climb the fence when the perimeter lights had failed. It was taken by two new prisoners without preparation or permission from the Escape Committee. They wore R.A.F. battle-dress which had not been altered. At about 8 p.m. on 20 September they noticed that the lights on the fence were fading and brightening. They decided to climb over if they failed completely and collected a quantity of chocolate and biscuits, a compass and a map; they also inserted wads of paper into their gloves to save their hands from being torn by the barbed wire.

The lights failed at about 9 p.m. and they climbed through the window of their barrack-room just after a guard, accompanied by an Alsatian dog, had passed by. They ran to the north-west corner of the compound where they climbed over the fence. Their intention was to make contact with Russian forces by travelling through Lithuania and Latvia but after three days they changed their plans and walked towards Memel. They were caught on the outskirts of that town on 26 September and returned to the camp later that day.

A most ingenious escape was made on 5 March, 1944, by Warrant Officer E. Callender, R.A.F. Information had been received that the north-west wash-house was to be closed off from the compound by a temporary fence while a new drainage system was laid by civilian workmen assisted by Russian prisoners of war. Callender approached the Escape Committee and proposed that he should hide in a twelve-foot long cylindrical wooden water-tank, fitted with a trapdoor entrance near one end, which was in the wash-house, and remain there until the enclosure round the wash-house was finished and a gap had been made in the perimeter fence to allow the passage of workmen and vehicles. He planned to leave his hiding place at a propitious moment, dressed as a workman, and walk through the gap. He

spoke excellent French and hoped to get help from French prisoners of
war at a camp near Konigsberg.

311

ESCAPE
FROM
GERMANY

*Stalag
Luft VI,
Heydekrug*

Acting on information received from a reliable German source, the
tank was emptied of water and Callender took up his position on the
evening before work was started on the erection of the fence around the
wash-house. A supply of food was placed there with him. He was dressed
in civilian trousers, a thigh-length civilian overcoat and a cloth workman's
cap. He had false identity documents and a travel permit authorising him
to travel from Heydekrug to Danzig via Konigsberg. He remained in the
tank for fifty-six hours, by which time the fence had been erected and a
gap made in the main fence. Then he appeared, acting the part of the
inspecting foreman, and eventually walked through the gap in the fence
and away from the camp. Russian prisoners, who were working in the
wash-house enclosure, removed all traces of his stay in the tank.

Callender's absence was concealed from the Germans for several weeks
until information was received from an unofficial German source that a
man claiming to be Callender had asked to be admitted to a French prisoner of war camp near Konigsberg. No information was received in the
camp from official sources. He is believed to have fallen into the hands of
the Gestapo and to have been shot.

Another escape was made during the alterations to the wash-house by
Warrant Officer E. P. Lewis, R.A.F., on 16 March, 1944. By this time the
Germans had dug a trench for the drain-pipes which ran from the wash-
house, passed under the enclosure fence and crossed the compound for a
short distance before passing under the west perimeter fence which separated the compound from the Vorlager. There was space between the tops
of the pipes and the bottom of each of the fences through which the civilian workmen frequently passed from the wash-house enclosure into the
compound and the Vorlager and vice versa. A guard was on duty at the gap
which had been made in the main fence which formed the fourth side of
the wash-house enclosure and through which Callender had escaped
about ten days previously.

Lewis was to pose as a civilian foreman. Early on the morning of the
selected day he put on his clothes and soon after the workmen had started
work he emerged into the compound from a barrack-room near the
north-west corner. At that moment several German civilians and Russian
prisoners were working in the trench within the compound. Lewis walked
to the trench, then along it as though he was inspecting the work. Finally
he stepped down into the trench and passed beneath the fence into the
Vorlager where he continued his "inspection." Presently he walked back
along the trench passing under the fence into the compound and eventually made his way under the fence into the wash-house enclosure.

All his movements were observed by the sentry patrolling the north

312

ESCAPE
FROM
GERMANY

*Heydekrug—
The Escape
Route*

fence near the gap leading into the enclosure. Lewis "inspected" the work being done around the wash-house then walked to the gap where he presented his pass to the guard. Although he knew only a little of the German language, he and the guard exchanged a few words before he walked off along the outside of the main fence.

Little is known of his subsequent movements except that he joined a working-party of British Army prisoners at Stolzenburg, between Konigsberg and Danzig, where he remained in hiding until about 29 July. During this time he tried to arrange a passage on a neutral ship through the agency of other British Army prisoners working in the Danzig area. He was arrested by a German guard while attempting to enter Danzig docks on the night of 31 July, 1944, and taken to the guardroom. Soon afterwards he was taken from there by an escort of two guards, presumably to a military barracks. It is understood that he attempted to re-escape and succeeded in getting away for a few moments, but was seen by a guard who shot him at close range. He died in hospital in Danzig a few hours later. It was some months afterwards that the Germans informed the Camp Leader of what had occurred.

The last attempt to escape from this camp took place in July, 1944. About a month before, information had been received from unofficial German sources that the camp was to be evacuated because of the advance of the Russian forces. Three prisoners approached the Escape Committee and proposed that they should build a hiding-place under the floor of one of the wash-houses and remain there until the camp was evacuated. The scheme was approved and a chamber built under a stove.

On the day of the evacuation of the camp these men, dressed in civilian clothes, were bricked into the chamber with sufficient food and water for fourteen days. Later that day they received a signal from a member of the Escape Organisation, by means of a series of taps on the bricks, that the last party of prisoners was about to be marched out of the compound. They remained in their hiding place until the evening of the following day when they emerged to find the camp absolutely deserted. They cut a hole in the fence and walked into Lithuania but were caught five days later by the Lithuanian Home Guard. Subsequently they re-joined the prisoners who had been evacuated from the camp.

## CHAPTER 31 · HEYDEKRUG—THE ESCAPE ROUTE

The results described in the last chapter were disappointing; nevertheless the Escape Committee nearly succeeded in establishing an organisation for escape which spread far beyond the boundaries of the camp and might have resulted in an established route to neutral territory.

313

ESCAPE
FROM
GERMANY

*Heydekrug—
The Escape
Route*

An analysis of the causes of the recapture of those N.C.O.s who had succeeded in escaping from the Centre Compound at Sagan had shown that, although all were able to speak German, they had been caught because of inadequate documents, unsuitable clothing, insufficient information about travel conditions, and also because of the effects of exhaustion upon the escaper's reactions. Action had already been taken by the Escape Committee to overcome the first three of these obstacles, but the last was the most difficult. What was needed was an address to which escapers could go and then rest and make final preparations for the last lap out of Germany.

About this time a member of the Escape Organisation received a letter from a friend of his family, an Englishwoman married to a Swede who lived in Stockholm. This letter contained a partly disguised message to the effect that her husband, the Captain of a Swedish merchant vessel, frequently visited "The Parson's House" near the camp when on visits to Germany. This information was passed to the Escape Committee and the conclusion was drawn that "The Parson's House" must be the name of an inn used by Swedish sailors in a Baltic Port, or the residence of a Swedish clergyman doing welfare work amongst Swedish sailors. In any case, here was an address where help might be forthcoming.

In order to try and find "The Parson's House" a trusted German named Munkert, whose activities already have been described, was sent to Memel to investigate. He made several visits and carried out exhaustive enquiries but without success. It was intended to send him to other Baltic ports but as this could only have been done during his periods of leave, at the end of which he invariably brought back quantities of valuable escape aids from his home, it was decided to postpone the matter for a time. Shortly afterwards one of the prisoners engaged in trading with Germans informed the Escape Committee that one of his "contacts," a Germanised Pole, was willing to shelter escapers in his own home and that he was connected with the Polish Underground Movement. The Escape Committee investigated this offer, came to the conclusion it was genuine and accordingly, about October, 1943, decided to organise an escape route by sending a prisoner to the Pole's home which he was to use as a base while visiting all the Baltic ports, until he found "The Parson's House." He was to be in communication with the Escape Committee by means of code messages in letters written in German to Munkert, who would pass them on to the Committee for decoding; messages in the reverse direction were to be sent in the same way, being posted outside the camp by Munkert.

As soon as the escape route was established, another prisoner was to be sent out to go to Sweden and arrange for the co-operation of Swedish seamen visiting German ports on the Baltic. This second man was to keep in touch with both the camp and the first man by code messages in letters

ESCAPE
FROM
GERMANY

*Heydekrug—
The Escape
Route*

written in English or German; the first letters from him would indicate how replies should be addressed. It was hoped that when all arrangements were complete prisoners would be able to leave the camp and proceed along the route from point to point until they would be taken on board a neutral ship and hidden.

When all the details of the plan had been worked out, two prisoners were selected by the Escape Committee. Both were members of the Escape Organisation, each was an experienced escaper and had succeeded in getting out of the Centre Compound at Sagan, and both spoke German. By mid-January, 1944, all was ready, the only decision which remained being the method by which the first man should escape from the camp. Arrangements were made with the driver of a horse wagon, a Pole, that the escaper should be taken out of the camp concealed in the boxlike compartment which served as the driver's seat. However on the appointed day, and for some weeks thereafter, this man failed to enter the camp with the wagon. After the escaper had waited fully dressed in civilian clothes for several days, this scheme was abandoned. Immediately after this, it was decided that he should repeat the performance of examining the new drainage system which was being constructed from the north-east wash-house and leave the compound disguised as a civilian foreman at the point where a trench passed under the fence of the wash-house enclosure. While the escaper was putting on his civilian clothes to do this the German Security Officer visited the site and gave orders that the trench should be filled in.

Undeterred, the escaper and the Escape Committee completed arrangements for a third scheme within a few hours. At this time, because of the comparatively mild weather, roll-call took place on the compound football field. Shortly before each parade a party of guards, usually about twelve in number, entered the compound and took up their allotted positions in various parts of it where they remained until the parade had been dismissed; whereupon they made their way individually through the compound and Vorlager gates to the guard-room. Afternoon parades took place at 3 o'clock and it was arranged that on this day the parade would last for about an hour instead of the usual twenty minutes, owing to artificially created miscounts. This would mean that the guards would leave the compound at dusk and it was planned that the escaper should leave disguised as one of them.

For many months the Escape Committee had been aware of the possibilities of escaping by this method, and all the equipment necessary for the operation of the scheme had been made and stored previously. It had not been intended that fluent German speakers should escape in this way but that it should be used, after the establishment of the escape route, by individuals able to speak only a limited amount of German.

Shortly after midday on 21 January, 1944, Warrant Officer G. J. W. Grimson, R.A.F., sat dressed in civilian clothes in the small office attached to the compound library. His outfit consisted of a good quality black jacket and waistcoat, dark grey worsted riding breeches, knee-length boots with laced fronts, white shirt and collar, black tie with white stripes and a R.A.F. officer's raincoat without belt or belt loops. When dressed, the legs of a pair of airmen's trousers, treated so that they were similar in appearance to German Air Force trousers, were pulled over the boots and riding breeches and pinned half-way up his thighs. On top of all this he wore a German Air Force greatcoat which had been made from two airmen's greatcoats, cross-belts, ammunition pouches and dummy bayonet. When dressed, Grimson lay down on a bed in a dimly lighted part of the room and was covered with a blanket. Meanwhile arrangements were made that the prisoners should be counted in their barrack rooms, ostensibly because of the colder weather, and for a prisoner who resembled Grimson to take his place pretending to be sick in bed. The arrangements worked smoothly and Grimson was counted as a man sick in bed. There were several miscounts and it was not until 4 p.m. that the whistle blew signalling the end of parade.

ESCAPE
FROM
GERMANY

*Heydekrug—
The Escape
Route*

At its sound Grimson rose, slung a beautifully made dummy rifle on his shoulder, put a German field-service cap on his head, and walked out through the compound and Vorlager gates without incident as the third or fourth "guard" to leave the compound. As there was no commotion when the last guard left it was obvious that the sentries on duty at the gate had not counted them as they passed. In the Vorlager, Grimson went to a lavatory close to the guardroom where he disposed of the dummy rifle. Then he walked across to a locked clothing store of which he had the key, where he found in a packing-case which had been taken there earlier in the day a trilby hat and a brief-case in which was packed all the documents and equipment which had been prepared for him. The packing-case also contained food for consumption on the spot. After removing the brief-case and food, Grimson took off his German uniform, and put it in the packing-case. On the following day this case was taken back to the compound by the Camp Quartermaster and a party of prisoners accompanied by Munkert.

Grimson remained in the store until an hour before the train on which he intended to travel was due to leave Heydekrug. After locking the store he left the key in a pre-arranged place to be picked up by his colleague next day. Dressed as a civilian he walked through the German camp to the railway station, a distance of about two miles. He bought a ticket and a few minutes later boarded the train for Insterbrug. He travelled by train, in stages, nearly four hundred miles to the home of a forester friend of the Polish guard at the camp who had offered shelter; this forester lived in

ESCAPE
FROM
GERMANY

*Heydekrug—
The Escape
Route*

woods in German-occupied Poland about ninety miles south-east of Danzig; the guard's home was in a nearby village. When Grimson arrived at the forester's house on 22 January, he was well received and stayed there for several days. During this time he wrote a letter to the Escape Committee which contained a message saying that he had arrived safely at the forester's house and had the nucleus of a good organisation already in being. He asked that tobacco and other things which he required for trading should be sent to him. This was done through a guard who went home on short leave soon afterwards. A few days later this man returned to the camp and conveyed a verbal message from Grimson to the effect that he was obliged to leave the forester's house because a woman relative of the family was talking too much to other Poles in the neighbourhood; also that he intended to try to find the "The Parson's House."

As had been explained, the Escape Committee had planned that a second man should escape and join Grimson when the latter indicated that he had made arrangements for him to be received and passed on to a Baltic port with a good chance of boarding a Swedish ship. After a lapse of two weeks, when no further communication was received from Grimson, a letter was sent to him which contained a message stating that the second man would be sent on 18 February to join him unless instructions to the contrary were received. This letter was taken by a guard who went home on three weeks leave who also carried a parcel of supplies for Grimson. The Escape Committee did not receive any reply to this message before 18 February and the second man escaped from the camp that morning as planned. Later that same day, the Escape Committee received a brief letter from Grimson which had been sent through Munkert. It contained the message "Send the second man but no route arranged."

On the following morning Munkert received a further letter from Grimson which had been posted in Memel. This contained a direct request to Munkert that he should meet him that day at a specified place in the town of Heydekrug at 6.30 p.m. Munkert took the letter to the Escape Committee and after the matter had been discussed, they told him to meet Grimson. He was given a written report of developments in the camp since Grimson's departure, including the instructions given to the second man who had escaped, and was told to give this to Grimson together with a parcel of supplies and a map of Danzig docks.

Munkert met Grimson in Heydekrug and handed over the report and supplies. Grimson gave him a written report of his activities since he had left the camp, also a personal note for one of the members of the Committee. These were delivered by Munkert the following morning. The gist of Grimson's report was that he had found "The Parson's House" in the seamen's quarter of Danzig and that the parson was a Swede. When Grimson had approached him, he denied all knowledge of the Swedish ship's

317

ESCAPE
FROM
GERMANY

*Heydekrug—
The Escape
Route*

Captain whom Grimson sought, and refused to help. Eventually he was persuaded to allow a search to be made of the register of Swedish seamen who had visited the parsonage, but no person bearing the required name had been there during the previous fifteen years. Afterwards Grimson had reconnoitred Danzig harbour and he gave details of the position of guards and Swedish ships. He stated that he had visited all the Baltic ports from Lubeck to Memel but had not been able to find another "Parson's House" nor to obtain any information about the ship's Captain whom he was seeking. He said that Memel was not used by Swedish shipping.

In his personal note to the member of the Escape Committee who had been his closest friend in the camp, Grimson described how he had spent the greater part of his time since leaving the camp in trains and snatching a few hours sleep in waiting-rooms whenever possible. He mentioned that he was suffering from a form of gastric influenza. He said that he was dissatisfied with the result of his work during the month he had been at liberty and felt that the Committee must be disappointed; he was prepared however to continue if the Committee thought he should do so. He had made contact with a number of Polish workers and outlaws in Danzig and district who might prove to be useful. Latterly, he had stayed occasionally at the home of the forester's brother, also a forester, in a wood some distance from his original shelter. He had been able to obtain food coupons from an inn-keeper who lived nearby and had paid for them with the chocolate and cigarettes which had been sent to him by the Committee. He concluded by saying that he wanted some more supplies, including clothes for the children of the man who was sheltering him, and that he would collect these the following week from Munkert whom he had arranged to meet at the same time and place. Finally he said that he was travelling to the original forester's house to meet the second man, as it was not safe for him to be in that area.

### Warrant Officer C. B. Flockhart

Meanwhile as already stated the second man, Warrant Officer (now Squadron Leader) C. B. Flockhart, D.C.M., R.A.F., had escaped from the camp. At this time, "E" Compound was nearing completion and a part of it was occupied by Americans and a few British. On 17 February, 1944, the clothes which Flockhart intended to wear and the false documents which he was to use were placed in a packing-case in "A" Compound and transferred, together with a number of other packing-cases containing supplies to "E" Compound. Later that day Flockhart and a member of the Escape Committee were escorted from "A" Compound to "E" Compound by a bribed German sergeant. After the sentries on the gates had changed the German took the Committee member back to his own compound and left Flockhart. While the prisoners in "E" Compound were being counted later

ESCAPE
FROM
GERMANY

*Heydekrug—
The Escape
Route*

that day, Flockhart hid under the bed in one of the barrack-rooms, and for the next six weeks his absence from his own compound was covered by the organisation.

Early on the morning of 18 February, Flockhart put on part of his disguise and, wearing a large-size Army greatcoat, walked to the north-west wash-house where he finished dressing. His outfit consisted of a civilian shirt, collar and tie, a green tweed jacket and grey riding breeches, both of which had been made in the camp from Italian uniform, black knee-length riding boots, a grey trilby hat and a R.A.F. officer's raincoat without belt or belt loops. He carried a canvas brief-case, also made in the camp, and in his hand a rolled-up plan of the camp and environs which had been made for him by surveyors amongst his fellow prisoners. The brief-case contained the usual equipment and in addition stage make-up materials and a book by one of the leaders of the Nazi Party about the superiority of the German race. His forged identity documents and passes described him as a Germanised Pole aged forty-five years, a surveyor working for the German Air Force. In order to create the impression of age, his hair had been cropped in the German fashion and shaved off at the temples as though it had receded; theatrical hair powder had been rubbed into the hair which gave it a grey tinge. Finally he had applied invisible black theatrical make-up to his face in such a way that combined with the alterations to his hair, he appeared to be quite fifteen years older than he was.

In accordance with the arrangements which had been made the previous day, the corrupt German sergeant arrived at the wash-house at 8.30 a.m. and met Flockhart, who told him to go to the small guard room just outside the nearby gate and engage the sergeant in charge there in conversation. After seeing that the towel, which indicated that there were no other Germans in the compound, remained hanging from a certain barrack-room window, he left the wash-house and walked past the end of the pathway leading to the gate.

The area east of this path was forbidden to prisoners and was marked by a single strand of wire patrolled by a sentry. As Flockhart approached this, the sentry had just turned at the opposite end of his beat, and when Flockhart waved to him to indicate that he was going to the east unfinished wash-house, he gave a signal of acquiescence. The pseudo-surveyor stepped over the wire and inspected the wash-house making notes on his plan. In a few minutes he entered the wash-house and continued the inspection, then emerged and walked slowly to the gate, rolling up his plan as he went. On arrival there, he showed his camp pass to the guard on duty, who merely glanced at it and stood aside to allow him to pass through the gate which he had unlocked as the "surveyor" approached.

Flockhart walked unhurriedly in a north-westerly direction to the site of a camp sewage farm which was being constructed near the river about

319

ESCAPE
FROM
GERMANY

*Heydekrug—*
*The Escape*
*Route*

two hundred yards from the gate. This was in full view of a number of the sentries in the watch towers around the compounds. He spent about ten minutes examining the excavations and pretending to make notes on his plan and to pace distances. There were no workmen on the site at the time and when he had ascertained that there were no Germans in the vicinity, other than the usual sentries, he put his camp plan into his brief-case and walked back towards the gate. However, he continued past it along the path beaten by the sentries patrolling outside the compound fence and turned south along the eastern camp boundary. When he passed the patrolling sentries and the few German Air Force guards whom he met he greeted them with the customary "Heil!" and the half-hearted Nazi salute then in fashion.

He walked to Heydekrug railway station where he bought a third-class ticket to Konigsberg, then entered the waiting room and whiled away the time by reading the German book which he had carried in his brief-case. Just before the arrival of the train, an hour-and-a-half later, several men entered the waiting room together. Flockhart recognised some of these as members of the Criminal Police who had conducted a search of the camp some time previously and in order to avoid having his identity documents examined, went to the wash-room where he stayed until he heard the train arrive.

He boarded the train and found that two of the policemen were in the compartment which he had selected. As he sat down in the only vacant seat, opposite a policeman, he began to wonder at what stage of the journey they would begin to check the identities of passengers. Almost immediately an old farmer sitting next to him began to talk about the weather, but fortunately was so garrulous that monosyllabic replies were sufficient to keep the discourse going. The policemen appeared to be uninterested and they left the train at Insterburg and disappeared without having checked any of the passengers on the train.

Flockhart also alighted at Insterburg and spent an hour in the waiting-room over a glass of beer waiting for the arrival of the train for Konigsberg. He continued his journey in stages to the forester's house. There was only one incident; while waiting at Marienburg station he sat in the crowded waiting-room feigning sleep. During the night two members of the Railway Police checked the identities of all those in the room, but when they reached Flockhart they paused, then passed on without disturbing him. Probably his dress, which was that worn by many middle-class Germans and higher officials including the Criminal Police and Gestapo, deterred them.

Flockhart reached the end of his train journey at about 9.30 a.m. and made his way on foot through the village to the forester's house where he believed Grimson to be staying. On arrival he discovered that the forester

ESCAPE
FROM
GERMANY

*Heydekrug—
The Escape
Route*

was not at home but his wife, who appeared to be very nervous, invited him to enter the house and wait, after he said he was a friend of the man who had arrived there a month previously. She stated that this man, Grimson, had gone on a journey some days earlier and she believed that he would not be returning. She began to prepare a meal and about an hour later the forester arrived. When he had satisfied himself concerning the identity of his visitor, he said that Grimson had gone to Danzig and Memel two days previously and as far as he knew would not be returning. Flockhart was unable to glean any further information from him and as he knew that the guard from the camp was at home on leave, he asked the forester to send for him. Within an hour this man arrived and said that he had delivered the letter and parcel from the Escape Committee to Grimson. He was unable to add anything to what the forester had said concerning Grimson's movements.

After a consultation in Polish, the two Poles stated that they had decided that Flockhart should go to the home of the forester's brother because it would be too dangerous to remain. Soon afterwards the guard led the way to the second forester's house, following haulage roads through the woods and footpaths across the snow-covered fields. On the way he explained that the first forester's wife was too talkative and that Grimson had left the district because of this. Upon arrival at the second forester's house, Flockhart was provided with food and a bed; the guard returned directly to his own home.

About 2 a.m. on 21 February Flockhart was woken up by his host and told that his friend had arrived. This was Grimson, who was accompanied by the guard. The two escapers discussed all that had happened during the previous month and Grimson explained that he had not succeeded in arranging a passage to Sweden but he believed it might be possible to board a Swedish ship in Danzig harbour. It was decided that they should travel to Danzig that day. After a few hours sleep they left, taking different train routes because their documents were almost identical. They met in the waiting room of Danzig railway station at 10 o'clock that evening as arranged. Grimson was familiar with the dock area and he led Flockhart to within a few hundred yards of a Swedish ship which was being loaded with coal. Flockhart then handed his money, papers, brief-case and raincoat to Grimson and arranged to meet him in the station waiting-room before daylight should he fail to get on board the ship.

While Grimson walked off towards the city, Flockhart entered the prohibited dock area through an open gate across a railway track and crawled fairly close to the side of the ship. There was quite a lot of activity on the quay side, which was illuminated by arc lamps, and a German sentry was posted on the end of the ship's gangway. Flockhart lay in the snow for about four hours seeking some means of boarding the ship unobserved.

Eventually he crawled to a position behind a crane about thirty feet from
the ship's side, but a few minutes later several workmen passed within
three or four feet of him on the other side of the crane. This narrow escape
from discovery, and the arrival of a railway engine in the vicinity, made
him decide that he could not board the ship that night. He returned to the
railway station and met Grimson, who informed him that the nightly
examination of identity papers had taken place some time previously. They
spent the remainder of that night in different parts of the waiting-room.

Next morning Grimson, who was an experienced oarsman, suggested
that it might be possible to board the same ship from a rowing-boat that
night. He proposed that he should search for a rowing-boat while Flockhart travelled to Gdynia to ascertain whether Swedish shipping used that
port. Flockhart went by train and found that it was a German Naval base
so heavily guarded that it was impossible to enter the harbour area in daylight. He returned to Danzig and met Grimson as pre-arranged but the
latter had not found a rowing-boat. However, he had seen another
Swedish ship in a different part of the docks and had discovered that this
might be reached through a hole in the fence.

After dark that evening Grimson conducted Flockhart by train and
ferry to a point close to the hole in the fence; this was about one hundred
yards from an anti-aircraft battery. Within a few seconds Flockhart had
handed over his raincoat and papers and lain down by the side of the road,
while Grimson continued walking. Flockhart crawled about one hundred
yards over snow-covered waste-ground to the fence, and after some
searching found a small gap. He crawled through and across railway tracks
towards the ship which Grimson had pointed out. This part of the harbour was well lit and eventually Flockhart was able to discern that there
were two ships flying the Swedish flag lying alongside the quay. He chose
the larger, a vessel of about three thousand tons, and reconnoitred from
the cover of some railway wagons. There was an armed sentry patrolling
near the ship's gangway. Flockhart walked some distance along the quay
away from the ship, keeping the railway wagons between himself and the
guard, then crossed to the water's edge and approached the ship. He was
helped in this by the cover afforded by the leg of a crane. He succeeded in
getting within about three yards of the gangway while the sentry was walking towards the opposite end of the ship, but he turned and saw him.
Flockhart was walking quite slowly, and when he saw that he had been
observed he stopped, had a look round, then sauntered slowly away. At
that moment two Swedish seamen arrived to go on board the ship and the
guard, being engaged in examining their papers, did not challenge Flockhart. The latter left the dock area immediately by climbing the fence some
distance from the hole through which he had entered.

He returned to the railway station and saw Grimson, but they

321

ESCAPE
FROM
GERMANY

*Heydekrug—
The Escape
Route*

ESCAPE
FROM
GERMANY

Heydekrug—
The Escape
Route

pretended not to recognise one another and sat in different parts of the waiting-room until morning, leaving about 7 a.m. Flockhart recounted his experiences and they discussed various means of boarding the ship under cover of darkness. Both men were suffering from lack of sleep, but Grimson wanted his colleague to make one more attempt that night. Flockhart, however, stated that he would prefer to make the attempt openly in daylight and asked the other to try to obtain a suit of workman's blue overalls, a black cap with a shiny peak, and one of the badges worn by Poles in Germany. Grimson said that he thought he could obtain these without difficulty from a cousin of the forester who was living in Danzig. They parted and about three hours later Grimson returned to the station with a parcel containing the clothes which were required.

Flockhart went into the station wash-room and put on the overalls over his civilian clothes, packed his trilby hat in his brief-case in case he should need it later, and substituted the peak cap. After a suitable interval Grimson knocked on the door of the compartment to indicate that there was no one else in the main room, and Flockhart handed him his raincoat as he passed. All Flockhart's papers, with the exception of his identity card and a permit to travel on the railway, were in one of the pockets as arranged. As Flockhart stood outside the railway station at a tram stop, Grimson, who had followed him, stood beside him for a moment and whispered "Good luck."

Flockhart travelled by tram and ferry to the dock area and walked to the hole in the fence which he had used the previous night. As he approached he noticed that a path had been trodden in the snow between the hole and the roadway. He assumed that this must be a short cut used by dock workers so followed the path and crawled through the hole. Although there were a number of people on the road, and soldiers were visible on the anti-aircraft gun site, no one displayed any interest. Feeling elated by the ease with which he had got into the dock, he walked across the railway tracks to a small wooden hut near a concrete mixer which he had observed the previous night. This was about two hundred yards from the larger of the two Swedish ships. He observed the quay through a knot-hole and, after hiding his brief-case under some wood in the hut, soiled his hands and face, then walked towards the ship. Some Russian prisoners were loading the bunkers with coal under the supervision of a guard, and a similar party was working on the quay near the smaller ship. As it was then midday, no other workers were about and Flockhart remained near these Russians for about half an hour in the hope that one of them might leave the others for a few minutes so that he could ask his help in boarding one of the ships; but this strategy was fruitless.

Noticing that the sentry on the larger of the two ships was walking up and down the quay near the gangway, Flockhart decided to try to repeat

his trick of the previous night and approach the ship along the water's
edge under cover of the crane leg. He returned to the hut by a circuitous
route and removed the Polish badge from his overalls. He approached the
ship noiselessly, and after ensuring that there was no one else near, stepped
from behind the leg of the crane when the sentry was walking in the opposite direction and began to examine one of the ship's moorings. He hoped
that when the guard turned and saw him he would assume that he was one
of the ship's crew who had descended the nearby gangway. When the sentry turned and noticed the man kneeling beside the bollard he displayed
no interest, whereupon Flockhart walked to the next mooring, which was
closer to the gangway, and examined it very carefully. As the guard walked
towards the other end of the ship he walked slowly up the gangway and
had almost reached the top when the sentry turned. However, he did not
take the slightest notice of the man in the dirty overalls.

In order to maintain the impression he had created in the sentry's
mind, he tidied up some ropes on the ship's deck for a few minutes before
seeking a hiding-place. The ship appeared to be deserted, and he spent
some time in his search for a suitable hiding-place. The ship sailed at 10
a.m. on 25 February, after having been searched by Germans, but Flockhart was not discovered. On the afternoon of the following day he went on
deck and revealed himself to a member of the crew, who took him to the
Captain. Upon learning the identity of the stowaway, the Captain stated
that his ship was in Swedish waters and would arrive in Stockholm the following day; he placed a cabin at Flockhart's disposal. On arrival in Stockholm at 7 p.m. on 27 February, the Captain handed him over to Swedish
plain-clothes police who boarded the vessel as soon as she docked. Next
morning he was conveyed to the British Legation and ten days later travelled by air to the United Kingdom.

During the week following Flockhart's departure from the camp, the
supplies which Grimson had asked for, and several additional copies of the
map of Danzig Docks, were taken to the surplus clothing store just outside
the camp with the connivance of Munkert. On the 26 February a letter of
encouragement to Grimson from the Escape Committee was handed to
Munkert together with the supplies, and when Munkert met Grimson that
evening in Heydekrug he received from him a written account of his activities since his previous report; Munkert delivered this to the Committee
the following morning and stated that Grimson had intended to spend the
previous night at the hotel in Heydekrug and had instructed him to meet
him again that evening. Grimson's report contained a detailed account of
all that had happened during the previous week. He stated that he had not
seen Flockhart again after his departure for the docks disguised as a Polish
workman. He had failed to learn whether or not he had been caught
although a number of his Polish acquaintances in Danzig had made

323

ESCAPE
FROM
GERMANY

*Heydekrug—
The Escape
Route*

324

ESCAPE
FROM
GERMANY

*Heydekrug—*
*The Escape*
*Route*

discreet enquiries. He expressed the opinion that Flockhart either had succeeded in getting aboard a Swedish ship or had been drowned. The report gave further valuable information about Danzig, and this was illustrated by annotations on the map which had been passed to him. He concluded by saying that he would meet Munkert the following evening and gave a list of his immediate requirements.

Later that day the Escape Committee's reply to Grimson and the things for which he asked were handed to Munkert for delivery. The letter contained the following message:—

"The Parson's House in Danzig is the one intended, but the parson has been changed—do not bother further. Make contact with Swedish seamen and endeavour to obtain their co-operation. Should the position become too difficult, get to Sweden and work from there."

On the following day, Munkert told one of the members of the Escape Committee that Grimson had gone back to the second forester's house. He had sent a verbal message to the effect that he would carry out the instructions contained in the letter and expressed the hope that the Committee were satisfied with what he had done.

During the following week arrangements were made by Sommers, a Polish photographer, that Grimson should stay overnight with friends of his at a house near Heydekrug on his subsequent visits to the area. Munkert and Grimson met at this house from then onwards.

Grimson again visited Heydekrug on the 4 March and weekly thereafter until the 13 April, 1944. On each occasion he gave to Munkert a written report of his activities, observations and plans, together with a list of his requirements for delivery to the Escape Committee. At the same time he collected his supplies.

In early March Grimson passed on an original permit authorising entry to Danzig harbour which he had borrowed from a Pole. He requested that it should be photographed and returned to him the following evening; also that a forged copy of it should be supplied to him the following week, together with a nondescript merchant seaman's outfit with a Swedish cap badge. All this was done and he was supplied with a modified Naval Petty Officers uniform including the peaked cap, to which a pseudo-Swedish badge had been attached in such a manner that it could be removed instantly if required. The permit was made in duplicate, one was completed with the details appertaining to a Dutch worker and the other for a Pole. Grimson used these items on many occasions to gain admittance to the Danzig dock area and at various times he borrowed rowing boats to enable him to reconnoitre the shipping.

The gist of Grimson's reports to the Escape Committee during March was that he had decided to confine his activities to the Danzig area because

325

ESCAPE
FROM
GERMANY

*Heydekrug—*
*The Escape*
*Route*

of the comparative abundance of Swedish shipping there and the fact that he had succeeded in obtaining lodgings which he considered to be reasonably safe. He was living on food obtained through black market sources and was forced to pay very high prices. About mid-March he stated that he had rented two other rooms in different parts of Danzig and that each contained a stock of food; the rents had been paid for some time in advance and they could be used for accommodating escapers until they could be put on board Swedish ships. In another report he stated that he had several Poles working for him and had established contact with helpful foreign workers who lived in a camp close to Danzig docks. Subsequently he outlined a scheme whereby any escaper from the camp who reached Danzig could establish contact with him. He intended to be at a specified place in Danzig railway station between noon and 1 p.m. and 7.30 and 8.30 p.m. daily. Should the escaper not find it possible to be there at either of these times, he should make a specified mark against a time when he would return there, on a particular ferry time-table in the harbour area. This notice-board would be under constant observation by one of his Polish helpers and the escaper would be met at the time he indicated on the board. In the report which he made towards the end of March, he stated that he had made some friends amongst Swedish seamen frequenting hotels in Danzig and that he was ready to receive escapers.

As related in the preceding chapter, Callender and Lewis escaped from the camp during March, but they were not given any information about Grimson's efforts to organise a route. The Escape Committee considered that it would be unfair to Grimson to have any escapers to handle before he had completed his arrangements.

At the end of March it was arranged between the Escape Committee and Grimson that the first man to use the route should escape from the camp on the 6 April. Grimson undertook to meet him at the house near Heydekrug and accompany him to Danzig. About the same time two members of the Escape Organisation proposed to the Escape Committee that they should escape together and proceed into Lithuania. It was their intention to explore the possibility of organising a route through that country to the Russian lines, or by fishing boat to Sweden, for use by non-German speaking escapers. The Committee approved this proposal on the condition that these two men undertook to remain in Lithuania for two weeks before travelling to Danzig to make contact with Grimson in the event of failure to establish a route. The details of Grimson's scheme for establishing contact in Danzig were explained to them after they had complied with the Committee's condition.

On 3 April, 1944, these two men, Warrant Officer R. B. H. Townsend-Coles, R.A.F., and Aircraftman, later Sergeant, J. Gewelber, M.M., R.A.F., were escorted from "A" Compound to "E" Compound by Munkert. They

ESCAPE
FROM
GERMANY

*Heydekrug—
The Escape
Route*

remained there, hiding during parades, until the afternoon of the follow-ing day, their absence from their own compound being covered by the Escape Organisation. Townsend-Coles spoke fluent German and Gewel-ber, who was of Polish birth, spoke excellent German and Polish and had some knowledge of Russian. About noon on 4 April they donned their dis-guises. Townsend-Coles wore a civilian shirt, collar and tie, black jacket and trousers, thigh-length overcoat and trilby hat. He was to pose as a civilian engineer. Gewelber wore the dress of a "ferret", which consisted of a dark blue boiler suit, German Air Force field-service cap, belt and short gaiters. Underneath this garb he wore a black civilian jacket and a pair of blue overall trousers and had concealed a civilian cap; this dress was to support the role of a Polish workman which he intended to adopt after leaving the camp. Both men were in possession of forged camp passes, identity cards and German money.

At 1 p.m. the compound was clear of undesirable Germans and the two escapers emerged from the room in which they had dressed. They walked to the gate in the north fence and showed their camp passes to the guard. Gewelber informed him that he was escorting the "engineer" to the sewage farm to inspect the work being done there. They passed through the gate without difficulty and on arrival at the sewage farm which was deserted, found a place which could not be seen from the camp. Gewelber removed his "ferret's" uniform and buried it; both men burnt their camp passes. After ensuring that there was no one about, they walked north-eastwards along the river bank, following it when it turned east. When they reached the Lithuanian frontier about six miles from the camp, near Nowemiasto, they decided it would be impossible to cross it because of the swampy nature of the ground which was covered with snow; also it was intensely cold.

They retraced their steps for a short distance and turned south into the woods, where they rested until 5 a.m. next day. They walked to a small rail-way junction near Jugnaten and after purchasing tickets boarded a train for Tilsit. They continued their journey by train in stages via Konigsberg to Danzig, where they arrived without incident about 7 p.m. on 6 April. They waited in the station at the place which had been specified by Grim-son until 7.30 p.m., but he failed to arrive. It was too late then to go to the ferry notice-board in the dock area and they decided that Gewelber should seek help from Poles. He spoke to three Poles standing at a street corner and explained who he was and requested assistance. One of them took the two escapers to his home where they stayed for two days, later moving to a foreign workers' camp where they lived in a room occupied by Poles. Some of their helpers endeavoured to arrange for them to be taken on board a Swedish ship but without success. They went to the ferry notice-board on 11 April and drew the sign specified by Grimson. In order to reach the notice-board they travelled on the ferry and noticed two Swedish ships in different parts of the harbour. During the next few days they visited the docks several times and endeavoured to persuade Swedish sailors to hide them on their ships but without success.

327

ESCAPE
FROM
GERMANY

*Heydekrug—
The Escape
Route*

Meanwhile Grimson visited Heydekrug on 6 April in order to pass on his report, collect supplies and escort the first escaper to use the route to Danzig as planned. He was informed that this man had not been able to escape that day because the forged documents which he was to use had not been completed and that they would be ready within a few days. Grimson arranged to return on 13 April. The Escape Committee informed him through Munkert that Townsend-Coles and Gewelber had escaped on 4 April and had been instructed to make contact with him in Danzig at the end of two weeks should they be unable to make their way through Lithuania. Grimson returned to Danzig.

On 12 April the first man selected to use the escape route was escorted from "A" Compound to "E" Compound by the same method as before. He was a fluent German speaker, having been a prominent member of the Escape Organisation as a "trader". He was in possession of forged identity documents and a camp pass. At about 11 a.m. on 13 April he put on civilian clothes, over which he donned a "ferret" uniform.

At noon he was advised that there were no Germans in the compound and left the barrack-room in which he had dressed. He walked to the gate in the northern fence and showed his camp pass to the guard. He was allowed to pass through, but when he headed towards the sewage farm the guard called out that he must "book out" at the guard room which was nearby. The bogus "ferret" replied that he did not think this was necessary but the guard was insistent. The escaper walked to the guardroom and reported to the sergeant in charge, who enquired whether he was new to the camp. This query was answered in the affirmative, whereupon the sergeant wanted to know to which Company he was attached. Without hesitation the escaper answered that he belonged to the third Company. At this juncture the sergeant examined the camp pass which had been presented for his inspection and expressed the opinion that the bearer must be a prisoner of war. He arrested the bogus "ferret" and took him into the guardroom. The escaper attempted to destroy his forged identity documents on the fire, but the untimely arrival of a member of the German Security Staff prevented their total destruction. After being searched he was marched off to the office of the German Security Officer and interrogated briefly. Later he was taken to the camp gaol where he was questioned by members of the Security Staff and a member of the Criminal Police.

That evening Grimson arrived at the rendezvous at Heydekrug and was met by Munkert and Sommers. They handed him a letter from the Escape Committee which explained the circumstances of the escaper's

328

ESCAPE
FROM
GERMANY

*Heydekrug—
The Escape
Route*

arrest earlier that day. Because of the similarity between Grimson's documents and those taken by the Germans that morning he was advised to return to Danzig and remain under cover for about two weeks. It was suggested that he should return to Heydekrug on 29 April.

Grimson gave a message to Munkert for delivery to the Escape Committee. The gist of this was that he had learned through one of his helpers just before he left Danzig that Townsend-Coles and Gewelber had arrived there. He proposed to return there immediately to make contact with them. He stated that travelling was becoming increasingly difficult because of much more frequent and closer examination of papers by Civil Police, Criminal Police, Railway Police and Gestapo officials. On one journey alone his papers had been inspected on twenty-seven occasions. He had tried to establish contact with various Allied nationals, including prisoners of war and workers in Germany, but seven attempts had been made to betray him. He concluded by saying that he would return on 29 April.

On the morning of 13 April Townsend-Coles and Gewelber visited the ferry notice-board and found a message from Grimson. This gave a time later that day and the initials "G.G." They returned at the time indicated but failed to see Grimson. Presently they noticed a man watching them and eventually he addressed them in Polish. After some discussion he stated that he was one of Grimson's assistants and gave them a parcel of food and arranged to meet them the following day; they returned to the worker's camp. They met Grimson's assistant on 14 and 15 April, when he informed them that he expected Grimson to return to Danzig that night with another escaper from the camp. They arranged to meet again that evening. They kept their appointment and met the Pole who was accompanied by Grimson. Grimson took them to an address in Gdynia where they were provided with accommodation by another of his assistants.

On 19 April Grimson escorted them to the docks and led them through the hole in the fence which had been used by Flockhart. He instructed them to board the Swedish ship which was lying there whilst he distracted the attention of the sentry guarding the gangway, then left them. He walked along the quay and engaged the sentry in conversation. Townsend-Coles boarded the ship quickly, but Gewelber approached more slowly and when he had reached Grimson's side, the sentry noticed Townsend-Coles moving on the ship. He went after him and on instructions from Grimson, Gewelber boarded the ship and hid. The guard caught Townsend-Coles, but Grimson remained on the scene and accompanied the party when Townsend-Coles was taken to an office for questioning. Later, the recaptured escaper was taken to a prison at Marienburg. The Germans searched the ship twice before she sailed on 21 April, but Gewelber was not discovered. He remained in hiding until the ship arrived in Sweden four days later, then got ashore without being observed and reported to the British

329

ESCAPE
FROM
GERMANY

Heydekrug—
The Escape
Route

Legation in Stockholm. He was handed over to the Swedish Police and repatriated to the United Kingdom, where he arrived on 8 May.

Immediately following the arrest of the prisoner who was trying to leave the camp disguised as a "ferret" on 13 April, the Escape Committee ordered the cessation of all escape activities and all equipment was hidden securely in anticipation of extensive searches. On the following day the man who had been captured was interviewed by the Camp Commandant and asked to make a statement about his intentions after leaving the camp. He refused and requested that his R.A.F. uniform should be brought to him. He was told that this was a matter for the Security Staff. On the following day he bluffed one of the cell guards into fetching his uniform from the compound and discarded his civilian clothing. He was detained in the camp gaol until 11 May, being interrogated daily, then released into the compound.

For a few days following his arrest, conditions in the camp were comparatively quiet but the Escape Committee learned through Munkert and other Germans that an investigation was being made about the forged documents which had been recovered from the guardroom fire. When it was discovered that some of these had been reproduced by photographic means, the camp photographer, Sommers, was suspected and questioned. It is believed that he was able to clear himself. At the same time Munkert was under suspicion because of his known association with the men who had attempted to escape. On about 19 April one of the members of the Escape Committee gave a message to Munkert for delivery to Grimson on the occasion of his next visit to Heydekrug. The message was:—

"Get out of the country, position hopeless."

Two days later Sommers arrived in the compound under escort and all the prisoners who lived in one of the barrack blocks were ordered to parade. Sommers scrutinised them but did not pick out anyone. At a propitious moment he pulled up one of his trouser legs which revealed that there were no laces in his boots. This was noticed by members of the Escape Committee, whom he knew, and it was concluded that he had instigated the identification parade in order to get into the compound so that they might learn that he was under arrest. Later he and the man being held in the camp gaol were confronted with one another, but each declared that he did not know the other.

About this time the Camp Commandant sent for the Camp Leader and the Senior Medical Officer, an officer of the Royal Army Medical Corps. He informed them it would be dangerous to continue escape activities at that time and requested the Camp Leader to hand over to him all existing copies of forged documents. He stated that the surrender of these would enable him to report to higher authority that the whole matter was closed;

330

ESCAPE
FROM
GERMANY

*Heydekrug—
The Escape
Route*

failure to do so would cause untold complications in the form of searches and arrests. The Camp Leader said he knew nothing about such matters but he would make enquiries in the compound. Upon his return there he consulted with the Escape Committee and it was decided that after a suitable interval he should return to the Commandant and inform him that there were no other forged documents in existence; this was done.

On 23 April a note from Munkert was conveyed to the Escape Committee by another German collaborator. The note stated that Sommers had asked him to inform the Committee that a colleague of his in the Polish Underground Movement had been killed in a shooting affray with the German Police, and that a message connecting him, Sommers, in his real name with this Movement had been found on the man's body. He had been in the hands of the Gestapo on a previous occasion and did not trust himself not to divulge information under interrogation. He desired the Committee to supply him with poison or a pistol so that he could commit suicide. The Committee conferred and decided that they could not meet this request; they prepared for the results of Sommer's disclosures.

Early next morning it was learned that Sommers had hanged himself in his cell during the night and later that day this information was confirmed. It was learned also, that the guard who had arranged accommodation for Grimson and Flockhart had been arrested at the same time as Sommers. They had occupied the same room in the German camp and were known to be associates. When arrested this man had broken away from his escort in an endeavour to get himself shot, but had been recaptured uninjured. However, he knew very little about the Escape Organisation within the camp or about Grimson's movements after he had moved to the Danzig area. He is believed to have been shot some time later.

On this day the Escape Committee learned from other Germans that Munkert was being watched very closely and virtually under open arrest. However, a few days later a note was received from him through the agency of a German who had not been very co-operative and whom the Committee did not trust. In the note Munkert stated that he was cleared of suspicion and wanted instructions for the meeting arranged between himself and Grimson which was to take place later that week. The Committee was reluctant to accept Munkert's assertion that he was cleared of suspicion, but decided that it was imperative to try to transmit a final message to Grimson. In order to effect this a letter was written giving full details of the developments within the camp during the previous two weeks and instructing Grimson to leave at once for Sweden; this was not signed. Grimson's friend on the Committee wrote a personal letter to Grimson and signed it. No Germans were mentioned by name in either of these letters. The letters and one thousand Reichsmarks were enclosed in an envelope and handed to Munkert's messenger at noon on 28 April. This

German did not return to his place of duty, the carpenter's workshop in the Vorlager, that afternoon.

331

ESCAPE
FROM
GERMANY

*Heydekrug—
The Escape
Route*

That evening one of the members of the Escape Organisation was informed by a "ferret" that Grimson, posing as a civilian working for the German Air Force, had been arrested at Insterburg; also that Munkert had been arrested that afternoon and removed from the camp. None of the Germans or Poles, Service or civilian, who had been really useful to the Escape Organisation were seen again in the camp after that day, but nothing is known concerning their fate.

On the following morning, 29 April, six prisoners of war, including the member of the Escape Committee who had signed the letter to Grimson, were arrested and placed in the camp gaol without being charged with any offence. Next day the Escape Committee learned that Townsend-Coles was being held in the cells, but was not allowed to make contact with any other prisoner in the gaol; also that he was still wearing the civilian clothes in which he had escaped. All efforts to get a R.A.F. uniform to him during the next few days were unsuccessful. However, it was learned that he was in possession of his prisoner of war identity disc. Despite the German precautions to prevent Townsend-Coles from communicating with his fellow countrymen, the member of the Escape Committee who had been arrested was able to converse with him for a few moments daily. He learned the main features of Townsend-Coles's story up to the time of his recapture at Danzig; also that Grimson had travelled as a passenger on the same train when he was being escorted from the prison at Marienburg to the camp. He had seen Grimson on several occasions, but they had not had an opportunity to speak because of the vigilance of his escort. He last saw Grimson when the train had stopped at Insterburg. He had learned from his guards that a country-wide check-up was being made to find Grimson.

On about 6 May Townsend-Coles was taken from the camp gaol under escort to an unknown destination, but a little later it was learned from one of the Germans in the camp that he had been seen in Tilsit Civil Prison. Subsequently the British Government made enquiries through the Protecting Power and a reply was received from the Germans to the effect that he had been charged with espionage and collaboration with the Polish Underground Movement; also that on 15 July, 1944, he had offered resistance at Tilsit and had been shot dead. The British Government demanded an enquiry, but before this could be carried out by the Protecting Power the area was occupied by Russian Forces, and no further investigation has been possible.

The six men who were arrested on 29 April were removed from the camp under escort to an unknown destination on 10 May. Subsequently it was learned from the Germans that these men were regarded by them as

ESCAPE
FROM
GERMANY

*Heydekrug—
The Escape
Route*

the Escape Committee. Although nothing was known in the camp at the time concerning their fate, they were split into two parties of three and sent to separate camps in other parts of Germany. Apart from periods of detention in cells, no further action was taken against them.

Little more is known about Grimson although extensive enquiries have been made. Nearly a year later, in another camp, one of the members of the Escape Organisation met a German whom he had known at Heydekrug. This man stated that about April, 1944, he had been a member of a party of guards which had escorted Grimson and Munkert from a military detention barracks, location not stated, to an undefined destination. He had not been a member of the firing party, but he believed they had been shot.

Although the Escape Organisation did not suffer any losses of equipment as a result of the German endeavours to smash the organisation, it was not possible to reorganise quickly because of the loss of the most valuable German and Polish collaborators. Those who remained at the camp were much too nervous to be of any real use. Shortly afterwards, rumours being current that the camp was to be evacuated, the Committee decided not to continue with any large-scale escape plans. The camp was evacuated in July, 1944.

The escaper who was arrested as he attempted to walk through the camp gate on 13 April was tried by Court Martial about January, 1945, at Stalag 357, Fallingbostel. He was charged with using forged documents to the confusion of the German military and civilian authorities. He was found guilty and sentenced to three months hard labour, but was not called upon to serve the sentence, probably because of the chaotic conditions prevailing in Germany at that time.

# Part Three

# Evacuation and Release

### CHAPTER 32 · EVACUATION

The invasion of France changed the attitude of most prisoners towards escape. To those who were stationed in the west of Germany the landing in Normandy and even more the break through at Avranches, brought the end of the war so close that to risk death in an attempt to gain a few weeks freedom seemed the height of folly. In those camps, with few exceptions, organised attempts at escape ceased, and for the rest of the summer the prisoners abandoned themselves to the pleasures of listening to the news, speculating on the date of their release, and dreaming of the joys that were to follow. No one questioned Mr. Churchill's hope that "before the leaves of autumn fell" the war would be over and prisoners would be home.

For those in the east of Germany and in Poland the position was different. They were a long way from the western armies, and with the Russians advancing towards them and every sign of panic beginning to appear among the civilian population, escape offered the chance of hiding until the arrival of the Russians and of being repatriated through Odessa. Prisoners to whom escape for some time had not seemed worthwhile began to think of it again and a few managed to hide and were eventually overtaken and repatriated by the Russians. The great majority stayed together. General Eisenhower's order, warning prisoners that it was dangerous to form guerilla bands and telling them to stay in their camps until formally relieved, had been received over the radio and camp leaders everywhere acted upon it. Instructions were often issued forbidding individuals to escape and plans were drawn up to deal with the emergency which might arise should German guards desert and the prisoners be left alone to meet retreating German and advancing Russian forces. In the officers' camps at Sagan and Barth full military discipline was imposed and detailed operational plans were drawn up. Parties were chosen to dig slit trenches as a precaution against air or ground attack and others were instructed to deal with fire and first-aid. Specially selected men were formed into "Commando" groups to take over the power stations and water installations which lay beyond the boundaries of the camps but were essential to the welfare of the prisoners, or to carry out reconnaissance and foraging for food. At Barth the plans included the taking over of the nearby aerodrome.

Meanwhile one camp was evacuated. Heydekrug, at the eastern extremity of East Prussia, was threatened by the Russians early in the summer of 1944. It was no surprise to the prisoners therefore when in the beginning of July they were ordered to get ready to leave. They were told that they could take with them only what they could carry and that no transport could be provided for baggage. A few days later they were marched out of the camp in two parties. The first of these, which was composed of more than nine hundred British prisoners and eleven hundred American N.C.O.s, entrained at Heydekrug and went to Libau. There they embarked on a small tramp steamer which took them to Swinemünde. The conditions on the ship were appalling. The prisoners were packed in the holds like sardines in a tin and they suffered from lack of air and thirst. No arrangements had been made for sanitation and they sweltered in the midsummer heat. The sick lay on the open deck without shelter of any kind. Upon arrival at Swinemünde, after four days and three nights, they were put in railway cattle trucks and sent to Kiefheide, in Pomerania, north-east of Stettin.

Although the new camp, Stalag Luft IV, Gross Tychow, was only three miles from the station of Kiefheide, the worst part of the journey was yet to come. When the prisoners detrained they were met by a party of German guards, accompanied by dogs, under the command of an officer who appeared to be mentally deranged. In the presence of the prisoners he harangued the guards, telling them that these were the "terror airmen" who had bombed their towns, destroyed their homes and killed their wives and children. The prisoners were ordered to march, then to run. Every man was laden with as many of his possessions as he could carry and was exhausted by the journey. They tried to obey the order to run and the prisoners' leader tried to remonstrate with the officer, but without avail. Within a few hundred yards many of the prisoners staggered and fell, whereupon the guards stabbed them with their bayonets, struck them with their rifle butts or caused the dogs to bite them, and forced them to continue. Hundreds were compelled to discard their packs while the guards, incited by their officer, shouted and jabbed those who lagged. This continued until the prisoners reached the camp gates. They discovered that the camp was occupied by approximately two thousand American N.C.O.s. During the following months further batches of new American prisoners arrived and when the camp was evacuated in February, 1945, the total strength was about ten thousand, of whom nine hundred were British.

The second party, composed of three thousand British N.C.O.s, went by train from Heydekrug to Thorn, then marched to Stalag 357, about one mile and a half from Thorn station. There were no incidents on the journey. Upon arrival they discovered that this camp was occupied by approximately seven thousand British Army N.C.O.s and other ranks. The Air Force prisoners were housed in a separate compound. Six weeks later, at the end of August, all the prisoners were transported by train to a camp at Fallingbostel, about thirty miles north of Hanover, which was re-named Stalag 357. There the Air Force prisoners were again put in a separate compound, but complete segregation was not enforced. Living conditions were bad because of dilapidated barracks, leaking roofs, and insufficient heating and lighting, and with the passage of time these conditions were worsened by over-crowding as further batches of Army prisoners arrived from other camps further east.

The movement of prisoners from East Prussia and Pomerania was only the prelude of what was to come. The failure of the assault at Arnhem in September dashed the prisoners' hopes of relief in 1944, and as the leaves on the trees turned from orange to brown and at last fell, Mr. Churchill began to talk of a final assault in the spring. In the east the Russian advance continued through the Balkans, but in the north, where the prisoners were, the line was stationary. The struggle for Warsaw dragged on, and though the Vistula had been crossed in many places there seemed little chance of a further big push in the winter. The length of the front and the need to police and occupy the Balkans seemed likely to absorb Russian reserves. Wearily, the prisoners braced themselves to face another winter.

And then suddenly the offensive began. In five days, on a front hundreds of miles long, the Russians advanced a hundred miles. By 21 January they had crossed the Oder south of Breslau and were approaching Sagan. Further north they took Lissa and Posen and advanced towards Stettin. All along the line, in front of their armies, a great trek of millions of civilians and hundreds of thousands of prisoners of war began. In mid-winter, with snow on the ground and a night temperature frequently twenty degrees below zero, the people walked or crawled in ox-wagons and the prisoners marched. It was one of the greatest movements of population and one of the severest tests of endurance in history.

It has not been possible to collect a detailed story of each of these marches. Tens of thousands of prisoners walked hundreds of miles, often spending nights in the open in the most extreme cold. Many were shot by their guards and many more died from exposure. Rations were always inadequate and sometimes non-existent. The camps to which they were sent were always over-crowded, and no sooner had they settled than they were often ordered out again to march once more away from the advancing Russians. Later, as the Allies advanced in the west, many of them had to retrace their steps eastwards. Under such conditions records were rarely kept; in only one instance, that of the march of the officers from Sagan, has a full account been available and the reason for its existence is undoubtedly that the march it records was one of the shortest, and the camps to which the officers were sent were better organised than those inhabited by other prisoners. Yet, fragmentary though it is, the Sagan story gives an idea of the experiences undergone by most Air Force prisoners in the last few months of the war and provides an epilogue to the struggle to escape which had preceded it.

The week beginning 21 January saw a steady crescendo of events. On that day a Russian tank unit crossed the Oder at Steinau to the north of Breslau and only 45 miles from Sagan itself. Rumour ran wild, and though the tanks were checked, for some days there was doubt whether a bridgehead had been firmly established. Further north the Russians took Bromberg, which had such vivid memories for some of those who had escaped from Schubin, and the Russians pushed towards the Baltic. Schubin itself was taken in the stride of the general advance, and rumour was received that the American officers who had been imprisoned there had been released.

Sagan itself had become a centre for refugees. Normally a town of 20,000 inhabitants, it was now said to be sheltering more than 100,000 people, and every day thousands more could be seen passing through by rail and road. The British officer in charge of Red Cross food parcels climbed to the top of the silo in which his parcels were stored just outside the camp, and reported that the stream of wagons from the east stretched out of sight on every road he could see. One train of open trucks, which arrived from Breslau, was filled with children who had been separated from their parents. After travelling through a night when the temperature had been many degrees below zero, some had died, and the condition of the remainder caused such indignation among the civilians that it gave rise to the first serious talk of rebellion that the prisoners had heard.

These events soon began to affect the German troops who were guarding the camp. Each man was at two hours' notice to be posted and hourly expected a call to the front. One or two of the officers and N.C.O.s, fanatics to the end, volunteered to join the paratroops and left immediately; the majority had given up all hope and desired only that the war should end quickly. To prisoners they talked openly of desertion and were constantly asking for news from the B.B.C.

Superficially, life within the compounds continued undisturbed. The weather was beautiful and skating went on to the mixed sound of Viennese waltzes played on the gramophone and distant gunfire. The reserves of bread which had been accumulated in the compound were taken by the Germans to feed the refugees, but daily rations were maintained, and it was decided to use up at once the reserves of Red Cross parcels. Every man received his full issue of one parcel for the week.

On Thursday, 25 January, it became certain that the Russians had crossed the Oder at more than one point north of Breslau and that their troops were within forty miles of the camp itself. No new orders were received from the Germans, but each Senior British Officer put his compound on an emergency footing. Strict orders were issued that no one was to escape or leave his unit without the permission of the Senior British Officer.

With the help of the increased rations the prisoners went into training; the circuits of the compounds were crowded throughout the day with prisoners walking in the snow to harden their feet. The prospect that any action, even the simple action of walking, might be useful, and the thought that men who had been spectators for so long might once again begin to take part in events was wonderfully stimulating. Pleasantest of all was the feeling that control was slipping from German hands. True the Germans still maintained guard and carried arms; true also that if they gave orders it was still necessary to obey them; but moral superiority lay within and not without the wire. It was the Germans who were harassed and worried; it was the Germans who were uncertain of their future.

As the week wore on, the blind confidence of Germans in their commanders turned to confusion. On 23 January every German guard at Sagan was issued with two days' hard rations, but whether this was to enable them to go to the front or to march west with the prisoners, no one knew. The following day the German officers on the staff became uneasy. They had already made tentative enquiries whether they should move their families and now, with the Russians only 30 miles away, they went formally to the Commandant to ask what instructions he had to give. He replied that they were to stay where they were and to get on with their jobs.

It was apparently not until Saturday, 27 January, that any orders were received from the German High Command regarding the prisoners of war. At 2 p.m. on that day the German Major in charge of the east compound told the Senior British Officer confidentially that the Commandant had that morning received instructions from the German High Command that the prisoners were not to be moved. This Major had been one of Germany's earliest airmen, and was able to act more independently than his colleagues whose positions depended on their show of allegiance to the Nazi Party. The senior officer among the Americans was also given this information unofficially, and though preparations to receive the Russians were pushed ahead during the day, it was agreed that no official announcement should be made until word came from the Commandant.

Six hours later this order was countermanded, and all compounds were informed that the prisoners were to leave that same evening. What happened in between is known only from reports from German N.C.O.s, but it appears that about 6 p.m. the Commandant was rung up from Berlin and told to get the whole camp on the march at once. A good many of his staff were in the town of Sagan at the time, and it was not until 7 o'clock that they were collected and that the prisoners were informed. Nine o'clock was given as zero hour for the American compound which was to lead the march. As the majority of prisoners did not know of the contradictory order given confidentially earlier in the day, and as they were used to such sudden decisions on the part of the Germans, the order to march was received with indignation but without great surprise.

In the North compound the dress rehearsal of the play "The Wind and the Rain" was in full swing when in the middle of a scene the curtains were slowly drawn and the Adjutant's voice rang out, "All pack up and be ready to move in an hour's time." In the East compound a play written by a member of the camp was under rehearsal when the Adjutant looked quietly in and said, "I'd be moving if I were you; we leave at 11 p.m." Protests were at once lodged by the Senior British Officer, but knowing that they would be futile every man was ready to move within the appointed time.

Inevitably there were delays. The short notice had given the German guards as little time to prepare as the prisoners, and it was more than an hour after the appointed time that the first American compound began to move. No rations had been issued by the Germans, but each prisoner collected a Red Cross parcel on his way out of the camp. This meant it was nearly midnight when the second American compound began to leave, and by then it was clear that the East compound, which was to be the last to go, would not leave until well on into the morning.

Meanwhile the prisoners made the best use of their time. As ever, the first consideration was food, and from the moment the order to move was received until the last man had passed through the gates, kitchen fires were burning and a steady succession of dishes of unprecedented richness were produced. Rows of tins which had been saved by messing officers for weeks were all opened together and eaten in whole or in part. Instead of thin slices of bread or tinned meat being divided into rations, everyone took as much as he could manage and left the rest on the table for anyone who might still have some gap in his stomach to fill. In the camp kitchens were stores of flour and a ration of newly killed meat; all this was distributed, and the smell of roast joints, a delicacy which prisoners normally experienced once every two months, pervaded every barrack. One enterprising party carried a leg of veal between them for the first two days of the march and then managed to have it cooked by a German woman in a village where they billeted. One could say with justice that never before had so much been eaten by so few in such a short time.

Sledges had second priority. The weather was still hard, snow covered the roads, and at midnight the temperature was already seven degrees below zero; by dragging even a small sledge a man could take more food and clothes than he could carry on his back, and the saving in burden was tremendous. Official permission for the construction of sledges had never been given by the Germans, but the N.C.O.s who were to accompany the march let it be known that provided progress was not held up they would make no objections. Every conceivable piece of timber which could be of any use was immediately employed, and hammering resounded throughout the compounds all night. When East compound finally left there was hardly a man who still had to carry his pack.

Had the compounds left on time, no one would have had much difficulty in deciding what to take. The minimum amount of clothes, the maximum amount of food and perhaps one book or some other treasured article was the common formula. Forty pounds was the maximum weight recommended. As the hours dragged on, however, men reconsidered their earlier decisions. Some had written books or parts of books or plays; others had collected drawings through the years; several had treasured carvings or other pieces of handicraft which they were loath to leave. These were piled on to sledges. Among the manuscripts brought out, several were eventually published as books, and more than one reached the London stage as a revue or a play.

What could not be carried was to be destroyed. According to the German guards a German Armoured Division was to move into the camp as soon as the prisoners had left it. At least they should not have extra clothing for nothing. The incinerators were soon alight and piles of old clothes, furniture, and anything else which might add to the comfort of the incoming Germans were burned steadily throughout the night. In the early hours of the morning there was an even greater glow in the sky as an entire barrack in the North compound went up in flames just after the compound was evacuated. But destruction apart, the wastage occasioned by the evacuation was tremendous. Twenty-three thousand Red Cross food parcels which the prisoners could not carry were left in the store. Clothes and blankets, many of them the property of the Red Cross, valued at £250,000, remained in storerooms and barracks. A quarter of a million books had been received in the camp in 1944 alone, and though many of these were Penguins and other cheap editions, thousands were valuable works of reference. The majority had been lent by the Y.M.C.A. and other international educational institutions, and many of them were out of print in the countries of origin. The total number of books in the camp of all kinds must have been nearly a million.

The loss of cigarettes was catastrophic. Cigarette parcels had arrived intermittently and large reserves had been built up to tide over lean periods. Two and a half million cigarettes were left in the North and East compounds alone and a far greater number had been received by the Americans. At the time much indignation was felt by the prisoners and a formal report of these matters was later presented to the Protecting Power.

## CHAPTER 33 · THE MARCH

The six compounds moved out in geographical order. The march was in a westerly direction and the most westerly compounds, both of which were American, left first. A 1 o'clock in the morning of Sunday, 28 January, the North (British and American) compound began to leave, the last man being clear of the camp at 3.45 a.m. The third American compound followed, and it was not until 6 a.m. that the East compound started moving. The British compound at Belaria, which was five kilometres away to the east, did not leave until the evening of that same day.

On his way out of the camp, each man collected a food parcel. For prisoners who had been short of food for so long to be given not merely a parcel each but to be told to open others and take out whatever they thought they could carry, was the refinement of torture. For many yards round the food store and for the first mile of the march the ground was strewn with tins of every description, a few opened and half eaten, but the great majority full. The food store of the East compound was just opposite the small cage in which sixty Russian prisoners were housed, and a constant fusillade of tins of milk, cheese, butter and anything else which the Russians asked for poured into their compound until the snow was completely covered. Never had the Russians eaten so well.

Those who had large sledges were able to carry two and even more food parcels per man, and at the sight of such wealth some people jettisoned almost all their clothing, determined at all costs to have a full stomach. But there were limits to what sledges would bear or men could carry and in the end parcels were being rifled for chocolate, cigarettes and coffee, which were light and useful as barter, and the rest was thrown away. Even before the prisoners were clear of the camp, German civilians and the girls of the censorship staff were out in the snow gleaning the harvest that had been left for them.

The night had been clear and the temperature at one point had reached twelve degrees below zero. Dawn was grey, but fine. When the last man of the East compound walked through the gates of the camp, which had enclosed him and most of his friends for nearly three years, the road ahead was already lined with the debris of those who had been lightening their loads in front. From the outset it appeared doubtful whether the

Germans had been able to make adequate arrangements for billeting or the provision of supplies, but a sense of adventure was uppermost, and to begin with nobody cared very much. The prisoners were outside the wire and the mere prospect of moving each day to some unknown destination gave a new purpose to life.

The first five columns all took the same road, marching first south and then in a westerly direction. In order to make way for those who came behind, the first American column was made to cover nearly thirty miles before it was allowed a night's rest; by then the last man in the last British column was still more than twenty miles behind. Each column marched under separate command having little contact with those in front or behind, and the experiences of each differed according to the distances it had to cover and the character of the Germans in charge. But to an observer in an aircraft the march would have appeared as a whole, 10,000 men moving in companies or straggling in groups, winding their way in a long procession over snow-bound roads through the forests and fields of Eastern Germany.

The chief enemy was the weather. Beautiful though the frost had seemed in camp, out in the open with no certain prospect of shelter, the cold became very formidable. With so many columns on the move the beaten snow on the roads made good going both for men and sledges, but it snowed frequently, sometimes to the strength of a blizzard, and on exposed stretches there was a biting wind. When a column halted, the cold soon became difficult to bear. Boots and clothing which had become coated with snow froze solid, and frostbite was common even during the first day. Any drink mixed with cold water would turn into a block of ice before there was time to drink it, and for several columns frost made the first day's bread rations uneatable.

Canadians and Americans had experienced such weather before and were adept at lighting fires with the barometer at 20 degrees below zero; they could also freely indulge their passion for ice-cream, which was only too easily made with a mixture of cocoa and powdered milk. But as each day wore on and the prisoners became tired, many of them reached a stage of numb indifference and wanted only to lie down in the snow and sleep. Regularly men had to be woken when the march was continued, and in the evenings when billets had been found, search parties were organised to collect those who might have dropped by the roadside during the final halt. Many lives were saved in this way.

In view of the weather, the absence of any proper organisation on the part of the Germans was serious. As far as could be ascertained no definite stopping places had been scheduled, and each German officer in command of a column had to make what arrangements he could towards the end of each day. It was quite plain that the Germans were prepared to leave the prisoners in the open each night, and it was only the energetic protests of the prisoners themselves which obtained some sort of roof over their heads.

No proper provision for the issue of rations had been made at all. A fraction of the first day's supply was carried in carts at the back of the column, but from then onwards the Germans in charge had to scrounge what they could from bakeries in the villages through which they passed. Had it not been for the reserve of Red Cross parcels which had been accumulated at Stalag Luft III, and for the snow which allowed so many extra parcels to be taken on sledges, the prisoners would have been hungry and many might not have survived. Medical arrangements were almost entirely lacking, and as far as the British were concerned only one small ambulance appeared to be accompanying the column, and that was never seen after the second day. The men who fell out were left in German houses and in German care, to be transferred to military hospitals as soon as possible. Fortunately there were very few who were not at least able to reach the penultimate stopping place, from which they could be taken in transport to the train.

Any attempt to guard the prisoners on the part of the Germans was abandoned almost immediately after the march began. Once or twice, as the columns left their compounds, a guard would force men to jettison some of their food because they were lagging behind, but most of the Germans were elderly men and soon found conditions so severe that it was all they could do to look after themselves. In several instances prisoners helped them by putting the packs of their guards on to their own sledges and hauling them with their own kit.

The guards had orders to shoot without warning anyone trying to escape, but with a biting wind blowing the snow into their faces they usually marched with their heads down and their eyes on the feet of the man in front of them, caring nothing for what went on around them. One guard who was in difficulties actually asked a British prisoner to carry his "tommy gun," and others put theirs on sledges with the prisoners' kit, only to have them thrown into the ditch the moment their backs were turned. By the second day many guards were unfit for duty, and later one was so severely frostbitten that he was taken to hospital, where he had to have both his legs amputated.

The discipline of the column depended almost entirely on the prisoners. In view of the orders which had been received from home that they were to stay together and that isolated fugitives who could not prove their identity would be an embarrassment to the advancing Allies, orders had been given that no one was to escape. But the orders would in any case have been unnecessary. There were many offers of a home and hiding place from Polish families and French prisoners who were billeted in the villages through which the columns passed, and had it seemed worthwhile, orders or no orders, many would have been accepted. But with German units and German refugees streaming back through the countryside in chaotic retreat, the prospect of being caught in some billet which the Germans themselves might wish to occupy, was uninviting. Many of the German troops were known to be in an ugly mood, and the refugees, who were perhaps even more desperate, were unlikely to be particular when it was a choice of their own or British prisoners' comforts. The weather made travel across country and the spending of nights in the open impossible. It is believed that two officers did drop out of the column and eventually reach England via Odessa. One or two others made the attempt, but abandoned it and rejoined the column later on.

The columns presented an appearance which only those who have seen mass movements of refugees would recognise. The predominance of khaki or Air Force blue might have given an observer some clue as to their identity, but clothes and packs were motley. On their heads men wore every type of woollen Balaclava, often crowned by a field service cap; some fortunate ones had wind jackets of various colours, and from each man dangled such an assortment of kettles, cooking utensils and other household goods that it was difficult to recognise the bent and bedraggled figures as those of military men.

The sledges would in any case have made marching in military order impossible. Men kept roughly to their companies, but each of these spread out over a mile or more. The prisoners travelled in ones and twos or, where a sledge needed more to pull it, in larger groups. Ropes had been unprocurable, and the makeshift harness of strips of linen or any other material torn and knotted together was continually giving way. Occasionally, when a group got so far behind that the wagons carrying the kit of the German guards caught up with it, there was an incident. One such group, which refused to move on until it had repacked its parcels, was fired at; another, which had been picnicking in a wood by the roadside, was accosted by a guard who was leading two Alsatian dogs. The prisoners began to collect their things, but the guard was impatient and set on the dogs. The result was unexpected, for after cantering up and licking the prisoners' hands, the dogs ate the remains of the meal and then went back to their master wagging their tails delightedly. The party left the guard cursing in the middle of the road.

But even without the sledges, orderly marching would often have been impossible owing to the streams of German refugees which blocked the roads. The long lines of covered wagons which had been seen passing the camp at Sagan in a westerly direction, were still on the move. They were indeed a pathetic sight. Old men and women dressed in black and muffled up to the eyes sat motionless on the front seat without speaking; children and pregnant mothers lay among the mattresses and furniture in the back; behind, tied to the wagon with ropes, came the two or three loose horses the family had been able to bring along. The elder boys and girls walked. Many of these refugees had already travelled more than a thousand miles from the steppes of the Ukraine, and most of them had still many hundreds of miles to go. Wherever they went they were unwelcome.

Every village in Eastern Germany had already received its quota of evacuees from the western towns which had been subjected to British and American bombing. Billets were not available; hospitals were overcrowded; the best that could be done for those in the wagons was to herd them into the market square at night, to provide fuel for fires, to offer them a little food, and to pass them on.

To the British prisoners these refugees showed nothing but kindness. The war for them had meant misery and their spirit was broken; they had a fellow feeling and were only too willing to help. As each column of wagons passed, prisoners would get up and sit beside the old couple who were driving the horse or clamber into the back and play with the children, enjoying the luxury of being carried for half-a-mile on a mattress. The refugees were too poor to do barter, but prisoners gave them chocolate and anything else they could spare.

Tolstoy's "War and Peace" had been a favourite book in the camp at Stalag Luft III, and the analogy between the scenes during Napoleon's retreat from Moscow and those the prisoners were now experiencing was striking. Soldiers, prisoners and civilians were intermingled, all were suffering the same hardships, and all were engaged in the struggle for survival. The movement was not a march but a migration, a gigantic retreat of armies and peoples before the oncoming Russians.

Two things only distinguished the prisoners from the others who were treading the same road; they had goods with which they could barter, and in spite of the cold, their faces were alive with hope. The amount of food which could be obtained from German civilians was never an adequate substitute for the lack of German rations, but in return for cigarettes, coffee, chocolate and particularly soap, it was often possible to obtain bread, potatoes, onions and occasionally eggs or beer. The civilians were always prepared to be friendly and besides bartering willingly fetched hot water or made pots of tea when a column halted near their houses. Those "messes" who had fluent German speakers among them, or someone who had enough energy to break off the road and make his way to a farmhouse, could count on considerable additions to their Red Cross food. Prices varied, but usually a 4-lb. loaf of bread would cost twenty to fifty cigarettes or a tin of coffee, a pound of potatoes five cigarettes, a litre of beer thirty cigarettes, a pound of onions or a single egg ten cigarettes. Sometimes German women refused to take food in exchange at all, but would gladly accept a bar of soap.

345

ESCAPE
FROM
GERMANY

*The North
Compound*

As a rule the German guards did not interfere. Occasionally, when an officer was around, they felt it necessary to be officious and once or twice a guard knocked a cup of tea from a prisoner's hand, telling him that he was not allowed to talk to civilians; he then turned and rated the civilians themselves. Sometimes guards who prevented the prisoners bartering on their own account took what the civilians had to offer for themselves.

The civilians were not always meek and would frequently shut their doors in the soldiers' faces; one woman who had been ordered to stop supplying hot water to prisoners retorted that her husband was a prisoner in England and had been well treated, and she wished to help the Englishmen in return. More obstructive than the guards were members of the S.S. or the local Nazi Party. Several times such men marched along the column as it dispersed along the village street during a halt, haranguing civilians and prisoners indiscriminately, accusing the civilians of disloyalty and describing the prisoners as beasts and child murderers who had destroyed German cities; but though this sometimes caused the column to be moved, the civilians were plainly either indifferent or hostile to what was said.

## CHAPTER 34 · THE NORTH COMPOUND

The three British columns marched separately from Stalag Luft III, but joined as the march proceeded, only to be divided again into two halves before they reached the entraining point of Spremberg. The column from the North compound, which at the outset included five hundred American officers, covered the distance in three stages. On the first day they marched thirty-three kilometres; on the second day less than thirty kilometres, and then after a rest of three days, they marched the remaining twenty-five kilometres in company with half of the East compound. The prisoners knew nothing of their destination as they left the camp, beyond the fact that the first halt was to be at the village of Halbau, seventeen kilometres to the south-west. It was dark, there was no moon, and the temperature was more than twelve degrees below zero. For the first few miles the absence of any agreement with the Germans about a regular system of halts caused a good deal of trouble, but very soon the cold, the darkness, and frequent snow storms made marching as difficult for the guards as for the prisoners, and when dawn came each man was trudging doggedly on, determined only to get to the other end and hoping for rations and rest at Halbau.

At Halbau the prisoners had their first taste of the complete disorganisation of the German command. No provision whatever for rations or even an issue of water had been made, and it was only the friendliness of the civilians, particularly the women, which enabled the prisoners to get

346

ESCAPE
FROM
GERMANY

*The North
Compound*

anything hot to drink at all. At Halbau the column was informed it was to billet at Friedwaldau, seven kilometres further on; but when this village was reached at about noon it was discovered that the only billets provided were two small halls capable of holding three hundred and fifty men each, and then only if they were packed so tight that no one could lie full length on the floor. The German officer in command of the column went in search of other accommodation, and meanwhile the column waited in the streets.

It was still bitterly cold, with snow falling intermittently, and the prisoners, for most of whom the march with heavy loads had been a severe test, were very tired. After an hour's wait, with their clothes gradually stiffening on them, some prisoners took matters into their own hands, and small parties began to reconnoitre the village to see what billets they could find. The village was full of evacuees from western Germany, and many were only too willing to give the prisoners shelter. They took them in at once, dried their clothes and prepared hot meals; but just as some of the more fortunate were sitting down to eat, shouts echoed down the village street and members of the S.S. and of the local police came to each house, ordering the prisoners out on the road. The truth about the war had not yet reached Friedwaldau; the Burgomaster was a fanatical Nazi and when he heard that British prisoners were "contaminating" his citizens he protested vigorously and enlisted the help of a local unit of the S.S. to drive them out. The whole column had to march a further seven kilometres to a village called Leippa, where it was rumoured that a large barn was available.

For this column the next few hours were the worst period of the march. The temperature had been steadily decreasing throughout the day. Clothes and packs, which became soaking wet while the prisoners were moving and the warmth of their bodies thawed the ice, had frozen solid during the wait at Friedwaldau, and many were suffering from frostbite. For those last seven kilometres the prisoners marched with bent backs, taking it in turns to haul on the sledge-ropes, or, if they were carrying packs, stopping every now and then to jerk the load higher on to their shoulders or bending double to let the pack lie horizontally and give a rest to their muscles. For the first time in his life each man became aware of a great weight on his feet. The only encouragement came from the sound of Russian guns in the distance and the rumours which were picked up as each village was passed. The Russians were said to have taken Frankfort-on-Oder; they were only twenty miles to the north and would overtake the column next day; Sagan itself was already being attacked. Though the prisoners had learnt to discount all rumours, each had sufficient probability to be worth passing on.

The village of Leippa was reached at 5 o'clock in the evening and it was at once discovered that the much talked of barn would hold at the most six hundred men. As many as possible were crowded in and the rest of the

347

ESCAPE
FROM
GERMANY

*The North
Compound*

column halted on the road. There they waited for the next four hours while some of the Germans tried to find other accommodation. The temperature was now approaching twenty degrees below zero and this night was, in fact, the coldest of the year. Clothes and boots froze stiff again and frostbite was spreading, but no medical assistance was provided by the Germans and the British doctors were under-equipped. As the likelihood of spending the night in the open under these conditions became apparent, the Senior British Officer offered to give parole that if further billets were found no one would escape from them. This parole was accepted, but by then most of the Germans had given up the search and retired to their billets for the night. It was mainly owing to the efforts of Glimnitz, one of the German staff sergeants, that eventually some sort of roof was found for all except fifty officers who spent the night in straw in the lee of a farmyard wall.

Meanwhile several officers were missing, and search parties were sent out. It was found that many had collapsed and were lying in ditches, wanting only to sleep where they were. Had they been left they would have undoubtedly died before morning. The barns in which the prisoners were housed were bare and there was little straw. They were so crowded that few could lie at full length, and each had to relieve nature or vomit where he lay.

The march was resumed at 8 o'clock next morning. It was still bitterly cold, and the column was kept waiting for nearly an hour while the Germans attempted a count. As it was entirely due to the determination of the prisoners themselves to keep together and survive that any number of them were there at all, this gesture seemed particularly futile and was eventually abandoned. Shortly before mid-day the town of Priebus was reached, where the column halted for half an hour. Here one of the American officers who had become hysterical with frostbite and had been dragged on a sledge for some miles was left in the hospital. Again no provision for rations or water had been made by the Germans, and again civilians came to the rescue. The column was now told that Muskau, another twenty kilometres ahead, was the destination for the day. It was reached by 6 o'clock in the evening, and at Muskau for the first time there was some evidence of an attempt by the Germans to provide reasonable accommodation.

Muskau is a picturesque town dominated by an immense palace belonging to the family of Arnhim, a member of which was in residence when the prisoners arrived. The column was met by the Burgomaster, who said that billeting was available and within two hours everyone had a roof over their heads. The riding school and the stables of the palace housed nearly five hundred, a laundry, a pottery and a French prisoner of war camp five kilometres outside the town accommodated the rest. The additional march to the French camp was more than some could manage, and rescue parties from the French camp had to be sent out to bring in those who had collapsed. One was the German guard who was so severely frost-bitten that he had to have his legs amputated.

In all the billets prisoners were very crowded and in several there was no heat or any facility for cooking. But the civilians in the town were only too anxious to help, and for the first time the bakery provided full rations of bread. Barter thrived, and once men had dried their clothes and eased their feet the column again began to treat life as a picnic. The stables at Muskau had been lavishly equipped to house racehorses. Hot and cold water was available and more than one prisoner managed to have a bath. Von Arnhim himself, a brother of the General who had fought in Africa, came and talked to the prisoners and did all he could to make them comfortable. He said that his house was full of fine pictures and furniture, but that he feared that within a week it would be taken by the Russians and everything removed or destroyed. His prophecy came true, but not until 17 April. Part of the stables was filled with the old carriages which had belonged to the family through generations, still beautifully painted and preserved.

In the rest of the town many prisoners made friends with German families and had delicious meals and much conversation. Perhaps because of the influence of the Arnhim family, there seemed to be fewer aggressive Nazis among the officials, and little attempt was made to keep prisoners and civilians apart. The Germans as a whole were longing for the end of the war but were terrified of the Russians, and the British prisoners were asked anxiously how the Russians were likely to behave and whether the civilians should join the flood of refugees or stay where they were.

It was at Muskau that the stories of the march of the first American column were heard. It had been their first stopping place since they left Sagan, and they had covered the distance of more than sixty kilometres marching through a day and a night. Many arrived in a hysterical condition, and one man who had been suffering from frostbite on entering a house and seeing a stove, was said to have rushed at it and clasped it in his arms, sobbing convulsively; luckily the stove was not alight. French prisoners in the town said that more than one American had died, but no confirmation of this was ever received.

The British were told that they were to wait for twenty-four hours; but it turned out that the North compound were at Muskau for three days and three nights. In the afternoon of Wednesday, 31 January, five hundred and twenty-three officers of the American Air Force who had marched with the British North compound left to join one of the wholly American columns which had been billeted in another part of Muskau, and which continued the march that day. Later that evening the British column from the East compound also reached the town.

The march of the East compound had been a little less severe. Instead of reaching Muskau in two stages they had taken three, and though no billeting arrangements had been made, the German officer in charge of their column was a man of some force of character, and had found somewhere to put the prisoners with rather less delay. On his own authority he informed the prisoners each day of their destination and the distance they were to march, and from their guards they knew even before they started that they were to entrain at Spremberg.

Halbau, the village at which the North compound had made its first halt, was the end of the first day's march for the East compound. Having started at 7.30 in the morning, they covered the distance of seventeen kilometres by 5.30 in the evening, a speed of little more than a mile per hour. That the prisoners went no faster was not due solely to their physical condition or to the amount they had to carry; from the start they were marching with columns of wagons of the German refugees, and the general disorder caused frequent delay. At the mid-day halt, which was taken in a bare stretch of country, the wind cut across the snowfields and drove the snowflakes into men's faces. A few fires were lit, but by the time they had been waiting for a quarter of an hour prisoners backs were covered in snow, and it was often difficult to distinguish a man from the pack against which he was leaning. An officer who had been to the Finnish war said that the scene reminded him of the Russian Division he had passed which consisted of corpses frozen solid on a forest road. At the end of half an hour the prisoners were more than ready to move on.

At Halbau, the East column suffered the same delay in finding billets that the North compound were experiencing further along the road. For four hours the prisoners stood in the streets of the town while their senior officer and the Germans sought shelter. To begin with they were told to occupy a church, but when the Senior British Officer opened the door he found it packed so tight with Americans who had arrived an hour or so before that he could not even squeeze himself inside. Finally, on his own initiative, the Senior British Officer visited the Burgomaster's office, where he found the German officer in charge already in consultation. Eventually a large school and another church were provided, and by 10 o'clock the prisoners were installed.

It was not the marching but the waiting in such bitter weather which had been hard to bear. After two or three hours almost all the men standing in the streets had been in physical pain from sheer cold. Civilians had attempted to give them hot drinks, but there were too many German refugees and soldiers already in the town to make it possible to provide anything on a large scale. At Halbau the S.S. were still arrogant and whenever they could prevented any help being given.

The church was a small building and was so cold that though the prisoners were packed like sardines, they could not keep warm. But the following day, which was spent at Halbau, the party in the church joined the main body in the school in the room of some Americans who had been billeted in the top floor and who had moved on. The school was a modern building with central heating and electric light, and though the passages were of bare concrete and most of the rooms were locked against the prisoners, it seemed comparative luxury.

From Halbau the East compound followed the same route as the North compound, passing through Freiwaldau and billeting for the second night at Leippa. The barns which the North compound had occupied had already been taken by Americans and after waiting for two hours in the bitter cold the British were billeted in a church and a school at the western end of the village. The church was so small that the prisoners had to sit upright in the pews through the night, and the only lighting for either building came from two candles which had been stolen from the altar and cut into sections. One mess camped round the altar itself and some of its members were able to sleep at full length on the steps and on the altar table. Another mess lit a fire in the font and were able to boil some potatoes. Those who billeted in the school found the coal store open and lit fires in the open at which they dried their clothes.

In Muskau the East compound was billeted in a large glass factory which consisted of a group of high brick buildings surrounded by a wall and looking from the outside something like an English county prison. To the prisoners who had suffered so much from cold, it was indeed a paradise. The main halls of the factory contained the furnaces in which the glass was made, which were continually at white heat; and in many of the other rooms which the prisoners took over, there was heat of one kind or another. The envy of the whole camp was the group which took up its quarters around the main boiler and slept with their backs to its padded sides. As the factory was in working order, run mainly by French prisoners of war, the kitchens were also in operation, and hot soup was provided within an hour or two of the prisoners' arrival. Bread rations in sufficient quantity were issued for the first time.

Meanwhile the prisoners made the most of their opportunity. There is a poem by Robert Service about a Canadian who worked in the Far North and who, having been cold for months on end, reached a spot where there was a factory furnace. He climbed inside and was slowly but happily burned to death. When the prisoners went into the main furnace room and saw the white flame inside the kilns, their feelings were only a little less ecstatic. Each kiln at once became a cookhouse. Not having had a proper hot meal since the march began, every sort of tin was ranged along the edges of the steel doors. The chance of dry clothes was almost equally

important and every pipe and surface which was not too hot was covered
with steaming garments of one kind or another. Many were burned
beyond repair, for prisoners enjoyed the heat so much themselves that
they frequently forgot their clothes until it was too late. All hoped that
they would stay in Muskau for at least forty-eight hours.

During the next twenty-four hours, however, two blows fell. First came
the thaw. The winter had been hard for so long that when the cold abated
a little no one thought anything of it; even when later in the evening the
snow began to melt on the roofs, few believed that it was more than a temporary change. By morning, however, a great deal of snow had disappeared and it had already begun to drizzle; the annual thaw had come
about a month before its time. Having endured the cold the prisoners
might have been expected to have been glad; but the slush on the roads
meant that sledges would not run and that packs would have to be carried
and this outweighed any other advantage. A search for handcarts and any
form of wheeled vehicle at once began, and a few were found, but the
majority trusted that in the open country the beaten snow would still be
on the roads and that sledges would still be useful.

Then in the afternoon the British columns were told that they were
once more to be divided, this time to go to different destinations altogether. The column from North compound and half the column from
East compound were ordered to march that night for Spremberg where
they were to entrain for Bremen next day. The remainder of East compound were to join the column from Belaria and to follow twenty-four
hours later to entrain, so it was rumoured, for Nuremberg.

Discussion at once arose as to which group was the luckier. Bremen
was nearest the Western Front, but with the Russians still advancing in the
south the chances of those who were to go to Nuremberg seemed brighter.
At the time there were many who wanted to exchange and a few were
allowed to do so. In the few hours remaining people said good-bye. Men
who had lived together in a series of camps for three and more years were
being suddenly parted without knowing when they were likely to meet
again. Many who had been devoted friends missed each other altogether
that night, and have never since met. But reluctant though many were to
leave Muskau, not one of those who marched that night would have
changed places with those he left behind had he known what the next
three months was to bring.

It was dark when the column, consisting of the North compound and
half the East compound, left the glass factory and assembled in the main
street of the town. The citizens had apparently received orders to stay in
their houses for windows were shut and only women accompanied by soldiers were seen on the streets. The Germans attempted a count, and in the
hour that was wasted prisoners sat on the pavements or in the doors of

352

ESCAPE
FROM
GERMANY

*The North
Compound*

shops and tried to sleep until pushed back into the road. It was still pitch dark when the column moved out of Muskau.

In the town what snow remained was a black slush and it was hard work pulling the sledges over cobbles. There was little talking and each man walked with his eyes on the heel of the man in front of him, pinning his hopes on the open country beyond. These hopes died as the column climbed the hill leading out of the town. Although there were still hard patches of snow, in the main the road was puddle and slush; one after another sledges were abandoned, and kitbags repacked and shouldered. A few groups pulling larger sledges struggled on for some hours unwilling to jettison their extra food parcels, but by the following morning only one officer, who had bought a genuine "Luge" which ran comparatively lightly over the wet roads, had persevered.

At midnight the moon came up and each man could see for himself what the column looked like. It was a fantastic cavalcade. Once the town of Muskau had been left behind guards had at once abandoned their duties and mingled with the prisoners as before. Of the prisoners, some marched in companies, halting at regular intervals and keeping formation in the belief that it helped morale; but as the night wore on, more and more split up into small groups and walked in their own time along the road.

North compound had taken the lead, but gradually, as one group after another rested by the wayside, the contingent from East compound caught up and the two became inextricably mixed. Old friends who had not seen each other for two years would suddenly recognise each other's voice in the night and continue the march together. The effects of frostbite and the weight of packs soon began to tell. Men were dog tired and at halts would fall asleep at once by the roadside until rounded up by their friends. One officer went to sleep on his feet and fell flat on his face as he walked. Nonetheless when dawn came and men found themselves alone in the country-side, with no trace of a German to order them about, their spirits lifted and the march again gave a taste of freedom.

One party had a slice of luck. Going into a public house to get some water in a village a few miles out of Muskau they met a unit of a Panzer Division which had just escaped from the Russians across the Oder. There was a camp guard with the prisoners, but he and the other Germans soon agreed that all should spend the night where they were and go on by lorry to Spremberg the next morning. They talked and drank the night through, and reached their destination long before the marching column.

The column itself reached the village of Grunstein at 6 o'clock on the morning of 2 February. Here they rested in barns until 11 a.m. Spremberg, a large depot for a German Armoured Division, was reached in the early afternoon. An hour later the column entrained for Bremen. The prisoners travelled in cattle trucks in the usual overcrowded conditions and had the

usual difficulties in obtaining water. But though there was no room to lie
at full length most men were so tired that they slept a good deal of the
time. The train arrived not at Bremen but at Tarmstedt, some 15 miles to the
north-east, at 5.30 p.m. on Sunday, 4 February, and the column marched
to a camp about three kilometres away which had been occupied throughout the war by officers of the Royal Navy and of the Mercantile Marine.

The end of the journey was in keeping with its beginning. Though
prisoners had been on the move for eight days and the German staff at
Tarmstedt had had rather longer notice of their arrival, nothing was ready.
The Commandant had ordered a personal search to be made of every man
before he came into the camp, and although it was raining the column
waited for four hours in the road outside the gates while some attempt was
made to carry out his orders. For many of the prisoners this wait proved
the last straw. Apart from exhaustion many were suffering from frostbite,
dysentery, and attacks of vomiting and several collapsed and had to be
taken to hospital; during the following fortnight more than sixty per cent of
those who had been on the march reported sick from one cause or another.

The camp itself was in a deplorable condition. Whether deliberately or
not, the members of the British Merchant Navy who had evacuated it had
been told that it was to be occupied by German refugees. As a result they
had gutted it thoroughly and taken away everything which could have
been of any conceivable use. There were no lights, hardly any stoves, no
fuel, hardly any beds, and practically no furniture. Barracks were damp
and the only "comfort" were piles of wood shavings thrown on to the floor
on which the prisoners were to sleep. This at least they did.

## CHAPTER 35 · TARMSTEDT

The camp at Tarmstedt was a great contrast to Sagan. It lay on a wide
heath with farmland rising away behind it to the north-east, and instead
of a horizon bounded entirely by fir trees, glimpses of long red roofs clus-
tering round church spires could be seen among the woods which
bounded the heather. A line of telegraph poles marked the only road in
sight. The woods themselves contained as much oak and birch as pine,
and green fields could be seen between them. Larks sang in the sky overhead and a variety of birds flitted in and out of the camp to the delight of
the ornithologists.

But for all its surroundings Tarmstedt was a bad camp. The buildings
were damp and there were never enough beds for each prisoner to have
one to himself, many people having to sleep on straw on the ground. Furniture was almost non-existent, the lighting hopelessly inadequate, and
what few stoves there were gave out little heat. The latrines stank, the

washhouses were too small and there was no sanitation in the barracks. Had there been any prospect of a long stay a torrent of complaints would have been made. As it was nobody cared very much. When the R.A.F. arrived the apex of the British front line was at Osnabruck, about sixty miles to the south-west, and the guns could be heard whenever the wind was in the right direction. For the moment the line was stationary, but everyone lived in daily expectation of the final advance. Escape was forbidden. It could have no possible military value and the only thing which mattered to any senior officer at this stage was to bring as many of his men as possible through to the end alive. When they were not haggling on the black market, foraging for wood or listening to the radio news, men walked the compound or lay on their backs in the sun listening to the distant gunfire, and daring for the first time to think seriously of what they would do in England that summer.

The black market was a legacy of the Mercantile Marine, and was far more highly organised at Tarmstedt than in any other camp which the R.A.F. had inhabited. Although the Nazi Party had done its best to squeeze the last drop of food out of the German farmer, in this remote district the farmers had always kept what they needed in reserve. Eggs were available, and a certain amount of extra flour, potatoes and other vegetables could usually be procured each week. When the R.A.F. arrived the standard price for an egg was two cigarettes, and for a 2-lb. loaf of bread, ten. As they had never experienced such wealth before and were well stocked with cigarettes, they at once caused a violent inflation. To the disgust of the Naval officers who had nursed their market through several years of war, prices soared and by the end of the first week the least for which an egg could be bought was six cigarettes, and loaves sold for anything from forty to sixty.

Exchange was conducted through the German guards, who were reserve Marines, thoroughly disgruntled and tired of the war; the bargain-counter was either the main gate or the wire fence between the German guard house and the compound. From dusk till the early hours of the morning prisoners would be seen hanging around both spots waiting for their pet guard, who, when his officers and N.C.O.s were out of the way, would creep up to the gate or fence and quickly pass packets through the wire and receive the cigarettes in exchange. Then some of the German N.C.O.s became jealous. They knew of the market's existence, but did not dare participate in it because for them the penalties would be higher if they were caught. One evening one of them came to the fence and shot through it two or three times with his revolver. Nobody was hurt, but a day or two later when a British officer had crossed the warning wire to conduct negotiations at another point another N.C.O., who happened to be passing, fired without warning and severely wounded him. Although penicillin was specially flown out by the Red Cross, he died a few weeks later.

The day after the shooting the market was closed, and private trading was forbidden. In future all exchange was done unofficially at an official level, eggs, extra bread, flour and vegetables being bought in bulk through German rations officer and distributed among the barracks in rotation. No further incidents occurred.

The weather was still cold in February and March and as the Germans had made no arrangements to provide the prisoners with coal, parties of officers were allowed to go out into the woods with a guard and bring back what they could pile on to a handcart. The woods were a mixture of fir and oak, and the thaw having come early, were already carpeted with flowers. Anemones, primroses, and fresh green moss were a sight that most men had not seen for years, and after collecting their share of wood, prisoners would wander off to some secluded spot and lie down to revel in the surroundings. The guards were only too glad of a rest and as they knew no one was contemplating escape, allowed the prisoners to go where they pleased. Army prisoners who had worked on farms or officers who had been allowed regular parole-walks might not have been particularly moved by the opportunity to wander alone in the fields; but for the past three years the R.A.F. had been confined practically without a break within wire, their horizons bounded on all sides by fir trees, their feet touching nothing but mud or dirty sand. The sight of grass, the movement of animals in the fields, the smell of flowers awakened emotions which because they had been crushed for so long were almost overpowering.

With the war so near its end radio was even more important than before, and within three weeks of arriving in the camp a special chamber lined with wood and beautifully equipped had been dug underneath the kitchen so that news could be listened to with safety at all hours. Even if the R.A.F. had not brought one with them, the acquisition of a radio set would have presented little difficulty. The neighbouring compound was occupied by the Mercantile Marine and, as they were internees rather than prisoners, the Germans had always connived at their having radios. The number in operation in February, 1945, was estimated at between fifty and sixty, and the sailors were only too willing to part with them in return for cigarettes. But the R.A.F. security was still essential since any set found would still have been confiscated. The number of sets was therefore strictly rationed and every precaution taken to prevent them falling into German hands. Preparations were also made to erect a transmitter in case of emergency.

But at Tarmstedt nothing that went on inside the camp was of more than secondary importance. Situated as it was only fifteen miles north-east of Bremen and forty miles from Hamburg, it was on the route for most of the daylight raids carried out by the R.A.F. at this time. Scarcely a day passed without some large force passing overhead. Sometimes the aircraft were American, flying at an immense height and leaving beautiful atmospheric streamers behind them in the sky; at others they were Lancasters, flying without formation, moving slowly in huge swarms from the south-west to bomb Bremen or Hamburg. Many of the bombs they were dropping at this time weighed ten tons, and each raid shook the camp and gave its occupants some idea of what it must have been like to be living in one of the targets. British fighters were also constantly in sight, sometimes at no more than five or six thousand feet, scouring the earth for any target that took their fancy. They never seemed to meet any opposition.

On one occasion two Mosquitoes circled the camp at less than two thousand feet and then made a series of attacks on a horse and cart which was carrying provisions between the R.A.F. compound and that of the Mercantile Marine. The attack was effective, the cart destroyed and the driver wounded; but as the direction of the aircraft was straight towards the camp and as the weapons used were twenty mm. cannon, every prisoner in the compound was flat at the time, and none witnessed the damage. Although grateful for the moral uplift, all hoped the operation would not be repeated.

Meanwhile the Intelligence Department, which at Tarmstedt worked under the command of the Navy, was reporting daily happenings among the Germans outside. Every boy of the age of ten upwards in every village had been conscripted, and "tank holes" were being feverishly dug along the side of every road. These were no more than little pits in which a man or boy could kneel or stand armed with a "Panzer Faust" to destroy an oncoming tank at close quarters. Diagrams of the "Panzer Faust" appeared in every school, and Germans, young and old, were told that if they did their part no armoured division would ever penetrate to their lines. Tank barricades made of tree trunks and rubble were erected at the entrance to each village and at Tarmnstedt itself four 88 mm. Cannon were observed in the woods.

The prisoners were apt to laugh at these preparations. The sweep of the Allied armies had been so overpowering that such puny resistance seemed futile. In a sense they were wrong. The "Panzer Faust" was never a contemptible weapon; but it was tragic that so many were operated by small boys who consequently lost their lives. The tank barricades were extremely effective; and the four 88 mm. cannon seen round Tarmstedt alone accounted for no less than nine British tanks on the day they finally joined battle. By then, however, the R.A.F. had been evacuated.

The British advance from Osnabruck began in February and continued throughout March. The firing was easily audible at Tarmstedt and accounts of the battle given by both the B.B.C. and the German radio were listened to by the prisoners daily; as always, it was the German description which was the more conservative and the more accurate. Before the end of

March the outskirts of Bremen had been reached and the whole basin of the Weser been occupied, and it seemed that the camp must be relieved within two or three days.

But at the river Weser the British armies paused. For a few days a campaign by radio was conducted against Bremen in the hope that the town would surrender, but against the wishes of the majority of the inhabitants the authorities refused, and preparations to storm the city had to be made. There were daily rumours that the British had crossed the river from the south at Verden, and that they were moving north-east along a line about fifteen miles south of the camp itself. But though these reports generally came from Germans who themselves claimed to have met the British and to have got away, they were not true. The British Army stopped at the Weser for at least a fortnight, and the German Camp staff who had made preparations for immediate flight began to speak of evacuation.

The possibility that the prisoners would once more be forced to evacuate their camp as the Allied armies approached had, of course, been discussed, but as so little of Germany was then left into which they could be withdrawn, the idea seemed preposterous. Most prisoners believed either that British troops would have cut off the camp before a march could be begun, or that the Germans would abandon the idea when it came to the point.

During the first week in April, however, the rumours of evacuation became more definite. To the east of Tarmstedt for a distance of seventy or eighty miles, lay what was called the Luneburg Heath, a great expanse of semi-waste land rather like the New Forest, and very thinly populated. According to the German guards, who were as strongly opposed to the idea of evacuation as the prisoners, the plan was to march the prisoners out of the camp and turn them loose on this great heath. The guards were to remain, and both they and the prisoners were somehow to feed themselves. It was hoped that this would in some way embarrass the advancing armies. There were other theories. Some guards said that the prisoners were being sent by train down to the "German Fortress" in the mountains behind Nuremberg; others had heard that they were going to Denmark. But in spite of the fact that the General in command of the area had declared he would hold out to the end, all hoped that at the last minute the camp Commandant would see the futility of moving, and would have the courage to disobey his superior.

As the rumours of evacuation became more positive the Senior British Officer approached the German Commandant, a reserve Naval captain who had been a police official in Berlin, and attempted to induce him to disobey the order should it be given. The Commandant was a fat genial little man, torn between two great fears, the punishment he might receive if he disobeyed his commanding officer and the reprisals that might be

358

ESCAPE
FROM
GERMANY

*The March
Eastwards*

taken if he displeased his prisoners. He was quite unable to conquer either of them, and remained in a state of agitated indecision. Some of his officers privately announced their intention of deserting if a march was ordered and many of the troops had made similar plans, but to the last minute no one was sure what decision the Commandant himself would take.

On the evening of the 6 April, a heavy cannonade was heard in the south, and the following day the rumours that the British had crossed the river at Verden seemed at last to have become a fact. Which way would they go? Hamburg lay to the north-east, and the direct line from Verden to Hamburg would lead the British forces some ten or fifteen miles south of Tarmstedt; provided they maintained their normal speed of advance their line must soon cut any route which the prisoners might be forced to take. On the 7 and 8 April news of the advance was frequent and contradictory. At one moment British troops appeared to be half-way to Hamburg and at another they were reported within five miles of the camp itself. Aircraft were everywhere, and Germans were still streaming back to the east. It was clear that light armour was fanning out a long way ahead of the main body of troops, but it was impossible to know with any accuracy what towns and villages had been occupied.

Then at some time on the 8 April a message was received by the R.A.F. from the Intelligence Officer in the Naval camp saying that he had been informed by a member of the German staff that one German officer and forty guards were to be left behind to guard the prisoners until the British forces arrived, and that the rest of the German troops would leave at any moment. The information was not broadcast to the camp, but it seemed so probable that those who knew of it believed it. Freedom was in sight at last.

## CHAPTER 36 · THE MARCH EASTWARDS

Early on the morning of 9 April the message which the Naval Intelligence Officer had sent the day before was repeated, and this time the news leaked out. Forewarned by experience, a few prisoners kept some mental reservations, but most people believed this course to be inevitable and true, and the camp was in a great state of excitement. Two hours later the whole situation was changed. From 10 o'clock onwards reports from all German "contacts" came pouring into the camp that the prisoners were to move in a few hours. By lunch time there was little doubt left in anybody's mind, and soon after 1 o'clock a definite order was received by the Senior British Officer that the camp was to be evacuated at 6.0 p.m. that evening.

A conference was held at once in the Senior British Officer's room to discuss the situation. As most of the German troops were still likely to obey their officers, outright mutiny was impossible. It was decided therefore to delay all movements as long as possible in the hope that British troops would reach either the camp or the marching column within a few hours or at least days.

359

ESCAPE
FROM
GERMANY

*The March
Eastwards*

At 2 p.m. the Senior British Officer called a parade at which he announced that the Commandant had ordered the prisoners to move. He also officially advised all officers not to obey the order unless compelled to do so by force. At 4 p.m. the Commandant and another of his officers themselves called a parade at which the order to move was again read out and advice given about what to carry. As every prisoner had already marched under much more difficult conditions, this was superfluous, but the announcement was interesting because a distance of twenty kilometres a day was mentioned. The usual warning against trying to escape was added, but no intimation whatever was given of the ultimate destination. When the German officers had finished speaking, the Senior British Officer stated publicly that he entirely disagreed with the order and held the German Commandant personally responsible for the safety of every member of the camp; his warning was translated into German. Zero hour for the move was given as 5.30 p.m.

Since the story of Sagan had been repeated it is of interest to record that in both cases quite contrary orders were received by the German camp staff on the very day that the evacuation took place. In the case of Stalag Luft III the contradictions originated with the German High Command; at Tarmstedt the Commandant was cut off from all except his own Area Commander, and it was he who, after allowing the Commandant to think that the prisoners were to remain, finally gave the order to move.

Immediately the parade was over, delaying tactics were adopted. The Senior British Officer and his staff took refuge in the underground radio room so that when German officers came to see him he could not be found and the rest of the prisoners cooked rather than packed and ate as much as they could.

At 6.30 p.m. two German officers came into the camp in great agitation, pointing out that the prisoners should already have been an hour on the road, and that most of them were not even ready to start. After much argument, zero hour was postponed to 8.30 p.m. Knowing that at some moment the Germans were bound to use force, the prisoners then got ready, but the Senior British Officer still remained in hiding, and gave no orders. Shortly after 8 p.m. Germans in steel helmets, armed with tommy guns and commanded by the officer who was to lead the march, came into the camp and began to drive the prisoners out of their barracks. With much shouting but without provoking any shooting, the prisoners straggled into the roadway. Gradually one squadron after another moved slowly through the gates out on to the road. By 10 p.m., when it was already dark, the Senior British Officer and his small staff, who brought up

360

ESCAPE
FROM
GERMANY

*The March
Eastwards*

the rear of the column, were clear of the camp. The Naval Officers' camp was to follow.

Then quite unexpectedly a car drove up and voices enquired for the Senior British Officer. The German Commandant stepped out and amiably but nervously explained that he was not happy about the march taking place at night. He wished to be careful of the prisoners' safety and felt that there was too great a danger of being strafed by aircraft without warning. He had therefore decided to send the prisoners back into the camp and to begin the move next day.

In high glee, every man believing that this must mean rescue before the morning, the whole column turned about and marched back into the camp. This had already been partially wrecked; not only had every tin of food been opened, but much of the furniture had been burned and all manner of rubbish was strewn everywhere. But with the British troops rumoured as close as Rotenburg, a small town less than twenty miles to the south-east, nothing except the news mattered. The next twelve hours might be decisive. The radio room was at once opened up and regular bulletins issued.

The march was supposed to begin again at 6.30 a.m. As it became light round about 5 o'clock the prisoners woke to find that no guards were in the towers or on the wire fence. For a moment the few who were awake had wild hopes that they had been relieved; but when they saw that the Germans were still guarding the gate and that there were no signs of British troops, they came to the conclusion either that the Germans were deserting or that the move was this time really to take place and that the guards were parading. For three officers, two of whom had been prisoners for more than five years, the temptation of unguarded wire was too much. Their orders were not to escape, but they possessed wire cutters, and without saying a word slipped away to a far corner of the camp before anyone was out of their barracks, and cut their way through. All three were later picked up by British troops.

At 8.30 a.m. hopes that the Germans were deserting were dashed. There was still no sign of the British, and the German guards came into the camp and once more drove the prisoners from their barracks. There was a good deal of noise but again no shooting, and within two hours the whole camp was once more upon the road. The Germans had made some attempt to count the prisoners, but the guards were inadequate and many of them so mutinous that all serious check upon numbers was soon abandoned.

The order to march had been carefully planned by the prisoners and was accepted by the Germans. With British aircraft constantly overhead the danger of being mistaken for German troops was considerable, and the column was therefore separated into squadrons marching at a distance of two hundred yards. The English system of marching for fifty minutes

361

ESCAPE
FROM
GERMANY

*The March
Eastwards*

and resting for ten was also agreed upon. At the rear of the column came the Senior British Officer with his interpreters, a few picked administrative officers, and some runners. All orders were transmitted by the Senior British Officer himself.

Compared to the march which had taken place rather less than three months before, that from Tarmstedt was a picnic. The weather was beautiful and the country bursting with spring, and although the prisoners were heading eastwards the distance that they could go was plainly limited by the sea on the one hand and on the other by the Allied advance which was gaining momentum every day. It was rumoured that the Germans meant to put the prisoners on trains and send them southwards from some station on the Elbe; but the advance of the Americans had made this plan impracticable before the camp had been evacuated, and with the Russians already north-east of Berlin, the furthest that any march could go was to some German port on the Baltic or to Denmark.

A few horse-drawn carts to carry packs had been provided and those who had drawn a lucky number walked light, but as handcarts had been almost impossible to acquire most people had to carry their packs. They were heavy and the column of ragged and bowed forms spread out over six or eight kilometres. From the air it must have looked much like a beaten army in retreat. From the ground it had a different aspect. Once again, prisoners who had been years behind barbed wire were out on the move, but this time instead of a temperature below zero the sun was shining, and instead of the Russians, it was British troops who were within a few miles and whose guns could be heard continually to the southward. Hope showed in every face, and though men cursed the slow pace of the march because it made their backs ache, they maintained it against every effort of the guards to hurry them, in the belief that at any minute rescue might be at hand.

The town of Zeven, from which provisions for Tarmstedt had come and which had been a name to all, was passed in the afternoon, but still the Commandant had given no destination for the day, and there was much speculation on what sort of billets the prisoners were likely to get. At 4 p.m. the small village of Heeslingen, nearly eighteen kilometres from Tarmstedt, was reached and here the prisoners were turned into a field and told they were to stay for the night.

Protests at lack of proper billeting were at once made, but as the weather seemed set fair and the Germans were obviously disorganised, there was little point in pressing them. It seemed better to treat the outing as a picnic, and to press for an immediate return to the camp. Water was available from a pump at a farmhouse, and wood to make fires from some wood stacks in a farmyard; in an incredibly short time the camp had taken on the appearance of a gigantic fair. Fires were alight in every corner, beds

362

ESCAPE
FROM
GERMANY

*The March
Eastwards*

of straw appeared as if by magic, pots sizzled, clothing was hung to dry, and even musical instruments came out. Then suddenly two shots rang out and several officers dashed out of a neighbouring farmyard. A minute or two later two other officers were carried out wounded. A young German N.C.O.—the same man who had shot and killed a prisoner in the camp only a week or two before—had found prisoners taking straw from a stack and had immediately shot without warning, wounding both men in the legs. The wounded men were at once taken to a German hospital, but feeling among the prisoners ran high, and when the Commandant arrived an hour or so later a heated discussion took place. Finally the Commandant promised that the N.C.O. should be sent away and he was not seen again until the column was relieved. He was then handed over to the British, and was last seen by a prisoner being driven away on a lorry. The prisoner was told he was going to his execution.

When the shooting incident had been disposed of, the Senior British Officer at once demanded that the whole "absurd" march be abandoned and the column sent back to Tarmstedt the following day. He pointed out that the guards were inadequate and of doubtful loyalty and with the British troops advancing so fast, he could not guarantee that his officers would not take matters into their own hands and attempt to join their own forces independently. This, he argued, would get the Commandant into even worse trouble than directly to disobey orders and to throw himself on the protection of the British. The Commandant was shaken, but answered that he had arranged for more guards the following day and that a contingent of field police were to join them. He said that he was a loyal German and that as his General had stated he was going to fight to the end, he felt bound to continue to obey orders. The march must proceed.

He did, however, grant one concession. A rumour had reached the camp that British aircraft had attacked the rear of the column by mistake and that some Naval officers had been killed. The Commandant had apparently not heard of this, but he agreed that when aircraft were close to the road on which the prisoners were marching, they could immediately take cover. This gave almost unlimited opportunity for further delay.

The night was fine, and though there was a heavy dew most people slept well and the camp was in good spirits next morning. The march was resumed soon after 9 o'clock, but again no destination was given. The field police, who wore green uniforms with badges of the S.S., were far better troops than the rest of the guards and adopted a reasonable attitude, helping the prisoners to buy perambulators and handcarts in which to carry their luggage. As the day wore on, even the little German Captain in charge of the march who had begun by being a martinet, thawed and expanded. He had been in the Infantry in the First World War and afterwards had been in turn a farmer and a commercial traveller. He was now nearly sixty,

and the march was telling on him. Although he did not divulge it, he had
been ordered to reach a point twenty kilometres away, but in the early
afternoon he sent the party in charge of the ration carts ahead to find a
convenient field in which to camp, and at 2 o'clock the column turned
into a field opposite a small factory and alongside a wood of fir trees at a
village called Bokel.

363

ESCAPE
FROM
GERMANY

*The March
Eastwards*

Throughout the morning British fighter aircraft had been carrying out
attacks very close to the column and in view of the rumours of the day
before there was a good deal of nervousness, and when aircraft came close,
everyone got off the road. By midday, however, it had become plain that
the aircraft must be aware of the prisoners' identity, for though they were
continually passing and re-passing and carrying out attacks on transport
and buildings within sight, they never went below two thousand or three
thousand feet when over the column itself. Spirits were high therefore as
the prisoners spread out across the field and turned it once more into a
second gigantic picnic. The weather was still glorious and parties scattered
into the wood to collect fuel, while others got straw from the farm or water
from the factory. The farmer's wife filled unending basins with hot water
for the prisoners to wash, and quickly ran out of her store of eggs and
potatoes. With half the day left in which to rest, the camp settled down to
enjoy itself.

In the evening the Commandant again appeared and was again interviewed by the Senior British Officer. He still denied that the rear of the column had been attacked, although the fact that three men had been killed
and seven injured had already been confirmed by other Germans. He still
refused to halt the march, but when pressed said that he thought the column was to go across the Elbe to a place called Pinneberg, just north of
Hamburg, from where the prisoners would continue by train to an unknown destination. When protests had ceased the Commandant in turn
asked why the prisoners had marched so short a distance. The Senior British
Officer explained that the prisoners were underfed, that their packs were
heavy, that their feet were not hardened, and that if the Commandant
wished the march to continue at all he must accept the fact that ten or
twelve kilometres a day was the most that could be managed. He also insisted that every second day should be one of complete rest, and this, too,
the Commandant accepted. There was no doubt that he himself hoped
that the British would overtake the column before it reached the Elbe.

Later that evening a smart Mercedes car drove up and a General of the
Air Force, in a black leather coat with a fur collar, got out and asked to
what unit the prisoners belonged. He was surprised to learn they were not
Germans. It was remarked with amusement that he was smoking English
cigarettes, using Swedish matches, and in between whiles, munching an
American biscuit.

364

ESCAPE
FROM
GERMANY

*The March
Eastwards*

When the march began next day the Captain in charge announced that he had been severely reprimanded by the Commandant for stopping so early the day before and that the column must at least reach the previous day's destination. He was quite cheerful, however, and began to ask what the prisoners thought would be the fate of elderly officers such as himself when the British captured them. From then onwards he was more of an ally than an enemy.

The distance to be covered was less than twelve kilometres, and though nothing unusual occurred on the march, it was the first day on which the Germans ceased to have any effective control at all. The police had already lost interest, the guards were tired, and instead of marching in companies men straggled in pairs and groups over the whole length of the column. The country was rich and well farmed and fruitful barter went on in every village and at every farm. In the small town of Harsefeld prisoners disappeared up every side street and walked into houses in search of eggs, flour and anything else the Germans had to offer in exchange for the usual coffee, cocoa or chocolate. One German who had several stacks of chopped wood did a roaring trade, and more than one prisoner drank beer in a "gasthaus" without exciting any comment.

A mile and a half beyond Harsefeld, in country not unlike parts of Salisbury Plain, camp was pitched in a field to the left of the road. For the first time there was no water nearby, and no wood, so that on the pretext of collecting both foraging parties were immediately organised and sent into every village within a radius of five miles. An hour after camp had been pitched a stream of men carrying bales of straw was coming from a village in which one barn was completely emptied, and feasts were cooking on a hundred fires. Rather than restrain the prisoners the German guards acted as runners collecting eggs and anything else they could persuade farmers to part with. By this time, however, the farmers were apt to be more generous to the prisoners than to their own men.

The camp at Harsefeld was better organised than its predecessors. On the previous nights the prisoners had bothered little about sheltering themselves and had lain in rows on straw huddled together under blankets. At Harsefeld the turf was good and enough spades and axes had been collected to allow sods to be cut and earthen walls to be built; with blankets or branches spread over the top and straw several inches deep on the floor they made snug shelters, and instead of a disorderly picnic the field looked almost like a village.

At Harsefeld the Naval contingent caught up with the Air Force, and the truth about the attack by British aircraft was learned. Two aircraft had circled the Naval contingent two or three times and finally dived on the ration cart at the back, round which were some of the senior Naval officers and a few Germans. The aircraft opened fire with cannon and two officers

365

ESCAPE
FROM
GERMANY

*The March
Eastwards*

were killed outright and a Surgeon Commander so severely wounded that he died shortly after. Presumably the pilots saw their mistake at once, for though they circled the column again they delivered no further attacks.

On Friday, 13 April, the column rested. Complaints had been received by the German guards overnight of the presence of prisoners in all the neighbouring villages, and a much smaller number dispersed in search of food in the morning; but there was a stream running by the camp where men could wash and with a cloudless sky most people asked nothing better than to lie in the sun and rest. As on every other day regular news bulletins were received from the ration party who were working the radio, and these were supplemented by the usual crop of rumours gleaned from German troops who straggled along the road. The British were said to be in Zeven, the town through which the column had passed on its first day's march; scout cars had been seen only five miles from Harsefeld; advance units were already level with the column on the autobahn, a few miles to the south. Less important but surprising, one of the mildest of the German camp officers was reported to have shot himself soon after Tarmstedt had been evacuated. None of these rumours was ever confirmed, but they added certainty to the general belief that the column would be overtaken before it reached the Elbe.

On the Saturday the march was over before lunch. The weather was as good as ever, and enough prams and handcarts had been acquired to enable most of the prisoners to push their packs rather than carry them. The scenery had changed, the road running through rolling hills which were cut into small fields by hedges; many orchards were in full blossom. With the Elbe getting nearer, the pace set was even slower than before and men constantly had to check their speed. The march became a stroll, guards and prisoners hoping that every car they heard approaching might turn out to be the van of the British army. Conversation varied between what each man would be doing in a week or ten days' time to the number of eggs or the quantity of flour that his mess had acquired at the last farm that had been passed. The guards had ceased altogether to assume the character of masters.

In the beautiful village of Heydendorf, situated on a rise overlooking the Elbe from which the spires of Altona and the docks at Hamburg could be seen in the distance, the column halted. After suitable camp sites had been found everybody set out to make the most of their surroundings. There were several villages and many large beech woods in the neighbourhood, and prisoners scattered far and wide; by the middle of the afternoon the camp must have been half empty. Occasionally German troops, who were themselves retreating and scrounging what food they could, refused to allow prisoners to enter houses, and in one village a fanatical Nazi stood cursing the English and vowing that he would have them all shot. But this

366

ESCAPE
FROM
GERMANY

*The March
Eastwards*

was the only unpleasant incident. By sundown piles of eggs and food were laid out on the grass, one Polish officer in particular having acquired two swans' eggs, several goose eggs and at least four dozen eggs of smaller varieties. The prisoners were still not free, and still entered German houses with a feeling of slight apprehension and bargained with the gentleness which perhaps only prisoners know; in the last resort the guards would still have opened fire; but it was generally agreed that freedom was being acquired in stages, and that the village of Heydendorf was the best stage so far.

On Sunday, 15 April, the march was longer. The column was to reach the Elbe, a distance of seventeen kilometres, and in order to make certain of his destination the Commandant had ordered farm carts to carry the prisoners' baggage. Before the camp was broken twelve long heavy carts, driven by farm workers and pulled by heavy horses still in excellent condition, came on to the field. The prisoners at once went in search of poles to extend the sides of the carts and within an hour a mountain of packs and kit bags had been loaded on to each. For the first time all the prisoners walked free. Once again the country was entirely different from that which had been passed through the day before. Coming down off the hill on which Heydendorf stood, the column entered the dead flat country which flanks the estuary of the Elbe on its southern bank. It is like the Fens in that the soil is black and it is heavily ditched and drained; the roads are laid on piles, but the fields instead of carrying corn are a mass of orchards, and in April the villages are half-hidden by blossom. Eggs were scarcer, but fruit was plentiful, and the villagers were as ready as ever to bargain. Air raid alarms sounded almost continuously through the morning, but the prisoners noticed with anxiety that far fewer Allied aircraft were in evidence and that the people seemed far less conscious of the closeness of the front. Fear began to grow that the Elbe would be crossed after all.

As the column approached the river, dykes grew higher and the road curved between high green banks. The village of Cranz was reached in the late afternoon and on being told to climb the dyke on their right-hand side, the prisoners found the Elbe in front of them. They were to camp between the dyke and the river, and to cross by ferry next day. At the sight of the river hopes of immediate relief sank. The spearhead of the British attack was known to be making for Hamburg, which was to the south, and few rumours of any activity in the immediate rear of the column had been received. It was as well the prisoners did not know the truth, for it was learned later that units of the 11th Armoured Division, which had gone north from Zeven, were still less than twenty miles away and might have relieved the column that very evening had they known of its existence or chanced to come that way.

The prisoners fanned out along the river bank and soon discovered delicious little sand beaches where they stripped and bathed. There were a

few ships to look at and even a sailing boat or two on the far side. The
usual shelters sprang up under the lee of the dyke and faggots of reeds
took the place of straw. In the evening the Captain of a Dutch dredger
anchored not far from the bank, came ashore and announced that the
Russians had begun their final attack on Berlin. In spite of the disappoint-
ment that no British troops had yet overtaken them the prisoners settled
down for the night still very much in the mood of schoolboys on holiday,
and were delighted when a German fisherman, some of whose poles had
been stolen, lost his temper and tried to recover them by force.

The Commandant had not appeared for three days, but before crossing the Elbe the prisoners learned that they were to camp within two or
three miles of the far bank, so that the march next day could not be far.
There were few farms in the village of Cranz, but the housewives of the
fishermen provided hot water and cups of tea in the morning, and many
officers enjoyed their first warm wash and shave for some days. The ferry
ran from a wharf beside a cafe, and two boats took the entire column across
in three hours. The crossing lasted twenty minutes and from the boat it
was possible to see the docks at Hamburg and the famous Fockewulfe aircraft works. Considering the amount of bombing they had received, it
seemed remarkable that so many of the great cranes were standing.

The prisoners disembarked in the small town of Blankenese, on the
north bank of the Elbe. It was then a charming little resort built on the cliff
which is formed by the north bank of the river and having narrow winding streets and balconied houses. The rendezvous was in the park at the
top of the bank in the centre of the town, and many prisoners spent several hours lying in the sun talking to the wounded from a German hospital. It was discovered that an English pilot who had recently been shot
down was also in the hospital, but he was not allowed to be visited. As the
day wore on, the Burgomaster of Blankenese, a dumpy and aggressive little figure in a brown-shirt uniform with scarlet arm band, came into the
park and made himself objectionable and ridiculous by driving the children away from the prisoners and shouting abuse at all and sundry. But
the people were still afraid to laugh at him openly.

The camp that night was pitched in the village of Sulldorf, three miles
beyond Blankenese and out of sight of the river Elbe. The country was
once more like the English Midlands, rich and well farmed, and eggs and
flour were again plentiful. Each day, from this time onwards, carts were
provided to carry the baggage, but still no one knew the column's ultimate
destination. Lubeck seemed likely, but many people believed they would
be turned north, to Flensburg and the Danish frontier. The Commandant
still failed to put in an appearance.

On Tuesday, 17 April, the column reached Ellerbeck and camped in
fields behind a bakery, which had unfortunately been closed. Here there

368

ESCAPE
FROM
GERMANY

*The March
Eastwards*

was a stream deep enough to bathe in, and more rich farms. But the war was a little further away, and that night such strong protests were made by the Nazi inhabitants of the villages nearby that the order was given that anyone found outside the camp after dark would be shot. The Naval contingent once more caught up with the column and camped at the other end of the village, and that night news of the Russian attacks on Berlin was received both on the radio and from Germans, and spirits, which had been slightly lowered by the crossing of the Elbe, rose again.

Next day was a day of rest. The weather still held, and in spite of complaints forage parties went far and wide. More than one prisoner was arrested by police or German troops and had to be reclaimed by the German guards, and a formal complaint against the Commandant was said to have been lodged in Hamburg by the local Nazis. But how close the end of the war had come was shown by an incident which occurred that evening. A German Squadron Leader and Flight Lieutenant having heard that a column of British prisoners had crossed the Elbe, came to tell the Senior British Officer that they had in their military jail on an aerodrome nearby eighteen British and American aircrew who had recently been shot down, and asked for an experienced prisoner to look after them. They admitted openly that the war was almost over. A British Squadron Leader was sent, only to find that at first none of his fellow captives would believe that he was not a traitor planted on them by the Germans. All of them were relieved within a few days.

The following day, 18 April, was uneventful and the camp was pitched at the village of Tangstedt, close to a German infantry training school. Training was in progress as the column arrived, and to the prisoners it seemed ludicrous to see young German boys of sixteen and seventeen being made to go through all the standard evolutions, rushing about and lying down to fire blank cartridges like public schoolboys on a field day, when Berlin was already encircled and most of Germany occupied. Many of the boys came to the camp in the evening and were pathetically anxious to know when the war would be over.

Next day the column reached the village of Elmenhorst on the main Hamburg/Lubeck road, and here for the first time the weather broke. It began to rain in the evening and as the German officer responsible for billeting had made no attempt to find accommodation the prisoners began to fend for themselves, and took over several barns. Disputes followed, until it was agreed that the following day should be a day of rest during which billets could be found. News came through that evening on the German wireless that the Russians were already in the suburbs of Berlin and that the Americans had crossed the Elbe; Germans who had remained Nazis were beginning to grow desperate. In some places where prisoners sought billets, German troops were already in occupation and incidents occurred. The S.S. were particularly truculent and one S.S. major paraded a party of British prisoners and marched up and down in front of them brandishing a whip and threatening to have them shot. From then onwards the German officer responsible for billeting went ahead of each day's march to make preparations.

On Saturday, 21 April, the prisoners were scattered through several villages; on Sunday they collected in Great and Little Barnitz, close to the autobahn running from Hamburg to Lubeck. Here a squadron of German fighters was seen flying at tree level towards the British lines loaded with five hundred pound bombs. Their speed was estimated and from the time they took to return it was calculated that their target could not have been more than forty-five miles away. The front line might have been considerably nearer.

Living in farms brought the prisoners even more closely into contact with the German inhabitants than before. In every village there were refugees from all over Germany, some of whom had come from as far as the Ukraine and had already travelled more than two thousand miles. Farmers who had been driven out of their land were found working as labourers and their wives as scullery maids; whole families from bombed-out cities were living in single rooms. The feeling towards the British prisoners was almost without exception friendly, and even farmers who were members of the local Nazi party, though they took care not to be seen bartering, made no pretence that they wished the war to go on. Their main concern was to know how far the Russians were likely to come and whether they would be well-advised to flee or not. They would ask questions about the British, and try to find out how much looting there was likely to be, but they generally assumed that they would be allowed to stay in possession of their farms. Tradesmen and labourers were anxious to know whether they would be permitted to go on working and whether they would be paid; but the chief fear of everyone was that they might fall into Russian hands.

Between Germans themselves tension was increasing daily. Most farmers had been compelled, at least outwardly, to declare themselves members of the Nazi party for fear of losing their land; but the inhabitants of any village knew exactly who were sincere Nazis and who were not, and at the first glimmerings of freedom revolt began to show itself. Men who had been forced to do fire duty against their will refused to answer the fire bell; fears were expressed for the safety of the village bull, which had usually been in the custody of the Nazi burgomaster and proposals made to put it in safer keeping; stories were told of the way certain farmers had treated their foreign labour, and in many cases the foreign labourers were still there to corroborate the evidence. They no longer hesitated to do so.

While billeted at Great Barnitz, the Senior British Officer had received

370

ESCAPE
FROM
GERMANY

*The March
Eastwards*

an order from the Commandant that the column was to march to Lubeck. This was at once disputed and a compromise reached by which the column was to billet in the two villages of Hamberge and Hamsfelder in the valley of the river Trave, about ten miles south-west of Lubeck, while the Senior British Officer himself was to go and examine the accommodation in the town. It was already known that Lubeck was greatly overcrowded, and the prisoners had themselves seen many columns of Belgians, Poles and French marching in that direction. An outbreak of typhus was rumoured. If it was possible without loss of life the Senior British Officer was determined to remain outside and to await relief in the open. That night the news bulletins announced that the Russians had taken the north-east and south-west of Berlin and that the Americans had taken Ulm and entered Augsburg.

The valley of the Trave was perhaps the most beautiful of all the lovely country through which the prisoners had marched. Green banks sloped gently up from the water meadows, fruit trees in blossom lined the hedges, and beech woods crowned the river banks in many places. There were boats in the stream, and the water was deep enough to bathe. So long as the Senior British Officer could manage to keep them out of Lubeck, every prisoner was more than content to stay where he was until British troops arrived.

On Tuesday, 24 April, the Commandant arrived for a conference armed with orders from General Rusof, who was in command of all prisoners of war and who was said to be still in Hamburg. The orders stated that the column must go to Lubeck, and the Commandant said he still dare not disobey. The Senior British Officer, however, had received a powerful ally in the presence of a German doctor who was high in the organisation of the German Red Cross, and who was able to take a more independent view of the war. He had arrived in a small Fiat at the village of Hamsfelde that morning and had immediately taken the side of the prisoners. At the conference he emphasised the dangers of typhus and came out openly on the British side. When reminded of the night's news the Commandant weakened, and after a certain amount of discussion agreed to put up the Senior British Officer's proposals to his higher command to allow the prisoners to remain where they were until he received the answer. On Wednesday morning the German doctor again drove into the village and said that General Rusof had agreed to the Senior British Officer's plans and had condemned the barracks at Lubeck as unsuitable accommodation. This news was the climax to what had been throughout a surprising march. Nine-tenths of freedom was already in the prisoners' hands and those who had wondered, perhaps rather morbidly, how they would react when they returned to normal life, ceased to wonder any more. They slept long and well in straw, ate eggs and vegetables in great

quantities, and bartered for bread, beer and wine. They bathed every day,
and when no one was bathing there were always one or two enthusiasts
who sat patiently fishing with an improvised rod and line. Overhead
British aircraft flew almost incessantly, making constant attacks with
rockets on the nearby autobahn but avoiding the villages, where giant letters R.A.F. and P.O.W. were decked out in the field in shirts, towels and any
other white material. With the exception of two jet aircraft, which were
said to be operating from the autobahn and were undoubtedly the fastest
things in the air, no German opposition was seen.

On Wednesday, 25 April, the last of the German Air Force guards left
the column and marched into Lubeck to be formed into units for the
front. One or two had been with the prisoners since the beginning of the
war. On the Thursday the Senior British Officer and the German doctor
went to see an estate called Trenthorst which belonged to a Mr. Raemtsma,
one of the directors of the Hamburg-America shipping line, where there
was said to be room for three thousand officers. Mr. Raemtsma had been
staying in Lubeck, and hearing that some two thousand five hundred
British officers were looking for a billet, had jumped at the chance of having them occupy his estate before the battle reached it and had made the
proposal to the Senior British Officer in person. Trenthorst proved to be
everything that was desired, and it was decided that the column should
move in on the following day.

## CHAPTER 37 · RELIEF

Trenthorst-Wulmenau, the last billet occupied by those R.A.F. officers
who had marched from Tarmstedt, consisted of two large estates about two
miles apart. The estates differed from an Englishman's "country seat" in so
much as the houses were small and instead of standing isolated in a large
park were surrounded by farm buildings. None the less, both Trenthorst and
Wulmenau were estates rather than farms. Mr. Raemtsma bred pedigree
Fresian cattle and his two herds had been lavishly equipped. The entrance
to Trenthorst consisted of a baronial courtyard; but the interior housed
animals and not humans. The herd at Trenthorst numbered 167 milking
cows and besides the courtyard there were eight immense buildings, the
largest of which was sixty yards long with a hayloft running its full length.
The herd at Wulmenau was only slightly smaller and the buildings were on
a similar scale. At Trenthorst there were three lakes which rose one above
the other, the upper two being surrounded by beautiful beech woods.

On Friday, 27 April, sixteen hundred Air Force officers moved in, six
hundred of them going to Wulmenau and the remainder to Trenthorst. At
first the Factor, a pronounced Nazi, tried to make stipulations about what

the prisoners could and could not do, but after a visit from Mr. Raemtsma this attitude changed. Up till that moment he had not realised that the war was lost. The prisoners did not interfere with the working of the farm nor steal much of the milk, but settled themselves into barns, distributed straw as they needed, washed their clothes in the lakes, and sent foraging parties over the countryside. Wood for fires was available in large quantities and Red Cross parcels were sent out from Lubeck, which had become the final Red Cross Depot for North Germany. The prisoners rested.

On 1 May desultory rifle fire was heard for the first time close to Trenthorst, but as there were no signs of British or German troops the firing seemed difficult to explain. It continued through the night and increased a little next morning, but it was never extensive enough to interfere with the prisoners' movements or to prevent their foraging expeditions. Then quite unexpectedly, at about 11 o'clock on the morning of 2 May, a prisoner on a bicycle rode breathlessly in from Wulmenau to say that two Comet tanks had just arrived. The excitement was terrific. The fear was expressed that two tanks might not be sufficient to ensure relief, but while a group gathered round the cyclist excitedly discussing the news, a scout car with three British soldiers in it drove into Trenthorst.

The scene that followed was unforgettable. Men swarmed over the scout car, cheering and clapping, and as the soldiers climbed out they were mobbed. Two of them were officers and the third a sergeant, and after all three had had their hands wrung many hundreds of times the senior, a captain, got back into the car to talk to his Battalion Headquarters while the prisoners gathered round to listen. There was dead silence while he gave his bearings and then the prisoners heard him say that he had found 1,600 Air Force officers and ask that the information be passed to PX, the branch that was dealing with British prisoners of war. Then, his hand still being shaken and his back interminably slapped, he walked off with his Lieutenant to the Senior British Officer's billet to have a cup of tea.

At once the German officer in command of the marine guards came to the Senior British Officer and formally surrendered himself and his men. They seemed thankful to hand over their arms. As the news of the scout car spread units of the S.S. also began to dribble in to Trenthorst to give themselves up, and it became plain that German resistance was at an end. The S.S. were well equipped and their mood was still bitter and aggressive, but communications had broken down and the British armoured spearheads were already to the north of them; unless they wished to throw away their lives there was nothing else they could do.

The officers of the scout car advised the prisoners to stay where they were until the PX organisation arrived. Then, having answered a thousand questions and dispelled all fear that the prisoners might be "recaptured", they left to continue the advance. Half an hour later a Comet tank appeared in Wulmenau and in a symbolic gesture mowed down the barbed wire which had contained the Russian troops who were working on the farm. After that even the most cautious prisoner knew that he was free.

Although neither the tank nor the jeep remained a stream of Germans continued to pour into Trenthorst to surrender, and it became necessary for the prisoners to set up an armoury and to search men and their belongings. Roles could not have been reversed more suddenly. During the next twenty-four hours a large collection of rifles, revolvers and automatic weapons of all kinds were collected into one of the modern pigsties and guards had to be set to prevent the ex-prisoners from taking them away. Bursts of firing again occurred within the neighbourhood of the camp, but it was impossible to tell whether fighting was in progress or whether exuberant members of the R.A.F. were practising at a tree.

Searching Germans was a more refined pleasure. British prisoners had so often been humiliated in this way that it would have been superhuman to expect them not to enjoy taking their revenge, and one German officer in particular who had been responsible for the alleged welfare of the prisoners while at Tarmstedt, but who had frequently imposed irritating and unnecessary restrictions on them, offered an irresistible opportunity. Having seen that capture was inevitable and knowing something of the privations which prisoners had undergone, he had carefully packed three large suitcases which he proposed to take with him to whatever "cage" he was sent. When he appeared before the searching party he was made to take out every single article from each of his suitcases and spread them all on the floor. A few things were confiscated and he was then told to repack. Having done so he was ordered to march to Lubeck and to give himself up at the first "cage" he found on the way. His face fell and of his three suitcases he opened one and began to discard much of what was in it so that it would be light enough to carry. When it was ready, with a salute but without speaking, he turned on his heel and disappeared down the road.

On 3 May the Colonel in charge of British prisoners for the area arrived at Trenthorst. The camp gathered round him and he made a speech from a farm cart in the courtyard. He announced that advanced units of the 11th Armoured Division had already by-passed the camp and that the main body of troops was only a few miles to the south. Lubeck had been taken by the single tank which had been through Wulmenau the day before, the Mayor having gone out to meet it to surrender the town. The Colonel also announced that the camp would be evacuated at the first moment possible, but that with the best will in the world it could not be done for a few days. He begged people to be patient and not to try and make their own way home. If they were found wandering about by British troops and were unable to establish their identity, they would end up in British jails and cause endless trouble.

With the arrival of the Colonel the last traces of prison psychology disappeared. Immediately after the arrival of the scout car the previous day the British camp doctors had visited the Poles and Russians who had been doing the work of the farm for the past two or three years and had given them food, and diagnosed their ailments. They had been living in very overcrowded conditions and the children particularly were suffering from serious illness. But it had not occurred to the prisoners to occupy the houses of the German farm workers. Now the Factor was ordered to give his best rooms to the Colonel and the Senior British Officer, and some of the other senior officers demanded rooms in other houses and gave themselves the luxury of a hot bath. The Factor himself, who had heard a rumour that the Poles whom he had maltreated were determined to kill him, and who knew of Germans on neighbouring farms who had been nailed to their doors with pitchforks, decided to flee with his wife and children.

Meanwhile British infantry who were following the armoured spearheads began to arrive in the camp and to take charge of the Germans who had surrendered. The marines who had been guards at Tarmstedt had already been sent off alone on the road to Lubeck to find their own way to a "cage"; the S.S. remained. They were paraded by a sergeant and marched off escorted by two men on motor-cycles. Those who saw him will not forget the Commander of the S.S. platoon who, though severely wounded and offered transport, insisted on marching with his men. No man who has been a prisoner can see others go into captivity without a qualm.

The arrival of the infantry introduced the ex-prisoners to a different aspect of war. The armoured and mechanised units which had preceded them were so engrossed in operations that they moved over the countryside as if across a map, intent only on getting from one place to another. The infantry, who had seen little fighting and were moving up to consolidate, took a different view. They looted houses, taking wine and whatever else they wanted, and they stripped men and women of their watches and jewels as they met them on the road. It was an ugly sight and many ex-prisoners resented it and ordered them away; but when told by the troops that they could take any car they found on the roads and use it as their own, the temptation was too great. There was an immediate exodus from the camp and by 6 o'clock that evening the courtyard at Trenthorst was packed with more than a hundred cars. As the night wore on parties of civilians walked wearily into the camp saying that their car had been taken and could they look for it, and one woman at least found hers and was allowed to take it away. But for the next two days the ex-prisoners had the time of their lives. They drove to Hamburg, they drove to Denmark, and on more than one occasion found themselves in advance of the advancing British line. Some of them started to drive home. It was said that it was partly due to the inconvenience they caused the fighting units that they were evacuated so soon.

On the evening of 5 May a column of Army lorries came to Trenthorst
and Wulmenau and the R.A.F. embarked for home. The first flush of freedom was over. As they left the farmyard and the surroundings in which
they had experienced the deepest joy they were ever likely to know, many
men vowed to return. But deep-seated feelings were rapidly giving way to
others and soon an overpowering impatience seized every man. The journey to the airfields was efficiently organised and for most people lasted
five days. The staffs of the transit camps had been warned that prisoners
were likely to be impatient, resentful of discipline, and not too particular
about rights of property. The staffs were kindness itself and the delays
reduced to a minimum, but to ex-prisoners any delay was unbearable and
many broke away and took any transport whose destination was an airfield, and some reached home as early as 8 May. The main body was broken up and despatched to two or three airfields between the Weser and the
Rhine, to await their turn for transport with the other services. The
arrangement was eminently fair, but to Air Force prisoners intolerable.
They had flown into Germany and they felt that they had first claim to be
flown out.

On 8 May a rumour reached them that Lancasters which had been sent
especially to take them home had been filled with ex-prisoners of the
Army and, though the rumour was never proved to be true, this was felt to
be too much to bear. In spite of the threat of a town Major that he would
put a thousand of them under arrest, the ex-prisoners sent an appeal to a
local aerodrome for transport, and on 9 May embarked in a column of
R.A.F. lorries. Although immediate air transport could not be guaranteed
all preferred to camp on the airfields rather than remain in the town.
About a hundred were flown home that night and, after a special effort by
Bomber Command, the remainder were taken to England next day.

## CHAPTER 38 · LUCKENWALDE

While their comrades who had gone to Tarmstedt were marching across
Germany the remnant of the R.A.F. prisoners who had evacuated Stalag
Luft III in January were having a no less eventful time. The five hundred
members of the East compound at Sagan who had been left behind at
Muskau that night at the beginning of February marched to the entraining point at Spremberg next day; there they were joined by the column
from Belaria, the sixth compound in the camp at Sagan.

The march from Belaria had been very similar to that of the other
columns except that they had started a day later and had one day more in
the thaw. They had taken a different route, billeting in villages slightly to
the north of those through which the other columns had passed. Being a

contingent of only a thousand men they had perhaps been luckier and in each village had slept in barns. As they had started from a point nearer to the Russians their hopes of relief had been correspondingly higher, and at one time they fell in with units of a German Panzer Division which was being chased by the Russians after escaping from Kippmanstadt. The German troops, who were very friendly and only too anxious to trade their rations for the prisoners' cigarettes or coffee, believed that the war would be over in a few days and were anxious to fall into the hands of the British or Americans.

Later in the day relations became suddenly strained. The Germans had stolen a goose, but when they came to eat their evening meal they found the goose gone. They at once presented an ultimatum to the British that unless the bird was returned strong measures would be taken. An appeal by the Senior British Officer was made, but the bird was never forthcoming for the good reason that it had already been cooked and eaten. After a heated altercation the affair was settled by a gift of a hundred cigarettes and a bar of chocolate to the German Officer in command.

Instead of going to Nuremberg as had been rumoured, this second half of the British column entrained for Stalag Luft IIIA, Luckenwalde, a camp forty miles south-west of Berlin. At Luckenwalde the R.A.F. were no longer isolated. Besides officers and men from the British army there were Americans, French, Russians, Italians, Jugoslavs, Czechs and Norwegians to the number of about 16,000. The senior Allied officer was a Norwegian, General Ruge.

The conditions were deplorable. For the first month after the R.A.F. arrived there no food was available from Red Cross parcels, and German rations did not amount to more than fifteen hundred calories a day. The camp was slowly starving. All equipment was inadequate, and an acute shortage of all forms of literature made the time pass even more slowly than before. The prisoners' spirits were maintained only by the news of the Russian advance, which was converging steadily on Berlin.

For one brief spell the R.A.F. contingent did resume its separate identity. There had been persistent rumours that when the Russians came close the R.A.F. would be moved to Southern Germany, and reserves of food had been collected against such a possibility. On 14 April the rumours came true and the column was ordered to march to the station. A train was waiting, and the prisoners were told they were going to Moosberg, near Munich, a prospect which would have been gloomy enough in any case, but was now positively dangerous in view of the Allied air attacks on German communications. Several trains containing prisoners had already been hit, with severe casualties.

The prisoners managed to persuade the Germans to allow them to paint the letters "R.A.F. P.O.W." in yellow on the roofs of the railway carriages, and were then locked in the train for the night. Hope did not die, however, because the train lacked an engine; and the German railway staff, who appeared to look on the whole escapade as a great joke, told the prisoners that the chances of an engine arriving to take them to Moosberg were very small. They said that the Americans had destroyed too many engines already and in any case American troops were in many places so near the line that it was highly improbable, even if an engine arrived, that the prisoners would finish their journey.

The prisoners remained in the train all night, but next morning, when no engine had arrived and none was expected, they were ordered out and told that they were to return to camp. By now, however, their attitude had changed. If the Germans could no longer move them where they wanted, the war was plainly so nearly over that the prisoners were in a position to take command. The Germans were unhappy and becoming obsequious, and when told that the prisoners were not going to carry their baggage any further and that they must provide the transport to take it to the camp, they not merely obeyed but loaded the kitbags on to the lorries themselves. For the prisoners the sweets of victory were very near.

Throughout the next week the situation at Luckenwalde became steadily more confused. A scheme for mutual defence in case the German guards deserted the camp was worked out and agreed to by each of the Allies in turn. The German staff became more and more polite, several of them asking for "good conduct" chits which they could present to the advancing army. Their chief hope was that the British and Americans would arrive first. Any morning the prisoners expected to wake up and find that the Germans had melted away. As it turned out they left formally and in broad daylight. On the morning of 21 April the prisoners noticed that the guard towers were no longer manned and about mid-day the Germans paraded just outside the main gate in full marching order. Just before mid-day the Commandant came into the camp to find General Ruge, but being unable to wait, handed over the camp to the most senior Allied officer he could see, who was an American. The Germans then marched off. They were seen again only behind Russian prison cages.

The prisoners were now in the position that they had so often imagined; German troops were in the woods all round them and the Russians were within a few miles; a battle might at any moment take place over their heads. At once parties of prisoners were posted as sentries round the perimeter of the camp to prevent anyone breaking in or out, and others went out on patrol. Both water and light had been cut off in the local town, but with the help of fire pumps enough water was obtained from static pools to maintain essential services. Returning from the town the patrol reported that all was quiet, that civilians were still being evacuated, and that the German Home Guard was still standing by. Patrols which met

Germans in the woods found them still full of fight against the Russians, but not unfriendly to the British and Americans, into whose hands they hoped to fall. The prisoners were warned that any act of hostility would bring immediate reprisals and in the afternoon a German General came into the camp to say that unless eight rifles which had been stolen from his men were returned, he would open fire on the camp. After an appeal the rifles appeared and were handed over. It is a tribute to the discipline of the Allied prisoners that no incident occurred in the camp itself, and that the whole defence scheme so hurriedly improvised worked well.

At 1 o'clock on the morning of Sunday, 22 April, a German aircraft strafed the camp. For many of the prisoners this was a new experience, and at the sound of firing, men sleeping in the upper bunks "baled out" at once and landed in a heap on the floor. Fortunately the pilot flew straight up the main street of the camp and none of his shells did any damage. That same night the Mayor of Luckenwalde came in and offered to hand over the town to the prisoners. This offer was refused by General Ruge.

At 5 o'clock that morning, with most of the prisoners already on the alert, a light Russian armoured car drove into the camp at high speed, pulling up sharply outside the camp headquarters. A small, very dirty Russian emerged and was at once mobbed. The excitement was tremendous. The prisoners were relieved and nothing else seemed to matter. All felt that they were already on the way home. The Russian seemed almost equally excited, and after having his hand shaken a hundred times himself got the infection, and grabbed everybody he met, kissing them and slapping them on the back. About twenty minutes later the car left, taking General Ruge to report to Russian Headquarters.

By this time there was continual firing in the woods round the camp, and it was remarkable that no bullets or shells seemed to land within it. At about 10 o'clock several Russian tanks and armoured cars swept up the main street between the barracks, bringing the news that the town of Luckenwalde had fallen. With the armoured cars was a large troop carrier filled with Russians armed with tommy guns, one of whom was an attractive 19-year old girl. She was dressed like a man in a short smock and breeches, and when asked what unit she belonged to, replied with obvious pride, "I am a soldier of the Red Army," and would say no more. The Russians were very friendly, and told the prisoners that the occupying troops would arrive very shortly and that they would then be released; they themselves were the spearhead and had no instructions. All the Russian prisoners, of whom there were about six hundred, were set free at once and ordered to find arms and go and shoot Germans. Several of them jumped on to the tanks to join the battle, and seemed surprised when the British declined to follow them. By mid-day most of these Russian troops had passed through and the camp settled down once more to comparative quiet.

The prisoners at Luckenwalde were free. It was not, however, for another six weeks that the British among them reached home. During that time they were visited frequently by Russians of all ranks, and lived under a loose Russian control. They foraged for food or had it brought to them in large but irregular quantities by Russian units. As first-hand evidence of the methods of the Russian army, the friendliness of the Russian people, and of the difficulty of dealing with the Russians at an administrative level, their experiences were of great interest. But to the prisoners they were exasperating.

On 26 April, Major-General Famin, the officer in command of repatriation on Marshal Koniev's staff, visited the camp and told the prisoners that he thought they would return via the West, but warned them that there was bound to be some delay. He was informed of the general impatience and was sympathetic, saying that his orders from Moscow were to get the prisoners home as quickly as possible. General Ruge, the senior Allied officer, left with General Famin, and the Senior British Officer was put in charge of the internal administration of the camp.

On 28 April a small Russian staff under the command of Captain Medvedev arrived to take over the administration of the camp with a convoy of thirty-three lorries. Among his staff were seventeen women, of whom two were officers. The lorries contained supplies, including fifty live pigs and twelve head of cattle, as well as clothing and musical instruments, and were unloaded under the direction of a female officer, who seemed efficient and kept the men hard at work. A staff of twenty-five Allied interpreters helped the Russians and organised their quarters.

Captain Medvedev, a Caucasian, twenty-four years old, with many decorations, was hard-working and conscientious, but had neither the experience nor the staff to take over a camp of sixteen thousand men. The administration, for all practical purposes, remained in the hands of the Senior British officer whom General Famin had put in charge. Though impressed by the way the Allied camp was organised and by the discipline, Captain Medvedev was horrified at the conditions in which the prisoners were living, and said at once that he knew of better German quarters within a few miles of the camp and that he intended to move the prisoners to them. As tactfully as possible Allied officers pointed out that as most of them had lived in these conditions for some years and hoped that their repatriation was only a matter of days, such a move would be more trouble than it was worth; but General Famin confirmed Captain Medvedev's view and insisted on the Senior British Officer accompanying him to the Adolf Hitler camp about six miles away.

Having been a German officers' camp, it was equipped on a luxurious scale with a sports stadium, swimming pool, officers' club, canteen and shower baths, and was situated among pleasant woodland surroundings.

It was large enough to take all the inhabitants of Luckenwalde without any overcrowding. After the visit General Famin gave the order that everyone except Poles and Italians at Luckenwalde should move to the Adolf Hitler camp as soon as possible. His concern for the prisoners' welfare was unquestionably genuine and no further objections could be made.

Meanwhile fighting had again broken out round the camp. The Russians estimated that there were about fifteen thousand Germans operating in disorganised bands around Luckenwalde and attempting to find their way through the Russian lines to the West, and on 30 April the Soviet forces began to round them up. As a result civilian refugees were turned off the roads, and besides two thousand Italian internees, who were drafted into the camp at Luckenwalde, about fifteen thousand French civilians found their way to the Adolf Hitler camp and proceeded at once to loot it thoroughly.

The advance party from Luckenwalde which arrived at the Adolf Hitler camp a few hours later found that much damage had already been done and that the prospects of moving were even less attractive than before. They also had great difficulty in persuading the French to evacuate the barracks which had been allotted to the British and American units and would have failed completely had it not been for a Russian woman interpreter named Maruska, who slung a tommy gun over the shoulder of her blue civilian dress and drove them out of the building in front of her. Each day, however, the stream of refugees increased, and though Maruska did her utmost many of them were armed and showed signs of fight. It became impossible to prevent them from occupying the barracks, and on 4 May the Adolf Hitler camp was finally abandoned.

Meanwhile at Luckenwalde people of all kinds appealed for shelter every day, but as there were no facilities for looking after women and children hundreds had to be turned away. In spite of the overcrowding, one barrack was set aside for the most distressing cases and everything possible was done to make them comfortable and find clothes for them from captured German stores.

Among the civilians who arrived was an English woman with her two children who had escaped from Berlin and with great difficulty come through the fighting lines. She was riding on a car through the town of Luckenwalde with two Dutch boys on her way to the American lines when she spotted the Union Jack on the British Liaison Officer's car. She shouted for the officer to stop and was brought to the camp to await repatriation. Her children, named John and Diana, aged 10 and 7 respectively, were in tremendous spirits and were suffering from nothing worse than blistered feet.

Among the first of the many Russians who visited the camp was a young and attractive girl interpreter, very smartly dressed in a tailored uniform and wearing Russian boots, named Sergeant Maya. She had only begun to learn English a few months before her arrival, but had made remarkable progress. Like many of the Russian officers, she remarked on the efficient way the camp was run, saying that it was much better than any other camp she had visited; she, too, considered the accommodation disgusting.

Russian officers who were not on duty were very willing to talk and to discuss politics. One Russian Major deprecated the pre-war propaganda which he said had misled both British and Russians in respect of each other. He said that the Russian people had a genuine respect and admiration for Mr. Churchill "whose personality was very sympathetic to them," and that they had also considered the death of President Roosevelt a great loss.

A party of Russian officers who came direct from Potsdam said that the town was not as badly damaged as Berlin, which they described as "ablaze from end to end." Asked why Marshal Stalin never came to England or went outside Russia to meet Mr. Churchill, they replied, "Mr. Churchill and the American President have only one job each, but Marshal Stalin is Commander-in-Chief of the Russian Forces, Prime Minister and leader of the nation, and he cannot possibly spare time to leave the Soviet Union." They did not like their political officers to be referred to as Commissars, saying that they were known in the Red Army as "Officers in Charge of Military Morale and Political Education."

A Russian Colonel who visited the Senior British Officer asked why the Germans fight the Russians to the death, but are anxious to surrender to the British and Americans. The British officer replied that this was due to German propaganda, which aimed at splitting the Allies, and also because the Germans were well aware of the devastation and terror they had spread in Russia and were afraid of reprisals. He added that surrender to the British and Americans would in no way protect them from their just punishment for their crimes in Russia. The Russian Colonel commented, "That is a very good answer."

Russians who came from Berlin seemed to have collected excellent transport, and many were seen driving past the camp in luxurious Mercedes-Benz cars. Most striking of all were some Russian women cavalry who passed through the town of Luckenwalde, looking very smart and well disciplined. Their uniforms were covered with long dark blue cloaks and they wore cavalry sabres at their sides. Their hair was cut short and they wore khaki field service caps.

The Polish officers at Luckenwalde received many visits from the Russians, including one from members of the Political Affairs Department. The Polish officers were told that the western boundary of the new Poland would be the Oder, that both East Prussia and Danzig would be incorporated, and that the eastern boundary was to be the Curzon line. The Russians promised that all the Poles in the camp should return home quickly and said that letters would be forwarded to their families in Poland; they also agreed to supply them with Russian and Polish newspapers if they could be obtained.

The fighting round Luckenwalde ceased after 2 May, but still there was no immediate sign of repatriation, and it had become obvious that the Russians had brought no supplies and were living entirely off the country. While the population of the camp had almost doubled, rations had been decreasing steadily since the Russians had arrived and the food position was causing considerable anxiety. Organised foraging parties of prisoners were allowed out to bring in what they could, and a certain amount of meat was brought in "on the hoof", but the neighbourhood, which had been short of food in any case, was becoming rapidly denuded.

The Burgomaster of Luckenwalde, a harassed, grey-haired little man with spectacles, did what he could to carry out the orders of the Russian Town Major. The latter, a rugged, middle-aged man well over 6 feet tall, sat beside the Burgomaster at the council table and told him quietly but firmly what he needed. Meat, food and water for the camp was to have priority over everything else, and he demanded an inventory of all food and livestock in the area. This inventory was never forthcoming and would have been useless in any case.

A touch of comedy was introduced when the Burgomaster asked if he might keep his radio set, all radios having been confiscated by the Russians. The Town Major asked why, and the Burgomaster said he wished to be able to know the correct time. The Town Major was highly amused and replied that the Russian authorities would be able to give the Burgomaster the correct time whenever he wished.

Illness was not yet serious; only thirteen hundred of the prisoners of war reported sick to the Russian woman doctor who asked for details. But with the influx of refugees the danger of epidemics was obvious.

Inevitably prisoners began to leave the camp on their own, hoping to find their own way west. Some got through, but the majority were picked up by the Russians and brought back. A few, not of British nationality, who were found lodging in German houses, were mistaken for collaborators and shot. Such attempts at escape were contrary to General Eisenhower's broadcast orders that all prisoners were to stay where they were and wait for orderly release and only made the task of organised repatriation more difficult. The Russians at once issued orders that no one was to leave the camp without a permit, and the Senior British Officer did his best to see that the orders were carried out.

On 4 May two American War Correspondents arrived in the camp from the American lines. They came in a jeep without any pass and had no trouble in passing the Russian lines. There was great excitement, everybody

feeling that their presence must bring release at once, and hurried letters
were written to relatives which the Correspondents promised to post.
There had been no mail since the Russians had arrived. After the Correspondents had left an announcement was made that a tentative arrangement had been made with an American officer who had come with them
that evacuation should begin next day and that the sick were to go first.

True to the agreement the next day an ambulance convoy under the
command of an American military doctor arrived, and, with the permission of the Russians, took away all the American sick and six British.
Everybody's hopes ran high.

On 6 May, Captain Sinkavitch, an American Liaison Officer, arrived
with a convoy of lorries and stated that he had orders to evacuate Americans, British, Norwegians and French, in that order. A meeting was held
with the Russian authorities, who pointed out that they had no orders on
the subject and therefore could not permit the evacuation to proceed.
Nobody could believe that Russian permission would be long withheld
and Captain Sinkavitch decided to try and carry out the evacuation as
intended. Headed by the Americans, the prisoners began to embark in the
lorries and some got away, but in the middle of the operation Russian
troops appeared and began firing over the heads of the prisoners, ordering
them out of the lorries. Part of the convoy was obliged to leave empty.

The spirits of the prisoners sank. After years of waiting, to see lorries
which had come to take them to freedom drive away empty was almost
too much to bear. In spite of the experience already gained of the Russian
administrative machine, the attitude of the Russians seemed incompre-
hensible and the prisoners began to suspect political motives. This seemed
to be confirmed a day or two later when the Russians broadcast that the
Allies were withholding 800 Russian officers who had been captured fighting with the Germans in Normandy shortly after D-day. The men began to
wonder whether they were to become pawns in an Allied struggle and to
remain in captivity indefinitely.

On 7 May another American officer, Captain Grant, arrived with
another convoy. The Senior British Officer persuaded him to go to Marshal
Koniev's Headquarters to see General Famin and try to get permission to
evacuate the prisoners. The convoy meanwhile was parked outside the
camp. On his way Captain Grant met some Russian Staff Officers who had
come directly from General Famin, and who said they were coming to
Luckenwalde with full instructions about repatriation. He therefore
returned with them, but on the following morning it became clear that these
Russian officers had in fact brought no instruction at all and it was decided
to fill Captain Grant's lorries with British and Americans and then make
one final attempt to get Russian permission for the lorries to depart.

The lorries were filled and the conference was held, but though the

Russians could give no indication of when evacuation would take place, they still refused to allow them to leave. In the middle of the conference a report came in that the lorries were driving off with prisoners inside. This must have been due either to some misunderstanding of the orders issued by Captain Grant or to ill-discipline on the part of the truck drivers. The situation was awkward and the Russians demanded at once that the lorries should be stopped. Most of them had gone, however, before the Senior American and British Officers arrived, unloaded the last few and brought the prisoners back to the camp. Had they not done so, it was clear that the Russians would have fired.

By this time there were only some hundred and eighty Americans and two thousand British left in the camp, about seventeen hundred having left during the past few days, mostly in the American lorries. But more and more individuals began to leave on their own, and as the Russian attitude towards those who were recaptured became more hostile, strict discipline had to be enforced and from the 10 May onwards no further unauthorised escapes were made.

For another comparatively uneventful week the British and American prisoners remained. One of the few interesting occupations was the investigation of all German files and documents which was carried out by a specially selected group of Intelligence Officers. Most interesting were the dossiers of individual prisoners. One file told of a prisoner charged with consorting with a German women and paying her in chocolate; the woman claimed that she was only exercising her profession, and on investigation this was found to be true; but since chocolate was rationed she was sentenced to a year's imprisonment and the prisoner to ten days' solitary confinement.

One of the propaganda files complained of the ill-timing of official leaflets. One day large placards were placed by the Germans in the camp at Luckenwalde saying "Will the enemy land? He has tried before. Dieppe is the answer. Let him come!" The Propaganda Officer complained that the enemy obeyed the invitation that very day and that this counteracted the intended effect.

Another file recorded that a prisoner had been charged with living at various times with twelve German women. The women denied the charge and the prisoner was acquitted; the comment made was that he must have been boasting. The German order on discipline read "The best way to maintain discipline amongst the Russians is to beat them, but as the High Command has forbidden this it should be done by the camp police." Another file contained complaints by the German officers about the behaviour of their Commandant, the chief of which seemed to be that he was bad-tempered at breakfast and refused to say "Good morning" to his officers. The Commandant was removed. In addition to reading German files, the prisoners compiled lists of German officers who had maltreated prisoners of war, to assist the Allies in the prosecution of war criminals.

Finally, on 19 May, twenty-nine days after their release by the Russian Army, the Colonel of the Russian repatriation staff arrived to announce that the remaining British and American prisoners were being taken to the Elbe the following day; and the next day a convoy of Russian lorries did actually arrive. The prisoners were taken to Coswick, near Wittenberg, and there handed over to the Americans. The British contingent were flown home within a week, arriving three weeks later than the other half of the column which in January had marched from Stalag Luft III.

So ended captivity. There can be few who would willingly live through it again, but there must be many who still draw inspiration from the knowledge that much can be endured and that to those who have once lost it, freedom has a value which is worth all the sacrifices which have been made for it.

# INDEX

## L

## M

## N

## O

**Acknowledgements** The Editor and Publishers would like to thank the following for their assistance: *Hugh Alexander*; *Catherine Bradley*; *Sebastian Cox*, Head of the Air Historical Branch; *Paul Johnson*; *Sheila Knight*; *Alan Rutter*; *Janet Sacks*; *Tom Wharton* and *Ken Wilson*.

**Photographic credits** The Publishers would like to thank the following for permission to reproduce their material in this edition: *Aircrew Association Archives* 5, 9, 12; *Michael Day* 2, 11, 13, 16; *Imperial War Museum* 1 (HU 8237), 4 (HU 48923), 6 (HU 20288), 7 (HU 20276), 8 (HU 21013), 10 (HU 20928), 14 (HU 47157), 19 (BU 7009); *The National Archives* 17 (ADM 1/15107); *RAF Museum, Hendon* 15, 18, 20.